To all the men and women around
the world who embrace
QUALITY
in everything they do.

THE
Ice Cream Maker

THE
Ice Cream Maker

AN INSPIRING TALE ABOUT MAKING
QUALITY THE KEY INGREDIENT
IN EVERYTHING YOU DO

SUBIR CHOWDHURY

CURRENCY   DOUBLEDAY

New York London Toronto Sydney Auckland

A CURRENCY BOOK
PUBLISHED BY DOUBLEDAY
a division of Random House, Inc.

CURRENCY is a trademark of Random House, Inc., and
DOUBLEDAY is a registered trademark of Random
House, Inc.

Book design by Michael Collica

Cataloging-in-Publication Data is on file with the
Library of Congress
ISBN: 0-385-51478-6

First Edition: November 2005
All trademarks are the property of their respective
companies.

SPECIAL SALES
Currency Books are available at special discounts for
bulk purchases for sales promotions or premiums.
Special editions, including personalized covers, excerpts
of existing books, and corporate imprints, can be created
in large quantities for special needs. For more
information, write to Special Markets, Currency Books,
specialmarkets@randomhouse.com

5 7 9 10 8 6 4

niversary, IIT featured Chowdhury as one of its top fifteen eminent alumni and CMU awarded him with its Distinguished Alumni Award (which has been bestowed upon only twenty-two alumni in its 100-plus-year history). Most engineering schools and business schools throughout the world include his engineering and management books in undergraduate and graduate programs. Chowdhury is frequently cited in the national and international media.

Chowdhury lives with his wife, Malini, and daughter, Anandi, in Michigan.

CONTENTS

1. A Bucket of Ice Water 1

2. Learning to Listen 21

3. The Secret of LEO 39

4. We Don't Need Steve Jobs 59

5. Striving for Perfection 75

6. Bringing It Home 97

Acknowledgments 111

THE
Ice Cream Maker

A Bucket of Ice Water

It was a Monday afternoon in May when my life changed forever.

I was working away at my job as plant manager for Dairy Cream, a regional ice cream company, when Reggie, one of our sales reps, came breezing through the door an hour earlier than I expected. He had a big appointment with Natural Foods, the booming national food chain that has had a branch here in town for ten years or so. I thought that perhaps he hadn't made his sales call yet, until he shook his head and with an easygoing shrug gave me a "thumbs down" signal. He'd failed again to sell even a half pint to Natural Foods. "We'll get 'em next time, Pete," he said nonchalantly, with the faith of a Cubs fan.

It was no skin off his nose, I could tell. After all, no one had really expected him to make the sale. We'd been trying for years. In fact, he seemed relieved. Going down there had become an annual chore I made him perform, and he had completed it. It was one less thing he had to do.

Only this year I had really been counting on making that sale. We'd come up with three new flavors using natural ingredients that I thought would knock their socks off. That was the way we'd originally made a name for ourselves—with radical new flavors that had gotten us not only local publicity and a surge in sales, but national attention. But my "new flavors" strategy seemed to have fizzled with Natural Foods.

What was worrying me most was something I couldn't tell Reggie or anyone else. Our boss and founder, Malcolm Jones, had recently expressed his disappointment to me at our lack of sales growth. Our profit margins were shrinking. Malcolm had told me if things didn't get better soon, he would have to make some serious changes. One solution, he said, would be to bring another management team on board. Or, he intimated, he might be forced to sell our factory outright to a national manufacturer, or scuttle the ice cream factory altogether by selling the land to a real estate developer. "I don't care what you have to do to turn things around, Pete. But get it done. I'm putting this on your shoulders." With suburban sprawl spreading past the highway belt encircling our city, I had no doubt Malcolm could make more money selling the land to a developer than he could running it with its current revenues. Either way, however, I would be out of a job. With a wife and two young kids, eight and six, Malcolm's rebuke jolted me out of my complacency.

Although I had grown up in town, I had taken the job at Dairy Cream only two years earlier, after spending ten years in a food manufacturing company in Denver. It seemed to me it was only recently that our family felt settled. My wife, Jean, had landed a job at one of the local bank branches, and our son and daughter had a growing circle of friends in the neighborhood. But there was no way we could swing the mortgage and everything else on Jean's salary alone.

And if I failed at Dairy Cream, what would I do? I wasn't necessarily the smartest guy in the room, but I worked hard at my job. I had come up with a number of management initiatives and employee morale programs to improve our manufacturing processes and increase production.

But lately, nothing seemed to make a difference. Our ice cream appealed neither to the high-end, premium buyers, nor was it competitive with the lower-priced budget brands. We were caught in the middle and getting squeezed from both ends.

I'd never failed at my job before, but I'd begun to run

out of answers. What could I do, I worried, to avoid this fate? What would happen to all the people under me if Malcolm sold the business—or the land?

That morning, I had held out hope that Natural Foods might be our savior. I knew that if we could sell our brand to just one branch of their chain, it would significantly boost our numbers. Their sales are so strong, they'd carry us with them. And then, of course, it would give us a foot in the door to try to land an account with the entire chain, multiplying our modest profits many times, overnight. And because Natural Foods has such a fabulous reputation for offering high-quality products and superior customer service, being picked up by them would signal to other retailers that we had earned the stamp of approval from the toughest judge in the food business, leading to more contracts.

So when Reggie returned to tell me we had gotten another "no go" from Natural Foods after an abbreviated ten-minute conversation with their buyer, my heart sank lower than my work boots. Reggie said he barely got his first sentence out when the buyer started asking questions he couldn't really answer.

"Such as?"

"Such as the density of our ice cream, the percentage of 'mix-ins,' in weight and volume, the success rate of our packaging . . . "

"The success rate of our packaging?"

"That's what I mean," Reggie said. "I'd never heard such questions before."

I was dumbfounded. How could Natural Foods make their decision on whether or not to carry our ice cream based on such arcane questions?

My disappointment, however, soon changed to determination. I couldn't just let this account go. Years ago I had known one of the higher-ups in the store. Darn it, I would go and make the pitch to them myself. Although I was scheduled to meet with our director of quality that day, I found myself taking off my safety goggles and lab coat, putting on my jacket, and grabbing my keys before I was even aware of what I was doing. I'm not a sales rep—I have absolutely no sales experience—but I knew how crucial this sale was. I *had* to get it. I hopped into my car—an SUV we had just bought two months earlier to help trundle the kids around town, I reflected ruefully, thinking of the payments—to visit Natural Foods myself.

Although I had always refused to shop at Natural Foods—because they had never bought our ice cream—I had no trouble finding their store, a huge building located at a major intersection. Essentially a fancy grocery store, it looks nothing like the Biggie-Mart I frequent. The storefront consists of huge windows framed in brick, making it look more like a bookstore than a grocery store. From across the parking lot you could see the thirty-foot-high rafters inside—the entire ceiling painted beige, not the depressing black or shocking white of most stores—and the friendly banners hanging above each cash register. Whether you cared about the products or not, the store's design had a way of drawing you in.

I wanted to not like the place, but I still couldn't help but notice the lengths Natural Foods took to make shoppers feel welcome. Despite my boycott, my wife still shopped there and often gushed about what a great place it was, gently mocking my stubbornness at refusing to cross its doors. I soon discovered what she was talking about.

I walked through the front doors—my wife claimed that if they ever closed them, she hadn't seen it—which are so expansive it's virtually impossible to bump into another customer, no matter how busy the foot traffic. A blast of invitingly cool air greeted me on this hot summer day. I walked past the shopping carts, all of them a shining, robust green, neatly organized in a fan design to allow maximum access and minimum hassle. I noticed an unmistakable fragrance, and looked to my left to see a veritable wall of flowers, like a scene from a rich impressionist painting. Soft, soothing music wafted down from above. The ten-second experience of walking into Natural Foods was as warm a welcome as a store can give you, transporting you to someplace inviting and exotic in just a few feet.

"Hello, how are you?" a friendly voice asked with such

genuine sincerity that I assumed she was a friend of mine. I
didn't recognize her, however, and must have looked puz-
zled. "Can I help you?" she asked.

"No thanks," I answered. She was clearly not an official
greeter, just a friendly employee doing her job arranging
the floral display while saying hello to as many customers
as she could. I soon heard a chorus of similar greetings
around the store, many of them quickly evolving into
longer conversations.

My first look inside revealed just how clean and fresh,
warm and welcoming the entire store was. It didn't feel at
all like my local chain grocery—and certainly not like our
factory. But I quickly dismissed the thought. After all, they
were in retail, and we sell to stores, not customers.

Just past the flowers I found the "Help Center," manned
by two cheerful employees, one of whom seemed free to
answer a question.

"Hello there," the information woman said. "I'm Jenny.
How can I help you today?" When I had gotten out of my
car I'm sure I was wearing a stubborn scowl, but I found it
impossible to maintain a downturned mouth in the face of
such a friendly smile. I had left the factory in such a rush
that I couldn't recall the name of the buyer Reggie had
talked to. But I remembered that one of my parents' neighbors had taken a managerial job at Natural Foods years before, and decided to give him a shot first.

"Does Mr. McMaster still work here?" I asked.

"Ohhhh, yes," she said, grinning. "I'm sure he's around here somewhere. Is he expecting you?"

"No," I admitted. "Is that a problem?"

"Not at all," she said. "He talks to lots of customers every day, and I doubt any of them have made an appointment yet."

"Well, actually," I said, "I'm not really a customer. I'm an old neighbor, from way back. I haven't seen him in, geez, probably ten years."

"Wow!" she laughed, joking, "Does he owe you money?"

"No," I said, smiling, unable to resist her humor. "Actually I'm here on a sales call."

"If you haven't seen Mike in a while, maybe I'd better take you to him."

Jenny stepped out from behind the counter, told her coworker she'd be right back, and led me through the store.

"Is his office in the back?" I asked.

"Mike's office will be our *last* stop. You're more likely to find him in the parking lot gathering carts, or at the entrance fiddling with the flowers, than sitting at his desk. Most of the time he's roaming the store, talking with customers and our team members."

We walked through aisles that were even wider than I

had imagined when I saw the store from afar in my car. They were immaculate and comfortably organized. The shelves were made of rich cherry wood, and cantilevered to break up the sterile, straight lines of most conventional stores. The lighting was softer, too, than the harsh fluorescent lighting of the typical grocery store, with a variety of lush green plants, making this huge box feel more like a cute coffee shop than the gigantic food franchise it actually was.

What I noticed most of all, though, was the number of employees we walked past—dozens, easily—stocking shelves, fashioning imaginative displays with coworkers, talking with customers. It was clear that rather than regarding their customers' questions as a nuisance, it was the favorite part of their jobs.

Jenny found Mike helping a customer in the pasta section, discussing the vast array of choices. He was undeniably older than I'd remembered, but he'd aged well, still lean and spry, with the same glint burning brightly in his eyes. Mike was asking the customer a detailed series of questions to determine exactly the kind of meal she was planning to prepare, and what pasta and sauce might work best for her purposes.

He gave us a "Just a moment" gesture, then asked the customer a few more questions about how often she visited Natural Foods (every week, she said), what she liked best (the selection and the service), and what she thought they could do better. "Hmmm," she said. "That's hard to say. I come here an awful lot, and I love it. But I suppose it'd be helpful if you had some sort of information card or sheet for your products, so I wouldn't have to ask a clerk like you every time I had a question."

"Ms. Truax, it's always a pleasure talking to our customers, but you have a very good idea. I'll see what I can do."

"Thanks," she said. "And please, call me Samantha."

"Samantha it is. Thanks for visiting our store."

When he turned to us, he said, "Now, you have to be Frank Delvecchio's son, Peter, aren't you?"

"Yes," I said, extending my hand. "You have an amazing memory. Last time I saw you, I was just home from college, with long hair and glasses."

He chuckled. "And I must have been thirty-five, with *some* hair, and *no* glasses!" He thanked Jenny for her help. "It's great to see you again, Peter. Can I buy you a cup of coffee?"

"Sure," I said. "Thank you. And call me Pete. I think only my mom still calls me Peter."

"And you can call me Mike."

"Mike it is," I said.

Mike started walking me toward the café in the front of the store, awash in sunlight pouring through the lightly tinted picture windows, and he found an open table where we could chat.

A friendly waitress came over to take our order. "Do you have latte?" I asked.

"Of course," the waitress said. "And you, Mike?"

"Make it two, Monica. Thanks." Then Mike turned his attention back to me. "So, to what do I owe this pleasure?"

"First, it's good to see you again," I said, suddenly a little embarrassed that I hadn't stopped in to see him before. I'd forgotten what a friendly neighbor Mike had been.

"Ditto," he replied. "But I've got a hunch you didn't come down here just to say hello!"

His remark disarmed me. He must be used to sales calls by now, I realized. "You're right," I said. "I'm the factory supervisor for Dairy Cream now. I've been there the last couple of years. And I've been dying to get our ice cream in your store for a long time. I remembered that you had helped Natural Foods' founder get the chain off the ground years ago, before relocating back here in town. So I thought I'd come in and see if you still worked here."

He spread his arms. "Now you have your answer!"

"What do you do here now?" I asked.

"Because I got in on the ground floor at Natural Foods—lucky timing—I rose to become one of the company's vice presidents. But ten years ago I decided I wanted to scale back my hours and my travel, so I asked

Glen Goodwell, our founder, if I could help start up a branch in my old hometown." He looked around the store. "And it's worked out very well."

"So you're the branch manager?"

"Yeah, I guess you could say that," he said. "Though a lot of our management ideas and decisions come from the people in the green smocks you passed throughout the store."

"Then do you decide what products to carry?"

"I have a lot of say in it, sure," he said, "though each department head usually makes those calls. I think I know where you're going with this, Pete. I have to tell you that your sales rep—Reggie, was it?—already came down here this morning and pitched Ike, our ice cream man, on the idea of carrying Dairy Cream. But I'm afraid he didn't make the sale."

"I know," I said. "That's when I decided to come here myself. But how did you know that?"

"I happened to be walking through the frozen foods section when they were talking," he explained, "so I joined the conversation."

"How did it go?" I asked. "I mean, I know Reggie didn't make the sale, but why, exactly, did your buyer decide to take a pass? I only know the punch line."

"Well, I could give you a number of reasons—we have half a dozen ice cream manufacturers pitch us every week,

INJUSTICES

The Supreme Court's History of
Comforting the Comfortable and
Afflicting the Afflicted

IAN MILLHISER

NATION
BOOKS
New York

Published by
Nation Books, A Member of the Perseus Books Group
116 East 16th Street, 8th Floor
New York, NY 10003
Nation Books is a co-publishing venture of the Nation Institute and the Perseus Books Group.

Books published by Nation Books are available at special discounts for bulk purchases in the United States by corporations, institutions, and other organizations. For more information, please contact the Special Markets Department at the Perseus Books Group, 2300 Chestnut Street, Suite 200, Philadelphia, PA 19103, or call (800) 255-1514, or e-mail special.markets@perseusbooks.com.

Designed by Trish Wilkinson
Set in 11.5-point Adobe Caslon Pro

Library of Congress Cataloging-in-Publication Data

Millhiser, Ian, author.
    Injustices : the Supreme Court's history of comforting the comfortable and afflicting the afflicted / Ian Millhiser.
        pages   cm
    Includes bibliographical references and index.
    ISBN 978-1-56858-456-0 (hardback) — ISBN 978-1-56858-457-7 (e-book)
1. United States. Supreme Court—History. 2. Political questions and judicial power—United States.—History. 3. Social justice—United States.—History. 4. Law—Economic aspects—United States.—History. I. Title.

KF8748.M475 2015
347.73'2609—dc23   2014049653

10 9 8 7 6 5 4 3 2 1

For Earl, Thurgood, and Ruth,
who proved that it does not have to be this way

Contents

Introduction   *ix*

PART I

THE CONSTITUTION OF STEPHEN JOHNSON FIELD

CHAPTER 1: How the Civil War Was Undone   3

CHAPTER 2: The Baron Outside Chicago   19

CHAPTER 3: The Two Constitutions   45

CHAPTER 4: The Price of a Coke   63

CHAPTER 5: You Load Sixteen Tons and
            What Do You Get?   82

CHAPTER 6: Men Feared Witches and Burnt Women   107

PART II

GETTING OUT OF THE WAY

CHAPTER 7: The Bottom Falls Out   129

CHAPTER 8: The Biggest Damned-Fool Mistake
            I Ever Made   158

CHAPTER 9: Should We Double Our Wealth and
            Conquer the Stars   176

PART III

THE BRIEF RISE AND RAPID FALL OF
CONSERVATIVE JUDICIAL RESTRAINT

CHAPTER 10: The Truce   195

CHAPTER 11: Rigging the Game   213

CHAPTER 12: The Final Word   238

CHAPTER 13: The Constitution Has Always Been at
             War with Eurasia   255

   EPILOGUE: The Gathering Storm   275

             Acknowledgments   *285*
             Notes   *289*
             Index   *333*

Introduction

The generally accepted notion that the court can only hear roughly 150 cases each term gives the same sense of reassurance as the adjournment of the court in July, when we know the Constitution is safe for the summer.

—Future Chief Justice John Roberts, April 19, 1983

On a porch in Colfax, Louisiana, eight wounded men lay shielded from the rain. Close to a decade earlier they'd been enslaved, toiling far away from the site where General Robert E. Lee would soon surrender his army. Five months earlier they'd cast ballots in a rigged election, then watched an ex-Confederate officer declare himself governor of their state. Two weeks back they'd been triumphant, emboldened by a federal judge's order to oust that false governor's loyalists and regain control of their local government from white supremacists. By morning, they would be gunned down by a racist mob.[1]

Eight decades later, in the autumn of Jim Crow, this mob's descendants would erect a historical marker commemorating this massacre: "three white men and 150 negroes were slain" in what the marker deems the "Colfax Riot," bringing the "end of carpetbag misrule in the South."[2]

The events this marker touts—the death of Reconstruction, the birth of Southern apartheid, and the near century of white supremacy that followed—did not simply emerge from a single day's slaughter. They were shepherded into being by one of the most powerful and most malign institutions in American history: the Supreme Court of the United States. Though a federal prosecutor achieved a nearly impossible task—he convinced a jury dominated by Southern white men to convict three members of the Colfax mob of violating the civil rights of African Americans—the Supreme Court tossed out these convictions in *United States v. Cruikshank* (1876).[3] Less than eleven years after Lee's surrender at Appomattox Courthouse, the justices gave their blessing to the campaign of white-on-black terrorism that would define the South for generations.

Cruikshank is hardly an anomaly in the Supreme Court's history. Just a few years before the Civil War, the justices delighted slaveholders and enraged abolitionists with its decision in *Dred Scott v. Sandford* (1857). More than just a proslavery decision, *Dred Scott* was rooted in the belief that men and women of African descent are "beings of an inferior order, and altogether unfit to associate with the white race." The Court examined "the condition of this race" at the time the Constitution was drafted, and determined that "it is impossible to believe that" the rights enjoyed by white citizens "were intended to be extended" to black people.[4]

A great deal had changed in the years between *Dred Scott* and *Cruikshank*, however. At the height of the Civil War, President Abraham Lincoln proclaimed that "all persons held as slaves" within the rebellious states "shall be then, thenceforward, and forever free."[5] Less than three years later, his armies vanquished the slaveholding Confederacy and accepted its surrender. By the time of the Colfax Massacre, five members of the Supreme Court were Lincoln appointees, and three were appointed by Lincoln's greatest general, Ulysses S. Grant. Although the Court did include Democrat Nathan Clifford, a "doughface" Northerner supportive of the Southern cause and the Court's lone holdover from before Lincoln's election, the doughface justice had only one of the Court's nine votes to offer the old Confederacy.

More importantly, the Constitution in 1873, the year of the Colfax Massacre, was a very different document than it was the day Lee surrendered to Grant. Since that day, the states had ratified three constitutional amendments. One of them, the Thirteenth Amendment, provides that "neither slavery nor involuntary servitude" shall exist in the United States, except as punishment for a crime. Another, the Fifteenth Amendment, calls for African Americans to be welcomed into the ranks of fully enfranchised citizens by forbidding states from denying the right to vote "on account of race, color, or previous condition of servitude."

The most sweeping of the three Reconstruction Amendments, however, was the Fourteenth Amendment. On its face, this amendment did not simply extend new rights to freedmen and their children, it transformed the very nature of American government. Prior to the Civil War, most of the rights embraced by the Bill of Rights were not "rights" in the way we understand that term today. Instead, the Constitution mostly prevented the *federal* government from taking certain actions against individuals. *States*, however, remained free to seize people's property without compensation, or to invade people's homes, or to establish an official state religion, just so long as the authorities did so in compliance with their own state's constitution.

The Fourteenth Amendment declared, for the first time in the nation's history, that Americans enjoy a broad array of rights simply because they are Americans, and that they keep these rights even as they travel across state lines. In the amendment's words, "no State shall make or enforce any law which shall abridge the privileges or immunities of citizens of the United States."

To ensure that states did not deny these new citizenship rights to freedmen, the Fourteenth Amendment also declared that all persons born in the United States and subject to its laws "are citizens of the United States and of the State wherein they reside," regardless of the station of their parents. And it proclaimed that there are some rights that citizens and foreigners both enjoy simply because they are human. No state may "deprive any person of life, liberty, or property, without due process of law; nor deny to any person within its jurisdiction the equal protection of the laws."

So the Fourteenth Amendment transformed the Constitution from a document that largely just assigned different roles to state and federal governments into one that recognized that certain liberties cannot be abridged by *any* government.

Though modern-day scholars disagree about what, exactly, the "privileges or immunities of citizens of the United States" are, the primary author of the Fourteenth Amendment had a fairly clear idea. In the words of that author, Ohio Republican Congressman John Bingham, "the privileges or immunities of citizens of the United States, as contradistinguished from citizens of a State, are chiefly defined in the first eight amendments to the Constitution of the United States. . . . These eight articles I have shown never were limitations upon the power of the States, until made so by the fourteenth amendment."[6] Thus, Bingham believed that his amendment would, for the first time, forbid the states from violating the Bill of Rights.

Yet Bingham's amendment was also fundamentally flawed. Whatever the Ohio lawmaker might have wished it to accomplish, the amendment's naked text offers no hint as to what the "privileges or immunities of citizens of the United States" could be. Similarly, it speaks in broad, undefined terms like "liberty" and "due process," then leaves the reader to guess what exactly these words mean as well.

By writing such open-ended language into the Constitution, Bingham and his fellow lawmakers delegated sweeping authority to the Supreme Court of the United States, as the power to interpret these and other ambiguous phrases within the Constitution ultimately rests with the justices who sit on that Court. The few men and even fewer women entrusted with this power have not often wielded it wisely:

- The Court spent the first three decades after the Civil War paving the way for Jim Crow, and it spent the next four decades shielding employers from laws protecting their workers from exploitation.
- The justices held that Americans could be forced into concentration camps based on nothing more than their race,[7] and that women could be sterilized at the state's command.[8]
- They held that children could be made to work in a cotton mill for as little as ten cents a day.[9]
- They relegated countless adults to dank sweatshops and deadly factories, with neither a union nor a minimum wage to protect them.[10]
- They gave billionaires a far-reaching right to corrupt American democracy,[11] and neutered much of America's most important voting rights law.[12]

And, throughout all of this history, the justices frequently ignored rights that are explicitly protected by the text of the Constitution. During World War I, for example, Congress enacted a sweeping censorship law that banned many forms of "disloyal" speech and even prohibited Americans from displaying the German flag.[13] Yet the Supreme Court showed little sympathy for the view that the First Amendment's "freedom of speech" protects individuals who speak out against their government during wartime. "When a nation is at war," the Court held in a unanimous opinion, "many things that might be said in time of peace are such a hindrance to its effort that their utterance will not be endured so long as men fight, and that no Court could regard them as protected by any constitutional right."[14]

The justices, in other words, have routinely committed two complementary sins against the Constitution. They've embraced extraconstitutional limits on the government's ability to protect the most vulnerable Americans, while simultaneously refusing to enforce rights that are explicitly enshrined in the Constitution's text. And they paved a trail of misery as a result. Few institutions have inflicted greater suffering on more Americans than the Supreme Court of the United States.

Nor is the Supreme Court redeemed by the brief period in the mid-1950s through the early 1970s, when the justices restored the Constitution's promises of equality, free speech, and fair justice for the accused. This anomalous phase in the Court's history was a historic accident. Indeed, if it weren't for a series of unpredictable events—including a fatal heart attack, a former Ku Klux Klansman's dramatic change of heart, and a decision that President Dwight D. Eisenhower later described as the "biggest damned-fool mistake I ever made"—then it is likely that the Court's 1954 decision declaring public school segregation unconstitutional would have gone the other way.

The justices of the Supreme Court are the closest thing America has to actual royalty. They serve for life and hold their offices due to presidential appointment—not because they earned a mandate from the people in an election. Unlike the president or any member of Congress, the justices go to work each day with no fear that they will be turned out of office if their decisions harm the country.

We trust them with this unchecked power because it ensures their independence. A just court will, at times, order an infamous man or woman to be freed from prison. It will shield hated minorities from their community's rage. And it will bring many of the nation's wealthiest and most powerful interests to heel before the law. Judges who fear their next election will be reluctant to enforce unpopular laws, or to tangle with politically influential litigants. As Alexander Hamilton wrote, "nothing can contribute so much to [the judiciary's] firmness and independence as permanency in office, this quality may therefore be justly regarded as an indispensable ingredient in its constitution, and, in a great measure, as the citadel of the public justice and the public security."[15]

Time and time again, however, the justices have taken the trust our Constitution places in them and wielded it to comfort the comfortable and to afflict the afflicted. They've read doubtful ideologies into the Constitution's vaguest phrases. And they've ignored provisions intended to protect the unpopular and the least fortunate.

Nor have many of the justices been particularly shy in their efforts to reshape the law in ways they find more agreeable. Not long after the Fourteenth Amendment officially became part of the Constitution, for example, two men—a former justice named John Archibald Campbell and a sitting member of the Court named Stephen Johnson Field—read the ambiguous words of that Amendment and saw an opportunity to reshape the nation. Campbell, a top wartime advisor to Confederate President Jefferson Davis, saw in an amendment intended to abolish American apartheid the power to sustain it instead. Field, meanwhile, was a deep skeptic of government regulation eager to write his own skepticism into the Constitution itself.

Both men would fail in their first effort to impose their vision upon the nation. And yet, before the twentieth century was more than a few years old, both men would achieve their wildest dreams.

PART I

THE CONSTITUTION OF
STEPHEN JOHNSON FIELD

Chapter 1

HOW THE CIVIL WAR
WAS UNDONE

T HE BATTLE TO reshape the Fourteenth Amendment did not begin in Colfax. It began nearly two hundred miles away in the dirtiest city in the nation.

Two years before the outbreak of the Civil War, the president of the New Orleans board of health described a city mired in filth. "Populous hotels poured their ordure from brimming sinks through the chief avenues of the city; gutters swelled with the blood and drainings of slaughter-pens; sugar refineries opened their sluices and whole streets reeked of rank odors; and every highway that chanced to be unpaved was broadcast with the rankings of gutters and the refuse filth of private yards and stables."[1]

Just a few years later, after Union forces captured the city in 1862, occupying General Benjamin Butler first encountered the odor of "putrefying filth" that filled the streets of New Orleans. After a carriage ride by a basin near Lake Pontchartrain, Butler complained that "the air seemed filled with the most noxious and offensive stenches possible, so noxious as almost to take away the power of breathing." Thick scum covered the surface of the water, and the remains of dead cats, dogs, and mules lined the banks.[2]

Indeed, the city Butler took charge of after it surrendered to Union forces in 1862 was the unhealthiest in the nation. At the middle of the nineteenth century, one in twelve residents of New

Orleans died each year, often from outbreaks of cholera or yellow fever. An 1851 study of New Orleans and Boston found twice as many deaths in the former city, despite the fact that Boston had thousands more residents than New Orleans. One physician described the city as a "great Golgatha."[3]

A major contributor to these conditions was the city's slaughterhouses, which were frequently built upriver of the intake pipes that supplied the city with water. Indeed, many of these slaughterhouses disposed of their waste by pumping water from the Mississippi River onto the killing floor. This water, now laden with blood and offal, would then be swept back into the current to poison the city's water supply.[4] Slaughterhouses built away from flowing water would drive leaking carts filled with animal waste through the city so that the waste could be discarded in the river. Others would discard their offal, in various states of rot and decay, into the streets and gutters of the city. Still more simply allowed their waste to fester on their own land.[5]

When Butler's troops arrived in New Orleans, Confederate loyalists widely expected his troops to be wiped out by one of the city's annual summer plagues. Motivated in no small part by fear that disease would achieve what rebel bullets could not, the occupying general ordered a massive cleanup of the city, putting thousands of men to work clearing garbage and closing down slaughterhouses along the river. His efforts were a huge success—the annual plagues ceased while Butler ruled over the city.[6]

Confederate defeat brought this occupation to a close, however, and Butler's reforms ended with the war. Slaughterhouses sprang up once again along the river, often providing jobs to former slaves trained to butcher cattle. Shortly after the war, New Orleans contained as many as 150 slaughterhouses[7] employing some one thousand butchers. In 1867, three thousand New Orleans residents died from the summer plague.[8]

As butchers polluted the Mississippi with the remains of dead cattle, newly enfranchised freedmen cast their first ballots to ratify a new Louisiana constitution proclaiming that "the citizens of this

State owe allegiance to the United States; and this allegiance is paramount to that which they owe to the State."[9] That same 1868 election elevated former Union officer Henry Clay Warmoth to the state governorship, and gave Abraham Lincoln's Republican Party commanding majorities in the state legislature. Thirty-five of the newly elected members of the state house were African American Republicans, just one fewer than the total number of Democrats.[10]

Louisiana's first integrated legislature soon turned its attention to the problem of slaughterhouses in New Orleans, and in March of 1869, they gave their solution the wordy title "An act to protect the health of the city of New Orleans, to locate the stock landings and slaughterhouses, and to incorporate the Crescent City Livestock Landing and Slaughter-House Company."[11] The act ordered all the city's slaughterhouses closed by the following June, to be replaced by a single grand slaughterhouse positioned so as not to pollute the city's water supply.

Though the act gave a monopoly to this single slaughterhouse, it also contained a detailed schedule of fees limiting how much the new complex could charge butchers to use its facilities, and imposed significant fines on the slaughterhouse's operators if they refused to allow a healthy animal to be slaughtered therein. All animals slaughtered at the new facility would be inspected by an officer appointed by the governor.[12] Thus, the act required all butchers to slaughter their cattle in a single location, but also guaranteed that all would have equal access to the grand slaughterhouse and that they would be charged only reasonable fees. An inspector would prevent diseased meat from entering the food supply, and the city's residents would enjoy clean water untainted by animal waste.

The city's slaughterhouse owners reacted with predictable outrage, but their rage was hardly limited to those businessmen impacted most negatively by the act. To many whites in New Orleans, the idea that black lawmakers and their Republican allies would presume to dictate any white man's business was itself an unforgivable outrage. As an editorial in the conservative *Daily Picayune* complained, whites "have been subjected to the terrible humiliation of seeing their former slaves, ignorant, brutal, and savage, placed above them in the political scale, and united with hordes of carpet-bag adventurers and robbers, coming down from the North, and now clothed with the law making power."[13]

No one felt this sentiment more deeply than John Archibald Campbell.

Campbell, who graduated from Franklin College (now the University of Georgia) with first honors at the age of fifteen, briefly studied alongside cadets Robert E. Lee and Jefferson Davis at West Point. Just two years into his military education, however, he abandoned it to pursue a career in law. After building a successful legal practice in Alabama, Campbell twice turned down appointments to the Alabama Supreme Court. When President Franklin Pierce offered him a seat on the Supreme Court of the United States in 1853, however, Campbell accepted and was swiftly confirmed.[14]

Campbell served just eight years as a justice, though that was long enough to cast a vote against the slave Dred Scott. He resigned from the Court less than three weeks after the first shots were fired at Fort Sumter, and his former classmate Davis—now the Confederate president—appointed him assistant secretary of war. In that role, Campbell was the highest ranking Confederate official to remain behind in Richmond, the Confederate capital, as the rebel government fled Grant's advancing army.[15]

By the time Louisiana's first black lawmakers took office, Campbell was a bitter man. During the war, Union troops destroyed nearly all of his possessions—including a substantial law library—and the former justice was laboring to build a new legal practice in New Orleans without them.[16] Having risen to become one of the most powerful men in the country, only to fall to the ranks of a nearly destitute traitor, Campbell gazed upon his state's new government with disgust. "We have Africans in place all about us," he wrote to his daughter in 1871. "They are jurors, post office clerks, custom house officers and day by day they barter away their obligations and duties." The South, Campbell warned, "will be a desolation until there is a thorough change of affairs in all the departments of government. . . .

Discontent, dissatisfaction, murmurings, complaints, even insurrection, would be better than the insensibility that seems to prevail."[17]

Yet Campbell also saw a path forward paved by the very words that were placed in the Constitution to guarantee equal rights to black citizens, and he soon started representing clients who would help him advance his white supremacist views. In one case, brought on behalf of a white businessman wishing to evade a state law requiring integrated theater seating, the former justice argued that the right to run a segregated business free from government interference was one of the unnamed "privileges or immunities" guarded by the Fourteenth Amendment.[18] In a challenge Campbell brought against the hated Slaughterhouse Act, he made a similar argument, believing he could convince his former Court to turn the Reconstruction Amendments against Louisiana's Reconstruction government.

Although Campbell's goal was white supremacy, he dressed up his challenge to the Slaughterhouse Act as a case about a domineering central government infringing upon the rights of small businessmen. "Can there be any centralization more complete or any despotism less responsible," Campbell asked in a brief to the justices, "than that of a State legislature concerning itself with dominating the avocations, pursuits and modes of labor of the population; conferring monopolies on some, voting subsidies to others, restraining the freedom and independence of others, and making merchandise of the whole?"[19] Tucked within the Reconstruction Amendments' mysterious unnamed rights, Campbell saw the right to be free from the Reconstruction government's slaughterhouse law just as clearly as he spied the right to separate white from black.

———

JUSTICE STEPHEN JOHNSON FIELD also sensed opportunity in what became known as the *Slaughterhouse Cases*, decided by the Court in 1873. If Campbell dreamed of a constitution that entrenched white people as America's master race, Field pined for a constitution that would shrink the government's power until it was completely incapable of threatening the power and fortunes of America's most fortunate few. Similarly, where Campbell viewed black men ruling over Southern whites as an affront to our nation's fundamental values, Field imagined a much older betrayal stretching back as far as the Federalist Party's ascendance during the John Adams administration.

Field, a Democrat at a time when Democrats were more likely to share his skepticism of government than Republicans, made a dark horse bid for his party's presidential nomination in 1880. During this race, Field's campaign published a pamphlet warning of "the chilling shadow of the empire" descending upon the American republic. "The old Constitution," Field claimed, "has been buried under the liberal interpretations of Federalist-Republican Congresses and administrations, grasping doubtful powers and making each step towards centralization the sure precedent of another." Field, the pamphlet went on to argue, was "the proper candidate of the party whose life-giving principle is that of local self-government."[20]

One of Field's fullest articulations of his antigovernment views arose from an attempt to protect farmers from price gouging. In the 1870s, nearly all grain grown in the Midwest made its way to the Chicago waterfront, where it was shipped via the Great Lakes to purchasers in the East Coast and Europe. While in Chicago, all of this grain was stored in just fourteen warehouses owned by nine firms that colluded among themselves to set prices.[21] Thus, for farmers in much of the country, the only way to access markets large enough to buy their crop was to pay a monopolist's rates to firms that could raise their prices virtually at will.

Yet, where the farmers saw entrenched businessmen bleeding their families dry, Justice Field saw property owners exercising a sacred constitutional right. When an Illinois law capping Chicago grain warehouse rates reached the Supreme Court, Field labeled this law a "bold assertion of absolute power by the State to control at its discretion the property and business of the citizen,"[22] and he called for businesses to be given sweeping immunity to regulation under the Fourteenth Amendment. For the moment, however, his views did not carry the day. Only Justice William Strong joined Field in dissent.

Though a Democrat, Field was appointed to the Supreme Court by Republican President Lincoln. After Lincoln's death, however, Field showed little interest in Reconstruction. Just over a year after the close of the Civil War, Field authored an opinion striking down an 1865 law preventing former Confederate officials from practicing law in federal court,[23] breaking with the Court's four other Lincoln appointees in the process.[24] Field's presidential campaign would later tout this opinion as proof that he would appeal to Southern whites if nominated for the White House.[25] (The victorious party in the Confederate officials case, Arkansas politician Augustus Garland, would go on to serve as Attorney General of the United States under President Grover Cleveland.)

Similarly, Field cared little for racial equality, although on this point he was often joined by his fellow justices. Three years before his death in 1899, Field joined the Supreme Court's nearly unanimous decision in *Plessy v. Ferguson* (1896), the segregated railcar decision that held that "the enforced separation of the races . . . neither abridges the privileges or immunities of the colored man, deprives him of his property without due process of law, nor denies him the equal protection of the laws."[26] In another opinion, Field mocked the very idea that African Americans cannot constitutionally be excluded from juries. If black people had such a right, Field chided, then states would have to give the same right to women![27]

Field showed similar indifference towards the anti-Chinese sentiment that plagued his home state of California. At the age of thirty-three, Field left a New York law practice to join the forty-niners seeking opportunity in the California Gold Rush.[28] He was joined there by thousands of Chinese immigrants. Yet, although California offered Field the chance to serve in the state legislature, to sit on its supreme court, and, eventually, to become its chief justice, the Chinese citizens who met him there typically found low-wage jobs, brutal working conditions, and racism.

In the years after Field left California to answer Lincoln's call, the Central Pacific Railroad hired as many as fourteen thousand Chinese workers to build the first leg of the tracks that would connect

America's two coasts. There, they labored under white foremen who often punished stragglers with the whip. A common task for Chinese crews carving railroad beds into mountainsides was to dangle a single man over ledges, in a basket thousands of feet above the ground, where the man would place a blasting powder charge in the face of the mountain, light the fuse, and pray that his companions pulled him up fast enough to escape death from flying rocks. During the wintertime, these same men would clear up to fifteen feet of snow just to begin each work day. Avalanches were a common cause of death.[29]

California rewarded these laborers with anti-Chinese laws often resembling those facing African Americans under Jim Crow. Chinese immigrants in California paid special taxes. They were barred from some professions and forced to obtain special licenses to engage in others. California's Chinese residents could neither sit on juries nor testify in court.[30] And the state actively lobbied for federal legislation restricting Chinese immigration.

An 1877 message to Congress prepared by an official committee of seven California state senators, warned that Chinese immigrants "seem to be antediluvian men renewed. Their code of morals, their forms of worship, and their maxims of life are those of remotest antiquity." The Chinese are "impregnable to all the influences of our Anglo-Saxon life," the senators' message complained. "There can be no hope that any contact with our people, however long continued, will ever conform them to our institutions, enable them to comprehend or appreciate our form of government, or to assume the duties or discharge the functions of citizens."[31]

The culmination of this anti-Chinese sentiment was the federal Chinese Exclusion Act of 1882, which barred Chinese workers from entering the United States,[32] and an 1888 act prohibiting Chinese laborers who departed the United States from returning, even if they'd previously been issued a certificate by the federal government granting them permission to do so. The Supreme Court upheld this later exclusion of Chinese workers in a unanimous decision by Justice Field.[33]

So when John Archibald Campbell told the Supreme Court that he stood for "Freedom. Free action, free enterprise [and] free competition" in calling upon them to strike the Slaughterhouse Act, he appealed to the one kind of freedom Field held most dear. Field's opinion in the *Slaughterhouse Cases* labels Louisiana's attempt to keep rotting offal out of the streets of New Orleans to be "similar in principle and as odious in character as the restrictions imposed in the last century upon the peasantry in some parts of France." Telling butchers that they must slaughter their cattle in a certain location downriver from the city was no less an affront to liberty, according to Field, than French lords prohibiting a man "to hunt on his own lands, to fish in his own waters, to grind at his own mill, to cook at his own oven, to dry his clothes on his own machines, to whet his instruments at his own grindstone, to make his own wine, his oil, and his cider at his own press, . . . or to sell his commodities at the public market."[34]

Field, however, wrote these words in a dissenting opinion. Though three of his colleagues shared his view that the Slaughterhouse Act was akin to peasantry, a majority of the Court joined an opinion by Justice Samuel Freeman Miller upholding the law.

———

THE FIRST OF TEN children born to poor Kentucky farmers, Miller nonetheless married the daughter of one of the preeminent attorneys of Barbourville, Kentucky. As a result of the marital property laws in effect at the time, Miller's marriage to Lucy Ballinger also gave him ownership of his wife's five slaves.[35]

Miller, however, soon fell under the sway of emancipationist politician Cassius M. Clay. Unlike the firebrand William Lloyd Garrison, who compared anything short of immediate abolition of slavery to telling a man "to moderately rescue his wife from the hand of the ravisher,"[36] Clay viewed slavery less as a moral affront to equality and more as a failed economic model. After a trip to New England, Clay returned home to Kentucky awestruck by the region's prosperity—in those free states, men and women lived "luxuriously" on land that, in Kentucky, "would have been deemed the high road to famine and the almshouse."[37]

This vision so resonated with Miller that he began freeing his slaves around 1846, just four years after his marriage to Lucy. When Kentucky enacted a proslavery constitution in 1850, Miller left the state for the free soil of Iowa, where he would start a successful law practice and help build the Republican Party. After Miller spent a dozen years in Iowa, President Lincoln placed him on the Supreme Court.[38]

Miller, however, did not begin his career as an attorney. Rather, he rose to prominence in Barbourville as a physician. A graduate of Transylvania University in Lexington, Kentucky, Miller rapidly grew disillusioned with the practice of medicine during an era in which treatments were often just as deadly as the diseases they were meant to cure. In Miller's age, the most feared disease was cholera, which could take a perfectly healthy man at morning, reduce him to violent vomiting and diarrhea at noontime, and leave him a corpse by sunset. In 1838, cholera took one-quarter of Barbourville's juvenile population.[39]

So Justice Miller was the ex-Confederate Campbell's ideal antagonist. More than just a staunch Republican, Miller knew better than anyone else on the Court how disease could ravage a town. When Campbell spoke of a hated monopoly denying New Orleans butchers their freedom, Miller could see hope that young doctors—like he had once been—would be spared from breaking the worst possible news to a dying patient's family.

Miller saw right through Campbell's efforts to recast the Reconstruction Amendments as a shield for Southern whites. "No one can fail to be impressed," Miller wrote in his *Slaughterhouse* opinion, "with the one pervading purpose found" in these three amendments. "Lying at the foundation of each" was "the freedom of the slave race, the security and firm establishment of that freedom, and the protection of the newly-made freeman and citizen from the oppressions of those who had formerly exercised unlimited dominion over him."

The target of Campbell's ire bore little relation to the "evil" these amendments were intended to remedy.[40]

Of the act itself, Miller wrote that "it cannot be denied that the statute under consideration is aptly framed to remove from the more densely populated part of the city, the noxious slaughter-houses . . . and to locate them where the convenience, health, and comfort of the people require they shall be located." The act's mechanism for doing so—mandating that all animals must be slaughtered in a single privately owned but highly regulated slaughterhouse—was "appropriate . . . stringent, and effectual."[41]

There was, however, a dark side to Justice Miller's opinion. Defying Congressman Bingham's expectation that the Fourteenth Amendment would reshape Americans' legal rights and forbid state lawmakers from violating the Bill of Rights, Miller rejected the notion that the Fourteenth Amendment fundamentally transformed "the relations of the State and Federal governments to each other and of both these governments to the people."[42] As Field correctly noted in dissent, Miller read the "privileges or immunities of citizens of the United States" protected by the new amendment so narrowly that he practically wrote them out of the Constitution. If Miller's reading of this constitutional language is correct, then the amendment was, Field wrote, a "vain and idle enactment, which accomplished nothing."[43]

Coincidentally, the Supreme Court decided *Slaughterhouse* just one day after the massacre in Colfax, effectively ratifying the Reconstruction government's health law the day after Louisiana's white supremacists proved they could seize power by force. The Court case that emerged from the Colfax Massacre would soon reveal the price of Justice Miller's narrow reading of the Fourteenth Amendment. Campbell's defeat in *Slaughterhouse* would lay the groundwork for a far greater triumph over Reconstruction.

————

As Campbell appealed to the courts to undermine the Reconstruction government, his fellow white supremacists resorted to voter suppression and outright violence in order to regain the levers of power in Louisiana. And, as Campbell awaited the Supreme Court's decision in the *Slaughterhouse Cases*, white Democrats recruited an unusual ally to their cause—the very man who signed the Slaughterhouse Act into law.

Republican Governor Henry Warmoth proved to be far more loyal to his own ambitions than he was to the former slaves who helped elect him. As the 1872 elections to choose his successor loomed, Warmoth struck a deal with Democratic leaders loyal to Campbell's cause. The Republican governor would throw his full support behind Democratic gubernatorial candidate John McEnery, a former Confederate army officer. In return, Democrats agreed to send Warmoth to the United States Senate (at the time, senators were selected by state lawmakers, rather than being popularly elected under the Seventeenth Amendment, which was ratified in 1913).[44]

Pursuant to this Faustian bargain, Warmoth installed loyal Democrats as voter registrars throughout the state. In a story that would play out again and again in the South for nearly a full century, these registrars then set out to ensure that the electorate would be as white as possible. Some registrars insisted that elderly black voters prove they were over the minimum voting age of twenty-one before they could register to vote—often an impossible task because former slaves had no birth certificates. Others changed voter registration sites but then notified only white voters of the relocations. Meanwhile, white landlords threatened to evict black tenants who voted Republican. And, when these efforts failed, election officials could always rely on old-fashioned ballot stuffing. In Grant Parish, the site of the Colfax Massacre, white officials snatched a ballot box, kept it overnight, and returned it the next day with a hole in its side where additional ballots could be dropped in.[45]

In the wake of this tainted election, both McEnery and his opponent, William Pitt Kellogg, a Republican and former Union army colonel, declared victory and began appointing their supporters to state offices. Kellogg eventually gained the upper hand after a pro-McEnery militia tried but failed to seize control of New Orleans police stations in March of 1873.[46]

However, a similar drama soon played out in Grant Parish with a very different outcome. At the same time that Democrats and Republicans fought over who would control the governor's mansion, competing slates of candidates in Grant Parish both claimed that they had the right to control various local offices. As both sides believed that they needed to control the parish courthouse in Colfax in order to govern, a group of Republicans quietly approached this building at night and snuck a young black boy into the courthouse through a window. The boy then unlocked the building from the inside, allowing the Republicans to occupy it.[47]

Three days later, on March 28, 1873, white Democratic leaders began plotting to retake the courthouse by force. When word of these plans reached the Republicans, armed black men started mustering at the courthouse to defend it against the white aggressors.[48]

Led by Christopher Columbus Nash, an ex-Confederate army lieutenant who was also the Democratic candidate for Grant Parish sheriff, Democratic forces marched on Colfax on April 13. Though the approximately 150 black men defending the courthouse slightly outnumbered Nash's men, the Republican forces were massively outgunned. About half of Nash's men were Confederate veterans, including four officers. Each of them was well armed, many of them with multiple guns, and they had even brought a small cannon to Colfax on a two-horse wagon.[49]

Meanwhile, as many as half of the black men protecting the courthouse had no guns whatsoever, and those with guns had only enough powder and ammunition to allow each man to fire about two rounds. The closest thing the freedmen had to artillery were three makeshift guns rigged from old steam pipes. When they attempted to fire one of these would-be cannons, the entire gun exploded.[50]

The result was a rout. White forces outflanked the freedmen, positioning their cannon behind the black army's trench line. Not long after the cannon started spewing buckshot at the exposed men around the courthouse, black combatants began to flee—only to be hunted down and captured or killed by white men on horseback. Though dozens of freedmen continued to fight from within the courthouse, Nash ordered the courthouse to be set ablaze. When the black Republicans laid down their arms and fled the burning building, many of them waving white flags of surrender, Nash's men opened fire.[51]

Nor did the killing stop there. Nash eventually ordered his men to cease fire, and the remaining freedmen were taken prisoner. Two hours before midnight, however, Nash left the prisoners under the control of a group of men led by Bill Cruikshank, a white supremacist cotton planter. Not long thereafter, Cruikshank ordered the captured freedmen to march away from the courthouse under armed guard. The column did not get far before Cruikshank's men drew their pistols and began executing their prisoners. A black man named Levi Nelson, who later served as a star witness against Cruikshank at his criminal trial, survived this death march only because Cruikshank tried to make sport out of murder by lining up Nelson and another man close enough together that they could both be shot with a single bullet, rather than spending two shots to ensure that both men would die.[52]

————

THE OSTENSIBLE ISSUE in *United States v. Cruikshank* was whether Cruikshank and two other members of Nash's army violated a federal law forbidding two or more people to "band or conspire together" to "injure, oppress, threaten, or intimidate any citizen, with intent to prevent or hinder his free exercise and enjoyment of any right or privilege granted or secured to him by the constitution or laws of the United States."[53] Yet, in rejecting these charges against Cruikshank and his fellow murderers, the Court did far more than simply resolve a single criminal case. If *Slaughterhouse* defied Congressman Bingham's expectation that his new amendment would transform the nation, *Cruikshank* practically mocked Bingham's high hopes.

In response to the prosecution's claim that Cruikshank tread upon his victims' First Amendment right to "assemble and to petition the government for a redress of grievances," the Court barely considered the idea that such a right was now encompassed by the Fourteenth Amendment. Instead, *Cruikshank* hold that "the people must look to the States" themselves to vindicate this right—they would find no protection from federal courts.[54]

The Court was similarly dismissive of a claim that Cruikshank and his fellow defendants could be prosecuted for assaulting their victims' Second Amendment right of "bearing arms for a lawful purpose." The Second Amendment, according to *Cruikshank*, "means no more than that it shall not be infringed by Congress."[55]

Much of the opinion relied on technical errors by the prosecution to toss out charges against the defendants. There is little doubt, for example, that Cruikshank joined Nash's army in order to undo ballots cast by black Republicans and restore white supremacist rule to his part of Louisiana. Yet the Court wrote that, even though "we may suspect that race was the cause of the hostility," the prosecution erred by merely making this claim "by implication."[56]

Nevertheless, *Cruikshank* swept far beyond technical rulings particular to this one case. Rather than fulfilling Bingham's hope that his amendment would give each citizen sweeping new rights that would be enforced by the federal courts, the Supreme Court denied the Bill of Rights to the freedmen. And they told these former slaves to "look to the States" to vindicate their rights.

It does not take much imagination to envision what happened next.

Governor Kellogg proved impotent in the face of violence led by the newly formed "White League," an anti-Reconstruction paramilitary organization that included many Confederate veterans. In Red River Parish, White Leaguers soon murdered six Republican officials. Emboldened by these killings, a militia of thirty-five hundred men captured the New Orleans city hall, statehouse, and arsenal. They left only after President Ulysses S. Grant sent federal troops to bolster Kellogg's government.[57]

Grant's successor, Republican Rutherford B. Hayes, took office under the most dubious of circumstances. Hayes had once been an advocate for enslaved black men seeking freedom. As an attorney in private practice, Hayes had argued dozens of cases on behalf of runaway slaves, often taking on clients offered to him by Levi Coffin, the president of the Underground Railroad.[58] But Hayes sacrificed this principle in order to shore up his path to the White House.

After Hayes lost the popular vote to Democrat Samuel Tilden and faced a highly disputed electoral vote, his supporters brokered a deal with Democrats: inaugurate Hayes, and the new president would end Reconstruction.[59] As a result of this deal, Grant's troops stood down, Louisiana inaugurated a Confederate brigadier general as governor, and former slaves were left only with the Court's admonition to "look to the States" for protection. By the time the sun set on the Hayes administration, Southerners no longer lived under the Constitution of the United States. They lived under the white supremacist Constitution of John Archibald Campbell.

And it wouldn't be long before the whole nation would live under the Constitution of Stephen Johnson Field.

Chapter 2

THE BARON OUTSIDE CHICAGO

I F THE CIVIL WAR had never been fought, and if chattel slavery had never existed within the United States, Abraham Lincoln would still rank among our greatest and most consequential presidents for a single bill he signed during the darkest days of the War Between the States. On the day Lincoln entered the White House, America was divided not just by a crisis of secession but also by what many maps referred to as the "Great American Desert." To reach the western states from Lincoln's new home in the nation's capital, the financial analyst Henry Varnum Poor warned that a traveler must cross two thousand miles

> through an uninhabited and, for the greater part, we may say an un-
> inhabitable country, nearly destitute of wood, extensive districts of it
> destitute of water; over mountain ranges whose summits are white
> with eternal snows; over deserts parched beneath an unclouded sky,
> and over yawning chasms which the process of disintegration since
> the volcanic fires were put out, has not yet filled up.[1]

In this land between worlds, wrote the newspaperman and future presidential candidate Horace Greeley, "famine sits enthroned, and waves his scepter over a dominion expressly made for him."[2] In the fertile soil of the Great Plains, few farmers tilled the soil and hardly any towns provided an opportunity to trade for food and supplies. Starvation stalked the traveler—and all too often it claimed its prey.[3]

To dodge this predator, many traveled instead by ship, either spending as much as four months rounding the southern tip of South America or availing themselves of a shortcut through the jungles of Panama. Those who took the latter option often regretted it.

Prior to 1855, a westbound traveler faced a potentially weeks-long layover in Panama, punctuated by trips up narrow rivers, wagon rides through the jungle, and the constant threat of fatal tropical diseases. One ill-fated vessel saw a third of its passengers drop dead from cholera and their bodies heaved overboard to prevent further spread of the disease. And even after a trans-Panama railroad improved conditions somewhat, the trip remained prohibitively expensive to many travelers and sometimes claimed thousands of lives in a single year.[4]

This is why, when President Lincoln signed the Pacific Railroad Act of 1862 and authorized the land grants and government bonds necessary to build a transcontinental railway, he fundamentally transformed the nation. As the *New York Times* proclaimed shortly after this railway's completion in 1869, "twenty years ago, 118 days were necessary" to round South America and reach the west coast. "Now, from ocean to ocean, a little over six days are consumed."[5]

Like any transformative innovation, railroads also made a number of men fantastically rich. One popular ranking lists Cornelius Vanderbilt as the second wealthiest man in American history, with a fortune of over $143 billion in 2007 dollars.[6] Jay Gould, who ranks ninth on the same list, controlled so much wealth that he and a partner nearly collapsed much of the nation's banking industry with an elaborate 1869 plot to corner the gold market. He was thwarted only after President Ulysses S. Grant intervened by selling massive amounts of the federal government's gold supply.[7] Leland Stanford not only amassed enough of a fortune to build the elite university that bears his son's name, he was also a dominant figure in California politics, serving two years as the state's governor and eight as a United States senator.

Meanwhile, workers in the age of Vanderbilt and Gould enjoyed few legal protections against their employers. Unions did exist among railroad workers, but they were typically small, exclusive groups of craftsmen with little real power relative to wealthy employers and no legal right to bring managers to the bargaining table. When disputes did arise between capital and labor, railroad workers typically had just two weapons in their arsenal—neither of which were particularly well honed. The first was the strike, which pitted workers against their own willingness to remain out of work and their bosses' ability to fire them in favor of scabs. The second was the boycott, which called upon outsiders to refuse to deal with the offending company until it agreed to higher wages or better workplace conditions.

And, on those rare occasions when a railroad feared it might bend to a strike or a boycott, the rail barons often had an ace in the hole—judges. In an opinion typical of this era, Judge William Howard Taft labeled an entire union a "criminal conspiracy against the laws of their country" after its members boycotted a railroad company.[8] Taft, of course, later served as President and then Chief Justice of the United States. Other judges wielded the Sherman Antitrust Act's prohibitions on monopolies and conspiracies "in restraint of trade or commerce" to shut down striking workers.[9]

In fairness, not every decision of this era prohibited strikes and boycotts—Taft and his fellow judges developed complex rules permitting strikes for some purposes and not for others[10]—but judicial orders halting labor actions were quite common. One scholar estimates that more than five hundred injunctions were issued against workers or labor unions just in the final two decades of the nineteenth century. By the 1920s, after watching an entire generation of judges' efforts to thwart the labor movement, American Federation of Labor president Samuel Gompers warned that "those who seek to retain the injunction evil and to expand it are doing the greatest disservice to our system of jurisprudence, and in fact to our system of democratic government."[11]

Against this legal backdrop, a young union, led by a man who would grow into one of the twentieth century's most prominent radicals, would challenge one of the nation's wealthiest men. As Stanford and Gould amassed fortunes and power that would have made a medieval lord blanch, another railroad baron came as close as any American has ever come to building his own personal fiefdom. Twenty-five years after a golden spike completed the first transcontinental railroad, this barony outside Chicago would be the staging ground for the most disruptive labor dispute in American history. And that dispute would cement the nearly boundless power of the United States Supreme Court.

THOUGH GEORGE PULLMAN'S name would become synonymous with first class railroad travel, he was born into far more modest circumstances. The son of a successful carpenter in western New York State, Pullman left school at age fourteen to work in a small general store and later in his brother's cabinet shop. Moreover, Pullman did not so much seek out his first business opportunity as have it foisted upon him by his father's death. After the state legislature voted to expand the Erie Canal, Pullman's father won contracts to move houses deemed too close to the canal's banks. When the elder Pullman fell ill and died in 1853, the task of completing these contracts fell to the twenty-two-year-old George.[12]

Pullman's ability to raise or relocate existing buildings was in high demand in America's fastest growing city. In 1850, when Pullman was still making cabinets for his brother's shop, just under thirty thousand people called Chicago their home. By Lincoln's election ten years later, Chicago's population was nearly four times that[13]—in no small part due to the city's emergence as a railroad hub and its proximity to navigable waterways. Yet much of Chicago's land also sat only a few feet above Lake Michigan, leading to persistent flooding of cellars and city streets. To combat this flooding, the city undertook a massive project to elevate the city's buildings and streets by four to seven feet in the affected areas. Pullman arrived in Chicago shortly after this project began to take advantage of the business opportunity it provided.[14]

Within three years, Pullman and his business partner were Chicago's leading provider of building elevations. At the age of twenty-seven, the former cabinetmaker supervised a team of a thousand men with five thousand jackscrews tasked with elevating the Tremont Hotel. According to one account, his team achieved this task without disturbing the people or the furniture, which remained in what was then Chicago's finest hotel as the entire structure was lifted from underneath. By the end of the year, Pullman's personal wealth exceeded the equivalent of a half million dollars in modern American currency.[15]

Pullman's fortunes could not last long, however, at least if he remained in this same line of work. With each building he raised, Pullman brought Chicago's overall project of raising the neighborhoods along Lake Michigan one step closer to completion. So it wasn't long before he found another line of work. When he was living in New York, Pullman formed a close friendship with former state senator Benjamin Field, a distant relative of the future Supreme Court justice. Field would soon introduce Pullman to the line of work that would transform the former cabinetmaker into one of the wealthiest men in the country.

A lengthy genealogy of the Field family claims that Benjamin "was the real inventor of the sleeping car, and it was of his thought and money that George M. Pullman availed himself to perfect one of the greatest inventions of the age."[16] This claim is hyperbolic at best. Sleeping cars existed well before Field and Pullman formed their partnership. Indeed, as early as 1854, an inventor patented a hinged chair that a mechanic could convert at night into a bed suitable for railway passengers. This convertible chair was intended to upgrade primitive early sleeping cars, in which travelers were confined to one of three wooden shelves permanently fixed to the side of the car.[17]

Yet, although sleepers existed before Pullman and Field formed their partnership, they were miserable, cramped environments that offered travelers all the comfort of a pinewood coffin. Pullman would later claim that he booked a berth in a sleeping car across New York State just to evaluate the quality of the experience. He discovered low ceilings and uncomfortable beds in which passengers were expected to lie fully clothed. Worse, the unventilated cars were heated by stove fires at either end, filling the air with choking fumes that Pullman described as "something dreadful." The young businessman rode in the topmost of three bunks, and the car's ceiling loomed uncomfortably close to his nose.[18]

Pullman and Field's first sleepers offered several improvements from these early accommodations. During the day, passengers sat on wide upholstered benches similar in appearance to the seating available to a first-class passenger engaged in a mere day trip. At night, these benches could be combined to form bunks for some of the passengers, while the remaining passengers would sleep on berths lowered from close to the ceiling. When not in use, these upper berths doubled as storage space for bedding.[19]

Not long after Justice Stephen Johnson Field authored his first opinion casting a wrench into the gears of Reconstruction, Pullman would assume full leadership of the company he began with the justice's kinsman. While New Orleans pondered its slaughterhouse problem, Pullman built larger and increasingly more luxurious sleeper cars. He also gave his company a name worthy of such luxury: the Pullman Palace Car Company.

By modern standards, Pullman offered travelers an almost comic degree of opulence. One early Pullman sleeper featured chandeliers, marble washbasins, and a black walnut interior.[20] Pullman built dining cars that offered steak, oysters, and a choice of wines to hungry passengers. By the 1870s a train equipped with a full complement of Pullman cars would include a barber shop, multiple libraries, a smoking room, and a fully functional organ, just in case passengers wanted to entertain themselves by playing music.[21]

Although this level of sumptuousness would be absurd in a modern train, Pullman tapped into a very real need for nineteenth-century travelers. The transcontinental railroad cut the length of a coast-to-coast trip from over three months to just under one week, but a week is nonetheless a long time to spend confined to a train car with nothing else to do but admire the scenery. Pullman built his fortune upon a singular insight: men and women who had already invested days of their life into a trip would happily pay a little more to make that trip bearable.

———

PULLMAN CRAVED WEALTH, and he craved the luxury it brought even more than the many travelers who lined up to ride his magnificent train cars. At a cost of as much as $12 million in modern dollars, Pullman built a mansion surrounded by the homes of Chicago's business titans (including retail magnate Marshall Field, another relative of the Supreme Court justice). There, surrounded by marble, teak paneling, and his own private pipe organ, Pullman and his wife would host truly enormous parties. When his daughter made her debut to Chicago's high society, a thousand guests greeted her at the Pullman home.[22]

After vacationing with President Grant and his wife, Julia, in the beach community of Long Branch, New Jersey, the Pullmans decided they needed a second mansion. Built in Long Branch, this additional house, named "Fairlawn," soon became their summer home.[23]

Yet, for all that he craved in terms of wealth, Pullman hungered just as intensely for dominion over the workers he employed and the railroads he served. Under his standard contract with a rail line, the Pullman Company maintained full ownership of its cars and merely leased them to the railroad for ten to fifteen years, although in some cases a railroad could purchase a half interest in the car itself. For each passenger who booked a ticket on a Pullman car, the railroad received nothing more than the cost of an ordinary fare. Every cent the passenger paid as a premium for Pullman's added luxury went right back to the Pullman Company.[24]

Pullman maintained an even tighter grip over his own workers. A passenger boarding a Pullman sleeping car would encounter two employees therein: an African American porter to service their needs and a white conductor to ensure their compliance with various regulations, such as the rule requiring them to remove their boots before climbing into bed. Though Pullman viewed this decision to employ black porters as a great service to freedmen seeking to escape agricultural labor, the Pullman Company's generosity extended only so far. At one point, white conductors earned nearly three times as much as the black porters who worked alongside them.[25]

Porters and conductors alike wore uniforms and were required to comply with their own detailed rule books. To ensure compliance with the rules, Pullman employed an array of undercover "spotters" who traveled the rails in search of messy washbasins or conductors sneaking a beer while on duty. Workers caught breaking the rules were fined.[26]

As time wore on, Pullman fixated on a quest to socially engineer the perfect workforce. He loathed saloons and alcoholism, not out of sympathy for the ruined men who dragged their way into his factories after yet another night of drinking, but because such men were frequently absent and were poor workers when they did show up.[27] Pullman also emerged as a leading benefactor of education for the working class. As an early president of the board of the Young Men's Christian Association, Pullman temporarily renamed the organization the "Chicago Athenaeum" and shifted its focus to low-cost courses in subjects like bookkeeping. Similarly, along with his friend and neighbor Marshall Field, Pullman served as a trustee of a school that trained working-class students to be mechanics.[28] Such efforts undoubtedly benefited the pupils trained in these programs, but they also helped ensure that the Pullman Company would have an abundance of skilled workers.

Nothing captures Pullman's quest for dominion over the perfect workforce, however, more than the model town he built to house his workers. Built on thirty-four hundred acres of land just a short train ride from Chicago, the town of Pullman reflected its namesake's vision of the ideal community—where skilled and unskilled workers lived sober lives together in the shadow of the factories where they labored.

Pullman's town, with its brick homes, wide streets, green lawns, and ubiquitous shade trees, was by all accounts beautiful. As *Harper's Magazine* described Pullman, Illinois, in 1885, "what is seen in a walk or drive through the streets is so pleasing to the eye that a woman's first exclamation is certain to be, 'Perfectly lovely!' It is indeed a sight as rare as it is delightful. What might have been taken for a wealthy suburban town is given up to busy workers, who literally earn their bread in the sweat of their brow."[29]

The town of Pullman had no saloons. Indeed, only one bar could be found in the entire community—and that was in the grand hotel where Pullman would entertain leading businessmen and politicians. Instead of drinking, Pullman expected his workers to entertain themselves at a library filled with hand-selected books, at a theater featuring plays screened by the company to exclude immorality, or at the park and athletic field built for residents' use. To recoup the cost of building the town, Pullman charged rents high enough to return a profit, although his rents were less than the cost of similar housing in Chicago—or at least, they started out that way.[30]

And yet, for all the enticements Pullman offered for his workers to relocate to this company town, it was ultimately a mechanism to ensure his dominion over them. Though Pullman employees were technically under no obligation to reside in their employer's town, promotions were often only available to workers willing to reside in company housing; workers who lived elsewhere were the first to be laid off in difficult economic times.[31] Every square inch of land in Pullman was owned by the company—workers had no option to buy their own homes—and its leases permitted the company to evict any resident on just ten days' notice. Thus, workers who displeased their bosses could find themselves homeless almost as quickly as they were rendered jobless.[32]

The town of Pullman's very layout also reinforced a rigid hierarchy. The residential portion of the town began at Florence Boulevard, named for Pullman's beloved daughter, where a dozen and a half homes housed Pullman Company executives. Beyond this block of Pullman's most expensive residences lay hundreds of two- to five-family row houses for skilled workers. At the outskirts of the community Pullman built ten tenements for unskilled laborers. Overlooking all of this was the Florence Hotel, built at the head of Florence Boulevard, where Pullman himself could watch over his domain from a suite built for his use.[33]

It was, in short, the closest thing that has ever existed to an American barony, with George Mortimer Pullman ensconced as its lord and master. As *Harper's* warned,

> the idea of Pullman is un-American. It is a nearer approach than anything the writer has seen to what appears to be the ideal of the great German Chancellor. It is not the American ideal. It is benevolent, well-wishing feudalism, which desires the happiness of the people, but in such way as shall please the authorities. One can not avoid thinking of the late Czar of Russia, Alexander II., to whom the welfare of his subjects was truly a matter of concern. He wanted them to be happy, but desired their happiness to proceed from him, in whom everything should centre.[34]

Yet, despite these warnings the town thrived in much the same way Pullman expected for over a decade. More than eight thousand residents filled its homes at night and the bulk of them filled Pullman's factories by day.

That is, of course, until the depression came.

———

EUGENE DEBS'S EARLY life offered few hints that he would emerge as America's most prominent socialist, that he would twice be imprisoned with the blessing of the Supreme Court, or that he would first become Pullman's greatest antagonist. Like Pullman, Debs was born into modest but comfortable circumstances; his parents were French immigrants who ran a successful grocery in Terre Haute, Indiana.

Debs's life leading up to his clash with Pullman tracked the evolution of the labor movement during the latter half of the nineteenth century. After a four-year stint as a railroad worker himself, Debs returned home to Terre Haute, where he became active in local politics—eventually serving a term in the state legislature as a Democrat—and an important figure in the Brotherhood of Locomotive Firemen.[35]

Like many of the old-line trade unions common in the years following the Civil War, the Brotherhood was small and exclusive to workers engaged in a very specific line of work. It recruited less through a promise of high wages achieved by solidarity and more because it offered members a low-cost insurance plan. Indeed, the Brotherhood actively discouraged confrontations with management. While serving as editor of the union's *Locomotive Firemen Magazine*, Debs himself wrote in 1883 that "we do not believe in violence and strikes as means by which wages are to be regulated, but that all differences must be settled by mutual understanding arrived at by calm reasoning."[36]

This model rendered the Brotherhood incapable of standing up to organized capital. Despite the words Debs wrote in 1883, the Brotherhood did partner with another union representing railroad engineers to strike the Chicago, Burlington and Quincy Railroad in 1888. What they learned was that the railroad could quite easily fire every single striking fireman and engineer and replace them with scabs.[37]

Faced with their own inability to stand against increasingly powerful employers, workers began to join together in larger and often significantly more inclusive organizations. This era saw the meteoric rise and spectacular flameout of the Knights of Labor, which rallied women and African Americans together with white male workers under the cry that "an injury to one is the concern of all." Moreover, unlike the trade unions with their rigid segmentation of the workforce, the Knights welcomed men and women from all occupations together under the same banner. At its height, the Knights boasted three-quarters of a million members and waged a successful strike against the ruthless Jay Gould. The organization soon collapsed, however, under the weight of weak leadership, internal racial tensions, and the administrative nightmare of managing its ballooning membership. The venerable American Federation of Labor formed amidst this collapse in no small part due to trade union dissatisfaction with the Knights.[38]

In 1893, Debs formed a new kind of labor organization. Neither as hyper-inclusive as the Knights nor as narrowly focused as the Brotherhood, the American Railway Union (ARU) welcomed any white person employed in the railways, regardless of their specific occupation, and permitted any ten of these workers to join together as a local union.[39] Within a year, the ARU boasted 150,000 members and had already won its first major victory. Indeed, that victory, which restored nearly all of the wages cut by executives of the Great Northern Railroad, seemed to vindicate the superiority of Debs's new model. The ARU succeeded in forcing concessions out of the Great Northern shortly after the old brotherhoods had tried but failed to achieve anything more than marginal gains.[40]

Not long after this victory, Chicago baron George Pullman would make similar wage cuts—spurring a conflict would have a very different outcome for Debs.

———

ON THE DAY Grover Cleveland placed his hand on a Bible and began his second term in the White House, America was already sliding into a deep depression. It would not recover until well after Cleveland left office. Unemployment more than tripled between 1892 and 1894, and it remained above ten percent for five years.[41] In light of this collapse, wage reductions and layoffs were inevitable at the Pullman Company. Rather than divide the impact of the depression among all of the company's stakeholders, however, George Pullman largely placed the weight of his company's lost revenues upon his workers' shoulders.

Between 1893 and 1894, the Pullman Company cut its payrolls by nearly 40 percent while simultaneously *increasing* the dividends paid to George Pullman and its other shareholders. Pullman cut his over seven million dollars in labor expenses nearly in half, while increasing dividend payouts from $2.5 million to nearly $2.9 million.[42] Similarly, the men who lived on Florence Boulevard and their fellow bosses remained immune to Pullman's pay cuts. As a federal inquiry into the Pullman Company later discovered, "during all of this reduction and its attendant suffering none of the salaries of the officers, managers, or superintendents were reduced."[43]

The worst effects of Pullman's cutbacks were felt outside of his personal barony. Pullman shut down a factory in Detroit, stripping jobs from eight hundred workers in the process.[44] Nevertheless, the residents of Pullman's chosen domain were hardly shielded from ruin. According to one railroad worker's account, workers who previously earned forty dollars a car for putting a decorating finish on the outside of a Pullman sleeper saw their pay cut to just eighteen dollars. Foundrymen and blacksmiths saw their work cut in half. When a group of women workers complained about receiving just three dollars per week in wages, a foreman reportedly told them that "if you cannot live upon the pay you are getting, go out and hustle for more. Why should we wonder that houses of prostitution find no difficulty in procuring inmates?"[45]

Pullman's workers saw their life savings evaporate. In just over a year, total deposits to the Pullman Loan and Savings Bank were nearly halved.[46] Yet, even as their wages tumbled, Pullman continued to charge full rents to the workers living in his company town. At the height of the depression, Pullman's rents were "from 20 to 25 per cent higher than rents in Chicago or surrounding towns for similar accommodations."[47] One woman claimed that, when her father died, the company stuck her with the bill for his unpaid rent and docked her pay until these debts were paid.[48] Another worker testified that he'd "seen men with families of eight or nine children to support crying" after receiving their paychecks because "they only got 3 or 4 cents after paying their rent." Workers lacking sufficient pay to cover both rent and sustenance would "drop down by the side of a car when they were working for want of food."[49] Yet tenants dared not leave the town of Pullman due to the company's practice of denying work to employees who lived elsewhere—a Pullman employee who moved just a few miles away to Chicago risked the same fate as Pullman's workers in Detroit.

The first gathering of the American Railway Union among Pullman's employees was held in secret, and it occurred several miles away from the town of Pullman in nearby Grand Crossing—workers feared that if their union activity were discovered, every single member of the union would be fired. Nevertheless, two hundred Pullman employees joined the ARU at that meeting, and additional wage cuts quickly drove more workers into the union's arms. Within a couple months of that first meeting, more than a third of Pullman's workforce belonged to the ARU.[50]

Emboldened by these numbers, the local union leaders revealed themselves in May of 1894, less than a year after Debs formed the ARU. Their initial demand to Pullman was not something his company reasonably could deliver—they asked for all wages to be fully restored to pre-depression levels even as the economic downturn was ongoing. But the workers gave ground and agreed to abide by any decision reached by a neutral board of arbitrators.[51]

The same cannot be said of Pullman. Initially, the railcar baron claimed that the company simply could not afford to pay higher wages if it wished to remain competitive, but this claim is highly dubious. As the federal inquiry into Pullman determined, the company benefited greatly from the continuous operation of its factories, even if it was temporarily doing so at a loss. The Pullman Company suffered these losses so "that its plant might not rust, that its competitors might not invade its territory, that it might keep its cars in repair, that it might be ready for resumption when business revived with a live plant and competent help, and that its revenue from its tenements might continue."[52] A protracted labor strike endangered each of these goals far more than restoring some share of the workers' wages.

In reality, the true reason for Pullman's unwillingness to bargain was later revealed by one of his most loyal lieutenants. In the words of Thomas Wickes, the Pullman Company's second vice president, "the policy of the company" was to refuse to bargain with unions over wages, lest they "force us to pay any wages which they saw fit." When asked if it was fair instead to require workers to accept whatever wages the company deemed fit, Wickes was unsympathetic—"but then it is a man's privilege to go to work somewhere else."[53] George Pullman's company had forced the greatest railroad companies to deal on his own terms. He'd built a fleet of immaculate monuments to opulence, and he'd driven saloons and sin from his own personal utopia. He'd be damned before he'd bend to the demands of mere workers. Like Czar Alexander before him, Pullman wanted his workers to be happy, but their happiness must proceed from him.

On May 10, Pullman fired three of the union's local leaders. The strike began the next day.[54]

———

AT LEAST AT first, the Pullman Strike was both peaceful and limited in scope. The local union posted three hundred men to guard Pullman's factories and ensure that they were not vandalized by strikers. Indeed, the town of Pullman itself remained free of violence even after much of the rest of the nation descended into bedlam. For more than a month, the town of Pullman was unusually quiet— although much of this quiet can be attributed to the fact that its factories were closed.[55]

Meanwhile, in nearby Chicago, George Pullman's offices swelled with dignitaries begging him to agree to arbitration. The Civil Federation of Chicago, made up of prominent businessmen throughout the city, twice urged Pullman to make peace with the union. Detroit's Republican mayor Hazen Pingree made a trip to Pullman's office, where he and Chicago's Democratic mayor John Patrick encouraged Pullman to arbitrate. The two men claimed to speak on behalf of fifty other large-city mayors, and yet still Pullman was unmoved.[56]

By the time the national ARU's convention convened in June, it was clear that local action would not sway George Pullman. Though Debs would later claim that the delegates gathered at the ARU convention voted unanimously in support of a boycott of the Pullman company,[57] this claim is almost certainly an exaggeration. In reality, the convention voted once to approve the boycott, and a second time to declare their decision unanimous after it was clear a majority supported a nationwide response to Pullman. Indeed, Debs quietly harbored misgivings about his union's ability to maintain such a bold action in the face of a depression, which gave managers plenty of potential scabs to do the jobs of workers loyal to the union.[58] Moreover, the union members' broad base of support for the Pullman strikers arose as much out of the boycotters' own personal grievances as it did out of their solidarity with the men and women in Pullman.

The Pullman Strike was, in many ways, a proxy war for a much larger conflict between capital and labor. George Pullman was hardly the only railroad baron who'd cut wages much deeper than the depression required. Additionally, as Debs later explained, many workers felt that railroad managers had deliberately exploited their patriotism during the Chicago World's Fair of 1893.

The World's Fair was one of the preeminent cultural events of the 1890s, with over twenty-seven million visitors descending upon Chicago during its six-month run. These visitors stressed the railroads and taxed its workers, many of whom believed that they were overworked and underpaid throughout the event. And yet the ARU prevailed upon its members not to strike, telling them that "it is your duty, your patriotic duty, to bear with patience any grievances you may have until the World's Fair is over."[59]

As the Fair wound down, however, railroad managers began widespread—and, it was later determined, orchestrated—wage cuts. As Debs explained, the workers subject to these cuts had lost faith in the old brotherhoods, "who had failed, in a single instance, to successfully resist these reductions that were gradually being made all over the country," and the ARU delegates arrived at the union's convention believing that their new, more inclusive union might be the only vehicle to resist mistreatment by their employers.[60] They were eager for a showdown with management to prove that they were no longer powerless in the face of the railroad barons' demands. George Pullman gave them their first opportunity to trigger this fight.

The union's strategy depended on isolating Pullman from his fellow barons. Under the terms of the boycott, ARU workers refused to handle Pullman cars or to assist in the passage of any train that contained a Pullman car. Eventually, they hoped, the railroads would be forced to disconnect these cars from their trains, and George Pullman would discover that American commerce could continue just fine without him—unless, of course, he came to the bargaining table.

What the union was not prepared for, however, was the General Managers' Association.

The Managers' Association included all twenty-four of the railroads centering in or terminating at Chicago. Together, they controlled over forty thousand miles of rail, and employed well over two hundred thousand workers. It was this association that orchestrated the system-wide wage cuts that so aggravated their workers. The Managers devised a "Chicago scale" for wages that would apply throughout all twenty-four of the railroads, encouraging each railroad to pay exactly the same as its competitors for labor.[61] Thus, on the Chicago lines, Wickes's proclamation that if a worker does not like his wages "then it is a man's privilege to go to work somewhere else" was largely an illusion. Railroad workers were likely to find the same pay schedule wherever they applied.

The Managers also recognized the implications of the Pullman boycott. Individual workers, and their decrepit brotherhoods, were impotent in the face of a united railroad industry and its threat that every worker who strikes can be replaced by a scab. But Debs's American Railway Union was an entirely different animal. With its tens of thousands of members, spread out throughout the industry and capable of shutting the engines of American transit down, the ARU presented the Managers with something they'd never faced before—an organization that could stare a railroad baron directly in the eye and force him to blink.

If the union's strategy was to surgically extract the Pullman Company from the nation's railways, the Managers ensured that the boycott was as disruptive as possible. The Managers intentionally manipulated their own schedules and let the blame fall upon the union. They gratuitously attached Pullman cars to freight trains and to short distance lines, thus forcing the boycotters to stop those trains and take the blame for halting commerce. And they specifically targeted mail trains for this tactic, thus ensuring that Debs's union would disrupt the federal government's central function of delivering the mail.[62]

––––––––

IT IS DIFFICULT to exaggerate the degree of collusion between the Managers and the federal government during the strike. The federal government appointed thirty-six hundred United States deputy marshals, each hand-selected and paid by the Managers, and placed them under the direct control of the railroads.[63] President Cleveland deployed federal troops to Chicago, against the strenuous protests of Illinois Governor John Altgeld and those of the soldiers' commander, General Nelson Miles, in order to break up the boycott.[64] While Miles's forces occupied Chicago, he set up his headquarters in the Pullman Building and met regularly with a top-level representative from the General Managers' Association.[65]

The Managers were able to achieve such cooperation from the United States government because they had an agent working for them within Cleveland's cabinet. Attorney General Richard Olney was a leading railroad attorney who'd twice turned down appointments to the Massachusetts Supreme Judicial Court in favor of the railroad clients who paid for his mansion in one of Boston's most prestigious neighborhoods. Although Olney accepted Cleveland's appointment as the nation's top legal officer, he did so only after the president agreed that he could also remain in private practice. Yet, rather than treating him as suspect because of his obvious conflict of interest, Cleveland viewed Olney's railroad ties as something that gave him insight into how to handle the strike. It was Olney who prevailed upon Cleveland to commit troops to Chicago.[66]

In other words, what began as a conflict between ordinary workers and one of the wealthiest men in the nation now pitted labor against the combined might of Chicago's railroad industry, the Justice Department, and the United States military. Eugene Debs was outgunned.

Confronted with a hostile army, the strike fell apart as spectacularly as can be expected. Although a federal inquiry later blamed the first wave of violence in Chicago on "hoodlums, women, a low class of foreigners, and recruits from the criminal classes," and not on the strikers or the union itself, there is no question that Miles's soldiers inflamed what had previously been a peaceful dispute into chaos.[67] What began as isolated individuals hurling rocks at the soldiers escalated into mobs setting fire to railroad cars. As many as ten thousand men tore through the Chicago stockyards, where they faced down cavalry and bayonets. Buildings left over from the World's Fair were set ablaze.[68]

As their hopes of reaching an accord with Pullman literally went up in flames, many strikers resorted to desperate tactics. As the federal inquiry later determined, "the strikers' experience and training were to be seen in the spiking and misplacing of switches, removing rails, crippling of interlocking systems, the detaching, side tracking, and derailing of cars and engines, placing of coupling pins in engine machinery, blockading tracks with cars, and attempts to detach and run in mail cars."[69] Public opinion turned hard against the union. The cover of *Harper's Magazine*, the same *Harper's* that once described Pullman as a feudal lord, now depicted Debs as a sulking king, sitting atop a disconnected bridge segment while all of Chicago's industry lay dormant behind him. When the strike broke, according to the president of the local union, Pullman blacklisted the union's leaders and ordered his workers to disassociate from the ARU.[70]

Olney required the trust of the president before he could set these events in motion, but he also required something else. Before General Miles's troops could unleash the dogs of war against the union,

Olney needed to win a much quieter battle in federal court. He needed an injunction that the troops could be called upon to enforce.

To battle the unions in federal court, Olney appointed another attorney who, like him, devoted his career to serving the railroad industry. Special Assistant United States Attorney Edwin Walker had thirty-five years of experience representing railroads. And just as Miles would work closely with the Managers in their shared goal of putting down the strike, Walker worked in equally close collusion with the judges who would decide the workers' fate.[71]

Shortly before President Cleveland would order troops to Chicago, Walker met with Chicago's United States Attorney and two federal judges to craft the document he would file formally requesting a federal court injunction. One of these two judges had recently given a speech warning that the emergence of even a single national union could "destroy the basis on which business in the long run can be successful and debase the man." When Walker filed this document on July 2, 1894, the two judges responded the very same day with an injunction that was simply breathtaking in its scope.[72]

Under the court order Walker worked with the judges to craft, the ARU was not simply barred from obstructing railroad traffic or hindering trains carrying US mail; Debs and his fellow union leaders were also forbidden from so much as merely inducing railroad workers to stop work. Under this order, simply asking a worker to strike or to picket a railroad were violations of the injunction. If Debs complied with this order, it would mean the immediate end of all the union's efforts on behalf of Pullman's workers.[73]

But Debs did not comply with the order. Three days later, President Cleveland cited the inability of the federal courts to execute this order "through the ordinary means" in a letter justifying his decision to deploy troops to Chicago.[74]

Meanwhile, Debs was rewarded for his defiance with a contempt citation and a trip to the Cook County Jail. His cell overlooked the location where four famous anarchists were hanged in 1887 after a bomb that was detonated by an unknown individual disrupted a labor demonstration in Chicago's Haymarket Square. As one scholar describes conditions in the jail,

> the corridors and cells were filthy with tobacco spit, body wastes, and moldy growths. Debs' own cell housed five other men, with bunks stacked three high against the two major walls. The mattresses were filled with bugs, and the inmates scratched the bug bites until they bled. Rats also ranged through the jail, and on one occasion Debs asked to borrow a guard's fox terrier in order to counterattack the rodents. Unfortunately, the rats frightened the dog more than the dog frightened the rats. With the dog whimpering and howling in fright, the guard removed it from the cell for its own protection.[75]

While in jail, Debs tried to recruit John Harlan—the son of the sole dissenting justice in the infamous "separate but equal" *Plessy v. Ferguson* decision—to join his defense team. Harlan declined, predicting that Debs's case would prove hopeless. "You will be tried," Harlan warned, "upon the same theory as were the anarchists, with probably the same result."[76]

———

BY THE TIME Debs's case was heard by the Supreme Court, he been released from Cook County's rat-infested cells on bail, then sentenced to six months in a different jail by another court order.[77] The union's campaign was lost. Pullman's factories were back to work, and the Managers stood triumphant. The man who once hoped to stand against the railroad barons and restore dignity to thousands of workers could now only ask the justices for one small thing—his freedom.

Yet, on the eve of the Court's arguments in his case, Debs had reason to be optimistic. Though Harlan had turned down his case, Debs was now represented by some of the finest lawyers of his age—including former Illinois Senator Lyman Trumbull, who authored the Thirteenth Amendment's ban on slavery, and a young, soon-to-be famous attorney named Clarence Darrow.[78] And, although the younger Harlan had deemed Debs a hopeless case, Harlan's black-robed father appeared to think differently. Justice John Marshall Harlan ordered Debs released on bail.[79] Moreover, though the union's hopes of defeating Pullman were lost, the Supreme Court could still hand labor an important legal victory. Debs was held in contempt of court for his failure to comply with the injunction against the ARU. So his lawyers attacked the validity of that injunction itself. If the justices held that the injunction was unlawful—or, at least, too broad in its scope—they could permanently weaken management's ability to obtain such injunctions in the future.

Whatever hopes Debs may have had prior to the Court's decision, however, they must have been dashed the instant he learned the identity of the justice who wrote the Court's opinion. The task of authoring this opinion fell to Justice David Josiah Brewer, the nephew of the now elderly Justice Stephen Field.

Justice Brewer joined the Court just seven months after his uncle upheld the expanded Chinese Exclusion Act, and the subject of Chinese immigrants was one of the few areas where Brewer pushed his Court to right injustices it was happy to leave untouched. Indeed, Brewer's greatest contribution as a justice was likely his dissents against the Court's mistreatment of Chinese men and women. As Brewer wrote in a dissent on behalf of several laborers of Chinese descent who claimed to be American citizens, Chinese workers built the backbone of our railways and China remained an essential trading partner. Should America's relationship with China be lost "and the most populous nation on earth becomes the great antagonist of this republic," Brewer concluded, "the careful student of history will recall the words of Scripture, 'they have sown the wind, and they shall reap the whirlwind,' and for cause of such antagonism need look no further than the treatment accorded during the last twenty years by this country to the people of that nation."[80]

Brewer's early life suggests that he would have been equally progressive in cases involving the rights of African Americans. As a young man, Brewer labeled *Dred Scott* "that last great satire on Constitutional logic," and shortly after graduating from law school he joined the exodus of antislavery New Englanders migrating to Kansas, which was at the time the focal point of tensions over the future of slavery.[81] Yet his record as a Supreme Court justice hardly matches his youthful opinions on race.

Brewer did not participate in the Court's decision in *Plessy*, ostensibly because he was away from Washington to attend his daughter's funeral, though it is worth noting that he did participate in several other cases that reached the Court during his absence.[82] Indeed, Brewer largely spent his time on the Court avoiding contentious issues regarding the rights of African Americans—typically in ways that left freedmen and their descendants out in the cold. Brewer upheld several black defendants' convictions, despite the fact that African Americans were systematically excluded from their jury pools, in large part due to a technicality regarding when the defendants' attorneys challenged these exclusions.[83] Similarly, when black plaintiffs accused the Commonwealth of Virginia of unconstitutionally denying them the right to vote in a congressional election, Brewer wrote for a unanimous Court that nothing could be done because the election had already happened and the winner—though likely elected on the back of Jim Crow—was already serving in Congress.[84]

In his speeches, Brewer largely laid the blame for African Americans' marginal position in society upon African Americans themselves. In one speech, he accused black Americans of being unable to "distinguish between liberty and license," or to understand "the obligations of morality and purity." In a speech to black college students, Brewer advised his audience that "no race is ever lifted up into a higher life simply through outside forces."[85] If black men and women wished to enjoy the full blessings of liberty, they must look elsewhere than the government to find it. Never mind that state governments were often the driving force behind Jim Crow, or that Brewer's Court was tasked with enforcing the Constitution's promise that no person shall be denied the equal protection of the laws.

Nothing animated Brewer's opinions more than this general suspicion of government—at least when government power was invoked on behalf of the powerless. Indeed, in this regard, Brewer displayed even greater skepticism of governance than his uncle Stephen Field. Brewer authored two opinions claiming that progressive taxation—in which the wealthy pay a greater percentage than the less fortunate—is unconstitutional.[86] He voted to strike down a Tennessee law forbidding employers from paying their workers in scrip redeemable only at the company store.[87] He claimed that an Arkansas law ensuring that coal miners are not denied part of their wages by their employers was unconstitutional.[88] And he twice attempted to revive the sweeping limits on business regulation that Justice Field embraced in the Chicago grain warehouse case.[89] "The paternal theory of government is to me odious,"[90] Brewer wrote in one of these opinions, comparing the government's efforts to protect farmers from unscrupulous businesses to *Looking Backward*, a popular 1888 novel by Edward Bellamy in which America transforms into a Marxist state.

To judges who shared Brewer's mindset, unions were no less odious than the governments that sought to control market forces—in fact they were in many ways viewed as more dangerous. Unions were not, in these judges' minds, coalitions of labor market participants joining together to improve their position at the bargaining table; they were competitors to the judiciary itself. The judicial decisions of this era routinely used words such as "tyranny" and "dictatorship" to describe unions engaged in strikes or boycotts.[91] Unions would declare employers to have sinned against the rights of workers, then impose sanctions upon those employers in much the same way that courts imposed consequences on lawbreakers. In this sense, Brewer and many of his fellow jurists perceived unions as creating their own alternative system of law—a law of labor, by labor, and for labor—that threatened to tear down the primacy of the law applicable in their courts.[92] This is why Justice Brewer's opinion in the *Debs* case proclaims that the American Railway Union exercised "powers belonging only to government" when it tried to separate the Pullman

Company from the channels of interstate commerce.[93] The courts must have the authority to reclaim their own dominance.

Taken in isolation, this was not an unreasonable impulse. Whatever else can be said about the Pullman Strike, about the justness of the workers' grievances, about the rapaciousness of the railroad barons, about the Goliath-like power of the General Managers' Association, or about the desperation of the army of Davids assembled under Eugene Debs's banner, one fact remains: the Pullman Strike endangered the backbone of the American economy and it did so in the midst of a devastating depression. At the height of the strike, *Harper's* claimed that the nation was "fighting for its own existence just as truly as in suppressing the great rebellion."[94] If the strike had continued unabated, this bold assertion could have proven correct.

Yet, in endorsing the steps taken to put down the strike, the Court asserted a simply breathtaking vision of its own power. The lower court that issued the injunction against the union relied largely on the Sherman Antitrust Act to justify its decision.[95] Justice Brewer's opinion, by contrast, relied on the law of "nuisance,"[96] a judge-made doctrine typically associated with property rights. Essentially, Brewer's opinion established that federal courts could issue sweeping injunctions with nationwide implications upon their own authority, regardless of whether elected officials had actually given them that power.

Just as important, no fair judge could have laid the full blame for the strike's disruptiveness at the union's feet. Pullman's workers chose to strike, but the Pullman Company made the decision to slash wages and increase dividends. The union chose to boycott, but it was the Managers who decided to intentionally disrupt their own train lines in order to turn the public against the union. The first stone was cast, not by a striking worker, but by a nameless thug— and that stone was met by bayonets ordered onto the scene by the President of the United States himself. The workers and their union resorted to disruptive tactics only because they had nothing else to fall back on. And with each escalation, management met them with overwhelming, even deadly, force.

When the Pullman Strike came to an end, Eugene Debs went to jail. The local union leaders were blacklisted. And Pullman's remaining workers returned at the same meager wages that triggered the strike. Meanwhile, the railroad barons went back to their mansions, where they remained among the wealthiest and most powerful men in the nation.

And the Supreme Court said this was right. Justice Brewer's opinion in *Debs* was unanimous.

Chapter 3

THE TWO
CONSTITUTIONS

As MUCH AS Justice David Brewer and his colleagues viewed unions as a threat to the rule of law, Brewer's Court was far more at peace with collusion among businessmen. Indeed, less than two months before its decision in *Debs* the justices sided with a company that obtained a virtual lock on the entire American sugar market—casting serious, if temporary, doubt upon whether anything could be done to break up such monopolies in the first place.[1]

Such monopolies, and similar conspiracies to set prices and maximize profits, were one of the defining elements of late nineteenth-century business. Prior to the invention of the railroad, much of the nation functioned as an archipelago of many different communities, each supporting a largely self-contained economy. Especially in communities apart from major natural waterways or canal systems, a farmer could spend his entire life farming the same plot of land, selling his crops to the same local customers, with minimal impact upon business in other states. After the growth of the railways, this same farmer's crops could travel to one of several central hubs, where the railroads could take them anywhere in the country or even to a port that would bring them overseas. The nation's economy was interconnected in a way that America's colonial ancestors could never have anticipated, and this unity made a new kind of business arrangement possible.

The very same railroads that enabled a farmer in Iowa to sell his crops in New York also placed him in competition with farmers throughout the nation—and the same was true of virtually every other business in the country. Timber mills, mines, and manufacturers who once supplied their entire community now risked being undercut by a business hundreds of miles away, and they also had a new opportunity to cut into that company's bottom line. It wasn't long before often-distant competitors began joining together in trusts and similar combinations to gain advantage over their smaller rivals.

The trust, in short, is a combination of ostensibly independent businesses acting together as a single unit. In a typical trust, several firms would place a majority of their voting stock under the control of a group of trustees, thus empowering the trustees to exercise full control over the companies subject to their oversight.[2] Though technically distinct companies, the parties to a trust would then set identical prices, avoid competing with each other, and otherwise work to either push out their competition or force them into the trust itself.

By the 1880s, trusts, along with less formal combinations such as the General Managers' Association, dominated the American marketplace. Newspapers and publishers bought paper at rates set by the American Paper Association, while homeowners decorated their walls at prices set by the American Wall Paper Manufacturers' Association. New York's bartenders bought beer at prices set by the Brewers and Maltsters Association of New York, while grocers in Boston contended with the New England Milk Producers' Association. Even the dead were at the mercy of the price-fixers—they were laid to rest in coffins priced by the National Burial Case Association.[3] Such collusion was so common by 1875 that, when a Pennsylvania legislative committee accused a railroad president of colluding to reduce production and drive up the price of coal, the executive did not so much deny the accusation as wonder why his one conspiracy was being singled out:

> Every pound of rope we buy for our vessels or for our mines is
> bought at a price fixed by a committee of the rope manufacturers

of the United States. Every keg of nails, every paper of tacks, all our screws and wrenches and hinges, the boiler flues for our locomotives, are never bought except at the price fixed by the representatives of the mills that manufacture them. Iron beams for your houses or your bridges can be had only at the prices agreed upon by a combination of those who produce them. Firebrick, gaspipe, terracotta pipe for drainage, every keg of powder we buy to blast coal, are purchased under the same arrangement. Every pane of window glass in this house was bought at a scale of prices established exactly in the same manner. White lead, galvanized sheet iron, hose and belting and files are bought and sold at a rate determined in the same way.[4]

Indeed, the greatest fortune ever amassed by a single American resulted from such efforts to control prices and eliminate competition. John D. Rockefeller was the only man in American history to surpass Cornelius Vanderbilt's vast wealth—eventually obtaining a fortune of nearly $200 billion in modern dollars—and he achieved this feat in no small part due to his collusion with Vanderbilt and other railroad barons. Rockefeller founded the Standard Oil Company in 1870, just one year after Louisiana's Slaughterhouse Act became law. Within a decade, Standard controlled 90 percent of the country's oil business.[5]

Standard achieved such dominance in large part due to a bargain it could strike with the railroads. In a typical contract, Standard would grant a railroad company exclusive rights to ship its oil over a particular route—thus denying any income from the nation's largest oil distributor to that railroad's competitors. The railroad, in return, agreed to ship Standard's oil at a discount, all while charging full price to Standard's competitors.[6] Meanwhile, the smaller refineries and local producers Standard sought to push out of the market could not offer the railroads enough business to strike a similar deal.

At their peaks, these discounts were absolutely crippling to Standard's rivals. The same railroad that charged $1.25 a barrel to ship non-Standard oil charged Rockefeller just ten cents. Another charged $1.90 per barrel to the public and as little as seventy cents to Standard—and these were only the rates that Rockefeller could achieve during ordinary times. At one point, Rockefeller convinced the New York Central railroad to wage war on a competitor by literally paying Standard for the privilege of hauling its oil.[7]

Soon, Standard Oil was the only company in many areas that could afford to sell oil at a profit, and it began to buy out its competitors at deep discounts. Rockefeller bought out one Cleveland refinery valued at $150,000 for just $65,000. He snatched up two others, worth $800,000, at a tenth of their value. And as Rockefeller seized greater and greater control of the oil market, he gained the ability to charge whatever price he wanted for oil. In 1880, Standard Oil paid just eleven cents per gallon to refine and transport its oil to Chicago. It then sold the oil for nearly twice as much.[8]

Congress eventually banned price discrimination by the railroads with the Interstate Commerce Act of 1887,[9] although this was far too late to prevent Standard Oil from cornering the nation's oil market. Broader legislation banning combinations "in restraint of trade or commerce" came three years later.

So collusion among businessmen was ubiquitous, and it wasn't exactly a big secret either. Muckraking journalists like the anti-monopolist writer Henry Demarest Lloyd worked hard to inform the public about the trusts that were building such vast fortunes.[10] Nevertheless, antitrust sentiment did not quickly find a home in either political party. First-term President Grover Cleveland was happy to indulge in anti-monopolist rhetoric. He warned Congress in 1888 that "as we view the achievements of aggregated capital, we discover the existence of trusts, combinations, and monopolies, while the citizen is struggling far in the rear or is trampled to death beneath an iron heel."[11] Yet he largely viewed such rhetoric as a useful tool to promote the Democrats' longstanding objective of tariff reform. The Democratic Party's 1888 platform claimed that "the interests of the people are betrayed, when, by unnecessary taxation, trusts and combinations are permitted and fostered, which, while unduly enriching the few that combine, rob the body of our citizens by depriving them of the benefits of natural competition."[12] "Unnecessary taxation," in this context, refers to excessive tariffs.

Meanwhile, the Republican Party's embrace of an anti-monopoly platform was likely driven as much by political necessity as it was by deeply held convictions. Cleveland's election in 1884 marked the first time a Democrat successfully won election to the White House since the disastrous presidency of James Buchanan. And, while Cleveland only triumphed over Republican Senator James Blaine by a very narrow margin, the 1884 race began to cement the GOP's reputation as the party of the wealthy and of big business.

A prominent former Republican helped shape this reputation. After losing command of the Union's forces in New Orleans, General Benjamin Butler began a successful career in politics—eventually serving ten years in the House of Representatives as a Republican and two years as the Democratic governor of Massachusetts. In 1884, he emerged as the Greenback Party's presidential nominee, tarring the Republicans he once served alongside in Congress as the "Party of Monopolists." Meanwhile, Blaine seemed determined to prove Butler right when he was fêted at a banquet—thrown by Jay Gould, Cornelius Vanderbilt, and other leading businessmen—that the *New York World* labeled "the Royal Feast of Belshazzar."[13]

So, when Benjamin Harrison took up the GOP's banner in 1888, an antitrust platform offered Republicans their best opportunity to escape being labeled the party of Vanderbilt and Gould. And, unlike Cleveland's Democrats, the Republican platform called for "such legislation as will prevent the execution of all schemes to oppress the people by undue charges on their supplies, or by unjust rates for the transportation of their products to market."[14] The Sherman Antitrust Act, named for the venerable Republican Senator John Sherman, became law just over a year after President Harrison took the oath of office.

There is an important epilogue to these events, however. Four years after Harrison's victory over Cleveland in 1888, the man Harrison vanquished became his vanquisher, and the conservative Cleveland returned to the White House shortly thereafter. In the Cleveland administration, the power to enforce the Sherman Act fell to Attorney General Richard Olney, who felt just as much contempt for antitrust as he did for the American Railway Union. After taking his spot at the head of the Justice Department, Olney wrote Treasury Secretary John Carlisle that a cabal of Boston bankers and merchants were willing to put their money towards repealing the Sherman Act, and he asked for a list of senators "who might be persuaded to see the thing in the right light."[15]

Meanwhile, President Cleveland had other priorities besides breaking up trusts—he still wanted reduced tariffs. Eventually, a tariff reform bill did become law, but it came at a price. Populist Democrats, led by Nebraska Representative William Jennings Bryan, inserted a modest income tax into the tariff bill that would impact just a small percentage of wealthy Americans. They hoped this tax would replace the revenues lost due to smaller tariffs. Although Cleveland objected to these new taxes, he viewed them as the unavoidable cost of a bill he dared not veto, so he allowed the bill to become law without his signature instead.[16]

Both of these laws, the antitrust act Olney loathed and the income tax Cleveland held his nose against but refused to veto, reached the Supreme Court in 1895, the same year that the justices pondered Eugene Debs's fate. And neither the president nor his attorney general would be disappointed by the pair of decisions announced by Chief Justice Melville Fuller.

———

IF FULLER HAD had his way, Abraham Lincoln would never have been president.

Born into one of Maine's most prominent Democratic families— his grandfather served as the state's chief justice—Fuller began his career as the editor of Maine's leading Democratic newspaper. In that role, he often jousted with the editor of a rival paper: future Republican senator and presidential nominee James Blaine. Following a broken engagement to his college sweetheart, Fuller decamped to Chicago, where he rose quickly in Democratic politics.[17]

Fuller arrived in his new hometown in 1856, two years after a Chicago native named Stephen Douglas tossed kerosene on the smoldering tensions between northern abolitionists and southern slave owners. Senator Douglas's Kansas-Nebraska Act created the two territories of Kansas and Nebraska and opened the question of whether each territory would permit slavery within its borders to determination by the territory's settlers. This act was immediately declared a betrayal by the antislavery lawmakers who would soon form the backbone of the Republican Party.

Prior to the Kansas-Nebraska Act, the Missouri Compromise of 1820 drew a line at the border between Arkansas and Missouri, north of which Missouri could be the only slave state. Thus, by even raising the possibility that Kansas or Nebraska could become slave territories, Douglas's proposal broke faith with free soilers who believed that the status of this region had already been settled. As a group of antislavery members of Congress wrote shortly after Douglas introduced his Kansas-Nebraska bill, "nothing is more certain in history than the fact that Missouri could not have been admitted as a slave State had not certain members from the free States been reconciled to the measure by the incorporation of this prohibition into the act of admission."[18]

Fuller, however, was not moved by these arguments. Though Fuller professed opposition to slavery—he attacked slavery's "tyrannical cruelties" while still a student at Bowdoin College—he cared far more about a kind of constitutional formalism than he did about ensuring that slaves were freed. Slavery, in the young Fuller's mind, was a state issue beyond the ken of the federal government.[19] Fuller viewed the Kansas-Nebraska Act as the appropriate remedy for slavery because he predicted that Northerners would soon outnumber Southerners in the contested territories—and that would give them the power to declare those territories free.[20]

Yet, by the time Fuller reached Chicago in 1856, it should already have been clear that this prediction was flawed. With Kansas's status as a free or slave territory in the balance, supporters of slavery flooded across the Missouri border, even as abolitionists traveled from as far as New England to settle in the contested lands. Violent outbreaks between the two sides were common. Yet, Fuller laid the lion's share of the blame for this state of affairs on one side. "The rascality of the Missourians," Fuller wrote from Chicago, "would have no opportunity to be displayed had it not been for the fanatical and hot-headed course of the abolition madmen."[21]

Fuller would become one of Douglas's top campaign surrogates. In his 1858 bid to remain in the Senate, Douglas found himself being squeezed at both ends. His leading opponent was an upstart former Illinois congressman named Abraham Lincoln. But Douglas's relatively moderate position on slavery also earned him the ire of one of his own party's most powerful members—President James Buchanan. At the same time that Lincoln's Republicans were attacking Douglas for reneging on the Missouri Compromise, Buchanan raged at Douglas for subsequently opposing Kansas's admission to the Union under a proslavery state constitution. To punish Douglas, Buchanan stripped him of his patronage and appointed new officeholders who actively campaigned against the incumbent senator. Fuller rose quickly in the new campaign organization Douglas built to supplant the patronage machine Buchanan took away, and the future chief justice soon found himself crisscrossing Chicago to give speeches on behalf of the senator. Fuller would play a similar role on a much larger stage when Douglas challenged Lincoln for the presidency in 1860.[22]

Though Fuller's patron died not long after his failed bid for the White House, Fuller's own political career was buoyed by a rise in anti-Republican sentiment while the Civil War appeared to be going badly for the Union. As a delegate to Illinois's constitutional convention in 1862, Fuller spearheaded an effort to gerrymander the state's congressional districts to benefit Democrats, and he voted to prohibit persons of African descent from settling in Illinois or casting a ballot in Illinois elections—the gerrymander was rejected by voters, but the racial provisions were approved. Similarly, while serving as a member of the state legislature, Fuller supported a resolution labeling the Emancipation Proclamation "unconstitutional, contrary to the rules of civilized warfare," and "calculated to bring shame, disgrace and eternal infamy" upon the nation. He also backed an amendment to the US Constitution preventing congressional interference with slavery.[23]

Though Fuller gave up on seeking elected office after an unsuccessful showdown with Illinois's Republican governor,[24] he remained active behind the scenes in Democratic politics, frequently attending the Democratic National Convention as a delegate. He also formed a fateful friendship with Grover Cleveland, then a rising Democratic politician. By the time Cleveland began his first term in office, Fuller was a leading member of the Illinois bar and he frequently traveled to Washington to argue cases before the Supreme Court. While visiting the nation's capital, he also made a habit of paying a social visit to his friend in the White House.[25] When the nation's top judicial job became vacant in 1888, Cleveland placed his friend on the bench.

Even before joining the bench, Fuller left a distinct paper trail suggesting he shared Cleveland's conservative views. While practicing law in Chicago, for example, Fuller published a revealing analysis of American political history:

> Two great parties have always divided the people of this country . . . the doctrine of the one is that all power not expressly delegated to the general government remains with the states and with the people; of the other, that the efficacy of the general government should be strengthened by a free construction of its powers. The one believes that that is the best government that governs least; the other, that government should exercise the functions belonging to Divine Providence, and should regulate the profits of labor and the value of property by direct legislation. The leader and type of one school of thought and politics was Thomas Jefferson; and Alexander Hamilton was the leader and type of the other.[26]

Although this passage is written in a far more measured tone than Justice Stephen Field's campaign pamphlet railing against "Federalist-Republican Congresses and administrations" grasping at "doubtful powers" to achieve imperial ends,[27] it reveals Fuller to be broadly sympathetic towards Field's narrow view of the role of government.

As early as George Washington's first term in the White House, Washington's cabinet split between two radically different visions of the Constitution. Broadly speaking, Treasury Secretary Alexander Hamilton believed that the Constitution gave the nation's leaders broad authority to regulate the national economy and to fund public works and general welfare programs,[28] whereas Secretary of State Thomas Jefferson would likely have viewed anything resembling the modern welfare and regulatory state as unconstitutional.[29] President Washington eventually backed Hamilton's more expansive understanding of the federal government's role when he signed a bill creating the First Bank of the United States over Jefferson's constitutional objections.[30]

In Fuller's mind, however, this struggle did not end with Washington's decision. By framing the entirety of American political history as a competition between the party of Jefferson and the party of Hamilton, Fuller transformed mere electoral wrangling into a grand battle over whether significant federal restraints on business could even exist—and he did so at the very moment that railroads were transforming the nation's commercial sphere from an atomized array of small farmers and merchants into a much smaller group of corporate titans powerful enough to rival the government itself. Moreover, as a proud member of the party of Jefferson, Chief Justice Fuller placed himself on the side that said George Washington was wrong.

———

WASHINGTON'S DECISION TO side with Hamilton's more expansive view of federal power is not surprising, as General Washington was among the former colonies' leading supporters of a strong central government. The Articles of Confederation, which preceded the

Constitution and governed the United States through much of the Revolutionary War, were a constant source of frustration to the revolutionary army's commanding general.

Unlike our present Constitution, which bound the states together under a powerful, if not entirely omnipotent, federal government, the Articles envisioned a "firm league of friendship" among states that largely retained their own separate "sovereignty, freedom and independence" from one another.[31] Congress, under the Articles, could not directly tax individuals or legislate their actions; delegates to this Congress had little authority to exercise independent judgment, as they owed their salaries to their state governments and could be recalled "at any time." Of particular frustration to a wartime general, the Articles gave Congress no real authority to raise troops or to provide for an army. Congress could request recruits or money, but it was powerless against states that denied these requests.[32] Indeed, at the height of the war with King George III, a frustrated General Washington wrote that "unless Congress speaks in a more decisive tone; unless they are vested with powers by the several States competent to the great purposes of War, or assume them as matter of right; and they, and the states respectively, act with more energy than they hitherto have done," he was certain "that our Cause is lost."[33]

Indeed, Hamilton likely knew that he was advocating to a sympathetic president when he clashed with Jefferson early in the Republic's history. As the war wound down, Washington had written to Hamilton that "unless Congress have powers competent to all general purposes, that the distresses we have encountered, the expences [*sic*] we have incurred, and the blood we have spilt in the course of an Eight years' war, will avail us nothing."[34] Later that same month, the future president reiterated that "no man in the United States is, or can be more deeply impressed with the necessity of a reform in our present Confederation than myself."[35]

By the time the Founding Fathers met in Philadelphia to replace the Articles of Confederation—in a Constitutional Convention presided over by George Washington—the delegates at that convention largely shared Washington's conviction that a stronger central government was needed if the United States were to prosper. Relatively early in the convention's proceedings, the delegates approved a resolution providing that the new Congress must be able to "legislate in all cases for the general interests of the Union, and also in those to which the States are separately incompetent, or in which the harmony of the United States may be interrupted by the exercise of individual legislation."[36] This resolution informed the convention's later efforts to define the federal government's powers with more specificity.

The resolution also reflected the Founding Fathers' understanding that certain challenges, such as the need to defend a large landmass or the need to regulate nationwide marketplaces, are national in character and must be met by an empowered national government. Later in the convention, a committee of the delegates drafted a laundry list of powers that Congress is permitted to exercise and that are now contained in Article I of the Constitution, such as the power to "raise and support armies" or to "establish a uniform rule of naturalization." Arguably the most significant of these powers is Congress's authority to "regulate commerce . . . among the several states."

As Chief Justice John Marshall explained in the very first Supreme Court decision to interpret it, *Gibbons v. Ogden*, this power to regulate commerce is quite expansive. There is "no sort of trade" that Congress cannot regulate, according to Marshall.[37] Moreover, Congress has "full power over the thing to be regulated," so courts should not question how the people's representatives exercise their lawful authority so long as they do not violate some other provision of the Constitution.[38] Congress's power is not limitless—the power to regulate commerce "among the several states" only permits federal oversight of commerce that "concerns more States than one"—but Marshall understood that national leaders must have the authority to tackle national problems and to regulate the nation's economy.[39]

Although the word "commerce" suggests to a modern audience that the framers only wanted to subject economic matters to the supervision of the federal government, Marshall also makes clear that this reading of the Constitution is too narrow. "Commerce,"

Marshall writes, "undoubtedly, is traffic, but it is something more: it is intercourse."[40] As Yale Law School's Jack Balkin explains, the founding generation understood the word "intercourse" to encompass a wide range of activities, including "travel, social connection, or conversation." Thus, "to have commerce with someone meant to converse with them, mingle with them, associate with them, or trade with them."[41]

This is why the problems presented by monopolies and trusts fit squarely within Congress's lawful authority to regulate—and why the Sherman Antitrust Act was clearly constitutional. The trusts were a national problem. They sought to control prices across the entire nation, and there can be no doubt that an effort to corner the market on oil or gold or wheat constituted something the framers would have understood as "commerce." To borrow Marshall's words in *Gibbons*, Congress should have had "full power over" the trusts, with their price-fixing schemes.

Chief Justice Fuller, however, did not feel especially bound by his predecessor's reading of the Constitution. The first antitrust case to reach his Court concerned the American Sugar Refining Company, which, by offering shares of its own stock to its leading competitors, bought all of these competitors out and seized control over 98 percent of the nation's sugar production.[42] With such a commanding share of the country's sugar refineries, this one company suddenly had the power to sell sugar for whatever price it wanted.

Yet, Fuller held that the sugar trust was completely immune to the federal government's efforts to restore competition to the marketplace. In contrast to the vision Marshall laid out more than seventy years before the *Sugar Trust Case* (1895), Fuller defined the word "commerce" so narrowly that it was practically meaningless. Congress's power over interstate commerce, in Fuller's view, meant little more than the power to regulate transportation of goods across state lines and the power to regulate the goods being sold or transported. "Manufacture, agriculture, mining, [and] production in all its forms" were not "commerce," according to Fuller, and thus could not generally be regulated by federal law.[43]

If this distinction appears confusing, that's because it is—and it certainly made no sense in the context of the sugar trust. Fuller maintained that, by taking control of nearly every single sugar refinery in the country, the American Sugar Refining Company merely obtained a monopoly over the manufacture of sugar, not over the actual sale of sugar—and thus the sugar trust was beyond the reach of Congress.[44] But the sugar trust did not form because it wanted to manufacture mountains of refined sugar and then store them in giant vaults; it formed for the very purpose of shipping that sugar across the country to be sold at inflated prices. And, thanks to Fuller's Court, it would be free to do so. Only Justice John Marshall Harlan dissented from Fuller's opinion that held the sugar trust immune from the Sherman Act.

The Supreme Court's opinion in the sugar trust case came just months before its unanimous opinion in *Debs* holding that courts can restrain workers from joining together to seek higher wages, even in the absence of any congressional authorization to do so. So, the justices twisted the Constitution in knots to protect combinations of capital at the same time that they were asserting unrestrained authority to thwart combinations of workers. But the *Sugar Trust Case* also should not be read solely as a boon for the trusts. With its holding that "manufacture, agriculture, mining, [and] production" typically could not be regulated by Congress, the Court took away the federal government's power to protect workers in factories, farms, mines and in other jobs removed from the actual transportation and selling of goods. Many of the most abusive workplaces in the country were now beyond the reach of federal officials.

If there was any doubt left that the most well-to-do Americans had a friend in the Fuller Court, that doubt was eliminated by Fuller's decision in *Pollock v. Farmers' Loan & Trust* (1895),[45] which was handed down in the few short months between *Debs* and the *Sugar Trust* decision.

The income tax that Cleveland begrudgingly accepted as the price of tariff reform was quite modest. The tax exempted the first $4,000 in income, more than $100,000 in modern dollars, and only required taxpayers to contribute 2 percent of their income beyond that point. In total, only the wealthiest one-tenth of one percent of all Americans would pay this tax, contributing less than four percent of the nation's revenues.[46] Yet Fuller's Court viewed even this modest tax as unconstitutional, and they relied on one of the Constitution's most confusing distinctions in order to strike it down.

As originally drafted, the Constitution forbade any "direct" tax from being laid by Congress "unless in proportion to the census." So if the state of New York housed seven percent of the nation's population, its citizens must pay exactly seven percent of any direct taxes enacted by federal law. Thus, if an income tax qualified as a "direct" tax, such a tax would be practically impossible to administer in the United States, as it would require the federal government to calculate and recalculate how much money it could raise from each state and enact a different tax system in each state to achieve that goal.

Moreover, as Fuller's opinion in *Pollock* makes perfectly clear, even the nation's founders were unsure what constituted a "direct" tax as opposed to some other form of taxation. Fuller devotes nearly fourteen pages of his opinion to conflicting quotes from prominent early Americans struggling to define the term "direct tax."[47] Future Chief Justice Marshall defined a direct tax as a tax on "lands, slaves, stock of all kinds, and a few other articles of domestic property,"[48] while Alexander Hamilton defined it more broadly to include "capitation or poll taxes, taxes on lands and buildings, general assessments, whether on the whole property of individuals, or on their whole real or personal estate."[49] Justice Samuel Chase, by contrast, doubted that taxes on "personal property" qualified as direct taxes.[50] And Justice James Iredell seemed to agree that only a "land or poll tax" can be considered direct taxation.[51] Theodore Sedgwick, a delegate to the Philadelphia Convention and future Speaker of the House, offered the unique view that taxes on "objects of luxury" could never be direct taxes[52]—a view that was soundly mocked by James Madison.[53]

In other words, the only thing that was clear from Fuller's lengthy catalog of quotes from the framers and their contemporaries was that the Founding Fathers themselves had no clear idea what distinguishes a "direct" tax from an "indirect" one. And yet Fuller concludes his list of quotations with one of the least self-aware passages ever to appear in a Supreme Court opinion:

> From the foregoing it is apparent: 1. That the distinction between direct and indirect taxation was well understood by the framers of the Constitution and those who adopted it. 2. That under the state systems of taxation all taxes on real estate or personal property or the rents or income thereof were regarded as direct taxes.[54]

The upshot of this opinion was that income from capital—be it land, stock, or commodities—was immune to taxation, but income from wages was not. John D. Rockefeller could sit in his office watching money pour in from his investments, the whole time comfortable in the knowledge that this income could never be taxed. His lowest-paid worker enjoyed no such security.

Indeed, in a concurring opinion, an elderly Justice Field was quite direct about the fact that he would declare this income tax unconstitutional specifically to protect the wealthy. "The present assault upon capital is but the beginning," Field warns. "It will be but the stepping-stone to others, larger and more sweeping, till our political contests will become a war of the poor against the rich; a war constantly growing in intensity and bitterness."[55]

———

POLLOCK WAS A massive departure from precedent. Early justices rejected an attempt to define "direct" taxes broadly as early as 1796,[56] and the Supreme Court upheld an income tax enacted during the Civil War just seven years before Fuller joined the Court—holding that direct taxes consisted of nothing more than "taxes on real estate" and "capitation taxes," a fixed-rate tax charging the same amount to every person regardless of wealth or income.[57]

The requirement that certain taxes be apportioned according to each state's population was also an anachronism by the time Fuller became a justice. Under the original Constitution, slaves counted as three-fifths of a person for purposes of determining how many representatives each state could send to the House, but they also counted as three-fifths of a person for purposes of apportioning direct taxes. The apportioning requirement was added as a compromise to entice Northern states to agree to give Southern states extra representation in Congress because Southerners would also have to pay additional taxes.[58] *Pollock* reached the Court in 1895, however, thirty years after slavery was abolished by the Thirteenth Amendment. With slavery forbidden, the apportionment requirement no longer served any purpose whatsoever.

The *Pollock* decision also did not survive very long. By 1909, support for an income tax—which enabled the burden of taxation to fall primarily on the wealthy—was so widespread that Congress largely divided upon whether to propose a constitutional amendment to overrule the Supreme Court, or whether to simply enact another income tax and dare the justices to strike it down again.[59] President William Howard Taft, having risen from the federal bench to the White House, endorsed the former option due to concerns that the latter would "not strengthen popular confidence in the stability of judicial construction of the Constitution."[60] Nearly eighteen years after *Pollock*, the Sixteenth Amendment—which clarifies that Congress has the power "to lay and collect taxes on incomes, from whatever source derived"—rendered Fuller's decision largely invalid.

Similarly, the protective dome Fuller erected around monopolists in the *Sugar Trust Case* began to crumble shortly after it was built. Just four years after *Sugar Trust*, the justices blessed a suit targeting six pipe manufacturers who joined together to fix the price of cast-iron pipe. The pipe-makers, according to the Court's decision in *Addyston Pipe & Steel Co. v. United States* (1899), violated the Sherman Act by trying to control the "sale and transportation" of iron pipes, not by trying to control the manufacturing of iron pipes. So a suit against the pipe-makers was entirely consistent with the Constitution.[61]

In reality, however, this distinction between the sugar trust and the pipe-makers' arrangement was entirely arbitrary. The pipe-makers were no less engaged in the manufacture of iron pipes than the American Sugar Refining Company was engaged in the manufacture of refined sugar. And the sugar trust formed to fix the price of interstate sugar sales just as surely as the pipe-makers joined together to fix the price of cast-iron pipes. Taken together, *Addyston* and the *Sugar Trust Case* stand for little more than the proposition that the Sherman Act is unconstitutional when the justices feel like saying that it is unconstitutional and it is constitutional when they want it to be constitutional.

No one felt this arbitrariness more than the American worker.

In the wake of the Pullman Strike, Congress enacted a law prohibiting railroads from firing workers solely because they belonged to a labor union. Because this law applied solely to railroads, which are, by their very nature, engaged in transportation and not manufacturing, it should have been well within Congress's authority even under the line drawn in the *Sugar Trust Case*. Yet the Court struck down this law in 1908, declaring that "labor organizations have nothing to do with interstate commerce" even if every single member of the union is engaged in interstate commercial activity.[62]

Similarly, after Congress enacted a law protecting collective bargaining and similar rights for coal miners, the justices struck down this law, in 1936, on the grounds that mining coal has nothing to do with selling coal.[63] Eleven years earlier, however, when a mining executive's attempt to de-unionize one of his mines broke out into an armed conflict between labor and management, the Supreme Court decided that it was perfectly acceptable for the federal government to regulate mining workers—at least when the regulation benefited management.[64]

This willingness to apply one constitution to management and another, inferior constitution to workers was not limited to these few cases involving miners and railroad workers. To the contrary, many victims of this double standard were barely old enough to spell their names.

Chapter 4

THE PRICE OF A COKE

I N THE EARLY years of the twentieth century, wedge-shaped build-ings dotted the "hard coal counties" of Pennsylvania, where heavy lumps of anthracite coal were crushed into marketable pieces. There, at the top of each wedge, iron rollers broke the coal and elaborate screens sorted it by size. Meanwhile, underneath this operation, machines of a different kind culled rock and slate from an endless stream of crushed coal pouring down the inside of the wedge. There, engulfed by clouds of black dust, dozens of children filled each of these coal "breakers," where they earned as little as forty cents a day for ten hours of labor.[1]

Chutes flowing with black anthracite formed the bowels of these breakers, while boys as young as eight years old sat on planks watch-ing the stream of minerals flow by their feet. Their job was to spot stray pieces of slate and other detritus that could impurify coal ship-ments and decrease their value. Men with sticks patrolled the boys, smacking the heads or shoulders of any boy who appeared to be slacking.[2]

Anthracite is difficult to distinguish from slate when it is con-stantly flowing by your feet in a rapidly moving stream—and when you are working in a room blackened with coal dust—so the boys bent low over the chutes to tell valuable coal from worthless slate. After just a few years of such labor, their backs began to hunch, their shoulders grew round, and their chests grew narrow.[3] As one visitor to the breakers observed, "most of them become more or less deformed and bent-backed like old men."[4]

When it was cold, the breakers were barely heated, so the boys donned scarves and hats and, if they could afford them, overcoats. Gloves, however, were forbidden, because the boys' jobs depended so much upon their sense of touch. At the end of the workday, even if they were bathed and costumed in the garb of a mine owner's son, a breaker boy could be immediately identified by his bleeding fingers and fingernails worn down to the quick by repeatedly plunging into the streams of hard coal. Many of these boys lost fingers. Some of them had entire limbs torn off by the machinery that drives the coal forward. Others slipped and fell down the refuse chutes—where, if they survived the fall, they were smothered to death by the piles of slate tossed in behind them.[5]

The boys who were not killed by the breakers eventually graduated to the inside of the mines, where they often began their careers by tending the mules that hauled the coal to the surface. Boys as young as ten served as "trap boys," who lifted heavy doors to enable a mule's passage to and from the mine. There, the boys faced even longer work hours and the kind of numbing isolation that today is reserved mostly to unfortunate prisoners. As one contemporary account explained:

> Think of what it means to be a trap boy at ten years of age. It means to sit alone in a dark mine passage hour after hour, with no human soul near; to see no living creature except the mules as they pass with their loads, or a rat or two seeking to share one's meal; to stand in water or mud that covers the ankles, chilled to the marrow by the cold draughts that rush in when you open the trap-door for the mules to pass through; to work fourteen hours—waiting—opening and shutting a door—then waiting again—for sixty cents; to reach the surface when all is wrapped in the mantle of night, and to fall to the earth exhausted and have to be carried away to the nearest "shack" to be revived before it is possible to walk to the farther shack called "home."[6]

When the sun rose on the twentieth century, twenty-five thousand boys under age sixteen labored in the mines and quarries of the nation, often rarely escaping these mines to see the sun with their own eyes. Ultimately, nearly every child who survived his early years in the breakers spent his adulthood cutting coal from the earth with a pick or shoveling just-mined coal into a mule's cart. Many of these boys would never even set foot in a school. Those that did were typically too exhausted from a day's work to benefit from their classes.[7] And if they were fortunate enough to avoid accidents and become fathers themselves, they often faced a future battling the disease they knew as "miner's asthma."

Black lung disease, and the havoc coal dust worked on a person's lungs after years in the mines, was hardly a mystery to the medical establishment of this era. As early as 1831, after performing an autopsy on a patient whose lungs "presented one uniform black carbonaceous colour, pervading every part of his substance," the Scottish physician James Gregory warned "those practitioners who reside in the vicinity of the great coal mines, and who may have charge of the health of the miners, to the existence of a disease, to which that numerous class of the community would appear to be peculiarly exposed." Yet the mine owners often deemed the elaborate network of blowers and fans necessary to protect their workers' health an unnecessary expense. The result was an environment in which children, who began shredding their lungs in the blackened air of the breakers, faced decades of breathing the same air in the mines—until their lungs began to emit a choking black substance that resembled ink or black paint.[8]

Though the mines typically did not employ women and girls, the breaker boys' sisters found employment in nearby knitting and silk factories, where as many as ten thousand girls produced socks, stockings, and underwear for an average of about forty-seven cents a day. Many of these girls earned far less than their brothers. One girl told a reporter for *McClure's Magazine* that she earned as little as $1.25 every week in the textile mill where she'd worked since she was nine years old, less than $2,000 a year in today's dollars. Another girl, who

lost her father to black lung disease and her brother to a mining accident, had to support her mother and a ten-year-old sister on just
$1.50 a week. As a factory inspector told *McClure's*, the mills were
located in Pennsylvania coal country specifically because "girl labor is
cheaper here than anywhere else."[9]

Unlike the breakers, which operated only during the day, the silk
mills ran day and night, with the girls divided into two twelve-hour
shifts. The mills were kept moist and hot, and the girls emerged
from this environment into the chilly Pennsylvania air at the end of
their winter shifts. Tuberculosis and bronchial diseases ran rampant
through the young workforce, as did anemia. And the work itself
was no less physically demanding than the conditions imposed upon
the breaker boys. As one girl described life in the mills,

> when I first went to work at night, the long standing hurt me very
> much. My feet burned so that I cried. My knees hurt me worse than
> my feet, and my back pained all the time. Mother cried when I told
> her how I suffered, and that made me feel so badly that I did not tell
> her any more. It does not hurt so much now, but I feel tired all the
> time. I do not feel near as tired, though, as I did when I worked all
> night. My eyes hurt me, too, from watching the threads at night.
> The doctor said they would be ruined if I did not stop the night
> work. After watching the threads for a long time, I could see threads
> everywhere. When I looked at other things, there were threads run-
> ning across them. Sometimes I felt as though the threads were cut-
> ting my eyes.[10]

THESE CONDITIONS WERE hardly limited to the mines and mills of
Pennsylvania's anthracite country. At the dawn of the twentieth century, more than seven thousand boys worked in glass factories, often
carrying red hot balls of glass to adults tasked with shaping them into
bottles. A typical boy's job required him to run three or four finished
bottles, still glowing red from the nearby furnace, to an "annealing

oven" where they were gradually cooled. The boy carried his load on a large asbestos shovel, constantly moving at a slow run to pick up more bottles and carry them to the oven. By one account, a boy would make seventy-two of these trips in a single hour, eventually traveling nearly twenty-two miles over the course of the day—back and forth, with a heavy weight that could burn his skin from his body.[11]

At first glance it was sometimes difficult to tell the glass factories where these boys worked from a prison. One observer described a glass factory as a "big wooden structure, so loosely built that it afforded little protection from draughts, surrounded by a high fence with several rows of barbed wire stretched across the top." When he asked the factory foreman to explain the purpose of the barbed wire, the foreman replied, "it keeps the young imps inside once we've got 'em for the night shift." These young imps earned an average of seventy-two cents a night for ten hours' toil behind the prison-like fence.[12]

At the oyster and shrimp canneries that lined the American coastline from New Orleans to Baltimore, entire families were shipped to the coast to prepare the day's catch to be canned. There, they were housed in dilapidated wooden shacks that sheltered as many as fifty workers in a single room. Outside their doorsteps, clouds of mosquitoes and sand flies filled the tidal marshes, and not far away were the docks and the ever-growing shell pile that marked the workers' progress each day.[13]

Boys and girls as young as four joined their parents to shuck oysters into pots, where an especially diligent child might fill as many as eight pots a day—and the days spent shucking oysters were the easy days. When the boys and girls were tasked with picking shrimp, they soon learned that the shrimps emitted a corrosive substance that could eat through their shoes and through the very tin cans in which the shrimps were put. The shrimp were also packed in ice that chilled the children's fingers, rendering them useless after only a few hours. For these reasons, the days spent packing shrimp were far shorter than the days spent shucking oysters. A day working shrimp ended when the worker's fingers could no longer function.[14]

For this work, a child could earn as much as a dollar a day, although children normally required several years on the job before they could turn around sufficient volume to receive an entire dollar. Few children under age twelve earned so much. The seven-year-olds typically received about a quarter for each day spent working at the cannery.[15]

And, for many children, ice and caustic shrimp were the least of the dangers presented by the workplace. In the unregulated stamping works of George Pullman's Chicago, boys were handed a short iron poker and tasked with keeping an endless series of cans in line as they traveled through a vat of molten metal solder. Though the boys wrapped their hands in cloth to protect them from the melted metal, this shielded them from little more than the most minor burns. The briefest splash would often cost a young boy his hand.[16]

Nicotine poisoning ran rampant through the children employed by Chicago's nearby cigar factories, and the gilding that many child workers applied to picture frames stiffened their fingers and left them susceptible to throat disease.[17] In the carpet factories of New York and Pennsylvania, child laborers soaked themselves in toxic dyes. One boy opened his shirt to a reporter to reveal a chest and stomach dyed a deep crimson. Others walked home night after night in clothes dripping with the red, blue, or green dye they'd worked with during their shift, leaving a brightly colored trail behind them in the snow.[18]

Children employed as varnishers in furniture factories inhaled poison fumes that led to a variety of intestinal maladies. Children in wallpaper factories slowly poisoned themselves with toxic paints. Naphtha fumes produced in the manufacture of rubber goods led to paralysis and decay. Children in leather works handled nauseating chemicals. Boys and girls working in match factories became sick with phosphorous necrosis—known as "phossy jaw"—a kind of gangrene of the lower jaw. Lead poisoning abounded in boys employed by foundries and stereotype printing operations.[19]

And even in workplaces where the air was clean and the dangers were readily apparent, children were endangered by the sheer exhaustion their long shifts worked upon their growing bodies. In a 1909 court case, a thirteen-year-old boy employed by an Indiana steel mill literally passed out with his leg crossing the rail of a track used to transport iron to his employer's furnaces. The boy had worked more than a week's worth of fourteen-hour night shifts in a row, and he remained unconscious with his leg across the track until it was crushed by a passing iron cart.[20]

———

CHILD LABOR WAS as much a Northern problem as it was a Southern problem, but in the South, cotton mill managers spoke openly of their hope that someday nearly all men would be unemployed—replaced by relatively cheap women workers and even cheaper children. A young boy would enter the mill at age six, earning as little as ten cents a day for his labor, grow to become a father himself, and eventually be laid off and replaced by his own six-year-old son.[21]

Within the mills, children worked twelve-hour shifts, day and night, while superintendents stood by to toss cold water in their faces if they began to doze off. Cotton dust filled the workers lungs, creating an epidemic of "brown lung disease," a coughing, wheezing disorder brought about by the dust inside the mill. Similarly, many children suffered from pneumonia, brought about by the sudden shift from the hot factory interior to the cool air of the early mornings and late evenings as they walked home from work.[22]

Yet the most striking ailment facing the children of the cotton mills may have been the premature seriousness that sets in when a boy or girl barely old enough to attend school is forced to spend nearly every waking moment in dreary monotony. According to one account, an Atlanta woman "thinking to give some of these little victims a treat, asked a number out to her place in the country and turned them into the woods to play. What was her distress and amazement to find that they did not know what the word or the thing meant."[23]

Though conditions inside the Southern mills were by no means harsher than those facing many child laborers in the North—indeed, they were often relatively safe compared to the poisonous, fire-filled environments of many Northern factories—conditions outside the mills gave the mill owners far greater ability to line their pockets at children's expense.

Unlike the North, where decades of industrialization and railroad construction gave parents at least some ability to seek work in communities where they would not toil alongside their young children, much of the Southern economy was little more than poor farmers barely earning enough to feed and clothe their families. A handbill circulated by a North Carolina cotton mill relied on the misery of nearby farmers' lives to recruit entire families:

> While you are on the farm toiling in rain and snow, feeding away what you have made during the summer and making wood to keep fires to keep your family from freezing, you could at the same time be in a cotton mill and in a good comfortable room, making more than you can make in the summer time on the farm. . . . At the mills, children over 12 years old, after they learn their job, can make more than men can make on farms.[24]

This was not a frivolous pitch to farmers who, in the handbill's words, "had only enough provisions and feed to carry [them] through making another crop, and no profit left" after a season spent raising hundreds of bushels of corn, wheat, oats, and hay.[25] Southern cotton mills could move into a town and essentially set their own terms with the state and with a local workforce that had no meaningful alternative to the drudgery the mills offered. For this reason, the South quickly became a gathering place for employers looking to exploit children for profit. Between 1880 and 1900, the percentage of workers outside the South who were less than sixteen years old declined from 15.6 percent to 7.7 percent, while during the same period, children made up one-quarter of all workers in the South.[26]

For this reason, many mill towns closely resembled the industrial barony George Pullman built outside Chicago. Several mill owners did not so much move into an existing community as build an entirely new village around their mill. And, like Pullman, Illinois, the company owned every building in these new mill towns.[27]

Similarly, the mill owners could demand and receive nearly any concession they sought from state lawmakers. In 1887, Alabama passed a law limiting child workers to an eight-hour workday. Seven years later, the state legislature repealed this law after a group of Massachusetts mill owners promised to open a factory in Alabama in return for its repeal.[28]

Indeed, Northern capital had almost as much of a stake in the South's mills as did Southern investors. One investigation of twenty-four Alabama mills found that eleven of them were owned by Northerners—and the Northern-owned mills employed twice as many children under twelve as those owned by Southern capital. Massachusetts, which barred child labor outright before the age of fourteen, had some of the strictest child labor laws in the nation. But wealthy Bostonians could evade these laws simply by shipping their capital down South.[29]

In other words, if child labor was to be stopped at all in the United States, it could not be stopped by the states acting individually. So long as one state permitted such exploitation of children, it would remain a haven for investors seeking to profit off of cheap child workers, and those investors would retain significant influence over the state legislature. And, even when restrictions on child labor were written into law, those laws could be just as deftly avoided if employers remained influential with the executive branch officials tasked with enforcing it.[30] Indeed, in many states where child labor laws did exist, families and employers routinely evaded them by obtaining certificates from local officials falsely attesting that a child was of sufficient age to work.[31]

Perhaps most significantly, the absence of child labor laws in one state would exert continuous pressure on the remaining states to repeal their laws in order to keep their businesses competitive. As Senator Albert Beveridge, for many years Congress's leading proponent of child labor regulation, warned in 1907, "even if in one, or a dozen states, good laws were still executed, the business man in the good state would be at a disadvantage to the business man in the bad state, because the latter could employ cheap child labor."[32] The states were, in the words of the Founding Fathers, "separately incompetent" to address the problem of children in the workplace.[33] A solution to this problem had to come at the national level or it would not come at all.

———

AN ATTORNEY AND historian of the Supreme Court—he won a Pulitzer Prize for his four-volume biography of Chief Justice John Marshall several years after he left the Senate—Senator Beveridge embraced the cause of child workers like a trial lawyer building the record that would save his client from the hangman's noose. When Beveridge introduced legislation imposing strict limits on mines and factories that employed workers below the age of fourteen, he held the Senate floor for the better part of three days. There, he read numerous reports compiled by journalists and opponents of child labor that described the terrible conditions facing children in coal mines, cotton mills, and factories across the nation. His indictment of child labor spans 106 pages of the *Congressional Record*.[34]

Yet, despite the thoroughness of Beveridge's presentation, his push for a nationwide child labor law initially garnered little support from his colleagues. When Beveridge presented his legislation to Congress in 1907, justices such as Melville Fuller and David Brewer still dominated the Supreme Court, and Fuller's opinion in the *Sugar Trust Case* raised a serious cloud of doubt over federal legislation seeking to improve the lot of workers. Southern senators, many of them loyal to the mills, interrupted Beveridge to express doubts that federal regulation of child labor was constitutional. In a statement typical of the opposition, Senator Augustus Bacon, a Confederate army veteran representing the state of Georgia, warned that if Congress had the "arbitrary power" to address child labor, its ability to control American lives would be "practically unlimited."[35]

(This claim—that if Congress has the power to enact a particular piece of legislation, then there would be no practical limit on its authority to enact other laws—would prove to be a common refrain repeated over and over again by opponents of progressive reform in the twentieth and twenty-first centuries.)

By October of 1907, even the nation's leading organization devoted to the eradication of child labor viewed federal legislation as a hopeless cause. Although the National Child Labor Committee initially endorsed Beveridge's bill, it withdrew that support after it became clear that the bill had no chance of becoming law.[36]

Just over one year later, the election of William Howard Taft placed an equally daunting obstacle in the path of child labor reformers. Although Taft won the presidency largely due to an endorsement by the progressive incumbent Theodore Roosevelt, Roosevelt quickly came to regret that endorsement. Though Roosevelt opposed the Beveridge bill during his time in the White House, that view was motivated as much by the lack of political support for child labor reform as it was by concerns over the bill's constitutionality. Roosevelt would later shift his views to support the bill after the political winds also shifted in favor of regulation.[37] Taft, by contrast, remained committed to the limited conception of federal power embraced by the *Sugar Trust Case*, labeling federal child labor laws a "clear usurpation" of states' rights shortly after departing the White House.[38]

By 1915, however, the landscape had shifted dramatically in favor of child labor reformers. Though Beveridge was no longer in the Senate—a Democratic sweep in Indiana's 1910 elections denied the progressive Republican a third term—Taft was also no longer in the White House. Granted, the new Democratic President Woodrow Wilson had himself opposed child labor laws during his tenure as president of Princeton University,[39] but public sentiment in support of reform would soon drive Wilson to openly lobby Congress to enact a child labor law.[40] A bill similar to Beveridge's proposal passed the House by a lopsided 233 to 43 margin, although it passed so near the close of the Sixty-Third Congress that its Southern opponents were able to block its passage in the Senate.[41]

Just as important, a wave of Supreme Court decisions affirming Congress's authority over the streams of national commerce gave reformers hope that a child labor law would survive contact with the nation's highest Court.

Recall that Chief Justice Fuller's opinion in the *Sugar Trust Case* relied upon an artificial distinction between "commerce"—narrowly defined as the sale or transit of goods—and other activities essential to commerce such as manufacturing, mining, or production.[42] Though the Fuller Court would not allow Congress to ban manufacturers outright from producing offensive goods in their factories, a trio of decisions held that Congress could prohibit businesses from transporting undesirable objects and persons across state lines. Thus, the justices upheld a federal law prohibiting interstate transport of lottery tickets in *Champion v. Ames* (1903).[43] And, in a pair of unanimous decisions handed down after the deaths of Fuller and Brewer, the Court upheld federal laws prohibiting the transit of adulterated foods in 1911[44] and prohibiting the transport of prostitutes[45] across state lines in 1913.

These three decisions provided the blueprint for the Keating-Owen Act of 1916, which passed both houses of Congress over little more than token dissent from a minority of Southern lawmakers.[46] Rather than banning child labor outright, the Keating-Owen Act prohibited manufacturers from shipping any good produced in a factory in which children under fourteen had recently worked, or where children under sixteen had recently worked more than eight hours a day.[47] Though this was undoubtedly a roundabout way to target child labor, it was also entirely consistent with the Supreme Court's decisions in *Champion* and later cases. The justices had opened a door, and the overwhelming majority of Congress walked through it.

———

ON THE DAY President Wilson signed the ban on child labor, even most mill owners conceded that the law was constitutional. David Clark, the influential publisher of the *Southern Textile Bulletin* later admitted that "it was the opinion of 75 percent of the cotton manufacturers and fully that percent of the lawyers that it was useless to contest the constitutionality of the laws." Only two members of the Executive Committee of Southern Cotton Manufacturers, a group Clark formed to defeat child labor laws, "really thought we had any chance of winning" a lawsuit attacking the Keating-Owen Act in the Supreme Court.[48]

The son of North Carolina's populist chief justice, Clark shared all of his father's ambition and none of his liberalism. Though ostensibly nothing more than the publisher of a regional trade magazine, Clark was the driving force behind the campaign against child labor reform and one of the South's most impactful conservative activists. Clark viewed the Keating-Owen Act in apocalyptic terms, at least by the standards of a region that once fought a war to maintain its peculiar labor practices and that still counted many veterans of that war among its most prominent citizens. If Congress can constitutionally ban child labor, Clark warned his readers, "it can take away from the States almost every power and every vestige of States Rights and Congress will control all our internal affairs."[49]

Under Clark's guidance, the Executive Committee recruited one of the giants of the American bar to lead the assault on child labor reform. Thirty-five years before Clark approached him to represent the Southern mill owner's cause, John G. Johnson turned down President James Garfield's request to nominate him to the Supreme Court.[50] Some years later he turned down the same offer from Grover Cleveland.[51] He denied President William McKinley's request to become attorney general. And between these decisions to spurn three presidents, Johnson argued and won the *Sugar Trust Case* and emerged as one of the business community's leading Supreme Court advocates.[52]

Indeed, Johnson was so sought after by the wealthy business interests that he amassed one of the finest art collections in the country (his nearly thirteen hundred paintings spanning the Renaissance to the nineteenth century now form the backbone of the Philadelphia Museum of Art's collection of European works). As the attorney for a holding company threatening to monopolize railroad traffic in the western United States, Johnson received a previously unheard of half-million-dollar fee—well over $12 million in modern dollars—to argue the holding company's case in the Supreme Court. Upon his death in 1917, the *New York Times* wrote that "in the opinion of some well qualified judges," Johnson was "the greatest lawyer in the English-speaking world."[53]

Unfortunately for the Southern mills, Johnson also died before their challenge to the child labor law could reach the Supreme Court, but not before he offered some important advice to Clark—"a judicial district should be selected in which the judge is a man of known courage. This is no case to try before a weak character."[54]

By "a man of known courage," Johnson meant a judge who rejected the consensus view that the Keating-Owen Act was constitutional—and Clark's new legal team soon found such a man in Judge James Edmund Boyd. A Confederate veteran appointed to the bench by McKinley, Boyd was widely perceived as an old-line conservative in the vein of Chief Justice Melville Fuller or Justice Stephen Field. He was also the sole federal district judge presiding over North Carolina's western federal district—a distinction that would ensure that any case filed within a large swath of North Carolina would wind up in his courtroom. To guarantee that Boyd would have the opportunity to declare the child labor law unconstitutional, Clark also recruited the father of two western Carolina child mill workers, Reuben and John Dagenhart, who would serve as the ostensible plaintiffs in the Executive Committee's case[55]—although Reuben and John would never appear in court or otherwise contribute much more than their names to the case.[56]

Just four days after the lawyers filed their final briefs in the case, Judge Boyd did exactly what the mill owners were counting on him to do and declared the ban on child labor unconstitutional. Though, in a sharp break from generally accepted judicial practice, he did not lay out his reasoning in a written opinion, thus avoiding the awkward task of having to explain how this result could be justified under the Supreme Court's decisions in the lottery, prostitution, and pure foods cases.[57]

By the time what was then known as *Hammer v. Dagenhart* (1918) reached the Supreme Court, Fuller, Field, and Brewer were all long dead, but the bench had largely been shaped in former President Taft's image. Taft promoted Justice Edward Douglass White, a conservative Cleveland appointee to the high Court, to the chief justice's seat. He rounded the bench out with Justice Willis Van Devanter, who would later emerge as one of the Court's most consistent antagonists against President Franklin Roosevelt's New Deal, and with Justice Mahlon Pitney, an undistinguished jurist who is best remembered—if at all—for labeling a state law protecting workers' right to organize as a "serious" interference with liberty.[58] Additionally, although Justice William Rufus Day joined the bench during Theodore Roosevelt's presidency, Day owed his job to his friendship with Roosevelt's successor. Taft and Day were intimate friends who served together as federal appellate judges, and Taft successfully lobbied Roosevelt to promote Day to the Supreme Court.[59]

Ultimately, however, the fate of the child labor law was sealed as much by a catastrophic choice by President Woodrow Wilson as it was by any effort by Taft to reshape the Court in his image.

Justice James Clark McReynolds was, in *Time* magazine's words, "a savagely sarcastic, incredibly reactionary Puritan anti-Semite."[60] McReynolds was lazy. He often would not even open the briefs lawyers filed to prepare him to hear a case until hours before the case was argued, and he frequently spent just a few hours crafting opinions that would govern all other courts in the country.[61] McReynolds was nasty. He labeled President Franklin Roosevelt "that crippled son-of-a-bitch . . . in the White House,"[62] and shunned his own nephew after the boy woke him up by playing jazz music on the radio.[63] McReynolds was a petty tyrant. He ordered his staff never to smoke tobacco even on their free time, and dictated where they were allowed to live.[64] During his frequent duck hunting trips, Justice McReynolds would bring along his longtime servant Harry Parker, and he would order Parker to wade through ice-cold water to retrieve the fallen animals in lieu of a bird dog.[65] Though the two men often saw eye to eye on the Constitution, Taft dismissed McReynolds as "inconsiderate of his colleagues and others, and contemptuous of everyone" after serving on the same bench with him.[66]

And, above all, Justice McReynolds was a bigot. He refused to speak to Justice Louis Brandeis for Brandeis's first three years on the Court because Brandeis was Jewish, and he forbade contact between his staff and the Jewish Justices Brandeis and Benjamin Cardozo.[67] There is no official photograph of the justices for 1924 because the Court's seniority-based seating chart required McReynolds to sit next to Brandeis, and McReynolds simply refused to be photographed next to his Jewish colleague.[68] When Brandeis offered his views in conferences, McReynolds would simply stand up and leave.[69]

On the rare occasions when a woman argued a case before McReynolds's Court, the justice would exclaim "I see the female is here" and walk out of the Courtroom.[70] When Charles Hamilton Houston, the Harvard-educated black attorney who mentored future Justice Thurgood Marshall as Dean of the Howard Law School, argued before the Supreme Court in 1938, McReynolds turned his back on the Courtroom to signal his disapproval.[71] McReynolds once warned one of his law clerks, who had grown close with Harry Parker, that the clerk "seem[ed] to forget that [Parker] is a negro." He advised the clerk to "think of my wishes in this matter in your future relations with the darkies."[72]

Though only President Wilson could know why he chose to place McReynolds on the nation's highest Court, it is widely believed that Wilson kicked McReynolds upwards in order to remove an unpleasant member of his own cabinet.[73] Despite his conservatism, McReynolds came to Washington as an effective trust-buster and head of the Justice Department's Antitrust Division under Theodore Roosevelt. After Wilson named him attorney general, however, McReynolds proved as difficult to deal with in the Cabinet Room as he would later be in the justices' conferences.[74] If nothing else, the Supreme Court was a convenient place to put McReynolds where he would have little daily interaction with the president.

Yet, by placing him there, Wilson also placed the balance of power between Taft's hand-picked justices and the dissenters in the child labor case in the hands of one of the most reactionary individuals who has ever served on the Supreme Court. Justice McReynolds was the fifth vote to declare the child labor law unconstitutional.

Justice Day's majority opinion in the *Dagenhart* case rested on a fine distinction between the Keating-Owen Act and the lottery, prostitution, and impure food laws previously upheld by the Court. In each of those cases, Day reasoned, Congress legislated because it wanted to ban a specific harmful item—be it lottery tickets, prostitutes, or adulterated foods—from traveling in interstate commerce.

The goods barred from commerce by the child labor law, by contrast, were not themselves harmful goods. Rather, Congress enacted the Keating-Owen Act because it objected to the way the goods were manufactured before they were loaded on a train to be transported across state lines. Under the lottery law, all lottery tickets were banned. But under the child labor law, one shirt might be permitted to travel in interstate commerce, while another, identical shirt would be banned because of the labor conditions in the factory where it was made. This, according to *Dagenhart*, was not allowed. The child labor law, Day wrote, "does not regulate transportation among the States, but aims to standardize the ages at which children may be employed in mining and manufacturing within the States. The goods shipped are of themselves harmless."[75]

This distinction, however, had no basis in law. As Chief Justice Marshall explained nearly a century before *Dagenhart*, Congress's power over interstate commerce—though limited only to matters that legitimately involve commerce among the states—is "plenary" with respect to those matters, a word that means that it is complete or absolute. Thus, when the Fuller Court held in the *Sugar Trust Case* that Congress could regulate transportation of goods across state lines, that meant that Congress could do so however it chose so long as it did not violate some other provision of the Constitution. In Marshall's words, Congress's authority over interstate commerce is "complete in itself, may be exercised to its utmost extent, and acknowledges no limitations, other than are prescribed in the constitution."[76] *Dagenhart* rested, in the words of the decision that overruled it decades later, upon "a distinction which was novel when made and unsupported by any provision of the Constitution."[77]

The *Dagenhart* opinion concludes with an argument similar to one that the Affordable Care Act's opponents would raise a century later in their nearly successfully quest to shut down Obamacare—the Court must strike down the child labor law to ensure that some limit remains on Congress's ability to regulate. Echoing David Clark's apocalyptic warning about an all-powerful federal government that will "control all our internal affairs" in the South, Justice Day claimed that the "far-reaching result of upholding" the ban on child labor "cannot be more plainly indicated than by pointing out that if Congress can thus regulate matters entrusted to local authority by prohibition of the movement of commodities in interstate commerce, all freedom of commerce will be at an end, and the power of the States over local matters may be eliminated, and thus our system of government be practically destroyed."[78]

In other words, *Dagenhart* stands for the proposition that, in order to prevent Congress's powers from becoming too expansive, the Court must create arbitrary new limits on that power—even if those limits have no basis in the text of the Constitution. The birth of the railroad, the dawn of the Industrial Age, and the growth of the modern economy linked the farthest reaches of the nation together into a single commercial web—with economic transactions in California now impacting prices in Virginia and vice versa. As a result, the Constitution's simple words—"the Congress shall have power . . . to regulate commerce with foreign nations, and among the several states"—now have far-reaching implications that their drafters likely could not have anticipated. But that neither changes the meaning of those words nor gives the justices of the Supreme Court unchecked authority to rewrite them. The Court in *Dagenhart* was so concerned with limiting elected officials' power that it never stopped to ask what the limits on the justices' own power should be.

FOR REUBEN DAGENHART, however, the case that bears his name stood for something else. Six years after the Supreme Court gave him the right to spend what remained of his childhood toiling in a cotton mill, a reporter asked Dagenhart what benefit he gained from his nominal victory before the justices.

"Look at me!" Dagenhart replied. "A hundred and five pounds, a grown man and no education. I may be mistaken, but I think the years I've put in the cotton mills stunted my growth. They kept me from getting any schooling. I had to stop school after the third grade and now I need the education I didn't get." Dagenhart was twenty years old when he gave this interview, and he swore that he would somehow save his sister from his own fate—"she's only 16 and she's crippled and I bet I stop that!"[79]

In return for their victory in the child labor case, Dagenhart's employer received a generation of cheap labor and the Southern mills won decades of freedom from federal interference. Dagenhart's own share of the spoils, however, was more meager. Reuben and his brother John "got some automobile rides when them big lawyers from the North was down here. Oh, yes, and they bought both of us a Coca-Cola."[80]

Chapter 5

YOU LOAD SIXTEEN TONS
AND WHAT DO YOU GET?[1]

Boys like Reuben Dagenhart faced a future nearly as grim as their childhoods. At the turn of the century, adult men earned as little as sixty-five cents a day laboring in Southern cotton mills—an annual wage of just $5,500 in modern dollars. And, despite Dagenhart's indignation at the mill owners who stole away his youth, his own job as an adult may have depended upon his willingness to consign his children to a similar fate. In some mill towns, the company would refuse to rent housing to its workers unless those workers signed a contract promising to send four or five of their family members to work in the mill.[2]

Without access to company housing, Dagenhart likely would have wound up homeless. Rather than building in established population centers and drawing labor from the existing community, mill owners typically built entire new towns where workers depended upon the company and a company-owned store for food, shelter, and clothing. Part Pullman, part plantation, the mill towns placed each worker's economic life—and much of their personal and spiritual life—in company hands. In many towns, both the police force and the church pastor were on the mill's payroll.[3]

Nor could Dagenhart expect to live a healthy adulthood. As one famous study of the American South explained, by 1900 the cotton-mill worker was a pretty distinct physical type in the South; a type in some respects perhaps inferior to even that of the old poor white, which in general had been his to begin with. A dead-white skin, a sunken chest, and stooping shoulders were earmarks of the breed. Chinless faces, microcephalic foreheads, rabbit teeth, goggling dead-fish eyes, rickety limbs, and stunted bodies abounded—over and beyond the limit of their prevalence in the countryside. The women were characteristically stringy-haired and limp of breast at twenty, and shrunken hags at thirty or forty. And the incidence of tuberculosis, of insanity and epilepsy, and, above all, of pellagra, the curious vitamin-deficiency disease which is nearly peculiar to the South, was increasing.[4]

In the North, wages were higher and workers typically enjoyed greater freedom, but few workers lived in comfort and many lived in poverty. In the relatively progressive state of Massachusetts, highly skilled workers such as masons, plumbers, and engineers could earn roughly the equivalent of $28,000 a year in modern dollars. Meanwhile, textile workers earned less than half that and operatives in other factories earned little more. According to one late nineteenth-century survey, families earning well over the mean income were still left with virtually nothing remaining after paying for food, shelter, clothing, and fuel. And even the poorest workers were better off than many of their neighbors. During the frequent economic downturns of this era, nearly 30 percent of the workforce was unemployed for at least part of the year.[5]

The factories of this era were, to put it bluntly, death traps. The beating hearts of American industry were high-pressure steam engines powered by massive boilers. Yet, despite the ubiquity of these boilers in factories that produced all kinds of goods, few engineers understood the properties of steam and hot iron well enough to operate the boilers safely, and poorly constructed boilers were common. Moreover, boiler attendants often lacked even the most rudimentary training. One sixteen-year-old worker hired by an uncle "who knew as little about a steam boiler as I did" learned how not to operate one safely when he added cold water to a hot, nearly empty boiler. The boiler immediately swelled and "steam began blowing from . . . every seam." Yet, unlike many other times a worker made this mistake, the boiler did not explode. Many workers were not so lucky. Between 1883 and 1907, an estimated seven thousand people died in boiler explosions within the United States.[6]

A labyrinth of gears, belts, flywheels, and shafts radiated from the steam engine at the heart of a factory, delivering power to every corner of the mill—and each one presented its own dangers to nearby workers. Belts could slip or break, catching unsuspecting bystanders in the process. Shafts turned at hundreds of revolutions per minute, and the screws protruding from them caught workers by the clothing and hurled them with deadly force. A thrown belt could wrap around unintended segments of the machine, snapping wooden shafts and often firing parts across the room. In one incident, a nine-ton flywheel measuring twenty feet in diameter tore free from the greater machine and rolled over twelve men, an armory, several railroad cars, an icehouse, and a hotel before it finally came to a stop.[7]

The single most dangerous moment of many workers' days was the moment they began working. Distributed around the factories were smaller machines that needed to be connected to the mass of whirling gears and pulleys or else they would lie idle. To start work, a worker had to manually shift a belt connected to the greater machine onto his smaller machine, thus joining it to the Rube Goldberg apparatus that powered the entire factory. Yet, because the central machine never stopped turning, the worker risked getting caught by the turning belt and crushed by the full force of the factory's steam engine.

Coal miners faced even greater dangers on the job. Often confined to "rooms" within the mines that could be no more than three feet in height, miners sometimes had to lie on their sides to chisel out portions of the mine face with their picks. Having done so, their next task was to bore several holes in the wall above the section they just dug out, fill them with black powder, light a fuse, and pray that the resulting explosion did not bring the entire mine shaft down upon their heads.[8] Many miners also lacked training in how to handle such explosives safely. Some died inspecting charges that they falsely believed to have misfired, only to discover that there had been no misfire when the charge detonated. Others opened metal powder kegs with their picks, creating sparks that ignited twenty-five pounds of powder at once.[9] And even when miners stood far away from these explosions, large slabs of slate could fall without warning from the ceilings, crushing any workers unfortunate enough to be standing below. In some cases, the surviving miners had to scrape the remains of their flattened coworkers off the ground with their shovels.[10]

Though falling roofs and similar collapses were the most common cause of death among miners, many mine workers lived in fear of an even more dramatic end. In just one month in 1907, more than seven hundred miners were killed in a series of explosions—over half of them in a disaster that wiped out all but five members of a mine's entire work force. Most mines produced methane gas, which is explosive even in fairly small concentrations. In an era when mine workers often relied on open-flame lamps for light, a miner could trigger an explosion merely by wandering into an area filled with gas.[11]

As the entire purpose of mining coal was to extract fuel that could be burned, the very coal dust that filled the mine's air and tore at the miners' lungs was also quite flammable. When a spark met a cloud of coal dust hanging in the air of the mine, the result could be a deadly chain reaction as flames danced from one cloud of dust to another a few feet away. Often, these chain explosions lasted several seconds as they traveled down narrow mineshafts, climaxing in an enormous tongue of flame where the shaft opened to the greater mine.[12]

Outside the mines, workers faced fewer dangers, but they often faced a dreary existence in towns and camps that existed for the sole purpose of supporting the mine. As late as 1925, 86 percent of coal-town houses in the states of Virginia, West Virginia, and Kentucky lacked running water—most relied on privies that emptied into a creek—and saloons, bordellos, and gambling halls were often the only after-work entertainment. Many Colorado mining communities, by contrast, enjoyed such luxuries as schools, theaters, and clubhouses, although these amenities came at a price that would make George Pullman blush. Colorado's mining towns were often surrounded by barbed wire and patrolled by company guards. If a union official wandered into the town hoping to organize the mine's workers, the guards tracked his every move until he departed.[13]

Yet this level of surveillance paled in comparison to the measures utilized to control workers in some communities east of the Mississippi. In Harlan County, Kentucky, the scene of a major Depression-era labor dispute that birthed the union protest song, "Which Side Are You On?" Sheriff J. H. Blair openly admitted that he "did all in my power to aid the coal operators." When miners elected a replacement for Blair, the new sheriff, Theodore Roosevelt Middleton, soon entered into a business partnership with the mine owners and obtained five mines of his own. He then appointed a small army of anti-union deputies, dozens of whom were convicted felons and nearly all of whom were on the mining bosses' payrolls. Jury service in Harlan County was limited to property taxpayers, and the miners all lived in rented company homes. Thus, mine workers or union officials arrested by Blair's or Middleton's deputies faced juries entirely devoid of their peers.[14]

Nor were these tactics limited to Harlan County. The Pittsburgh Coal Company employed over three hundred police charged with strikebreaking and union busting. Mine owners in Logan County, West Virginia, paid tribute to Sheriff Don Chafin—who returned the favor by naming hundreds of mine guards as his deputies.

Chafin met every train that stopped in his county and physically assaulted union sympathizers arriving on these trains.[15] Eventually, these tactics led to open warfare between Chafin and Logan County's miners. In 1921, thousands of armed miners clashed with a smaller but better-equipped army loyal to Chafin. The battle continued on and off for days, even after Chafin employed aircraft to drop bombs filled with nails and metal shrapnel upon the miners. Hostilities ceased after federal troops arrived and disarmed the miners.[16]

So, while the adult Reuben Dagenhart and his counterparts in factories and mines would have enjoyed somewhat higher wages than the children who shared their workspaces, they still looked forward to a string of miserly paychecks, deteriorating health, potentially deadly working conditions, and systematic efforts to render them powerless against their employers. And, like so many of the hardships visited upon the workers of this era, the courts played a significant role in maintaining these conditions.

———

ON A WINTER'S day in turn-of-the-century Chicago, John Zolnowski climbed inside one of the Illinois Steel Company's enormous furnaces in order to reline its walls. He was joined in this task by a co-worker named Behrens, and a torch flame to light the furnace's dark interior while the two men worked. After several hours of work, a column of gas shot into the furnace, erupting into a tongue of flame fourteen feet long when it touched Zolnowski's torch. Behrens immediately burnt to a fatal crisp. Zolnowski survived, but he was left disfigured and permanently disabled.[17]

Any number of precautions by Illinois Steel could have saved these two men from this fate. A lock could have been placed on the valve that opened the flow of gas into the furnace, for example, or a guard could have been stationed at the valve to ensure that it was not turned. Yet the Illinois courts held that the steel company owed nothing to the men burned in their service. Zolnowski would spend the rest of his life covered in horrific burns, but he would receive no compensation for his injury.[18]

The upshot of cases such as this one is that businesses had few incentives to keep workers safe—men and women could be maimed or killed in their service, but such accidents cost the company nothing more than it cost to hire a replacement worker. Installing machine guards, training workers in safe practices, and providing them with appropriate clothing and safety goggles, by contrast, could be quite costly. And even relatively kind bosses had to compete with companies that cared little about their workers' lives. Too much attention to safety placed a factory at a competitive disadvantage if the courts refused to order employers to compensate their injured workers.

And, lest there be any doubt, Zolnowski's inability to obtain compensation was hardly isolated. One 1910 study of workplace fatalities determined that over half of widows and children left behind after a fatal accident received either nothing at all from their deceased loved one's employer or else they only received enough money to pay for funeral expenses. Of the remaining families, only a small fraction received more than what the lowest-paid worker earned in a year.[19]

Men like John Zolnowski were at the mercy of flexible legal doctrines developed over the course of centuries by British and later by American judges. In Zolnowski's case, for example, Illinois Steel would be deemed negligent, and therefore liable for Behrens and Zolnowski's injuries, if a "prudent person prior to the accident" would have taken additional precautions to prevent the gas from entering the furnace.[20] Other cases rested on equally ambiguous questions, such as whether a worker assumed the risk that they would be injured when they stepped into a potentially dangerous environment, or whether the worker also behaved negligently in a way that might cancel out their employer's own neglect. Because of these open-ended doctrines, judges had broad discretion to decide whether to deny relief to injured workers, or even to toss out jury verdicts favoring the injured.

It should be noted that judge-made doctrines such as the law of negligence still make up the backbone of much of American law governing injuries, contracts, and other matters that occupy the lion's share of every modern law student's first year in law school. Moreover, these "common law" doctrines, as they are known, have an important virtue—they can be modified by elected lawmakers or even replaced completely by laws more protective towards the vulnerable. By 1917, every major industrial state legislature enacted a workman's compensation law guaranteeing that workers injured on the job would receive payment from their employers.[21] Though the payments were often meager compared to the cost of spending an entire life without an arm, a leg, or an eye—a worker with an amputated limb received as little as $18,000 in modern dollars—they were high enough to change the attitudes of factory owners concerned only with their own bottom line. Suddenly, the cost of permitting frequent injuries exceeded the cost of machine guards, safety gear, and adequate training for workers. As one Ford executive admitted, the "awakening consciousness on safety came at about the same time as compensation laws."[22]

So, while the judges of this era often showed little concern for workers, this lack of concern could be overcome by elected officials. That is, of course, unless the judges forbade those officials from lawmaking. At the same time that Melville Fuller, Stephen Field, and David Brewer championed elaborate legal doctrines that hobbled the federal government's ability to legislate, their counterparts on state supreme courts across the country erected their own barriers to state legislation.

To Fuller's fellow travelers on the state bench, a law protecting Wisconsin workers' right to organize was "legalized thralldom, not liberty."[23] A law ensuring that Ohio coal miners would be paid for every ounce of coal that they mined was an "object of socialism."[24] A Missouri statute prohibiting employers from paying their workers in scrip redeemable only at the company store "introduce[d] a system of state paternalism which is at war with the fundamental principles of our government."[25] And a Colorado law prohibiting mine owners from overworking miners was "subversive of the right to enjoy and defend liberty, to acquire and possess property, and to pursue happiness."[26]

The Wisconsin opinion was typical of this genre of cases. Just as John Archibald Campbell looked to the ambiguous language of the Fourteenth Amendment and found in there the means to protect white supremacy, the Wisconsin justices gazed into the words of the Declaration of Independence and found in there the power to free businessmen from having to deal with unions. Under the Wisconsin

Supreme Court's decision in *Zillmer v. Kreutzberg* (1902), the state legislature must be hobbled in its ability to enact laws protecting workers, because these laws limit the kind of labor contracts an employer can offer to an employee.

The Wisconsin Constitution begins with an homage to the Declaration—"all men are born equally free and independent, and have certain inherent rights; among these are life, liberty and the pursuit of happiness; to secure these rights, governments are instituted among men, deriving their just powers from the consent of the governed."[27] Yet it is unlikely that the men who gathered in Philadelphia to sign the Declaration and provide their justification for war with Britain could have anticipated how their words would be used by judges more than a century later. Relying on nothing more than their state constitution's statement that all men have an inherent right to "liberty," the Wisconsin justices concluded that one of these so-called liberties is the right of every worker to be bound by nearly any contract they enter into, regardless of whether the worker is actually capable of bargaining effectively with a far mightier employer. If a worker's employer threatens to fire him unless he agrees to quit his union and never again seek the benefits of collective bargaining, then it is the worker's right to be forced to capitulate to his bosses' demands.[28]

To reach this conclusion, the Wisconsin justices looked to some of the leading conservative thinkers of the nineteenth century, men such as the British Social Darwinist Herbert Spencer and the influential American scholar Christopher Tiedeman. In fact, the court's opinion borrows its definition of liberty from Tiedeman's writings—"it is the right of every one to determine whose services he will hire," and thus to deny a job to anyone who joins a union. "Governments, therefore, cannot exert any restraint upon the actions of the parties."[29]

Yet, while the judges of this era relied heavily on scholars and theorists like Spencer and Tiedeman—Tiedeman bragged in the second edition of one of his treatises that "the first edition of the book has been quoted by the courts with approval in hundreds of cases"[30]— the notion that the law cannot shield a worker from oppressive labor contracts was introduced to American legal audiences by a much more famous and powerful figure, Justice Stephen Johnson Field. In his *Slaughterhouse* dissent, Field claimed that the Fourteenth Amendment protects what he labeled the "right of free labor." When the state enacts a law that limits which kinds of labor contracts are permissible, Field wrote, using language he borrowed from the seminal economic philosopher Adam Smith, such a law is a "manifest encroachment upon the just liberty both of the workman and of those who might be disposed to employ him."[31]

So when state supreme court justices held that mine owners could deny miners the full value of their work, or that laborers could be paid only in scrip, or that anyone who joined a union could be denied employment altogether, they effectively rewrote the history of the *Slaughterhouse* dispute and declared Field the winner—at least within the borders of their own state. The Constitution of Stephen Johnson Field may not yet have become the law of the land, but it was the law in Wisconsin, Ohio, Colorado, and numerous other states.

As Field's narrow vision of government power took hold in state after state, few writers captured the spirit of the judges who implemented this vision better than Tiedeman. Professor Tiedeman warned that "the conservative classes stand in constant fear of the advent of an absolutism more tyrannical and more unreasoning than any before experienced by man—the absolutism of a democratic majority." To combat this risk that democratically elected lawmakers might believe that the will of the people gives them a mandate to govern, Tiedeman urged the courts to "lay their interdict upon all legislative acts" that violated his conception of liberty, "even though these acts do not violate any specific or special provision of the Constitution."[32] Many judges were more than happy to comply.

———

THE UNITED STATES Supreme Court's opportunity to take up Tiedeman's call emerged from a much more mundane setting than the factories, railroads, and coal mines that so often symbolized work

in the industrial age. Yet, although New York City bakeries featured none of the technical marvels that snaked and spun and turned
throughout turn-of-the-century factories, they were often just as un-
healthful and as oppressive to their workers as the mills where Reuben Dagenhart spent his childhood.

Though primitive, New York's bakeries were as much creatures of
the industrial age as the cotton mill and the railroad. In rural America, few families cared to pay for another to bake their bread when
they could simply do so at home. Yet the tenements that housed New
York's many poor workers often lacked ovens or were too crowded
with multiple families to permit home baking. As a result, the number of bakery workers increased more than eightfold during the latter
half of the nineteenth century in order to meet city dwellers' growing
need for bread.[33]

The new bakeries, however, resisted modernization because of the
nature of the product that they were selling. Unlike crackers, hard-
tack, and other, less perishable baked goods that were well-suited
to mass production, bread has a limited shelf life and is best served
fresh. So, although cracker bakeries grew, automated, and built factories just like many other major industries, for several years into the
twentieth century bread bakeries remained tiny shops catering only
to neighborhood customers.[34]

The upshot of this divide within the baking industry is that, while
cracker barons could spend lavishly on modern factories with state-
of-the-art machinery, bread bakeries typically saved costs by locating
in the basements of the very tenements that they served. In the early
twentieth century, nearly nine out of ten New York bakeries were
basement operations.[35]

These basement workplaces enabled bakery owners to save
on rent, but they also obscured conditions that would have made
their customers gag on their bread. As one New York City inspector documented after visiting several of these bakeries, "filth, cob-
webs and vermin" filled these basements, as did colonies of rats and
mice. Worse, the tenements' sewer pipes typically ran through the
basement bakeries, often leaking their raw contents on whatever lay

was an impossibility, and even socializing outside of the four or five coworkers who shared the basement with them was a rare luxury.[40] They were, in this sense, even worse off than Reuben Dagenhart.

In the face of these conditions, the state of New York enacted "an act to regulate the manufacture of flour and meal food products" in 1895. Most of the law targeted the unsanitary conditions that pervaded basement bakeries. The law required adequate drainage and plumbing in bakeries. It required bakery floors to be constructed of cement, tiles, or "wood properly saturated with linseed oil." It regulated how flour must be stored and how washrooms must be kept, and it mandated that the "sleeping places for the persons employed in a bakery shall be separate from the room or rooms" where bread was baked.[41]

New York's lawmakers, however, did not just protect the public from unhealthy bread, they also sought to better the lot of the men who baked this bread. In an act that would set up one of the most important court battles in the nation's history, the New York law limited a baker's hours to sixty per week and no more than ten in a single day.[42] The days of bakers working twenty-four-hour shifts were over.

Or, at least, they would have been over if it were not for the Supreme Court.

––––––––

SIX YEARS AFTER New York placed a limit on bakers' hours, the state fined a bakery owner named Joseph Lochner fifty dollars for overworking an employee. Four years later, Lochner's case reached the Supreme Court. Yet, despite the fact that it took a decade for the maximum-hours law to reach the justices, the fact that the law was doomed became obvious the moment Chief Justice Fuller announced that Justice Rufus Peckham would deliver the Court's opinion in *Lochner v. New York*.

Fuller and Peckham were, in many ways, ideological twins. Just as Fuller opposed the Emancipation Proclamation and tried to pro-

below. In one bakery, "the sewer pipes leaked into the bake-
and I really saw the contents flow into the ferment tub which
tains the yeast used in the production of bread." In another, a
tive sink leaked waste water all over the floor of the bakery, "c
pools of putrid water and piles of mud, exhaling odors so v
the desire to escape to the side-walk became irresistible." A
third, roaches lined the walls with such density that "the wat
walls were literally black" with the insects.[36]

Windows were small or nonexistent and ventilation of
from just a handful of horizontal grates, leaving the bakers
dungeons lit by a hot oven, as the air filled with flour dust a
rising from the oven's flames. Moreover, the ceilings in tl
ments sometimes rose no higher than five and a half feet
floor, forcing many workers to crouch in order to fit into
cated workspace. Some basements lacked any flooring to s
the bakers were compressed between short ceilings and
Other bakery workers stood on wood floors rotten from f
riddled with rat holes.[37]

And they worked long hours in these squalid conditio
age bakery employee worked between 13 and 14 hours a
longer hours were far from infrequent. One shop's bake
hours a day, five days a week—in addition to a 24-ho
Thursday.[38] Another imposed a 126-hour workweek
leaving them with only 6 hours a day to do anything o
bread. Indeed, the hours in New York's bakeries we
that, when the bakers struck in 1881, they demanded
reduced to just 12 hours a day. And for these labors the
more than a poverty wage. At the turn of the cent
earned more than 12 dollars a week—approximately
in modern dollars.[39]

Even when they weren't working, bakers rarely
day. Bakery owners typically required bakers to sl
where they worked, often on the very tables wher
kneaded the dough—and the price of these sleeping
was then deducted from their pay. For many baker

hibit federal incursions upon slavery as an Illinois state lawmaker, the young Rufus Peckham was a Democrat who opposed secession but who also had no love for black slaves. "I am proud I believe in no negro equality," Peckham wrote his brother the same month Abraham Lincoln was elected president. Two years later he railed against "the radical abolitionists" who were "making it a war for the freedom of the slaves, in spite of the Constitution and if necessary in spite of the Union."[43]

Peckham remained similarly dismissive of African Americans after becoming a judge. As a justice, Peckham voted to uphold segregation in *Plessy*. He sided with Alabama's suspicious decision to prevent over five thousand black citizens from registering to vote.[44] And he backed a Georgia county's plan to tax black families to pay for white schools without providing similar school facilities to black children—although, in keeping with the frequent disregard of turn-of-the-century justices for civil rights, the Court's decision in *Cumming v. Richmond County Board of Education* (1899) was unanimous.[45]

His most revealing race case, however, may be a silent dissent Peckham offered on behalf of a skating rink owner claiming that a law prohibiting race discrimination in "places of amusement" violated the owner's supposed right to do what he wanted with his property.[46] Though Peckham did not explain why he believed the rink owner should have the right to deny admission to black patrons, his dissenting vote matched a long record of skepticism regarding the power of elected officials to rein in business. Peckham's laissez-faire outlook animated even the most routine cases he heard as a state court judge. When a fourteen-year-old girl employed by a laundry crushed her hand between the two heavy rollers of a machine used to press collars, Peckham scoffed at the idea that her employer had any obligation to prevent such accidents or to compensate the victims of such injuries. By merely "accepting this work and entering upon the employment about this machine," the young girl assumed the risk that she might be injured by it. According to Peckham, workers like this permanently disabled girl "cannot call upon the defendant to make alterations to secure greater safety."[47]

Justice Peckham, like Chief Justice Fuller, owed his high position to his friendship with the conservative President Grover Cleveland. Early in Cleveland's first term in the White House, the new president exerted his considerable influence in his home state of New York to help place Peckham on the state's highest court. Nearly a decade later, Cleveland favored his friend with an appointment to the nation's highest Court.[48]

Yet, for all that the two justices shared in common, Peckham was, if anything, even more conservative than the chief justice. Seven years before *Lochner* reached the Supreme Court, a mine owner brought a similar lawsuit challenging a Utah maximum-hours law governing miners. Even Fuller agreed that this law was constitutional, joining six of his colleagues in deferring to the state legislature's determination that the hazards of mine work required a shorter work day.[49] Peckham and the archconservative Justice Brewer found themselves in a lonely dissent.

And Peckham combined his staunch conservatism with an overarching distrust of democracy. When the city of Buffalo passed an ordinance replacing several gas street lamps with electric lighting, Peckham responded with a dissenting opinion, calling this act a "plain, bald, useless waste of the property or funds of the public" and insisting that his court should keep the gas lighting in place. To Peckham, even a question as routine as whether a particular avenue should be lit by gas flames or lightbulbs cannot be trusted to elected officials, and it was the sacred duty of judges to veto those officials' decisions if the judges deemed them unwise. No other judge joined Peckham's dissent in the electric lights case.[50]

In other words, Peckham was the perfect justice to take up Professor Tiedeman's crusade against "the absolutism of a democratic majority" and to write Justice Field's conservative vision into the Constitution. Six years after Field's death and just eight years after his retirement from the bench, *Lochner v. New York* would be more than just a victory for Joseph Lochner, it would be the culmination of Field's life's work.[51]

Peckham's *Lochner* opinion in many ways maps the state court opinions invalidating attempts to better the lot of workers. Just as the Wisconsin justices read a right to be bound by some of the most oppressive labor contracts into their state constitution's invocation of the word "liberty," Peckham found a similar freedom from laws improving workplace conditions within the Fourteenth Amendment's vague language. "The general right to make a contract in relation to his business is part of the liberty of the individual protected by the Fourteenth Amendment of the Federal Constitution," Peckham wrote—despite the fact that this so-called right is never mentioned in this amendment—so judges must treat any effort to protect workers from exploitation with great skepticism.[52]

Although the *Lochner* opinion did place some limits on this extra-constitutional right to contract, Peckham showed nothing but scorn for the idea that protecting workers is, in and of itself, a legitimate task for lawmakers. In Peckham's mind, "the question whether this act is valid as a labor law, pure and simple, may be dismissed in a few words. There is no reasonable ground for interfering with the liberty of person or the right of free contract" by preventing bakeries from overworking their bakers. Peckham also had no sympathy for the fact that a poor tenement dweller with no means to buy his own bread is hardly in a position to negotiate for decent wages or reasonable hours. "There is no contention," the *Lochner* opinion asserts, that bakers are unable to "care for themselves without the protecting arm of the State."[53]

In reality, of course, New York's bakers worked fourteen-hour shifts in roach-infested basements, slept on their work tables, and then woke up the next day to do it again before the "protecting arm of the State" intervened.

Though *Lochner* deemed mere sympathy for workers to be an illegitimate impulse on the part of lawmakers, Peckham did leave the door open to some forms of labor regulation. Laws protecting the "safety, health, morals and general welfare of the public" were still permitted under *Lochner*. So a state could still, in theory, protect workers from injury or disease.[54]

Yet even this limited universe of health and safety laws could be vetoed by the courts. As Justice John Marshall Harlan explained in a dissenting opinion, many turn-of-the-century health researchers believed that bakeries were unusually unhealthy work environments, and that bakers' health risks were exacerbated by long hours. Quoting an unnamed source, Harlan details the many health hazards contemporary medical science attributed to work in a bakery:

> The constant inhaling of flour dust causes inflammation of the lungs and of the bronchial tubes. The eyes also suffer through this dust, which is responsible for the many cases of running eyes among the bakers. The long hours of toil to which all bakers are subjected produce rheumatism, cramps and swollen legs. The intense heat in the workshops induces the workers to resort to cooling drinks, which together with their habit of exposing the greater part of their bodies to the change in the atmosphere, is another source of a number of diseases of various organs. Nearly all bakers are pale-faced and of more delicate health than the workers of other crafts, which is chiefly due to their hard work and their irregular and unnatural mode of living, whereby the power of resistance against disease is greatly diminished. The average age of a baker is below that of other workmen; they seldom live over their fiftieth year, most of them dying between the ages of forty and fifty. During periods of epidemic diseases the bakers are generally the first to succumb to the disease, and the number swept away during such periods far exceeds the number of other crafts in comparison to the men employed in the respective industries. When, in 1720, the plague visited the city of Marseilles, France, every baker in the city succumbed to the epidemic, which caused considerable excitement in the neighboring cities and resulted in measures for the sanitary protection of the bakers.[55]

Peckham, however, dismissed these risks. "It might be safely affirmed that almost all occupations more or less affect the health," the justice wrote in *Lochner*, but "there must be more than the mere fact of the possible existence of some small amount of unhealthiness to warrant legislative interference with liberty." Having dismissed the evidence that too many hours working in a bakery was unhealthy, Peckham then wrote Tiedeman's fear of democracy into the Constitution itself—"it is unfortunately true that labor, even in any department, may possibly carry with it the seeds of unhealthiness. But are we all, on that account, at the mercy of legislative majorities?"[56]

The upshot of this debate between Peckham and Harlan was that workplace health and safety laws were allowed, but only at the sufferance of unelected judges. Rufus Wheeler Peckham had no popular mandate to legitimize his exercise of power. He also had neither training as a physician nor any background in the sciences. Yet he took it upon himself to decide which workplaces were healthful and which ones dangerous enough to justify state intervention. And his opinion in *Lochner* was an invitation for every other judge in the country to do the same.

———

IT IS WORTH noting that not every judge, or even every justice who joined the majority opinion in *Lochner*, was as skeptical of government action as Justice Peckham. Though judges like Peckham weren't exactly rare during the decades surrounding the *Lochner* decision, a more subtle philosophy drove many of Peckham's contemporaries as well.

Judges, and the lawyers who someday become judges, are creatures of precedents and common law rules that developed through a slow, deliberative process, often over the course of hundreds of years. This breeds a kind of conservatism that is less rooted in antigovernment ideology than it is in traditionalism. As Alexis de Tocqueville wrote in the mid-nineteenth century, lawyers "are secretly opposed to the instincts of democracy; their superstitious respect for what is old, to its love of novelty; their narrow views, to its grandiose plans; their taste for formality, to its scorn for rules; their habit of proceeding slowly, to its impetuosity."[57]

Indeed, de Tocqueville likened the legal profession to something akin to the English gentry. "If you ask me where American aristocracy is found," he wrote in *Democracy in America*, "my reply would be that it would not be among the wealthy who have no common link uniting them. American aristocracy is found at the bar and on the bench."[58]

Admittedly, the legal profession's aristocratic character began to fade after state lawmakers started relaxing the requirements necessary to be admitted to the bar during the early 1800s. By the second half of the nineteenth century, however, these relaxed requirements led to a kind of class struggle between old-line aristocratic lawyers and the less-refined crop of men, many of them immigrants, who began earning a living as attorneys. Justice Brewer complained in 1895 that "a growing multitude is crowding in who are not fit to be lawyers, who disgrace the profession after they are in it, [and] who in a scramble after livelihood are debasing the noblest of professions into the meanest of avocations." One president of the New York State Bar objected that "men are seen in almost all our courts slovenly in dress, uncouth in manners and habits, ignorant even of the English language, jostling, crowding, vulgarizing the profession."[59]

The American Bar Association (ABA) was founded in 1878 largely as an effort by the "best men" of the bar to reassert control over their profession, in part by raising the standards of legal education and other requirements necessary to become an attorney. Indeed, the ABA was largely the brainchild of one of the most pedigreed members of the legal profession—Simeon Baldwin, a Yale Law School professor and son of a former United States senator. Baldwin would go on to serve as chief justice and then governor of Connecticut.[60]

Laissez-faire attitudes were hardly uncommon among the men who heeded Baldwin's call to organize America's elite attorneys under a single bar association. Tiedeman and Brewer were both early members of the ABA, as were several very conservative lawyers who would later serve on the Supreme Court.[61] But the prevailing attitude among these legal elites was less one of generalized skepticism about government and more a fear of rapid change. James Broadhead, the first president of the ABA, compared the development of the law to the slow, Darwinian process of natural selection. New Jersey Governor John Griggs, a future United States Attorney General, echoed this sentiment in a speech to the ABA:

> The contemplation of the history of the system of English law which we inherit is to the lawyer a cause of enthusiasm and a lesson in conservatism. To trace the growth of this system from the earliest beginnings, from the proto-plasmic cells, so to speak, of village and tribal customs among the primeval fens and forests of Saxony, or the bogs and crags of Jutland, on through centuries of progressive evolution upon English soil and under English skies until we see its mature development is well calculated to arouse the admiration and enthusiasm of the lawyer and statesman as well as of the mere student of history.[62]

This evolutionary process was, above all things, gradual. As ABA president Charles Manderson explained in 1899, "nature, in her evolutionary processes, moves with a deliberation only equaled by her precision. Her motto seems to be, 'make haste slowly!'"[63]

To legal elites who believed that the proper development of the law takes centuries, legislatures—with their power to cast aside longstanding principles of the common law and replace it with an entirely novel legal regime—were downright terrifying. One early ABA president proclaimed that the United States could "endure all its other dangers with less apprehension than the action of its federal and state legislation inspires." Another ABA president fretted that "when a state legislature meets, every great corporation within its reach prepares for self-defense, knowing by bitter experience how hospitably attacks upon its property are received in committees and on the floor." ABA speakers labeled elected lawmakers as "'reckless politicians' who truckled for 'the unthinking vote'; 'social agitators' who sought office for 'self advantage, not for the public weal'; [and] 'professional demagogues' who filled the land with 'ill-considered and impractical theories' and engaged in 'gross, persistent, flagrant and sometimes corrupt dereliction.'"[64]

The judiciary offered these legal elites the gradual, evolutionary process they found so comforting, whereas democracy represented the greatest single threat to this gradualism. In their minds, long-standing principles of the common law had served Americans and their English forefathers well for generations, so why should upstart lawmakers be allowed to simply cast these principles aside?

Yet the answer to this question should have been obvious. Even setting aside the fact that legislators are elected, and judges, at least at the federal level, are not, the nineteenth and early twentieth centuries saw a complete transformation of the American economy and in the ways that Americans were able to interact with each other. Railroads knitted the nation together. New technology enabled rapid—and, eventually, instantaneous—communication between merchants. Factories and other industrial workplaces created economic challenges and physical dangers for workers that simply did not exist in the colonial era. Towns became cities and then metropolises. Legal doctrines that took centuries to evolve were rendered obsolete by technological innovations that could sweep across the nation in a few years.

In the end, it took an alliance of two very different kinds of conservatives to produce opinions like *Lochner*: those who viewed democracy as a threat to liberty and those who believed, as Edmund Burke once wrote, that society must show "infinite caution" before tearing down longstanding institutions.[65] The lawyers and judges of this era did not need to be disciples of Christopher Tiedeman—although many of them were—in order to stand athwart democracy and yell, "stop!"[66] They just had to be protective of a legal regime that was designed for an era when it took four months to travel from New York to California.

———

THE FACT THAT not every justice who agreed with *Lochner*'s result shared an unforgiving ideology sometimes meant that plaintiffs invoking the so-called "liberty of contract" doctrine did not prevail. Indeed, *Lochner*'s most strident modern-day apologist defends the opinion on the grounds that the Supreme Court upheld most of the laws challenged under this doctrine.[67] Yet, while this claim may be true, it is too dismissive of the sweeping impact of many decisions that did strike down laws protecting workers—or the completely arbitrary reasoning that the justices would often apply when deciding whether a law violates *Lochner*'s freedom to contract.

Three years after *Lochner*, in a case known as *Muller v. Oregon* (1908), the justices considered an Oregon law providing that "no female (shall) be employed in any mechanical establishment, or factory, or laundry in this State more than ten hours during any one day." Rather than reject this law as just another incursion upon the supposed right to contract, the nine men on the Court concluded that the "inherent difference between the two sexes" justified the Oregon law.[68]

"History discloses the fact that woman has always been dependent upon man," Justice Brewer explained on behalf of a unanimous Court. Man, Brewer continued, "established his control [over women] at the outset by superior physical strength," and then he compared women to children. Much like "minors," the supposedly frailer sex

> has been looked upon in the courts as needing especial care that her rights may be preserved. . . . Looking at it from the viewpoint of the effort to maintain an independent position in life, she is not upon an equality. Differentiated by these matters from the other sex, she is properly placed in a class by herself, and legislation designed for her protection may be sustained, even when like legislation is not necessary for men and could not be sustained. It is impossible to close one's eyes to the fact that she still looks to her brother and depends upon him.[69]

Setting aside the Court's dismissive attitude towards women, this passage is hard to square with the logic of *Lochner*. The economic theory underlying *Lochner* is that government shouldn't regulate the workplace, because workers will do a better job of looking out for their own interests if they are free to negotiate over their working conditions with their bosses. That's why the *Lochner* opinion described New York's maximum-hours law as a violation of each baker's right "to enter into those contracts in relation to labor which may seem to him appropriate or necessary for the support of himself and his family."[70]

But if *Lochner* is right that workers are best served by fewer labor laws, and if women in the workforce truly are handicapped in their ability to "maintain an independent position in life," then the appropriate response is to give them even *fewer* legal protections in the workplace than men enjoy. If it were actually true, as the justices would later claim, that the right to work every waking hour for a dollar a day is "as essential to the laborer as to the capitalist,"[71] then why isn't this so-called right even more essential to working women at the margins of society?

Rather than follow this liberty-of-contract rabbit hole to its end, however, Brewer offers another reason why women should not be overworked. The need to ensure a woman's "proper discharge of her maternal functions—having in view not merely her own health, but the well-being of the race—justif[ies] legislation to protect her from the greed as well as the passion of man." Long hours, Brewer writes, tend "to injurious effects upon the body, and as healthy mothers are essential to vigorous offspring, the physical well-being of woman becomes an object of public interest and care in order to preserve the strength and vigor of the race."[72]

Here, at least, Brewer appears to rest upon *Lochner*'s conclusion that a labor law can sometimes be allowed when it serves the public health, but he offered no citation to the Constitution itself to support the proposition that men have different constitutional rights than women—and, indeed, he could not have offered one even if he had tried. As in *Lochner*, the fate of the Oregon law had nothing to do with the Constitution's text and everything to do with the medical judgment of nine unelected lawyers.

A dozen years after *Lochner*, the justices seemed tired of playing doctor. In a 1917 decision upholding a law limiting men's and women's hours to thirteen a day and requiring overtime pay after ten hours, the Court barely discussed whether such a law was necessary "for preservation of the health of employes [*sic*]." What little analysis they did offer was limited to a brief statement suggesting that the justices would defer to state officials' judgment regarding which laws were necessary to safeguard health.[73]

Nevertheless, the justices resumed their role as the nation's chief physicians just six years later. In *Adkins v. Children's Hospital* (1923), a decision striking down the District of Columbia's minimum wages for women and children, the Court disavowed *Muller*'s chauvinistic rhetoric about the health needs of future mothers—or, at least, disavowed it as much as was necessary to prohibit lawmakers from ensuring that women receive an adequate wage. "While the physical differences" between men and women "must be recognized in appropriate cases," the Court concluded that, "we cannot accept the doctrine that women of mature age . . . require or may be subjected to restrictions upon their liberty of contract which could not lawfully be imposed in the case of men under similar circumstances."[74]

Lochner Era justices, in other words, forbade maximum-hours laws—except when they didn't. They viewed women as frail creatures justifying special protections, except when those protections included a fair wage. And they deferred to the legislature's judgment, but only when they wanted to. More than just the nation's top physicians, these justices appointed themselves America's censors, and they frequently embraced Tiedeman's charge to undo majoritarian action "even though these acts do not violate any specific or special provision of the Constitution."[75]

Indeed, a case handed down just a month before they upheld the Oregon law in *Muller* demonstrates just how far these justices were willing to go in order to turn the Constitution on its head. In *Adair v. United States* (1908), the Court held that employers have a constitutional right to forbid their employees from joining unions—relying again on the so-called liberty of contract. "The right of the employe [*sic*] to quit the service of the employer," according to majority opinion in *Adair*, "is the same as the right of the employer, for whatever reason, to dispense with the services of such employe [*sic*]."[76]

With this one line, the justices placed opponents of labor unions on the same plane as the abolitionists and Lincolnian Republicans who wrote the Confederacy's "peculiar institution" out of the Constitution. Workers have a constitutional right to quit their jobs, because the Thirteenth Amendment provides that neither "slavery nor involuntary servitude" may exist in the United States. So, by equating a company's so-called right to fire a unionized employee with that employee's countervailing right to escape involuntary servitude by leaving the company's service, the Supreme Court essentially declared that laws protecting workers' right to organize are no less repugnant to the Constitution than slavery.

Nor did the Court stop there. The right to contract, according to *Adair*, forbids government from compelling "any person in the course of his business and against his will to accept or retain the personal services of another, or to compel any person, against his will, to perform personal services for another."[77] More than half a century later, President Lyndon Johnson would sign a law compelling employers to cease discriminating against women and minorities, and compelling segregated lunch counters to begin serving African Americans. If the justices who decided *Adair* and *Lochner* had survived to see that day, they would have declared the Civil Rights Act of 1964 unconstitutional.

Chapter 6

MEN FEARED WITCHES AND BURNT WOMEN

CARRIE BUCK WAS an imbecile, and the mother and the daughter of an imbecile to boot.[1] In the words of the superintendent of the state mental institution where Buck was sent to live as a young woman, her family belonged "to the shiftless, ignorant, and worthless class of antisocial whites of the South."[2] And, perhaps worst of all, Buck was promiscuous—a trait that was alone sufficient reason to have her institutionalized. Indeed, the evidence of Buck's promiscuity was hard to deny as it literally grew inside her. At the age of seventeen, Carrie Buck was pregnant, and she needed to be sent away.[3]

This is the picture of the young woman that would reach the justices sitting 150 miles away from her new institutional home near Lynchburg, Virginia. It also bore no resemblance to reality. Indeed, Buck's case would come to symbolize the dangers of judicial inaction no less than *Lochner* stood for judicial overreach. Taken together, the two cases reveal just how drastically judges empowered to decide the scope of constitutional rights can miss their mark. The justices invented a right to work long hours for little pay virtually out of thin air, yet they could not move themselves to stop one of the most intrusive invasions of a woman's liberty in all of American history.

Far from falling behind her peers intellectually, Buck performed quite well in school. Rather than claiming Buck could be intellectually disabled, a teacher wrote a note indicating Buck was a strong student—"very good-deportment and lessons"—her final year in school.[4] Though Buck was forced to drop out during the sixth grade, this had little to do with her so-called "feeblemindedness" and far more to do with her living conditions. Carrie Buck's father died shortly after her birth in 1906, and she was removed from her mother Emma's care and placed in a foster home at the age of three. Her foster family, however, viewed her as little more than an indentured servant. The younger Buck's foster parents, a couple named J.T. and Alice Dobbs, pulled her out of school so she would have more time to focus on the household chores they assigned to her— and so that Buck could be "loaned" out to the neighbors.[5]

And Buck was not promiscuous. She was raped. By her foster mother's nephew.[6]

Carrie Buck spent her entire young life being used for others' purposes. She was used by the Dobbses as an unpaid servant. She was used by Alice Dobbs's nephew for sex. And she would soon be used to legitimize a nationwide effort to create an American master race. Heredity, according to a Virginia law enacted just two months after Buck was institutionalized, "plays an important part in the transmission of insanity, idiocy, imbecility, epilepsy and crime."[7] Therefore, the solution to imbeciles or criminals was to remove them from the gene pool entirely.

Less than a year after arriving at the Virginia State Colony for Epileptics and Feebleminded in 1924, Carrie Buck would be given a show trial intended to prove that she was genetically unsuited for breeding. Her attorney would be one of the state's leading supporters of eugenics—selected for his willingness to collude with the Colony's officials and to work against his client.[8] One of the star witnesses at this trial was a nurse who would diagnose Carrie's eight-month-old daughter as a "not quite normal baby" based upon little more than "a look about" baby Vivian Buck.[9] Another key witness was a mental hospital director who moonlighted as a poet composing rhyming couplets about eugenics ("Oh why do we allow these people / To breed back to the monkey's nest / To increase our country's burdens / When we should only breed the best?"[10]). His testimony would liken

Carrie Buck to a lame mare or a stunted pig—the farmer "breeding his hogs, horses, cows [or] sheep . . . selects a thoroughbred." So why is it that "any sort of seed seems good enough" when human beings breed?[11]

In just five hours of testimony, lawyers, doctors, social workers, and eugenicists erased any trace of a perfectly intelligent young woman born into unfortunate circumstances, and recast her as the second of three generations of feebleminded offspring. Yet, although the result of Carrie Buck's trial was all but predetermined, her fate was sealed by a much higher Court. In its nearly unanimous decision in *Buck v. Bell*, the Supreme Court proclaimed that "three generations of imbeciles are enough."[12]

Five months later, a surgeon cut Carrie open and removed her fallopian tubes.

———

EVEN THE MOST upstanding bloodline, according to an influential early twentieth century study on eugenics, will produce offspring corrupted by drunkenness, feeblemindedness, criminality, and degeneracy if it is mingled with the "bad blood" of a defective family.[13] So it is somewhat fitting that eugenics was itself the offspring of a marriage between sound science and sociological quackery.[14] Eugenics was born in an era when scientists were just beginning to grasp evolution and biological inheritance. Yet it is as much a reaction to this era's social Darwinism as it was to the publication of Charles Darwin's *On the Origin of Species*.

Eugenics arose, at least in part, from an overreading of Gregor Mendel's seminal experiments studying the heritability of genetic traits in pea plants. Though the eugenicists who set their eyes on Carrie Buck relied upon Mendel as justification for their own forays into selective breeding, they showed little understanding of the fact that human ability is shaped by factors far more complex than the genes that determine whether a plant will produce smooth or wrinkled peas.

One study that was widely cited during Buck's trial, for example, examined the offspring of a Revolutionary War soldier given the pseudonym "Martin Kallikak." The Kallikak bloodline diverged during Martin's military service, when he met a woman the study identifies only as "the nameless feeble-minded girl," and impregnated her after drinking in a tavern. Sometime later, Martin married another woman, considered by the study to come from superior genetic stock, and fathered another line of children with his wife.[15]

Martin's legitimate offspring grew up to become upstanding members of society—"doctors, lawyers, judges, educators, traders, landholders"—and almost none of the legitimate line of Kallikaks demonstrated the kind of undesirable traits most loathed by eugenicists. "There have been no feeble-minded among them; no illegitimate children; no immoral women; [and] only one man was sexually loose." Epileptics, criminals and "keepers of houses of prostitution" are all absent from Martin's legitimate descendants.[16]

Meanwhile, Martin's illegitimate son—who the study colorfully labels the "Old Horror"—reportedly begot a line of criminals, deviants, and drunks. The study purports to examine the intelligence of nearly two hundred of the Old Horror's offspring, labeling more than three-quarters of them "feeble-minded." Meanwhile, two dozen were alcoholics. Three dozen were illegitimate. And nearly as many were "sexually immoral persons, mostly prostitutes."[17]

What's remarkable about the Kallikak study is that it attributed the entirety of the one Kallikak line's prosperity and of the other line's failures to the genetic distinctions between Martin's wife and his one-time lover. Indeed, the study's author barely even considered the possibility that there might be some explanation other than genetics that could explain why a child who grows up in a stable two-parent home outperforms the illegitimate offspring of a woman abandoned by her child's father—or why the poverty of circumstance facing the less fortunate child could be passed down from generation to generation. To the contrary, the Kallikak study deems Martin's tainted bloodline to be largely irredeemable—"no amount of education or good environment can change a feeble-minded individual into a normal one, any more than it can change a red-haired stock into a black-haired stock."[18]

Lying beneath this belief that our worth is determined by our genes, however, was an even more sinister social theory that gazed upon poverty and starvation and saw purifying flames.

Though the term "survival of the fittest" is often associated with Charles Darwin, it was actually coined by the philosopher Herbert Spencer[19]—the same Herbert Spencer the Wisconsin Supreme Court quoted in its 1902 decision striking down that state's law protecting union rights.[20]

"Inconvenience, suffering, and death," according to Spencer's most famous work, "are the penalties attached by nature to ignorance, as well as to incompetence." They are also "the means of remedying" these traits. "By weeding out those of lowest development," Spencer explained, "nature secures the growth of a race who shall both understand the conditions of existence, and be able to act up to them. . . . Nature demands that every being shall be self-sufficing. All that are not so, nature is perpetually withdrawing by death."[21]

Far from proving nature's cruelty, Spencer believed that this deadly game "purif[ied] society from those who are, in some respect or other, essentially faulty." If a man or woman is "sufficiently complete to live," then they should live. But if "they are not sufficiently complete to live, they die, and it is best they should die."[22]

Charity, in Spencer's mind, should be viewed with suspicion—though he would allow it in limited circumstances—because it impedes nature's ability to purge the unfit from the ranks of humanity. "There is unquestionably harm done when sympathy is shown without any regard to ultimate results," according to Spencer's widely read book, *Social Statics*. "Instead of diminishing suffering," such charity increases it by enabling "the multiplication of those worst fitted for existence." Rather than lift up the weak and the desolate, kindness "tends to fill the world with those to whom life will bring most pain, and tends to keep out of it those whom life will bring most pleasure." Needless to say, Spencer saw no place for what he labeled "acts of parliament to save silly people."[23]

Though he was an Englishman, Spencer's works were wildly popular among American elites. In the four decades following the Civil War, Spencer sold nearly 370,000 copies of his books to American readers—a figure that is virtually unheard of for an author producing difficult works of philosophy and sociology.[24] When Spencer toured the United States in 1882, he received all the fawning treatment often associated with traveling celebrities. Hotel managers and railways competed for the opportunity to serve him, while reporters clamored for interviews. At a banquet honoring Spencer at New York's Delmonico's restaurant, Carl Schurz, a former US senator and member of President Rutherford B. Hayes's cabinet, even suggested that the Civil War could have been avoided if the South had been more familiar with Spencer's *Social Statics*.[25] (This last claim is less ridiculous than it sounds. Spencer, for all his faults, opposed slavery.)[26]

After nearly two months in the United States, Spencer offered a grand assessment of America that seemed straight out of a eugenic tract. "From biological truths it is to be inferred," Spencer explained, "that the eventual mixture of the allied varieties of the Aryan race forming the population will produce a finer type of man than has hitherto existed." For this reason, he concluded that "whatever tribulations they may have to pass through, the Americans may reasonably look forward to a time when they will have produced a civilization grander than any the world has known."[27]

Yet, despite his considerable influence on the men who sterilized Carrie Buck, Spencer's prescription for extermination by neglect was quite distinct from the remedy offered by eugenicists.

In 1883, Sir Francis Galton—a cousin of Charles Darwin's—coined the word "eugenics" by combining the Greek words meaning "well" and "born." Like Spencer, Galton saw a path towards a stronger, better-suited human race. Indeed, during a lecture Galton delivered in Spencer's honor a few years after the latter man's death, Galton acknowledged a "personal debt" to Spencer, who had often offered a sounding board for Galton's ideas during games of billiards at London's Athenaeum Club.[28]

Nevertheless, Galton's vision differed from Spencer's in at least one important way. While Spencer wrote that we should simply ignore the least fortunate and allow nature to kill them off, Galton preferred a more active approach. "What Nature does blindly, slowly and ruthlessly," according to Galton, "man may do providently, quickly and kindly."[29]

In one sense, Galton offered a more moderate alternative to Spencer's genocidal libertarianism, as he did not argue that the least fortunate should simply be allowed to die. "I do not," Galton explained, "propose to neglect the sick, the feeble or the unfortunate." To the contrary, he promised to do everything he could "for their comfort and happiness." This charity, however, came at a steep price: "I would exact an equivalent for the charitable assistance they receive, namely, that by means of isolation, or some other drastic yet adequate measure, a stop should be put to the production of families of children likely to include degenerates."[30]

This was the vision behind the Virginia law enabling Carrie Buck's sterilization. According to that law,

> the Commonwealth has in custodial care and is supporting in various State institutions many defective persons who if now discharged or paroled would likely become by the propagation of their kind a menace to society but who if incapable of procreating might properly and safely be discharged or paroled and become self-supporting with benefit both to themselves and to society.[31]

By sterilizing Carrie Buck today, Virginia believed it could spare itself from caring for generations of "defective persons" tomorrow.

———

JUSTICE OLIVER WENDELL Holmes was not like his fellow justices. A staunch believer in democracy, Holmes doubted nothing more than his own ability to second-guess the will of the people. Holmes once wrote Harvard law professor (and future Supreme Court justice) Felix Frankfurter that "a law should be called good if it reflects the will of the dominant forces of the community even if it would take us to hell"—though he added his suspicion that the "community would change its will" if the law performs poorly.[32] Indeed, Holmes measured his worth as a judge according to his willingness to uphold legislation he despised. "It has given me great pleasure," he once explained, "to sustain the Constitutionality of laws that I believe to be as bad as possible because I thereby helped to mark the difference between what I would forbid and what the Constitution permits."[33]

Holmes's greatest opinion was only a little more than two paragraphs long. Rather than engage in the sparring match between Justices Rufus Wheeler Peckham and John Marshall Harlan over whether bakeries were sufficiently unhealthy workplaces to justify regulation, Holmes's dissenting opinion in *Lochner* disclaims altogether the idea that judges should be setting America's labor laws:

> A constitution is not intended to embody a particular economic theory, whether of paternalism and the organic relation of the citizen to the State or of *laissez faire*. It is made for people of fundamentally differing views, and the accident of our finding certain opinions natural and familiar or novel and even shocking ought not to conclude our judgment upon the question whether statutes embodying them conflict with the Constitution of the United States.

Holmes also accused the majority of writing social Darwinism into the Constitution: "the Fourteenth Amendment does not enact Mr. Herbert Spencer's Social Statics."[34]

Holmes's personal views resembled Spencer's more than his dissent in *Lochner* suggests. He "loathe[d] the thick-fingered clowns we call the people," and his radical majoritarianism grew, not from a moral understanding that these "thick-fingered clowns" have a right to govern themselves, but from his belief that the ballot box and the legislature were the appropriate battlefields to resolve a Darwinian struggle between political factions. "In the last resort a man rightly prefers his own interest to that of his neighbors," Holmes wrote in 1872. "The more powerful interests must be more or less reflected in legislation; which, like every other device of man or beast, must tend in the long run to aid the survival of the fittest."[35]

But, above all, Holmes possessed the rarest of traits in a man whose job it is to judge his fellow citizens—a profound lack of faith in his own wisdom. "I am so skeptical as to our knowledge about the goodness or badness of laws," he once wrote a friend, "that I have no practical criticism except what the crowd wants."[36] "Truth," according to Holmes, "was the majority vote of the nation that could lick all others."[37]

Holmes learned this skepticism after three violent brushes with death.

The son of a famous physician and author, the young Holmes grew up surrounded by such luminaries as Henry Wadsworth Longfellow, Ralph Waldo Emerson, and Nathaniel Hawthorne. Herman Melville was his neighbor at his father's summer home.[38] When Abraham Lincoln won the White House in 1860, Holmes was finishing his studies at Harvard. Yet he dropped out of school just two months before graduation to join what he expected to be a very brief war against the Confederacy. The newly commissioned Lieutenant Holmes joined several of his classmates for a champagne dinner at Delmonico's on his way to the front. Servants accompanied him on his trip.[39]

So Holmes arrived at the battlefield with the kind of naïve certainty that can only come with great intellect, extreme privilege, and no exposure whatsoever to the sacrifices required to defeat a rival possessed by similar certainty. He began the war as a staunch abolitionist. Six months later, a Confederate soldier shot him in the chest.

By the end of the war, Holmes would endure another wound to his neck and a third to his heel. At the height of the war's slaughter, he wrote to his family about the "indifference one gets to look on the dead bodies in gray clothes . . . the swollen bodies already fly blown and decaying." When he was wounded the third time, he secretly wished that it was serious enough to require amputation, because then he would be spared having to return to war.[40]

After the war ended, Holmes blamed the certainty he once held regarding the righteousness of abolitionism for the horrors he endured. "When you know what you know," he would write close to the end of his life, "persecution comes easy. It is as well that some of us don't know that we know anything."[41]

Holmes's unwillingness to substitute his own judgment for the law made him a hero among progressives who loathed cases like *Lochner* and *Dagenhart*. Yet, just as Justice Samuel Freeman Miller's *Slaughterhouse* decision beat back one effort to undermine Reconstruction only to deny freedmen the constitutional rights they would need to resist white supremacy, Justice Holmes's single-minded defense of majority rule also came at a terrible price.

In an era when the Supreme Court was notoriously indifferent to African Americans, Holmes urged his colleagues to show even greater deference to white Southern lawmakers. Several Southern states replaced slavery with a "peonage" system in which workers were indebted to their employers and then forced to work for them until the debt was paid. In many cases, employers could show up at their county jail, pay off the bonds of any prisoners they wished to indenture, and then treat their new worker as if they were his master.[42]

In Alabama, workers who were paid in advance for their work, and who then did not repay that money with cash or with their labor, were presumed to have committed crimes. Moreover, the rules of evidence in that state forbade any persons indicted under this law from testifying in their defense. The result, in the words of the black educator Booker T. Washington, was that "any white man, who cares to charge that a Colored man has promised to work for him and has not done so, or who has gotten money from him and not paid it back, can have the Colored man sent to the chain gang."[43]

Though the Supreme Court struck down this peonage system as a violation of the Thirteenth Amendment's ban on "involuntary servitude,"[44] Holmes treated Alabama's indentured peons in much the same way that Justice Peckham treated New York's bakers. "Breach of a legal contract without excuse is wrong conduct, even if the contract is for labor," Holmes wrote in a dissenting opinion. "If a State adds to civil liability a criminal liability to fine, it simply intensifies the legal motive for doing right, it does not make the laborer a slave."[45]

So Carrie Buck never had a chance before Justice Oliver Wendell Holmes. More than just an opportunity to tout his majoritarian *bona fides*, and more than just an appeal to his Darwinistic outlook, *Buck v. Bell* tapped into Holmes's self-image as a man who came face to face with death in the service of his country. "We have seen more than once that the public welfare may call upon the best citizens for their lives," Holmes wrote in his opinion permitting forced sterilizations. "It would be strange if it could not call upon those who already sap the strength of the State for these lesser sacrifices, often not felt to be such by those concerned, in order to prevent our being swamped with incompetence."

Holmes's opinion was the triumph of Sir Francis Galton's vision. "It is better for all the world," the justice wrote in words that could have been authored by the British eugenicist, "if, instead of waiting to execute degenerate offspring for crime or to let them starve for their imbecility, society can prevent those who are manifestly unfit from continuing their kind."

———

JUSTICE HOLMES'S OPINION in *Buck* is an indictment of his donothing approach to judging. Yet it is also an indictment of conservatives who viewed the government with such skepticism when it sought to improve the lives of workers, but who suddenly couldn't be bothered to save a woman from state-sanctioned mutilation. Holmes may have authored the Court's opinion, but his opinion was joined by conservative Chief Justice William Howard Taft and his even more conservative brethren Willis Van Devanter, James McReynolds, and George Sutherland.

Of the Court's nine members, only Justice Pierce Butler dissented, albeit without an opinion to explain his reason for doing so. Butler was unquestionably a conservative—he would later ally with Van Devanter, McReynolds, and Sutherland to form the Court's "Four Horsemen," a bloc of conservative justices determined to thwart President Franklin Roosevelt's New Deal. Nevertheless, Butler's opposition to eugenics likely stemmed more from his devout Catholic faith than from a philosophical objection to government action.[46] Certainly, this was the spin Holmes placed on his colleague's lone dissenting vote. "He knows the law is the way I have written it," Holmes remarked on Butler's dissent, "But he is afraid of the Church. I'll lay you a bet that the Church beats the law."[47]

Next to Holmes and the racist McReynolds, Taft's vote in *Buck* was probably the least surprising of the nine justices. In the space between his tenure as president and as chief justice, Taft served as a board member and later as chairman of the Life Extension Institute, an organization that eventually became a leading provider of eugenic counseling to families considering marriage or children.[48] During his tenure as board chair, Taft authored a forward to the institute's ambitiously titled self-help treatise *How to Live*. Though the bulk of this text offered mundane advice such as "the air we breathe should be sunlit when possible," or "most people in America eat too rapidly," *How to Live* also recommends "sterilization of certain gross and hopeless defectives, to preclude the propagation of their type."[49]

The intellectual leader of the Court's right flank also cast his vote against Carrie Buck. A former American Bar Association president and United States senator from Utah, Sutherland emerged as a powerful force for conservatism almost as soon as he joined the Court in 1922.[50] On the day Sutherland received his judicial commission from President Warren G. Harding, many Court observers believed that *Lochner* was on life support, as the Court had recently handed down a series of decisions upholding workmen's compensation laws, maximum-hour laws for railroad workers, and overtime pay for factory workers.[51] After just seven months on the bench, however, Sutherland successfully rallied four of his fellow justices behind his opinion in *Adkins v. Children's Hospital* (1923), which breathed new life into *Lochner*'s so-called freedom to contract. Laws abridging this supposed freedom, according to Sutherland's opinion in *Adkins*, "can be justified only by the existence of exceptional circumstances."[52]

Eleven years later, Sutherland took on a distinctly Spencerian tone in a dissenting opinion scolding the millions of Americans cast into destitution during the Great Depression.[53] To Sutherland, these millions were less victims of global economic forces than they were of their own inability to adapt. The "vital lesson" they failed to learn, according to Sutherland, was that "expenditure beyond income begets poverty." And just as Spencer had once urged lawmakers not to enact "acts of parliament to save silly people," Sutherland insisted that "indiscretion or imprudence was not to be relieved by legislation."[54]

Yet, even as Sutherland railed against government overreach when lawmakers tried to improve the lot of workers or poor people, he saw no overreach whatsoever in Virginia's decision to sterilize Carrie Buck.

In the end, Sutherland's decisions, and the decisions of the other justices willing to declare forced sterilization sacred and the minimum wage profane, reveals the tragic flaw at the core of the Fourteenth Amendment. By describing the scope of American's individual rights in such imprecise terms—What are the "privileges or immunities of citizens"? What is the "liberty" that cannot be denied "without due process of law"?—the drafters of this amendment delegated the power to define these rights to the nine justices on the Supreme Court. And those nine men were so inapt to the task that they placed the right to be exploited by a rapacious employer on a higher plane than a woman's right to do what she wants with her own body.

The same justices who embraced *Lochner*'s fabricated freedom to contract also placed this imaginary right on a higher plane than many rights that were explicitly laid out in the Constitution itself. The *Lochner* Era was not simply an age when the justices seized the power to censor economic regulation, for example; it was also one of the high points of an entirely different form of censorship. Though the Constitution's First Amendment explicitly protects every American's right to speak freely, the justices who were so active in striking down progressive labor laws could not actually be bothered to enforce the right to speak out against the government.

———

"DISLOYALTY," PRESIDENT WOODROW Wilson warned in his address seeking a declaration of war against Germany in 1917, "will be dealt with with a firm hand of stern repression." Indeed, he envisioned a nation in which immigrants would strike out at their own neighbors if storm clouds of dissent formed in their communities. German Americans, the president predicted, "will be prompt to stand with us in rebuking and restraining the few who may be of a different mind and purpose."[55]

Yet Wilson had good reason to fear dissent from his decision to bring America into a distant conflict that had already massacred much of Europe's male population. Indeed, during his successful bid for reelection in 1916, Wilson explicitly appealed to antiwar sentiment, campaigning on the slogan "he kept us out of war." Though the president changed his mind after a German submarine blockade seeking to cut off trade to England and France sank three American vessels, Wilson's decision to go to war spurred angry objections. One senator proclaimed that "we are committing a sin against humanity and against our countrymen." After Wilson asked for civilians to be drafted into his war, House Speaker Champ Clark, a Democrat like Wilson, protested that "there is precious little difference between a conscript and a convict."[56]

Nevertheless, Congress voted by a wide margin to give Wilson his declaration of war, and then they gave him far more. By the time the Allied Powers met at Versailles to sketch out the terms of Germany's surrender, Congress had made it a crime to "willfully utter, print, write, or publish any disloyal, profane, scurrilous, or abusive language" about America's Constitution, its military, its flag, or its form of government. Or to argue against the draft. Or to publicly claim that Germany was on the right side of the First World War. Indeed, the mere act of displaying a German flag could be punished by up to twenty years in prison.[57] "May God have mercy" on dissenters, Attorney General Thomas Gregory proclaimed, "for they need expect none from an outraged people and an avenging government."[58]

At Gregory's urging, armies of volunteers arose not just to fight the enemy abroad, but to spy on potential dissidents at home. The American Protective League employed literally hundreds of thousands of members to report rumors of disloyal neighbors directly to the Justice Department. Other, smaller groups bore names such as the "Knights of Liberty," the "Sedition Slammers," and the "Boy Spies of America." Gregory bragged that these domestic spies enabled the government to "to keep scores of thousands of persons under observation."[59]

And the nation's judges were no more merciful than Gregory and his prosecutors. The editor of a Jewish socialist newspaper received ten years in prison for uttering the twelve words "I am for the people and the government is for the profiteers." Thirty German Americans were convicted for asking South Dakota's governor to reform Selective Service procedures and threatening to vote for his opponent if he refused to do so. A filmmaker, who produced a movie about the Revolutionary War that depicted British soldiers committing atrocities, received a ten-year sentence. "History is history, and fact is fact," the trial judge wrote about the film, but "this is no time" for films that may sow seeds of "animosity or want of confidence between us and our allies."[60]

In just one week, in 1919, Justice Holmes handed down three unanimous decisions blessing these kinds of prosecutions.

In the first, the Court upheld the conviction of a Socialist Party leader named Charles Schenck who mailed thousands of leaflets to men conscripted into military service urging them to oppose the draft.[61] Though the flyer blamed "Wall Street's chosen few" for the government's decision to institute the draft, the bulk of its text offered several reasons why Socialists believed conscription to be unconstitutional. It opened by quoting the Thirteenth Amendment's ban on slavery and forced labor, then argued that a conscript is "forced into

involuntary servitude" no less than a slave. "If you believe in the com-
mandment 'thou shalt not kill,'" it added, "then that is your religion,
and you shall not be prohibited from the free exercise thereof." The
first page closed with a call to "join the Socialist Party in its campaign
for the repeal of the Conscription Act," and offered a few ways that
conscripts could reach out to their members of Congress to express
their opposition to the draft.[62]

Such language, Holmes insisted, would be entirely permissible
"in many places and in ordinary times." Yet these were not such
times. "When a nation is at war, many things that might be said in
time of peace are such a hindrance to its effort that their utterance
will not be endured so long as men fight, and that no Court could
regard them as protected by any constitutional right." A leaflet urging draftees to turn against the very law that would ship them to the
front lines was a bridge too far in time of war.[63]

Seven days later, Holmes authored a pair of similar decisions
treating antiwar speech as a criminal act. The first targeted an obscure
editor at a German language newspaper convicted for publishing
twelve articles opposing the war and the draft.[64] The second, however, re-imprisoned a man who had risen to become the most prominent leftist in the country—the former union leader, Eugene Debs.

———

WHILE HE WAS jailed due to his involvement with the Pullman
Strike, Debs discovered the works of Karl Marx and emerged from
prison as a devoted socialist.[65] He would eventually run for president on the Socialist Party's ticket on five separate occasions—on
two occasions winning almost a million votes. By the time Congress
voted to declare war on Germany in April of 1917, Debs was among
the best-known men in the country, beloved by thousands of workers and loathed by the capitalists and industrial barons who stood
to lose the most in Debs's utopian vision for society. Ultimately,
however, Debs returned to prison not because of his radical plans to

overthrow capitalism but because of his far more banal opposition to the war.

Admittedly, Debs's socialism and his pacifism were tightly intertwined. As Wilson prepared to lead the nation to war, Debs was well into his sixties and was too sick to travel to an emergency convention called by Socialist Party leaders in St. Louis. Yet he wrote the party's executive secretary to urge his fellow partisans into a strong stance against this and all other wars. "To be consistent with its revolutionary character and true to its international principles," according to Debs, the party "is morally bound to stand squarely against every war save and alone the war against war, the war of the world's enslaved and exploited workers against the world's enslaving and exploiting masters."[66] After progressive Senator Robert La Follette cast an unpopular vote opposing the build-up to the war, Debs sent a pithy telegram to the senator denouncing the "Wall Street Wolves and Their Prostitute Press" that he saw as the instigators of American involvement in this war.[67]

Despite his strong feelings, Debs was largely absent from the public fight against the war for a full year after American troops began shipping overseas to Europe. While his friends and fellow socialists protested and went to jail for having the audacity to protest, Debs spent much of his time regaining his strength at a sanatorium in Colorado.[68] So, it was not until June of 1918, during a Socialist Party convention in Canton, Ohio, that Debs delivered the speech that would earn him a ten-year prison term.

Debs began his speech with a blunt acknowledgment of the danger he faced merely by expressing his views aloud. "I realize that, in speaking with you this afternoon," he told the crowd of approximately twelve hundred people, "there are certain limitations placed upon the right of free speech. I must be exceedingly careful, prudent, as to what I say, and even more careful and prudent as to how I say it." Nevertheless, he also acknowledged that he had freely chosen to go to jail before he would silently comply with the Wilson administration's censors—"I would rather a thousand times be a free soul in jail than to be a sycophant and coward in the streets," the defiant Debs proclaimed.[69]

Indeed, much of Debs's speech, which earned him the ire of Wilson's censors, was devoted to denouncing those very efforts at censorship. Debs delivered his speech shortly after visiting three Socialists who were, in his words, "paying the penalty for their devotion to the cause of the working class." These men, Debs warned, "have come to realize, as many of us have, that it is extremely dangerous to exercise the constitutional right of free speech in a country fighting to make democracy safe in the world." In a similar vein, Debs told his audience to "think of sentencing a woman to the penitentiary simply for talking"—a reference to the Socialist orator Kate Richards O'Hare, who received five years in prison for an antiwar speech in North Dakota. "The United States, under plutocratic rule, is the only country that would send a woman to prison for five years for exercising the right of free speech."[70]

The irony of sending Debs to prison for a speech denouncing censorship did not appear to be lost on the Justice Department. When United States Attorney Edwin Wertz wrote the Justice Department's war office to advise them of Debs's speech, the head of that office wrote back that "the Department does not feel strongly convinced that a prosecution is advisable."[71] Yet, even if the Wilson administration was divided on whether to pursue Debs—Wertz prosecuted the union-leader-turned-socialist despite the war office's ambivalence—the Supreme Court had no qualms about Wertz's decision. Once again, Justice Holmes's decision upholding the conviction was unanimous.[72]

———

THERE WAS A somewhat hopeful epilogue to Holmes's three opinions upholding censorship. In the summer following *Debs*, a small group of the nation's leading judges and legal scholars successfully lobbied Holmes to change his mind.[73] The next fall, Holmes rejected the Wilson administration's attempt to criminalize the "surreptitious publishing of a silly leaflet by an unknown man," albeit in a dissenting opinion.[74]

"Persecution for the expression of opinions seems to me perfectly logical," Holmes wrote in an opinion that now stands with his *Lochner* dissent as among his greatest contributions to American law. "If you have no doubt of your premises or your power and want a certain result with all your heart you naturally express your wishes in law and sweep away all opposition." Nevertheless, Holmes explained,

> when men have realized that time has upset many fighting faiths, they may come to believe even more than they believe the very foundations of their own conduct that the ultimate good desired is better reached by free trade in ideas—that the best test of truth is the power of the thought to get itself accepted in the competition of the market, and that truth is the only ground upon which their wishes safely can be carried out. That at any rate is the theory of our Constitution. It is an experiment, as all life is an experiment. Every year if not every day we have to wager our salvation upon some prophecy based upon imperfect knowledge. While that experiment is part of our system I think that we should be eternally vigilant against attempts to check the expression of opinions that we loathe and believe to be fraught with death, unless they so imminently threaten immediate interference with the lawful and pressing purposes of the law that an immediate check is required to save the country.[75]

Just as he viewed democracy as the best vehicle to mediate a Darwinian struggle among competing factions, Holmes now understood that a similar competition occurs in the marketplace of ideas. Justice Holmes would not allow the law to upset this struggle any more than he believed his fellow justices were entitled to set the nation's economic policy.

Holmes's conversion, however, was cold comfort to the men and women imprisoned for disagreeing with the government. Only Justice Louis Brandeis, a man who would later compare government censorship to literal witchhunts—"men feared witches and burnt women"[76]—joined Holmes in supporting free-speech rights. The other seven justices stood firmly for the right of the government to jail dissidents.

This was the law that the Supreme Court had made by the onset of the Great Depression. Dissent was dangerous. Sweatshops enjoyed the blessing of the courts. Children labored from dusk until dawn in the deadliest factories. And women could be mutilated according to the whims of the government.

PART II

GETTING OUT
OF THE WAY

Chapter 7

THE BOTTOM FALLS OUT

IN 1929, A generation after the Supreme Court embraced Justice
Stephen Johnson Field's vision of a government powerless against
America's most fortunate, the bottom fell out of the American economy. In three short years, half a million families lost their homes.
The Ford Motor Company laid off more than two-thirds of its Detroit workforce, as car sales fell by just as much nationwide. Farm
income fell from $6 billion in 1929 to $2 billion in 1932, and iron
and steel production fell 60 percent. Some communities became
wastelands where full-time labor all but ceased to exist. In Birmingham, Alabama, only 8,000 members of the town's 108,000-person
workforce enjoyed full-time employment. Chicago stopped paying
its teachers for an entire winter because it simply ran out of money.[1]

Many workers gave up on the United States of America entirely.
One hundred thousand of them sought work in Soviet Russia.[2]

Lorena Hickok, a journalist (and, according to some historians,
a romantic partner of Eleanor Roosevelt's) was hired by a federal
agency to chronicle the human costs of the Great Depression. She
described brutal hardships and humiliations visited upon American
families. A young man in Baltimore walked twenty miles into the
city's center and back, stopping at every door along the way "and asking if they didn't need somebody to work—at anything." A woman
on a South Dakota farm boiled thistles into soup in order to ward
off hunger—"it don't taste so bad, only it ain't very filling." Children

in Houston refused to go to school lest they be teased for wearing the black-and-white striped pants passed out to families on relief. A trained architect told Hickok how grateful he was to find work as a day laborer on a road crew because "at least my children can tell the teacher their father is working," though he added that "they don't have to say what he is doing."[3]

One man, an unemployed fur worker in Pittsburgh, described the downward spiral facing so many families. "You just can't know what it's like," he explained to Hickok, "to have to move your family out of the nice house you had in the suburbs . . . down into an apartment, down into another apartment, smaller and in a worse neighborhood, down, down, down, until finally you end up in the slums."[4]

Indeed, no corner of life was too personal, no crevice of the home too private, to remain untouched by the Depression. One California woman lamented what she described as "this *thing* of having babies":

> You've got no protection at all. You don't have any money, you see, to buy anything at the drugstore . . . and there you are, surrounded by young ones you can't support. And always afraid . . . I suppose you can say the easiest way would be not to do it. But it wouldn't be. You don't know what it's like when your husband is out of work. He's gloomy all the time and unhappy. You haven't any money for movies, or anything to take his mind off his troubles. You must try all the time to keep him from going crazy. And many times—well, that is the only way.[5]

The nation's marriage rate fell 22 percent. Americans could no longer afford to have families.[6]

The Depression ruined once-prosperous workers, but it utterly devastated communities that were already struggling when the nation fell off the cliff. Well before the Depression, diesel engines were already replacing coal-fueled boilers in ships and locomotives, while gas, oil, and electric heaters replaced the once-ubiquitous coal furnaces that heated American homes closer to the turn of the century.

When the Depression hit, miners were forced to beg for jobs that paid only a seventh of what they once earned. Many of them subsisted on nothing more than "bulldog gravy," a concoction of water, flour, and lard.[7] In the coal country of West Virginia, Hickok saw families that were so hungry that their bodies were starting to break down: "some of them have been starving for eight years. I was told there are children in West Virginia who never tasted milk!"[8]

And this devastation was hardly limited to coal towns and other regions that were as much victims of a natural ebb in demand for their products as they were of the Depression itself. Throughout the nation, in booming cities and in decaying company towns, thousands of seniors lived in a permanent state of poverty long before the Depression caused their children to join them. The day a man retired, he often sentenced himself to destitution.

———

THE UNITED STATES, a former Union general named Isaac Sherwood told his fellow Members of Congress in 1917, was "the only great nation, either in Europe or America, except Russia, that has no old-age pension for its worn-out worthy workers."[9] As a result, Americans typically moved in with their own adult children and depended on them for support when they were no longer able to work—thus limiting those children's ability to save for retirement because they were now caring for an additional dependent.[10]

Not all children were able or willing to care for their parents, however. Elderly mothers often fared far better than their husbands during their twilight years. Though the sexism that pervaded the early twentieth century provided men with better jobs and far more economic opportunity during their working years, an elderly mother who spent her adulthood raising children and performing household chores was often viewed as a useful hand to have around the house. An aged father, however, with his body worn out from a lifetime working in a mill, a mine, or a railroad, was more likely to be viewed as a charity case. Grandmothers could offset the cost of their care by helping raise their grandchildren, but grandfathers were often simply discarded by their families when they were no longer able to work.[11]

And for many of these men, getting turned away by their own children was the final insult after decades of slowly watching their bodies fall apart. As a 1930 report by a New York commission explained, "a very marked lessening of earning power begins around age 50," in large part because workers' worn-out muscles could no longer handle the kind of heavy labor that once supplied their livelihood. In some industries, men started to fall apart even younger. "In the building trades," a 1918 Pennsylvania commission determined, "one-half of the workers have suffered partial or total impairment of earning power at age 54. Among glass blowers, this is true at age 51; among steel workers age 46, and among railway workers at age 39." The heavy industrial work that offered many fathers their only way to make a living simply "burns men up."[12]

Some of the elderly shut out by their own children wound up homeless,[13] but a common fate was life in the poorhouse. Though the poorhouse faded from American memories many decades ago, every state but New Mexico had such homes at the dawn of the Franklin D. Roosevelt administration providing housing of last resort to individuals on the furthest margins of society. Most of the inmates in these houses (and poorhouse residents were typically labeled as "inmates") were elderly. A 1910 report in Massachusetts, for example, found that 92 percent of poorhouse inmates took up residence after age 60.[14]

Though conditions varied, poorhouses were often wretched, dirty environments with little capacity for long-term care and few, if any, staff trained to provide for the infirm. A New York commission unanimously concluded that "with a few notable exceptions, our present public almshouse care of the aged . . . is inadequate and altogether unsuited to meet the varying needs of the poor." Often, no effort was made to segregate the sick, the frail, or even those with communicable diseases into facilities suitable for their care. "Worthy people are thrown together with moral derelicts, with dope addicts, with prostitutes, bums [and] drunks" the New York commission explained. "Sick people are thrown together with the well, the blind, the deaf, the crippled [and] the epileptic." And even healthy residents had little to occupy their time.[15]

Able-bodied residents had few opportunities to work if they wished to do so, and many poorhouses residents had no access to a radio or similar source of entertainment. The only reading materials available were the books, pamphlets, or magazines donated to the poorhouse by generous individuals or organizations, and the food was typically bland and repetitive. Sick inmates received barely any care for their conditions, and healthy residents could do little more than wait to die.[16]

In some facilities, conditions crossed the line from neglectful to horrific. An Ohio commission described crumbling poorhouse infirmaries where "the inside of the buildings was unclean and slovenly; the walls had not been painted in a generation and no attempt had been made to repair cracks or other defacements." Worse,

many old persons suffer from foul smelling disorders and when a number of them congregate in small groups, the resulting bad odor is very noticeable to a person unaccustomed to it. Lack of attention regarding personal cleanliness, poor ventilation and over-heating tend to accentuate the odor. In many of the buildings inspected, sections occupied by the inmates were so foul smelling that they were almost unbearable. The inmates frequently were unclean, the beds dirty, the bed covers old and worn and ventilation poor. Those who were unable to care for their physical needs and demanded constant attention, had to depend on other inmates for the most urgent wants. Often these improvised attendants were feeble-minded or at least ignorant and inattentive. In the entire group there was virtually no medical supervision.[17]

Faced with such a future, some workers celebrated their retirement with suicide rather than spend the rest of their lives in a poorhouse.

A sixty-year-old man in Cleveland threw himself from a bridge onto the street 125 feet below because he feared his own old age.[18]

————

ON THE DAY Franklin Roosevelt took office, however, the new president's first concern wasn't the state of poorhouses or even the millions of workers cast out of their jobs by the Depression. A more immediate concern threatened to strip even the most frugal and fortunate Americans of their life savings. Three years of Depression set off more than five thousand bank failures, with each collapse leading more and more depositors to withdraw their funds from banks that needed that money in order to stave off their own failure. By Inauguration Day, thirty-two state governors ordered their states' banks closed down to prevent this death spiral from continuing. In many other states, depositors could access only a tiny percentage of their funds—often just 5 percent. Texas forbade withdrawals exceeding ten dollars a day.[19] Meanwhile, businesses across the country had to find a way to pay their remaining workers when their customers couldn't even touch the assets they needed to pay for goods and services.

The president's solution to this crisis was a flurry of activity that would simply be unimaginable in a more recent era of filibusters and hyperpolarized political parties. Roosevelt took office on March 4 (the Twentieth Amendment, which moved that date to January 20 for future inaugurals, had not yet taken effect). The next day, he ordered all banks closed for four days and called Congress into special session at the end of this banking holiday—both of which were actions Hoover unsuccessfully pressed Roosevelt to endorse when Roosevelt was the president-elect. That gave a Treasury Department still largely populated by holdovers from the Hoover administration less than a week to come up with a bill to calm the nation's jitters. Working round the clock, the Hoover holdovers devised a plan to supervise the banks, provide additional funds to cash-starved banks on the verge of collapse, empower the Federal Reserve to expand the money supply, and ratify the actions Roosevelt took on his first full day in office. Before the clock struck 9 p.m. on the day Congress convened, President Roosevelt signed the Emergency Banking Relief Act into law. He'd been president for less than five days.[20]

Roosevelt's first major act as president was a huge success—the banking bill quelled the nation's fears and depositors soon began moving their money back to the banks.[21] The remainder of the reforms Roosevelt pushed during his famous first one hundred days in office, however, ranged from inspired to untested to downright ham-handed.

The president's decision to take America off the gold standard saved the nation from a longer and even more brutal downturn—according to future Federal Reserve Chair Ben Bernanke, "no country exhibited significant economic recovery" during the Great Depression "while remaining on the gold standard."[22] At the same time, however, Roosevelt's first attempt to provide workers with the fair wages and collective bargaining rights denied by cases like *Lochner* was a morass of industry-specific codes that practically wrote Congress out of the lawmaking process entirely. It was also declared unconstitutional in a unanimous decision joined by both the liberal and conservative wings of the Supreme Court.[23]

Indeed, there was a great deal of incoherence to Roosevelt's earliest efforts to calm the Depression. He signed bills appropriating billions in infrastructure spending and putting millions of unemployed to work for the government, yet he also slashed veterans' benefits.[24] The new president seemed unsure whether he should stimulate the economy with new spending or push for a balanced budget.

Franklin Roosevelt did not come to Washington with a comprehensive plan. What he did promise the voters who placed him in office, however, was an entirely new approach to policymaking. "The country demands bold, persistent experimentation," he told the graduating class of Oglethorpe University one month before he accepted the Democratic Party's presidential nomination. "It is common sense to take a method and try it: If it fails, admit it frankly and try another. But above all, try something. The millions who are in want will not stand by silently forever while the things to satisfy their needs are within easy reach."[25]

Roosevelt's plan to turn the government into a laboratory was wildly at odds with his predecessor Herbert Hoover's vision, who warned in one of his final campaign speeches that his opponent would "destroy the very foundations of our American system" by extending "government into our economic and social life."[26] But, more important, Roosevelt's ideas were a direct assault on the vision that dominated the Supreme Court.

When the justices created a constitutional right to fire unionized workers, or when they declared the minimum wage to be off limits, or when they held the United States of America powerless to purge the nation of child labor, they did far more than simply set the nation's labor policy. They declared that many of the most important and controversial questions left to lawmakers were instead answered by the Constitution itself, and that the kind of experimentation Roosevelt proposed was strictly off limits. The battle that emerged between Roosevelt and the Supreme Court was about far more than whether the New Deal would stand or fall. It was about whether the solutions to America's most vexing problems were preordained— and whether the American people had the right to prefer Roosevelt's bold experimentation to Hoover's stoic confidence in the old ways.

———

EARLY IN HIS presidency, Roosevelt was, at best, an ambivalent supporter of the right to unionize. The president preferred laws providing direct help to workers—whether through pensions, unemployment benefits, or a minimum wage—to laws improving their ability to bargain collectively for better wages and benefits. He supported Senator Robert Wagner's National Labor Relations Act of 1935, which built the backbone of modern union law, but he did so somewhat reluctantly.[27]

Nevertheless, on the day President Roosevelt signed this act into law, he might as well have taken the presidential limousine to the Supreme Court and personally slapped each of the Four Horsemen across the face. The act began with a direct rebuttal to these justices' notion that workers will thrive if we just free them from government and allow them to sign any labor contract that's placed in front of them—and it laid much of the blame for the Great Depression directly at the feet of the so-called right to contract:

> The inequality of bargaining power between employees who do not possess full freedom of association or actual liberty of contract, and employers who are organized in the corporate or other forms of ownership association substantially burdens and affects the flow of commerce, and tends to aggravate recurrent business depressions, by depressing wage rates and the purchasing power of wage earners in industry and by preventing the stabilization of competitive wage rates and working conditions within and between industries.[28]

Collective bargaining—not the one-on-one arrangements between hungry laborers and mighty corporations favored by the decisions that applied *Lochner*—was the act's remedy for depressed wages and unequal bargaining power in the workplace. And the act went further than any federal law had ever gone to ensure that workers could organize to bargain collectively. Though the Supreme Court had twice struck down relatively unambitious laws forbidding labor contracts that prohibited union membership,[29] the National Labor Relations Act did that and far more.

"Employees," the new law proclaimed, "shall have the right to self-organization, to form, join, or assist labor organizations, to bargain collectively through representatives of their own choosing, and to engage in other concerted activities for the purpose of collective bargaining or other mutual aid or protection." Employers, meanwhile, were forbidden from refusing to bargain with the union chosen by their workers.[30] George Pullman's tactic of simply waiting out his workers until they agreed to work on his terms would no longer be allowed.

It would have been difficult to design a law more offensive to the ethos that dominated the Supreme Court in the years following the Pullman Strike. The National Labor Relations Act defied decades of precedent enabling employers to thumb their noses at unions. It brought sweeping, nationwide oversight of the labor market at a time when the federal government wasn't even permitted to keep six-year-olds out of cotton mills. And it benefited the one group of Americans who had fared the worst under the Supreme Court—ordinary workers.

Just over a month after Roosevelt signed this labor law, he fired another shot across the steps of the Supreme Court. In May of 1935, while the president was working to pass his Social Security bill authorizing a nationwide old-age pension system, a 5–4 Supreme Court handed down an opinion declaring a similar pension law for railroad employees unconstitutional.[31]

Although there were strong legal arguments distinguishing Social Security's pension system from the railroad law that had just been struck down by five justices, it is difficult to read these justices' decision in *Railroad Retirement Board v. Alton Railroad* (1935) as anything other than a warning to the president that Social Security would not be greeted fondly by the conservative justices. Worse, *Alton Railroad* suggested that these justices were moving even further to the right than their predecessors from the *Lochner* Era.

Even at the height of its skepticism to federal regulation of employers, when the Supreme Court gave its blessing to child labor in *Hammer v. Dagenhart*, the justices still maintained that Congress had robust authority to regulate the transportation of goods across state lines.[32] Under this theory of the Constitution, Congress was at the apex of its power when it regulated the railroad industry, because railroads were in the very business of interstate transportation of goods.

Nevertheless, *Alton Railroad* claimed that a law providing pensions to the workers engaged in interstate commerce "is not in purpose or effect a regulation of interstate commerce within the meaning of the Constitution."[33] If the Court was willing to bend its own already quite restrictive rules in order to deny pensions to railroad workers, then this was not a hopeful sign that it would embrace something as transformative as Social Security.

Yet, despite the very real likelihood that it would be struck down, President Roosevelt signed the Social Security Act. If the justices were going to doom another generation of the least fortunate seniors to the poorhouse, then they would have to do their own dirty work.

————

THE LOOMING SHOWDOWN between Roosevelt and the Supreme Court was, in many ways, a microcosm of a much larger battle between the president and many of the nation's wealthiest businessmen. Indeed, the conflict over what kind of Constitution the United States would have—a Constitution that allowed the American people to choose their own government or one that sharply limited the government's ability to help the least fortunate, regardless of what the voters preferred—was one of the central questions presented by the 1936 presidential election. By defeating Roosevelt, many of the most privileged men in the nation hoped to permanently discredit his vision for activist government, and maintain their all-important grip on the Supreme Court in the process.

The rich man's campaign against Roosevelt began with a single letter from one wealthy businessman to another. "Five negroes on my place in South Carolina refused work this spring," an agitated Ruly Carpenter wrote a former colleague in 1934, and "a cook on my houseboat in Fort Myers quit because the government was paying him a dollar an hour as a painter." Carpenter's correspondent was John J. Raskob, a former chairman of the Democratic Party and current vice president of the DuPont company, where Carpenter had himself been a senior executive. The purpose of his letter was to urge the politically connected Raskob to speak with Roosevelt about where the president was taking the country.[34]

Raskob, however, had another plan. "You haven't much to do," he wrote to his recently retired friend, "and I know of no one that could better take the lead in trying to induce the DuPont and General Motors groups, followed by other big industries, to definitely organize to protect society from the sufferings it is bound to endure if we allow communistic elements to lead the people to believe that all businessmen are crooks."[35]

The former party chair was right about Carpenter's abilities. More than just a retired executive in one of America's great chemical companies, Carpenter was a member of the du Pont family by marriage and the brother-in-law of two of the nation's wealthiest men—Pierre and Irénée du Pont. Indeed, what began as one man's annoyance that he could no longer hire cheap African American workers would eventually grow into one of the most prominent organizations in the country. At its peak, the American Liberty League even rivaled the Republican Party as the focal point of American conservatism. Many observers believed that the League would eventually replace the GOP altogether.[36]

Carpenter's project achieved such success in no small part due to the enthusiastic support of his brother-in-law Irénée. Irénée du Pont, who viewed the New Deal as "nothing more or less than the Socialistic doctrine called by another name," was a former president of the company that built his family's massive wealth. Founded early in American history as a gunpowder supplier, the DuPont company's products could be found in nearly every household in the country by the time President Roosevelt took office. Packaged food was wrapped in DuPont cellophane, and radios built with DuPont plastic. Movies were filmed on DuPont cellulose and cars colored by DuPont paints. The soldiers Woodrow Wilson shipped off to Europe fought the Great War armed with DuPont munitions.[37]

In July of 1934, Irénée and his brothers Pierre and Lammot convened a group of their friends and fellow businessmen to, in Irénée's words, form a "property holder's association" to provide "information as to the dangers to investors" presented by the New Deal. Yet the captains of industry who heeded the du Ponts' call were wise enough to know that they would have a difficult time selling their message to the public if it was framed as an effort to protect their own fortunes. Thus, the American Liberty League would present itself as a vigorous defender of the Constitution—or, at least, the Constitution as America's most fortunate sons saw it. By selling themselves as guardians of America's founding document, Irénée predicted that they could ally with other organizations that, in his mind, were also defenders of the Constitution—organizations such as the American Legion or "even the Ku Klux Klan."[38]

Yet, for all the League's efforts to wrap itself in the mantle of the Constitution, it was unable to disguise exactly what kind of Constitution the League preferred. As one early League supporter wrote in a letter obtained by the *New York Times*,

> I believe in the Constitution of the United States; I believe in the division of power that it makes, and that it is the duty of every public officer to observe them [*sic*]. I believe in the rights of private property, the sanctity and binding power of contracts, the duty of self-help. I am opposed to confiscatory taxation, wasteful expenditure, socialized industry, and a planned economy controlled and directed by government functionaries.[39]

Absent from this Apostles' Creed of belief statements about the Constitution was any reference to the freedom of speech, or the freedom of religion, or the right to be free from discrimination. This was not the Constitution that would free Eugene Debs from jail or rescue Carrie Buck from the surgeon's knife. This was the Constitution of George Pullman and Stephen Johnson Field.

This was the Constitution that locked Reuben Dagenhart in a cotton mill.

———

MUCH OF THE League's membership drew from the unsuccessful "Stop Roosevelt" movement that threw its support behind former New York Governor Al Smith at the Democratic Party's national convention in 1932. Smith, who preceded Roosevelt both as his party's presidential nominee and as New York governor, bore a smoldering grudge against Roosevelt over a series of perceived slights—one of which was the fact that Roosevelt did not offer Smith a seat in the cabinet.[40] Smith would emerge as one of Roosevelt's most vocal critics, likening the president to an American Lenin. "There can be only one Capital—Washington or Moscow," he told a Liberty League gathering in an election-year speech denouncing the New Deal. "There can be only one flag, the Stars and Stripes, or the red flag of the godless union of the Soviet. There can be only one national anthem, the Star Spangled Banner or the Internationale."[41]

The true spirit of the Liberty League, however, rested not with the resentful Smith but with the former New York governor's own predecessor as the Democratic presidential nominee. John W. Davis was a former congressman, ambassador, and Solicitor General of the United States. He emerged as the 1924 Democratic nominee for the White House after a disastrously fractured convention that required 103 ballots to settle on a candidate. Davis would go on to lose to President Calvin Coolidge in a landslide.

Though a failure as a presidential candidate, Davis was arguably the most accomplished legal advocate of his generation. As solicitor general and as an attorney in private practice, Davis argued 140 cases before the Supreme Court, including one of several challenges to the National Labor Relations Act.[42] When a vacancy opened up on the Supreme Court shortly after Davis returned to private practice, he was widely touted as a leading candidate to fill that vacancy—several of the justices themselves urged him to seek a seat alongside them on the nation's highest bench. Davis brushed off these requests that he leave his lucrative legal practice, however, explaining to a colleague that he took "vows of chastity and obedience but not of poverty."[43]

Davis is probably best known, however, for his final argument before the justices, in which he defended South Carolina's segregated school system. After the Court announced that he had lost, in the famous *Brown v. Board of Education* (1954) decision, Davis declined to bill South Carolina for his services. The state's governor gifted him a silver tea service to thank him for his work defending segregation, on behalf of "the People of South Carolina."[44]

In denouncing Roosevelt, Davis spoke of the Liberty League's vision of the Constitution in religious terms, denouncing men and women who would abandon it as "those who worship false gods."[45] In a speech to the New York Bar Association that was reprinted as a Liberty League pamphlet, Davis warned that the New Deal would drain the states of their "life-blood," eventually rendering them irrelevant even to "the mapmakers." "Surely there is something deeply humiliating in the present spectacle of a steady procession of mendicant Governors, Mayors, Boards of Trade and private pilgrims marching on Washington, like beggars with their tin cups, for a share of Federal alms."[46]

Yet Davis saw far more than humiliation and a breakdown of his treasured states' rights if the New Deal were allowed to continue. "With every eye turned toward Washington and every hand outstretched for what Washington has to give," Davis predicted that "our federal system will soon lose all vigor." Worse, "when that time comes, there must eventuate a union torn apart by the clash of group and sectional interests, or a despotism—under what name it matters not—strong enough to maintain our continental unity by force."[47] Smith gazed upon Roosevelt and saw an American Bolshevik; Davis saw a man planting the seeds of either civil war or fascism.

This kind of rhetoric—at times denouncing Roosevelt as either a communist or a fascist, or sometimes both in the exact same sentence—pervaded the Liberty League's indictments of the president. One creatively anachronistic League pamphlet argued that the Founding Fathers cast off the chains of colonialism to abolish a system of central planning similar to fascism or communism—and that Roosevelt was bringing the central planners back. Laws such as the National Labor Relations Act and the Social Security Act "all fit into a scheme under which economic planning is carried out," this pamphlet warned. "Only the Constitution stands in the way of complete government control of industry and agriculture, of workers and farmers."[48]

And the League offered the philosophy of Irénée du Pont as the antidote to Roosevelt's colonial Marxist fascism. "Real progress and prosperity can come only through private enterprise," one League pamphlet proclaimed.[49] Another laid out a laundry list of proposals ranging from "the government must cooperate with business men [and] remove every obstacle possible from their paths" to "the government should remove itself in every way possible from business activities." Roosevelt's plans to improve people's lives through governance were a fool's errand. "There is no easy road to recovery," the League insisted. "There is no way in which the people in general can spend or borrow their way into a sound recovery."[50]

In the South, the League offered a targeted message appealing to regional resentment. "The movement to discredit and then destroy the Constitution," one member of the League's National Lawyer Committee warned, "would threaten an era worse than the period of Reconstruction in the South." The New Deal would "dry up [the South's] industry, and destroy any chance of harmony among its people." Indeed, the League predicted a kind of militant economic struggle resulting from Roosevelt's policies. They would "rend the South into armed economic camps" with "agricultural labor organized against the farm proprietor" and "town arrayed against country."[51]

In a thinly veiled appeal to racism, the League also warned of an age when white Southerners would lose their grip on the franchise. In the new armed struggle for control of the South, "suffrage qualifications" would be overturned.[52]

Outside the South, Social Security became the centerpiece of a desperate, last-minute plot to remove Roosevelt from office. In the final weeks of Republican Kansas Governor Alf Landon's unsuccessful bid to unseat Roosevelt, placards suddenly appeared in Detroit factories announcing that "You're Sentenced To A Weekly Pay Reduction For All Your Working Life. You'll Have To Serve The Sentence Unless You Help Reverse It November 3." On the Friday before the election, workers across the country discovered an unexpected surprise in their pay envelope—a note informing them that

we are compelled by a Roosevelt "New Deal" law to make a 1 percent deduction from your wages and turn it over to the government. Finally, this may go as high as 4 percent. You might get this money back . . . but only if Congress decides to make the appropriation for this purpose. There is NO guarantee. Decide before November 3— election day—whether or not you wish to take these chances.[53]

The Liberty League's attacks on Social Security were more subtle but no less certain that it would lead to disaster. Mass inflation would result from excessive New Deal spending, a Princeton economist and member of the League's National Advisory Council insisted, and the new benefits for unemployed and retired workers would be devoured by this inflation. Social Security, the League warned, "is no more secure than the value of the dollar in which its benefits are payable."[54]

The League, in other words, cast the 1936 election as a stark choice: vote Roosevelt, and risk an apocalyptic descent into communistic fascism; or vote Landon and preserve the values that justices like Field, Brewer, McReynolds, and Sutherland have relied upon to guide the nation.

———

ROOSEVELT WON REELECTION in one of the biggest landslides in American presidential history. Only a little more than a third of the nation cast their ballots for Landon, and the incumbent President Roosevelt won forty-six of the nation's forty-eight states. In a send-off of a once-common political adage that "as Maine goes, so goes the nation"—Maine used to hold statewide elections in September and was viewed as a bellwether state for political observers trying to predict the outcome of the next November's election—Roosevelt's campaign manager quipped that "as Maine goes, so goes Vermont."[55]

Less than two months later, FDR placed his hand on a Bible and recited the presidential oath for a second time. In his inaugural address, he offered a stern rebuttal to the justices who might try to strip him of the mandate a landslide election had given him—especially after the Liberty League had cast that election as a referendum on Roosevelt's understanding of the Constitution:

This year marks the one hundred and fiftieth anniversary of the Constitutional Convention which made us a nation. At that Convention our forefathers found the way out of the chaos which followed the Revolutionary War; they created a strong government with powers of united action sufficient then and now to solve problems utterly beyond individual or local solution. A century and a half ago they established the Federal Government in order to promote the general welfare and secure the blessings of liberty to the American people. . . .

Nearly all of us recognize that as intricacies of human relationships increase, so power to govern them also must increase—power to stop evil; power to do good. The essential democracy of our nation and the safety of our people depend not upon the absence of power, but upon lodging it with those whom the people can change or continue at stated intervals through an honest and free system of elections. The Constitution of 1787 did not make our democracy impotent.[56]

Roosevelt's words echoed General George Washington's much older warning that "unless Congress have powers competent to all general purposes" then the blood spilt in the Revolution will "avail us nothing,"[57] but the truth was that, even at the zenith of his popularity and influence, President Roosevelt had few tools at his disposal that would allow him to restore his first predecessor's vision of a robust national government if the justices were determined to hold the line for the Liberty League.

Perhaps the most obvious solution to a Supreme Court that read Washington's vision out of the Constitution is an amendment explicitly writing it back into the document. In the midst of an economic crisis, however, this simply was not an option. The constitutional amendment process is an unwieldy procedure that requires the consent of three-quarters of the states to complete. After Chief Justice Melville Fuller's opinion declaring the income tax unconstitutional in 1895,[58] it took nearly two decades to ratify the Sixteenth Amendment and undo Fuller's handiwork. Similarly, though Congress proposed an amendment restoring its power to ban child labor in 1924, only six states signed on to the amendment by 1930. By the time Roosevelt delivered his second inaugural address in 1937, only about half of the states had ratified the Child Labor Amendment.[59] If Roosevelt offered a new amendment shoring up Congress's ability to regulate the labor market more broadly and to provide for Americans' retirement, his own children could be eligible for Social Security before enough states got around to ratifying the amendment.

The opposition to the Child Labor Amendment revealed two other challenges facing anyone seeking to amend the Constitution. Constitutional amendments can have unpredictable results—just look at how the Supreme Court treated the Fourteenth Amendment—and this unpredictability can lead to opposition from unexpected sources. Conservative groups recruited parents to oppose the amendment by claiming that it would lead to a federal ban on household chores. One of the leading opponents of the amendment was the Catholic Church, which feared that it would allow Congress to regulate parochial schools on the theory that schoolwork was a form of "labor." The Boston archdiocese even claimed that the Child Labor Amendment was "more in keeping with Soviet Russia than with the fundamental principles of the American Government."[60]

This tendency to stir opposition points to a related problem facing proponents of a constitutional amendment. No other constitutional democracy—nor, for that matter, any of the fifty states—has a constitution as difficult to amend as the United States Constitution.[61] With rare exception, such as when Congress refused to seat senators or representatives from rebel states that refused to ratify the Fourteenth Amendment[62] or the unusual case of Prohibition, the American Constitution is impossible to amend unless there is a widespread national consensus supporting the amendment across nearly every region and every sector of the nation. Determined opposition from an interest group that is powerful in just a small minority of states can be enough to derail an amendment.

Of course, the Child Labor Amendment faced opposition from far more than just misguided parents and Catholic bishops. Southern cotton mills had an obvious interest in keeping the tiny laborers who worked their looms. Newspapers fretted that they could lose their paperboys. Family farmers worried that their children would no longer be able to work the fields.[63] And this was nothing compared to the opposition that would face any plan guaranteeing workers' right to organize. If Roosevelt sought an amendment ensuring that Congress could protect collective bargaining, he would face the wrath of nearly every single business group in the country.

And even if lawmakers did rally behind his amendment with such enthusiasm that it was ratified literally overnight, that wouldn't change the fact that the Constitution is interpreted by the very same Supreme Court that took an amendment intended to abolish apartheid and transformed it into a means to bust unions. The nation's lawmakers could propose and the states could ratify an amendment explicitly authorizing Social Security or the National Labor Relations Act, only to have the justices reveal some novel and spurious reason to strike these laws down regardless.

For all of these reasons, a constitutional amendment simply wasn't a workable solution to a hostile Supreme Court—and Roosevelt knew it. In a letter to a friend, the president warned that no "controversial amendment, especially one which in effect is opposed by a political party, has ever been passed within a short space of time." He told a top aide that "moneyed interests" could easily "buy up enough legislatures" to prevent an amendment from being ratified.[64]

Nor could Roosevelt simply wait out his antagonists on the Supreme Court. Though all of the Four Horsemen were in their seventies on the day Roosevelt won reelection, the president could neither force them into retirement nor predict the dates of their deaths (as it turned out, three of the four would survive Roosevelt's second term). And even if one of them did leave the Court while FDR was still in the White House, that could be after the nation spent five, six, or seven years watching an ineffective president fight losing battle after losing battle against the Supreme Court. By the time Roosevelt moved the Court in his direction, he could be a lame duck drained of all the political capital he enjoyed after his reelection.

"When I retire to private life on January 20, 1941," the president once lamented—at that point unaware that he would win two more terms in office—"I do not want to leave the country in the condition Buchanan left it to Lincoln."[65]

———

LEFT WITH FEW good options, Roosevelt committed what was probably the biggest legislative blunder of his entire presidency. Though the Constitution provides that America's judicial power "shall be vested in one Supreme Court, and in such inferior courts as the Congress may from time to time ordain and establish," it nowhere defines how many justices shall comprise the Supreme Court. When John Jay took his seat as America's first chief justice, he was joined by only five associate justices on the nation's highest bench. The nine-justice Court came about due to an antiquated practice that divided the nation up into multiple judicial "circuits," assigned one justice to each circuit, and required each justice to spend the majority of their time hearing ordinary cases within their assigned circuit. By 1837, the nation had grown large enough to support nine circuits—and thus Congress established that there would be one justice for each of these nine judicial regions.[66]

The Court's membership briefly rose to ten during the Lincoln administration—Congress created a tenth circuit encompassing California and Oregon, and Lincoln made the disastrous decision to appoint Justice Field to the additional seat on the Supreme Court.[67] Not long after Lincoln's assassination, Congress shrank the Court to just seven justices in order to prevent the loathed President Andrew Johnson from appointing anyone to fill its vacant seats. When Johnson left office, Congress restored the Court to nine seats.[68]

So the size of the Court ebbed and flowed a great deal during the Republic's first century, largely for administrative reasons, but occasionally for political reasons as well. Nothing in the Constitution prevented Congress from altering the Court's size again to dilute the votes of the justices loyal to cases like *Hammer* and *Lochner*.

Roosevelt's inspiration for what was soon derided as his "Court-packing plan" came from an unlikely source. While researching a book on the history of the Justice Department, Attorney General Homer Cummings uncovered a proposal offered by one of his predecessors as the nation's top attorney—the odious Justice James McReynolds. Elderly judges, McReynolds had complained in 1913, "have remained on the bench long beyond the time that they are able to adequately discharge their duties." The solution to such superannuated judges, at least according to McReynolds, was to permit the president to appoint a younger judge every time a sitting jurist reached the age of 70, regardless of whether the sitting judge actually retired from the bench.[69]

McReynolds was speaking about lower court judges when he laid out this recommendation, but it formed the basis of Roosevelt's plan to grow the size of the Supreme Court. By applying something similar to McReynolds's plan to the Supreme Court, Roosevelt would be able to appoint up to six new justices right away—more than enough to force the Four Horsemen to live out the rest of their careers in dissent.

President Roosevelt's speech announcing his Court-packing plan to the press was a masterwork of disingenuity. The president offered few hints at his real motive for seeking to add new judges and justices to the nation's courts. Instead, he warned the press that "a lowered mental or physical vigor leads men to avoid an examination of complicated and changed conditions." Adding new seats to the bench, according to Roosevelt, would "vitalize the courts" through a "constant and systematic addition of younger blood."[70]

By obscuring his true reason for wanting to appoint additional justices, Roosevelt may have hoped to avoid a debate on whether the Supreme Court had become such a malign force that utterly eradicating its legitimacy was an appropriate solution, but few people were fooled by his performance. In the ride back to the Capitol, after Roosevelt summoned congressional leaders to the White House to learn of his proposal, House Judiciary Chair Hatton Summers turned to his colleagues and announced, "boys, here's where I cash in my chips."[71] A Gallup poll taken just weeks after the proposal was announced showed 53 percent of the nation opposed to it.[72]

The plan also exposed rifts between Roosevelt and many members of Congress that the president had largely been able to avoid due to the popularity of his programs. In 1937, the South was still largely a one-party region—literally every single US senator and virtually every representative from the South was a Democrat. Many African Americans were denied the right to vote altogether, and white Southerners weren't exactly inclined to support the party of Lincoln.

Because they faced little to no risk of being turned out of office by a Republican, Southern Democrats had an outsized influence on Congress—even though they were increasingly out of step with the rest of their party. Committee chairmanships were largely awarded on the basis of seniority, and a Southern lawmaker could hold the same office for decades. The one-party South could offer a newly elected senator or congressman something very close to life tenure.[73]

Many Southern lawmakers looked at the New Deal and saw President Roosevelt building a power base within their states that could eventually rival their own. Public works programs sponsored by the Tennessee Valley Authority and other agencies were slowly modernizing the South's economy and bringing desperately needed jobs to the region in the process.[74] And the president was wildly popular as a result. In Mississippi, Roosevelt triumphed over Landon with an absurd 97 percent of the popular vote. Meanwhile, the growing federal influence spawned by the New Deal offended old-line Southerners who viewed states' rights almost as a religious creed.[75] If Roosevelt controlled the Supreme Court he could grow powerful enough to render the South's longstanding power structures irrelevant.

Though Roosevelt's record on race was mixed at best—nearly two-thirds of African Americans were ineligible for Social Security under the bill Roosevelt signed in 1935, because it excluded farm and domestic workers[76]—Southern lawmakers also feared another consequence if conservatives lost their grip on the Supreme Court. North Carolina Senator Josiah Bailey wrote a friend shortly after the Court-packing bill was announced complaining that the president "is determined to get the Negro vote, and I do not have to tell you what *this* means." What it meant was that a liberal Supreme Court might abolish segregation.[77]

Meanwhile, many of the Senate's progressives gazed upon the Court-packing plan and feared an all-powerful president unchecked by any other institution. "We're on the road to Fascism," Senator Hiram Johnson wrote his son one day after Roosevelt announced his proposal. Progressive Senator Burton Wheeler, who already resented Roosevelt for, among other things, not giving him the vice presidential nomination, became one of the plan's leading opponents.[78]

The Court-packing plan, in other words, gave the president's foes—and people who had not yet figured out that they were his foes—an unpopular plan to rally against, and it stoked legitimate fears that Roosevelt was claiming too much power for himself. But it was also a terrible blunder for a wholly different reason: it was completely unnecessary.

———

ON THE DAY Roosevelt announced the plan, a close associate of the president drove to the Supreme Court building to give the aged liberal Justice Louis Brandeis a warning about the proposal. Brandeis read a copy of the press release announcing the plan, and then turned to the White House's envoy with a warning. "Tell your president," Brandeis said, "he has made a great mistake. All he had to do was wait a little while."[79]

Brandeis knew something Roosevelt didn't know. Justice Owen Roberts, the Court's fifth conservative and a largely consistent ally of the Four Horsemen, had defected.

Justice Roberts was not Herbert Hoover's first choice for the Supreme Court. That honor fell to Judge John J. Parker, a North Carolina judge opposed by labor for upholding an injunction prohibiting unions from organizing many West Virginia mine workers and by the National Association for the Advancement of Colored People for labeling "the participation of the negro in politics" as "a source of evil and danger to both races" that is "not desired by wise men."[80]

As a judge, Parker later proved to be relatively moderate on the issue of race, at least as compared to other white Southerners. He authored an opinion in 1952 holding that a South Carolina school district had not lived up to the "equal" prong of "separate but equal," and he ordered the state "promptly to furnish to Negroes . . . educational facilities and opportunities equal to those furnished white persons."[81] Nevertheless, the NAACP's opposition to Parker was vindicated three years later, when he handed down an influential opinion interpreting the Supreme Court's desegregation order in *Brown v. Board of Education* to permit segregated schools to remain segregated so long as the school district gave students the option of voluntarily transferring to another school.[82] African American students, intimidated by pervasive Klan violence in the South, rarely availed themselves of such opportunities to attend a white school.

For much of his life, the man Hoover chose to replace Parker was a fairly obscure figure who served as a senior prosecutor in Philadelphia and as a law professor at the University of Pennsylvania. Prior to joining the Court, Justice Roberts was a conservative Republican, and up until the day that Roosevelt unveiled his Court-packing plan, Roberts's outward behavior as a justice largely mirrored his politics. Justice Roberts authored the Court's opinion striking down the railroad pension law in 1935,[83] and he authored another opinion blocking part of the New Deal's agricultural policy in 1936.[84] Indeed, just five months before Roosevelt's reelection, Roberts joined the Four Horsemen in a sweeping reaffirmation of *Lochner*'s so-called liberty of contract.

In *Morehead v. Tipaldo* (1936), Roberts provided the key fifth vote for an opinion holding that laws abridging this supposed liberty "can only be justified by the existence of exceptional circumstances." *Tipaldo*, however, did more than simply reaffirm a principle the Court's conservatives had clung to for over three decades; it was an homage to the idea that an employer's wealth is beyond the reach

of a populist government. Minimum-wage laws, such as the one at
issue in *Tipaldo*, exact "from the employer an arbitrary payment for
a purpose and upon a basis having no causal connection with his
business or the contract or the work the employee engages to do; the
declared basis is not the value of the service rendered but the extra-
neous circumstance that the employee needs to get a prescribed sum
of money to insure her subsistence, health and morals."[85]

Tipaldo, however, would prove to be one of the shortest-lived
precedents in Supreme Court history. What Brandeis knew, and
Roosevelt didn't, on the day the president unveiled his Court-
packing plan was that Roberts had already voted to reverse himself.

Shortly after they hear arguments in a pending case, the justices
typically meet in a private conference to reveal their votes to their
colleagues. The actual opinion-drafting process, however, typically
takes weeks or even months, especially if there is a dissenting opinion that the majority feels compelled to rebut. Thus, the justices and
their law clerks may know that a major precedent is about to be overruled for months before they let the rest of the world in on the secret.
In December, the justices heard oral arguments in *West Coast Hotel
v. Parrish* (1937), a minimum-wage case that was virtually identical
to *Tipaldo*. Yet, when the justices met to confer on the case, Roberts
announced that he was switching sides.

When the moment came for the justices to reveal their secret
to the nation, a bitter Justice McReynolds rose from his seat at the
bench and stormed out of the Supreme Court courtroom. Chief Justice Charles Evans Hughes, a moderately progressive Republican
who had served as governor of New York and who nearly defeated
President Woodrow Wilson as the GOP presidential candidate in
1916, repudiated *Lochner* just a few minutes later.

"The Constitution does not speak of freedom of contract," Hughes
proclaimed in his opinion for the Court. Because the law at issue in
Parrish was a minimum wage applicable to women, Hughes's opinion spoke to the ability of states to protect women from exploitation
in the workplace. "What can be closer to the public interest than
the health of women and their protection from unscrupulous and

overreaching employers?" Hughes asked. "And if the protection of women is a legitimate end of the exercise of state power, how can it be said that the requirement of the payment of a minimum wage fairly fixed in order to meet the very necessities of existence is not an admissible means to that end?" Rather than having its decisions second-guessed by unelected judges,

> the legislature of the State was clearly entitled to consider the situation of women in employment, the fact that they are in the class receiving the least pay, that their bargaining power is relatively weak, and that they are the ready victims of those who would take advantage of their necessitous circumstances. The legislature was entitled to adopt measures to reduce the evils of the "sweating system," the exploiting of workers at wages so low as to be insufficient to meet the bare cost of living, thus making their very helplessness the occasion of a most injurious competition. The legislature had the right to consider that its minimum wage requirements would be an important aid in carrying out its policy of protection.

Even if the Court disagreed with a legislature's judgment, "even if the wisdom of the policy be regarded as debatable and its effects uncertain, still the legislature is entitled to its judgment." The Supreme Court of the United States would no longer serve as America's highest lawmaking authority, and the justices would now respect the people's right to govern themselves through their elected representatives.[86]

Two weeks later, Hughes dropped an even bigger bombshell. The right to engage in collective bargaining is a "fundamental right," according to the majority opinion in *National Labor Relations Board v. Jones & Laughlin Steel* (1937). A "single employee," Hughes continued, is often "helpless in dealing with an employer." If that employee quits their job, the employer may experience a brief inconvenience, but the worker could lose entirely the ability to provide for self and family. Only by joining together can many workers hope to negotiate effectively with their bosses. Unions, in Hughes's words, are "essential to give laborers opportunity to deal on an equality with their employer."[87]

Just as important, *Jones & Laughlin Steel* dealt a mortal blow to Chief Justice Fuller's pronouncement that "manufacture, agriculture, mining, [and] production in all its forms"[88] were beyond the reach of Congress. "Experience has abundantly demonstrated that the recognition of the right of employees to self-organization and to have representatives of their own choosing for the purpose of collective bargaining is often an essential condition of industrial peace"—an experience, of course, that stretched back at least at far as the Pullman Strike. Failure to maintain that peace threatens "immediate," even "catastrophic," disruptions of the nation's commerce. The Court could no longer pretend that the power to protect workers is beyond Congress's authority to "regulate commerce."[89]

Justice McReynolds, for his part, was left to repeat the familiar conservative complaint that, if Congress had the power to enact the National Labor Relations Act, then there would be no limits to its power. "Almost anything," McReynolds claimed in dissent, including "marriage," "birth," or even "death" could now be controlled by the federal government.[90]

By the time the justices handed down the final cases of the term that June, they would hand Roosevelt another major victory, upholding Social Security in a pair of opinions enabling Congress to continue weaving America's safety net.[91]

Years later, McReynolds's own law clerk would write that, if the Four Horsemen had not lost their majority—if Justice Roberts had not set aside his discomfort with a liberal president's broad new agenda—then "these four conservative Justices would have permanently wrecked the Supreme Court as it was then constituted."[92] If destroying the Supreme Court were the only way to save the nation, the Court-packing bill might have passed.

But destroying the Supreme Court was not necessary to free the nation from its yoke. Roberts did flip his vote, and several months later, one of his colleagues ensured that Roberts could not undo this decision even if he had another change of heart. On May 18, 1937, nearly a week before the Court upheld Social Security, conservative Justice Willis Van Devanter wrote the president to announce that he would "retire from active service" at the close of the Court's present term.[93] Roberts's vote would no longer be needed to save the New Deal, as Roosevelt would name Van Devanter's replacement.

Thus, for the first time in more than a generation, the Supreme Court would no longer have enough votes to hamstring democracy. *Lochner* was dead, Social Security and the National Labor Relations Act were very much alive, and Roosevelt would no longer need to seek the justices' permission before he and his partners in Congress exercised their mandate to govern. Roosevelt would be the first president in more than a generation to preside over a nation in which the will of the people trumped the will of five men in robes. His plans to lift up workers and free America from the poorhouse would rise or fall on their own merits.

Chapter 8

THE BIGGEST DAMNED-FOOL MISTAKE I EVER MADE

CONGRESSMAN JIMMY BYRNES was a bigot. He had to be if he hoped to win election in a Jim Crow state whose very constitution spun a web of literacy tests, poll taxes, residency requirements, and all-powerful election managers—all intended to prevent South Carolina's black majority from casting a ballot.[1] So Byrnes played the role of the Southern race-baiter to great effect. "Rape," he told his fellow members of Congress in 1921, "is responsible directly and indirectly for most of the lynching in America."[2] He opposed a national conscription act during World War I, fearful that it would lead to white Southerners serving alongside African Americans in the same unit. When an epidemic of racial violence broke out shortly after the war, Byrnes blamed it on black veterans and called for African Americans who advocated racial equality to be deported.[3]

Despite these views, Byrnes was a relative moderate on race compared to his contemporaries at the top of South Carolina politics. Not long after his first election to Congress in 1910, Byrnes sought the favor of "Pitchfork Ben" Tillman, the one-eyed farmer-turned-senator who'd driven the last vestiges of racial equality out of his state with the barrel of his gun. Within a few years, the two men would grow so close that the elderly Tillman would delegate much of the responsibility for managing his massive patronage operation to the young congressman.[4]

Though Tillman did not serve in the Confederate Army due to an infection that eventually cost him his left eye, he was no stranger to the use of arms to defend white supremacy. Three years after the Colfax Massacre in 1873, Tillman joined what President Ulysses S. Grant would describe as a "barbarous massacre of innocent men" in the town of Hamburg, South Carolina.[5] After a tense standoff between white farmers accused of forcing their way through a black militia parade at gunpoint and the militiamen who were themselves accused of leveling bayonets at the farmers, white "rifle clubs" descended upon the town of Hamburg to provide armed resistance to the militia. One of the rifle clubmen was a twenty-nine-year-old Ben Tillman.

In a smaller-scale reenactment of Colfax, the rifle clubs surrounded the black militiamen and took them prisoner during a violent exchange in which one man on each side was killed—the fallen black man was a town official Tillman described as "more hated by whites of the surrounding county than any other individual of his race."[6] "It was agreed," Tillman later said of this exchange of a life for a life, "that we could not have a story like that go out as the record of the night's work." So the rifle clubs selected five of their black prisoners to be marched "a little ways down the street and shot." When one of the executioners ran out of rifle cartridges, Tillman lent the white man his gun.[7]

Yet for all of his racism—Tillman was elected captain of his rifle club, and he personally ushered his state's Jim Crow constitution through an 1895 convention[8]—Pitchfork Ben offered his followers more than just white supremacy. Though he provided South Carolina's black residents with little more than violence and disenfranchisement, Tillman also embraced a kind of Southern populism that promised a far better life for his state's poor whites. As governor, Tillman built two state colleges—one for men and one for women—and he backed maximum-hours laws benefiting cotton mill workers.

As a senator, he sponsored the first national legislation forbidding corporate donations to political campaigns. Indeed, Byrnes would hyperbolically describe Tillman as the "first New Dealer."[9]

So Byrnes learned a kind of bigoted populism from his mentor Ben Tillman—a politics that showed compassion for lowly whites while simultaneously treating black men and women as subhuman. In response to a political opponent who accused him of being led by "alien prophets of socialism and bolshevism," Byrnes offered an unapologetic retort. "I admit I am a new dealer," he proclaimed while campaigning for reelection to the US Senate in 1936, "and if it takes money away from the few who have controlled the country and gives it to the average man, I am going back to Washington to help the president work for the people of South Carolina and of the country."[10]

Indeed, President Franklin D. Roosevelt so trusted Byrnes that he would eventually place the South Carolinian in charge of managing the nation's domestic readiness for World War II. When Roosevelt traveled abroad to confer with Winston Churchill and Joseph Stalin, he left Byrnes with a safe full of signed, blank executive orders in case an emergency arose while the president was out of the country. Byrnes's official job title was Director of the Office of War Mobilization, but the press gave him a more descriptive title—the "assistant president."[11]

And yet, this was not the only high appointment Roosevelt offered the one-time protégé of Pitchfork Ben Tillman. Jimmy Byrnes served only a little more than a decade in the Senate, leaving in 1941 to accept Roosevelt's appointment to the Supreme Court of the United States. He would leave the bench just over a year later to sit at Roosevelt's right hand in the White House.

Five years after Roosevelt's death, South Carolina would elect the former congressman, senator, Supreme Court justice, and assistant president to a four-year term as governor. In that role, Governor Jimmy Byrnes would hire the nation's top advocate to defend public school segregation. When John W. Davis lost his final argument before the Supreme Court, it was Byrnes that sent him a silver tea service on behalf of "the People of South Carolina."[12]

If Byrnes had kept his seat on the Supreme Court—if Roosevelt had not chosen the avowed segregationist to be his top lieutenant—then it is all but certain that he would have rejected the Court's conclusion that "separate educational facilities are inherently unequal."[13] Indeed, if Justice Byrnes had remained on the Court, *Brown v. Board of Education* could have been decided the other way.

————

BYRNES WAS IN many ways emblematic of Roosevelt's approach to the Supreme Court. The president did not so much wish to stack the Court with justices who shared Byrnes's views on race as he was indifferent to how the Supreme Court might decide questions of racial justice. Roosevelt's appointees included staunch civil libertarians like Frank Murphy, liberal activists like William Douglas, and skeptics of judicial power like Felix Frankfurter. So long as his nominees could be counted on to reject *Lochner*ism and permit New Deal lawmakers to govern, Roosevelt was not particularly concerned with how they would decide other matters.

Indeed, six of Roosevelt's justices were responsible for one of the most widely reviled decisions in the Supreme Court's history. At the height of the Second World War, more than one hundred thousand people of Japanese descent, most of them Americans, were ordered to leave their homes and eventually relocated to internment camps. Though no one doubted the loyalty of the overwhelming majority of these detainees, the Justice Department told the Court that this sweeping and indiscriminate action was necessary because it was impossible to separate loyal Japanese Americans from the few disloyal ones.[14]

We now know these claims were false. Among other things, the Justice Department suppressed an intelligence report that revealed that "only a small percentage of Japanese Americans posed a potential security threat, and that the most dangerous were already known or in custody."[15]

Nevertheless, the Supreme Court refused even to probe the question of whether mass internment camps were necessary to combat the threat of disloyal Americans. Relying on a previous decision that upheld a mandatory curfew for persons of Japanese descent, the Court's infamous opinion in *Korematsu v. United States* (1944) explained that "we cannot reject as unfounded the judgment of the military authorities and of Congress" that some Japanese members were disloyal. "There was evidence of disloyalty on the part of some," the Court concluded, "the military authorities considered that the need for action was great, and time was short. We cannot—by availing ourselves of the calm perspective of hindsight—now say that at that time these actions were unjustified."[16]

The Court would defer to military authorities even when they committed one of the most egregious violations of the Constitution's ban on race discrimination in American history, and Justice Murphy was left to complain in dissent that this decision "goes over 'the very brink of constitutional power' and falls into the ugly abyss of racism."[17]

Korematsu was authored by Roosevelt's first nominee to the Supreme Court, former Alabama Senator Hugo Black. On the surface, Senator Black appeared to be an equally racist and even more populist version of Jimmy Byrnes. A month after Roosevelt won his first election to the White House, Black tried to preempt the first round of New Deal legislation with a bill that would have limited the nation's workweek to just thirty hours—the idea was to create new jobs by spreading existing positions across more workers.[18]

Yet, although Black spent many of his Senate years tacking to Roosevelt's left on economic issues, he'd sold the state of Alabama a very different package in order to win election to the Senate in the first place. As a defense attorney in Birmingham, Black defended a Ku Klux Klansman who had murdered a Catholic priest for marrying the Klansman's daughter to a man of Puerto Rican descent. Before shooting the priest, Black's client told the clergyman that he'd "acted like a low down, dirty dog. . . . That man is a nigger."[19]

Black gave his client exactly the kind of defense that was likely to appeal to a jury stacked with Klansmen. Puerto Ricans, Black told the jury, were of mixed race and should be considered black. The Catholic priest had stolen his client's daughter away from her parents' faith. In his closing argument, Black quoted the official Klan prayer.[20]

The jury voted to acquit, labeling the murder self-defense.

In 1923, Black joined the Klan himself, anticipating that membership in one of his state's most influential organizations would prove advantageous when he ran for statewide office. He was right. The Klan's Grand Dragon of Alabama served as Black's de facto campaign manager during his first run for the Senate. Black won by the widest margins in areas with the highest Klan membership.[21]

When the newly confirmed Justice Black was forced to repudiate his past ties to the Klan in a national radio address, Black told the nation that "many members of the colored race" are his friends and that "some of my best and most intimate friends are Catholics and Jews."[22]

Unlike Byrnes, however, Black eventually abandoned many of his racist views after Roosevelt placed him on the Court. Indeed, decades after John Archibald Campbell's crusade to halt Reconstruction, Justice Hugo Black would do as much to dismantle Campbell's legacy as any other man in American history.

———

"WE WILL NOT suffer future dictation from the North as to what we are to do about the Negro," the Arkansas poet John Gould Fletcher complained in 1933, after a rare Supreme Court decision tossed out the convictions of several young African American men railroaded into rape convictions after little more than a show trial. "We will take the law into our own hands," Fletcher warned, "by a resort to violence" if necessary. "If a white woman is prepared to swear that a Negro either raped or attempted to rape her, we see to it that the Negro is executed."[23]

The case that drew Fletcher's rage was the first of two Supreme Court decisions questioning the state of Alabama's treatment of several black teenagers who became known as the Scottsboro Boys. In March of 1931, these nine young men were traveling on a freight train through Alabama when a fight broke out between them and a group of white boys who shared the same train. Eventually, the larger group of black teenagers prevailed, throwing all but one of the white boys off the train.[24]

Their victory was short-lived, however. Before the train reached the nearby town of Scottsboro, word of the fight had already reached local authorities, and a sheriff's posse seized the nine Scottsboro Boys. Two white girls, who were also passengers on the train, accused the nine young men of raping them.[25]

What followed bore only a passing resemblance to a judicial trial. In a precaution against mob violence from the surrounding white community, the sheriff called out the state militia to protect the defendants from would-be lynchers. The Scottsboro Boys were escorted to and from court proceedings by military guards. Their trial began just six days after they were indicted, and no lawyer was named to represent them until the morning of their trial. Death sentences soon followed.[26]

This kind of sham trial defined Southern justice for much of the twentieth century. From the era of the Pullman Strike until the early days of the Hoover administration, the number of lynchings in the South plunged more than 90 percent. A major factor in this drop, however, were state laws intended to placate white mobs by rushing black defendants from arrest to execution.[27] Arkansas's law, for example, provided that a trial must begin within ten days after a sheriff notified the local judge that the "crime of rape, attempt to commit rape, murder, or any other crime calculated to arouse the passions of the people" had occurred[28]—the defendant's right to secure counsel and prepare a defense be damned.

Once the trial began, defense attorneys rarely sought continuances for fear that their client would be murdered. Prosecutors told juries to convict in order to reward mobs for the restraint they showed by allowing the trial to move forward. Some governors even refused clemency requests on the grounds that a death sentence was necessary to ward off a lynching.[29]

This, in other words, was the world that had emerged from the Supreme Court's Reconstruction decision in *Cruikshank*. The lesson of the Colfax Massacre was that violent mobs could enforce white supremacy with near-impunity. And because *Cruikshank* effectively freed the states to ignore the Bill of Rights, nothing prevented states like Alabama from transforming their courts into agents of the mob.

Admittedly, by the time that Hugo Black joined the bench, the Court had begun to roll back this lawlessness at the margins. The two Scottsboro cases established that state capital defendants have a right to counsel.[30] And they reaffirmed the rule, first articulated by the Court in 1880,[31] that a state cannot systematically exclude black jurors[32]—although jury discrimination would linger for many decades after Scottsboro.[33] In another case, the Supreme Court tossed out several confessions extracted through torture, including that of one black man who was repeatedly hanged from a tree and then let down to gasp at the air, then tied to the tree and whipped, and finally taken into custody and whipped again while being told that it would continue until he confessed.[34]

But Justice Black was the first modern justice to argue that the fully panoply of safeguards contained in the Bill of Rights—including the right against unreasonable searches and seizures, the right to an impartial jury trial, the right to an attorney, and the right to be free from cruel and unusual punishments—must be honored by the states as surely as the federal government. "To hold that this Court can determine what, if any, provisions of the Bill of Rights will be enforced," Black wrote in a dissent laying out his vision for a Bill of Rights restored, "is to frustrate the great design of a written Constitution."[35]

To Black, the sin that led to decisions like *Cruikshank* and *Lochner* was the Court's failure to root its opinions in the Constitution's text. Under these decisions, "the power of legislatures became what this Court would declare it to be at a particular time independently of the specific guarantees of the Bill of Rights. . . . Neither the contraction of the Bill of Rights safeguards nor the invalidation of regulatory laws" by *Lochner* and similar decisions, "would readily be classified as the most satisfactory contribution of this Court to the nation."[36]

Thus the former Ku Klux Klansman who President Roosevelt appointed to tear down the last vestiges of the *Lochner* Era would come to view safeguarding black men from abusive state governments as an essential prong of the same battle. The way to ward off *Lochner*, with its extra-textual freedom of contract, was to hew precisely and absolutely to the rights that were actually safeguarded by the Constitution.

And, although Black would be an old man before many parts of his quest to apply the Bill of Rights universally to the states were achieved, he would live to see nearly all of his dream fulfilled. By the time an elderly Black left the Court in 1971, he and his fellow justices held that nearly every one of the Bill of Rights' safeguards extended over state law.

———

WHEN THE JUSTICES convened in 1952 to discuss the fate of public school segregation, Justice Black had no illusions about what would happen if the Court sided with equality. Months earlier, when his son Hugo Jr. was considering a bid for Congress, the justice wrote his namesake to warn him that the elder Black was about to do something that would make it very difficult for his son to have a political career. Black told his fellow justices in conference that "violence" would undoubtedly follow if the Court held segregation unconstitutional. And he relayed his old friend Jimmy Byrnes's warning that, if the Court ordered South Carolina to integrate its schools, the state might "abolish [its] public school system" first.[37]

Yet there was also little doubt how the former Klansman would decide the case. The purpose of the Fourteenth Amendment, Black told his colleagues, was the "protection of the negro against discrimination," and Black understood that segregation existed to foster such discrimination.[38]

The Court as a whole, however, viewed *Brown v. Board of Education* with far less clarity. Recalling the day of the initial conference when the justices met to discuss the case, Justice William O. Douglas later wrote that only four members of the Court—himself, Black, and Justices Harold Burton and Sherman Minton—were certain votes to abolish public school segregation. Chief Justice Fred Vinson and Justice Stanley Reed, according to Douglas, both thought that the Court's pro-segregation decision in *Plessy* was correctly decided, and Justice Tom Clark was "inclined that way." The two remaining justices, Felix Frankfurter and Robert Jackson, "expressed the view that segregation in the public schools was probably constitutional."[39]

To be fair, the reality is probably somewhat more nuanced than Douglas's notes suggest. Among other things, Douglas loathed Frankfurter and he may have wished to paint his rival in an unfavorable light. Shortly after the Court handed down its *Brown* decision, Frankfurter claimed that the initial vote was 5–4 *in favor* of ending discrimination, with Frankfurter himself casting the key fifth vote.[40]

But there were few signs that the Court would eventually achieve the unanimity that marked its decision in *Brown*. The Southerners Vinson, Reed, and Clark—Vinson and Reed both hailed from Kentucky, Clark from Texas—were all reluctant to upend the expectations Southern whites had relied upon for generations. As Clark put it during conference, "we had led the states on to think segregation is OK and we should let them work it out."[41] Meanwhile, the Roosevelt appointees Frankfurter and Jackson seemed to have overlearned the lessons of the *Lochner* Era. They were so committed to making sure that the Court did not impose its views upon the nation that they were reluctant even to strike down Southern apartheid.

As a Harvard law professor prior to joining the Court, Frankfurter was one of the nation's leading liberal intellectuals. A founder of the American Civil Liberties Union, Frankfurter signed a report denouncing a series of Justice Department raids in 1919 and 1920 that targeted thousands of alleged anarchists and communists. These raids, according to the report, were "utterly illegal acts which have been committed by those charged with the highest duty of enforcing the laws."[42] Frankfurter would later emerge as one of the nation's highest-profile defenders of Nicola Sacco and Bartolomeo Vanzetti, two Italian American anarchists convicted of murder under dubious circumstances.[43]

Frankfurter's views on race were similarly progressive. In the 1930s, he served on the NAACP's National Legal Committee. And he was the first member of the Court to hire an African American law clerk.[44] In a 2005 interview, the clerk, William T. Coleman, recalled one incident when his boss learned that Coleman was not able to dine at a popular hotel's restaurant because he was black. When Coleman returned to Frankfurter's chambers after the incident, "the justice had tears in his eyes" because he was so upset that his own law clerk was denied service because of his skin color.[45] (Coleman would go on to serve as secretary of transportation under President Gerald Ford.)

Yet, there was another side to Frankfurter's progressivism even before he joined the Supreme Court. Coming of age in an era when it was unimaginable that the Court could be anything more than a hindrance to progressive reform, Frankfurter lionized Justice Oliver Wendell Holmes and Holmes's restrained approach to judging. Indeed, Frankfurter quickly emerged as a one-man public relations firm for Holmes, praising him to his fellow legal academics as a judicial saint who was uniquely capable of setting aside his own political views and respecting the judgments made by the people's representatives.[46] After joining the Court himself in 1939, Frankfurter was determined to emulate Holmes's approach to the law.

The perfect opportunity to prove his devotion to Holmes's narrow approach to judging arose just over a year after Frankfurter's appointment to the bench. In *Minersville School District v. Gobitis* (1940), two Jehovah's Witnesses' children were expelled from a public school after they refused to salute the flag and recite the Pledge of Allegiance, an act that they believed to be akin to worshiping an idol.[47] Frankfurter looked at *Gobitis*, however, and saw neither a free speech case nor a religious liberty case; he saw a matter best left to school officials' judgment.

"The wisdom of training children in patriotic impulses" through compulsory activity such as the flag salute, "is not for our independent judgment." "Perhaps it is best," Frankfurter acknowledged, "to give to the least popular sect leave from conformities like those here in issue." But such leave was not Frankfurter's to give. "The courtroom," he concluded in an opinion joined by a majority of the Court, "is not the arena for debating issues of educational policy. . . . So to hold would in effect make us the school board for the country. That authority has not been given to this Court, nor should we assume it."[48]

Within weeks of the Court's decision in *Gobitis*, the FBI received hundreds of reports of violence against Witnesses. Six days after the *Gobitis* decision, a mob of twenty-five hundred surrounded a Jehovah's Witnesses Kingdom Hall in Maine and burned it to the ground.[49]

Yet, when a contrite Supreme Court overruled *Gobitis* just three years later, Justice Frankfurter viewed that decision as a personal affront. "One who belongs to the most vilified and persecuted minority in history is not likely to be insensible to the freedoms guaranteed by our Constitution," Frankfurter wrote in a reference to his Jewish roots. "But as judges we are neither Jew nor Gentile, neither Catholic nor agnostic. . . . As a member of this Court I am not justified in writing my private notions of policy into the Constitution, no matter how deeply I may cherish them or how mischievous I may deem their disregard." Even after the consequences of a too-narrow Constitution had been laid bare for him, Frankfurter would not acknowledge that our founding document could embrace values he had spent much of his career fighting to uphold.[50]

Indeed, Frankfurter was often unwilling to second-guess state lawmakers even when those lawmakers' actions or inaction did nothing more than entrench their own power at the expense of the electorate. In the 1960s, the state of Tennessee had not redrawn its legislative districts since the turn of the century, despite the fact that significant migration had occurred from rural to urban districts. The result was a state legislature that could hardly be described as a representative body. Tennessee's most populous state senate district included more than five times as many voters as its least populous one, while the most populous state house district included more than eighteen times as many voters as the most sparse district.[51]

And yet Frankfurter balked at the notion that the courts should step in to ensure that every vote counts equally. "There is not under our Constitution," he lectured his fellow justices from dissent, "a judicial remedy for every political mischief, for every undesirable exercise of legislative power."[52]

So Frankfurter approached *Brown* with trepidation, fearful that his own personal disdain for segregation might color his approach to the law. "However passionately any of us may hold egalitarian views," he wrote while *Brown* was pending, a judge "travels outside his judicial authority if for this private reason alone he declares unconstitutional the policy of segregation."[53]

Justice Robert Jackson was a frequent ally of Frankfurter's who, like the former Harvard professor, was placed on the Court to bury the judicial activism of the *Lochner* Era. Also like Frankfurter, Jackson's personal politics were relatively liberal on the subject of race. Yet he also shared Frankfurter's concern that those personal views must not guide his approach to the *Brown* decision.

Jackson's law clerk, the future Chief Justice William Rehnquist, advised him that "if this Court, because its members individually are 'liberal' and dislike segregation" vote to abolish it in *Brown*, then "it differs from the McReynolds court only in the kinds of litigants it favors and the kinds of special claims it protects." (Rehnquist, for what it is worth, disavowed this memo shortly after he was nominated to the Supreme Court in 1971, claiming that "the memorandum was prepared by me as a statement of Justice Jackson's tentative views for his own use.")[54]

Though Jackson did not go quite as far as Rehnquist did in his memo—Rehnquist specifically stated that "*Plessy v. Ferguson* was right and should be reaffirmed"[55]—the justice undoubtedly shared some of his law clerk's reluctance to overrule decades of precedent permitting segregation. Jackson noted that "almost a century of decisional law rendered by judges, many of whom risked their lives for the cause that produced" the Reconstruction Amendments "is almost unanimous in the view that the Amendment tolerated segregation by state action."[56]

"Policy decisions by the least democratic and the least representative of our branches of government are hard to justify," Jackson warned. Like Frankfurter, Jackson was born into an era when the Supreme Court stood for low wages and child labor. As a justice himself, Jackson's self-image depended upon his belief that he was engaged in something more than simply deciding what he wanted the law to be and writing those preferences into the Constitution.[57] This is what made him better than men such as Fuller, Brewer, McReynolds, and Sutherland, and it was the best shield he could offer against the excesses of his predecessors.

Even when faced with a question as simple as whether the Constitution's ban on race discrimination permitted black children to be excluded altogether from the facilities offered to white children, Jackson feared that he would repeat the sins of the *Lochner* Era if he defied precedent to reach a result he personally favored.

———

A FATAL HEART attack conspired to break this impasse. Nine months after the Court first heard arguments in *Brown*, while the justices were still wrestling with how to decide the case, Chief Justice Vinson died suddenly at the age of sixty-three. Shortly after hearing of the chief's death, in a sign that the former Harvard professor had already decided to cast his vote to end school segregation in *Brown*, Justice Frankfurter reportedly quipped that Vinson's death was "the first solid piece of evidence I've ever had that there really is a God."[58]

President Dwight Eisenhower, in what may have been payback for political maneuvering by California Governor Earl Warren that helped Eisenhower clinch the Republican presidential nomination in 1952,[59] named Warren as Vinson's replacement. When the newly constituted Warren Court met once again to discuss the fate of *Brown*, the new chief justice immediately cast his lot against Jim Crow. "We can't set one group apart from the rest of us and say they are not entitled to [the] same treatment as all others," Warren told his new colleagues. The Reconstruction Amendments "were intended to make equal those who once were slaves."[60]

The significance of Warren's pronouncement was obvious to each of the other eight justices. A year ago, under Vinson's leadership, there were only four certain votes to end school segregation. Now the only question was whether the justices would stand together when they stuck the knife in Southern apartheid.

The value of unanimity was not lost on the members of the Court. Justice Clark announced that he would support a decision striking school segregation—provided that the Court did not require the South to change too quickly—almost immediately after Warren's vote made the outcome in *Brown* inevitable. Justice Frankfurter told a former law clerk that he feared a divided decision could trigger such resistance from the South that the Court's order would become unenforceable. When Justice Reed was the lone holdout preparing a dissent upholding segregation, Warren dissuaded him with a warning—"Stan, you're all by yourself in this now." Not wanting to bear the blame for the South's backlash against *Brown*, Reed signed onto Warren's opinion.[61]

Justice Jackson, who'd been confined to a hospital bed for nearly two months due to a heart attack of his own, defied his doctor's orders and returned to the bench for the day *Brown* was announced. He, too, wanted to present a united bench on the day the Court struck down one of the core elements of Jim Crow.[62]

And so on May 17, 1954, the Supreme Court of the United States grievously wounded the Constitution of John Archibald Campbell—and they did so unanimously. For several reasons, however the wound was not yet mortal.

The first is that, although the Court was willing to declare school segregation unconstitutional, it wasn't yet willing to do much about it. One year after *Brown*, the justices handed down another unanimous decision holding that desegregation need only move forward "with all deliberate speed." Local judges, many of whom owed their jobs to their relationships with segregationist senators, would supervise school integration. And local officials would have the "primary responsibility" for determining how to implement *Brown* in light of the unique conditions within their school districts.[63]

White Southerners received this decision as if Earl Warren had personally ridden on horseback to Appomattox Courthouse in order to surrender the Union's armies. Florida lawmakers broke into cheers when they learned of the decision, and a Louisiana legislator labeled it "the mildest decree the Supreme Court possibly could have handed down." A Virginia politician mused that "the court has not the courage of its previously avowed convictions," and a segregationist from Florida decided that the Court "realized it made a mistake in May and is getting out of it the best way it can."[64]

Though Southern resistance to *Brown* was inevitable, the Court's timid implementation order undoubtedly emboldened the resisters. Eighty-one Southern members of Congress signed a "Southern Manifesto" pledging to "use all lawful means to bring about a reversal of this decision which is contrary to the Constitution."[65] Several schools in Virginia refused to open entirely rather than permit black students to be educated alongside white ones.[66] After Governor Orval Faubus deployed the Arkansas National Guard to prevent nine black students from attending Little Rock Central High School, President Eisenhower had to deploy twelve hundred paratroopers to Little Rock to protect the students.[67]

And the South's campaign of resistance was wildly successful for many years. In 1959, just forty of North Carolina's three hundred thousand African American students attended integrated schools. Forty-two of Nashville's twelve thousand black students attended desegregated schools in 1960.[68]

After a Virginia county closed its public schools and set up an elaborate scheme to thwart desegregation by means of tuition grants to private academies, the Court finally admitted that its call for gradual implementation of *Brown* was not working. "There has been entirely too much deliberation and not enough speed," a frustrated Justice Black wrote in his majority opinion—an opinion issued ten years after *Brown*. The original desegregation plaintiffs, Black noted, "have doubtless all passed high school age."[69]

Yet, despite the Court's initial reluctance to ensure that *Brown* would be meaningfully enforced, it is easy to imagine a much darker opinion emerging from the Court's deliberations over public school segregation. If Jimmy Byrnes had remained on the Court, the vote Justice Minton cast for integration would have instead belonged to the man from South Carolina. Similarly, if President Herbert Hoover had succeeded in appointing Judge John J. Parker to the Court, that may have added another vote in favor of segregation. If Hugo Black had behaved more like a former Klansman might have been expected to behave, and if Chief Justice Fred M. Vinson had not died when he did, then *Brown v. Board of Education* might now be remembered as one of the greatest civil rights defeats of the twentieth century.

Indeed, history would have been quite different if only President Eisenhower had been more diligent in screening his Supreme Court nominees.

Although Eisenhower respected the rule of law enough to order troops to Little Rock in order to enforce the Supreme Court's order, he was privately unamused by Chief Justice Warren's most famous opinion. Southern whites, Eisenhower told Warren at a White House dinner, "are not bad people. All they are concerned about is to see that their sweet little girls are not required to sit in school alongside some big overgrown Negroes."[70] Eisenhower later described the Warren appointment as the "biggest damned-fool mistake I ever made."[71]

In spite of the slow progress achieved by *Brown*, the nearly sixteen years that Earl Warren served as chief justice were nonetheless one of the most transformative periods in American constitutional history. For the first time since Reconstruction, the justices gave real meaning to the Constitution's ban on racial apartheid. The Warren Court invigorated the Bill of Rights. It gave dissenting voices the freedom to speak openly without fear of arrest.[72] It barred police from indiscriminately listening in on people's phone calls.[73] And it restored democracy to states that had abandoned the basic rule that every person gets one, and exactly one, vote.[74] Constitutional rights that had lain dormant for nearly a century roared back to life thanks to the Warren Court, and the Fourteenth Amendment finally represented something more than a shield over the rich and the powerful.

The Warren Court was one of the great anomalies of American history—a brief period when the Supreme Court read the Constitution and saw some of the many ways it was intended to make American lives better. And we owe this period to a series of historical accidents. If Byrnes had remained on the Court; if Black hadn't rejected his racist past; if Vinson hadn't died; or if Eisenhower hadn't made two damned-fool mistakes—he later listed his appointment of Justice William Brennan, a reliable vote in favor of the Warren Court's landmark decisions, as a second mistake akin to the Warren appointment[75]—then the constitutional revival of the Warren era could have never happened.

Like all anomalies, this revival could not last forever. Future presidents typically put a great deal more thought into their Supreme Court nominations than President Eisenhower did.

Chapter 9

SHOULD WE DOUBLE OUR WEALTH AND CONQUER THE STARS

O N THE EVE of their trip to Mississippi, hundreds of young civil rights volunteers gathered in Ohio to be trained in how to educate Southern black children and how to register their parents to vote.

They were taught to assume the fetal position when they were being beaten, rolled into a knot with their arms protecting their head.[1]

They were taught not to wear sandals, and that "a T-shirt will save you some skin if you are being dragged on your stomach."[2]

They role-played how to behave when confronted by an angry white plantation owner with a shotgun. Or by white state troopers on a lonely highway. Or when they received a phone call warning them to leave town by midnight or else the black family they were staying with would be attacked and their house burned down.[3]

The volunteers were forbidden from carrying guns, civil rights leader Bob Moses explained to them, because Southern police might murder armed civil rights workers and then claim self-defense. But Moses also told them something else: "if you were in a house which was under attack, and the owner was shot, and there were kids there, and you could take his gun to protect them—should you? I can't answer that. I don't think anyone can answer that."[4]

Moses did not hide the dangers these young volunteers would face in the heart of Jim Crow—"the way some people characterize this project is that it is an attempt to get some people killed so that the federal government will move into Mississippi."[5] If generations of lynchings, show trials, Klan violence, and outright massacres could not inspire Washington to act, then maybe seeing the blood-soaked children of white Northerners beaten on the nightly news would be enough to trigger action.

Four years earlier, three black men and women walked into a burger joint in Nashville and asked to be served at a whites-only lunch counter. The black patrons were not served. Instead, the waitress poured a bucket of water on their heads and dumped detergent down their backs. She turned a hose on these customers and then jacked up the air-conditioning as high as it would go in an effort to freeze them out of the building.[6]

The three black patrons remained at that lunch counter until they were relieved by two other black men—one of whom was future Congressman John Lewis. Upon seeing his new customers, the manager announced that the restaurant was closed, locked the two black men inside, and then turned on a fumigator intended to kill vermin.[7]

The only thing that saved Lewis and his companion from the choking fumes was a passerby who, mistaking the toxic cloud spewing from the restaurant for smoke, called the fire department. When he saw firefighters about to break through the restaurant's windows, the restaurant's manager unlocked the door, freeing the two black men from his makeshift gas chamber.[8]

Nor was this the only time Lewis faced death at the hands of Southern racists. In one of the most famous instances of Southern violence during the civil rights era, Lewis and fellow civil rights leader Hosea Williams led a voting rights march of six hundred people in 1965 across the Edmund Pettus Bridge in Selma, Alabama, where they were confronted by what Lewis later described as "a sea of blue-helmeted, blue-uniformed Alabama state troopers."[9]

Shortly after the marchers knelt and began to pray in front of the line after line of policemen sent to stop them in their tracks, they were beset by men armed with billy clubs, bullwhips, tear gas, and, in at least one case, a rubber hose wrapped with barbed wire.[10] Lewis still bears visible scars from when a state trooper struck him in the head.

Meanwhile, Southern resistance to *Brown* continued to bear fruit for segregationists. In 1964, the year that Justice Black lamented that there'd been "entirely too much deliberation and not enough speed" in response to the *Brown* decision, just over one Southern black child in one hundred attended a racially integrated school.[11]

Ultimately, the first ten years of *Brown v. Board of Education* did more to demonstrate that the Supreme Court was either unable or unwilling to tear down Jim Crow than it did to establish the justices as grand defenders of civil rights. What finally turned the tide against massive resistance to *Brown* wasn't Hugo Black's frustration over too much deliberation, but the fact that Congress decided to get off the sidelines and join the fight for integration on the side of African Americans.

The landmark Civil Rights Act of 1964 empowered the Justice Department to file suits against segregated school systems—a role that previously had been left almost entirely to lawyers at the NAACP Legal Defense Fund—and it enabled federal officials to withhold funding from segregated schools. As a result, segregation finally began to buckle. The percentage of Southern black children attending integrated schools increased nearly sixfold in the first two years after the Civil Rights Act took effect. Admittedly, this meant that only a little more than six percent of black children were educated in desegregated schools. Within five years, however, nearly a third of Southern black children attended integrated schools. By 1973, as many as 90 percent did so.[12]

Nevertheless, Jim Crow's reach extended far beyond segregated school districts. It was a monster nurtured by widespread terrorism against African Americans, and fed as much by private sector discrimination as by official state action. It also thrived on the sheer creativity of Southern racists. As President Lyndon Johnson warned in his 1965 address responding to the bloody march in Selma, "every device of which human ingenuity is capable" was used in the South to deny African Americans the right to vote.[13]

These devices proved quite resistant to judicial remedies, as did racism stemming from private businesses. Only Congress, acting pursuant to authority that the *Lochner* Era Court would never have permitted it to exercise, proved capable of desegregating workplaces and lunch counters and of protecting African Americans' right to vote.

Indeed, in the end, the most important thing the Warren Court did to advance racial justice was not the *Brown* decision. It was its willingness to get out of the way once Congress decided to confront Jim Crow.

———

THE WARREN COURT completely abandoned *Lochner*ism and the broader idea that judges should set the nation's economic policy—as a unanimous Court announced in 1955:

> the day is gone when this Court uses the Due Process Clause of the Fourteenth Amendment to strike down state laws, regulatory of business and industrial conditions, because they may be unwise, improvident, or out of harmony with a particular school of thought. . . . For protection against abuses by legislatures the people must resort to the polls, not to the courts.[14]

The Warren Court's embrace of democracy did not eliminate the factions who believe laws intended to protect the least fortunate to be un-American or unconstitutional; it merely shifted the battlefield where they would make these arguments.

As Justice Robert H. Jackson's law clerk, William Rehnquist appealed to his boss's fear that a decision ending school segregation would replicate the sins of the *Lochner* Era. The New Deal Court, Rehnquist wrote in his memo urging Jackson to reaffirm *Plessy*, "called a halt to" justices "reading [their] own economic views into the Constitution." Similarly, Rehnquist claimed that the plaintiffs in *Brown* asked the Court to "read its own sociological views into the Constitution."[15]

More than a decade later, however, the future Chief Justice of the United States sounded a whole lot like Justice Stephen Johnson Field and the Liberty League. By 1964, Rehnquist had moved to Phoenix, Arizona, and entered the private practice of law. That year, the Phoenix City Council considered an ordinance that would ban race discrimination at lunch counters and other places of public accommodation. To the man who once defended *Plessy* to Justice Jackson, this ordinance was nothing less than an attack on "the right to manage your own affairs as free as possible from the interference of government." Rehnquist was one of only three people who testified against the proposed ordinance before the city council, claiming that "there has never been this sort of an assault on the institution" of private property. Business owners, he insisted, could not be told "who can come" into their place of business.[16]

When the ordinance passed despite Rehnquist's objections, he authored a letter to the editor of the *Arizona Republic* that laid out his objections in more detail. In one respect, Rehnquist's letter was more moderate than his claim as a law clerk that "*Plessy v. Ferguson* was right and should be re-affirmed."[17] Race discrimination by the government itself, Rehnquist wrote in his letter, was out of bounds: "all of us alike pay taxes to support the operation of government, and all should be treated alike by it, whether in the area of voting rights, use of government-owned facilities, or other activities."

Yet, although the somewhat older Rehnquist rejected state-sponsored racism, he also believed discrimination by private businesses to be an entirely different animal. Phoenix's anti-discrimination ordinance, Rehnquist complained, "does away with the historic right of the owner of a drug store, lunch counter, or theatre to choose his own customers."[18] More than just an attack on property owners' rights, Rehnquist suggested that the anti-discrimination ordinance was fundamentally un-American. "The founders of this nation thought of it as the 'land of the free' just as surely as they thought of it as the 'land of the equal,'" and when laws "substitute for the decision of each businessman as to how he shall select his customers . . . we give up a measure of our traditional freedom."[19]

Though Rehnquist's letter does not explicitly mention either the Constitution or the Supreme Court, his vision of property owners free to exclude anyone they choose from their businesses finds strong support in the *Lochner*ism Rehnquist once denounced in an effort to convince his boss to sustain *Plessy*. Just three years after *Lochner*, the justices claimed that government may not "compel any person in the course of his business and against his will to accept or retain the personal services of another" in order to strike down a law prohibiting discrimination against unionized workers.[20] More than half a century later, Rehnquist made virtually the same argument—that government may not compel any person in the course of business to serve another—to explain his opposition to a law prohibiting discrimination against racial minorities.

If Rehnquist had not gained the ear of a prominent senator, it is possible that his belief that property rights trump civil rights would have been forgotten not long after his letter appeared in the *Arizona Republic*. Rehnquist, however, had an especially well-connected friend within his state's Republican Party. One of the named partners at his law firm was Denison Kitchel, who had run Barry Goldwater's first successful bid for the US Senate and gone on to serve as general counsel for the Arizona State Republican Committee. Kitchel would also run Goldwater's far less successful campaign for the presidency in 1964.[21]

Two years before that presidential campaign began, President John F. Kennedy ordered federal troops to Oxford, Mississippi, to quell a wave of violence sparked by James Meredith's effort to become the first black student at the University of Mississippi. Senator Goldwater immediately denounced the Kennedy administration's efforts on behalf of Meredith. "I don't like segregation," Goldwater claimed, "but I don't like the Constitution kicked around, either."[22]

Not long after Goldwater declared Kennedy's actions unconstitutional, Kitchel asked Rehnquist to draft a brief evaluating whether the senator was right about the Constitution. To his credit, Rehnquist concluded that Goldwater was not correct—Kennedy acted lawfully when he stood with Meredith and against Jim Crow—and Rehnquist's brief convinced even Goldwater to change his mind.[23]

When Goldwater had to decide whether to vote for the Civil Rights Act of 1964, with its bans on discrimination by employers, hotel owners, restaurants, and many other private businesses, Goldwater turned again to Rehnquist for advice on whether the act was constitutional. This time, Rehnquist offered an opinion similar to the one he had expressed in the *Arizona Republic*. The Constitution did not permit bans on private discrimination.[24]

On the surface, Barry Goldwater seemed an unlikely champion for the cause of segregation. Goldwater was not a white supremacist. Nor did he believe in separating white people from people of color. Goldwater supported the civil rights legislation that passed Congress in 1957 and in 1960. And his presidential campaign literature touted his support for integrating the Arizona Air National Guard when he served as its chief of staff, as well as his support for desegregating Phoenix's municipal facilities when he served on its city council.[25]

In the end, however, Goldwater embraced Rehnquist's view that the Constitution places racist business owners on a higher plane than the people excluded from their businesses. After hearing Rehnquist's advice, Goldwater sought a second opinion from Robert Bork, the Yale law professor whom President Ronald Reagan would try, unsuccessfully, to place on the Supreme Court in 1987.[26] Yet Goldwater must have known what Bork would tell him about the Civil Rights Act. In a 1963 article published in the *New Republic*, Bork echoed Rehnquist's distinction between laws forbidding official racism and laws targeting private discrimination. "It is one thing," the Yale professor wrote, "when stubborn people express their racial antipathies in laws which prevent individuals . . . from dealing with those who are willing to deal with them, and quite another to tell them that even as individuals they may not act on their racial preferences in particular areas of life." Bork then authored a passage that would play a prominent role in the campaign to keep him off the Supreme

Court more than two decades later. The principle behind a federal ban on whites-only lunch counters "is that if I find your behavior ugly by my standards, moral or aesthetic, and if you prove stubborn about adopting my view of the situation, I am justified in having the state coerce you into more righteous paths. That is itself a principle of unsurpassed ugliness."[27]

Goldwater's speech on the Senate floor announcing that he would oppose the Civil Rights Act shared little of Bork's stridence. Yet it reached a very similar conclusion. Though Goldwater began his speech by claiming that he is "unalterably opposed to discrimination or segregation on the basis of race, color, or creed," he had decided that abstract principles were more important than freeing African Americans from Jim Crow. The senator singled out the act's two provisions prohibiting private businesses from engaging in discrimination, saying that he could find "no constitutional basis for the exercise of Federal regulatory authority in either of these areas; and I believe the attempted usurpation of such power to be a grave threat to the very essence of our basic system of government."[28]

At least initially, the "grave threat" Goldwater perceived was subtly different from the concern for racist business owners forced to do business with African Americans that Rehnquist and Bork expressed in their public writings. In his Senate floor speech, Goldwater worried that if the *federal* government, as opposed to state lawmakers, had the power to forbid whites-only lunch counters and race discrimination in employment, then this power would undermine a system "in which 50 sovereign States have reserved to themselves and to the people those powers not specifically granted to the Central or Federal Government."[29] Where Rehnquist and Bork claimed that property rights must triumph over civil rights, Goldwater was far more concerned about states' rights. (Though, it should be noted that he subsequently delivered another speech in which he claimed that the civil rights law also violated the "freedom not to associate.")[30]

In essence, Goldwater felt the same fear that drove the Supreme Court to ban federal child labor laws nearly a half century earlier. Just like Goldwater, the five justices responsible for *Hammer v.*

Dagenhart worried that if they were to permit federal regulation of employment, then "the power of the States over local matters may be eliminated, and, thus, our system of government be practically destroyed."[31]

Nevertheless, there is an important distinction to be drawn between Goldwater's actions and those of the justices who decided cases like *Dagenhart* and *Lochner*. Goldwater misunderstood the Constitution, and his decision to place states' rights ahead of civil rights was morally myopic. But there is nothing illegitimate about a US Senator voting against a particular bill for whatever reason they choose. The premise of a representative democracy is that the electorate chooses men and women who will have wide discretion to vote for the bills that these representatives deem good and to vote against bills they deem wicked or wrongheaded. Goldwater's mandate flowed from an election that he won in the state of Arizona, and that electoral victory gave him the constitutional legitimacy, if not necessarily the moral right, to cast a vote against civil rights.

The same cannot be said about the justices of the Supreme Court, however. Justices are not elected, and their mandate flows from the Constitution's text and their duty to interpret it in good faith. What makes *Lochner* and *Dagenhart* so offensive is not simply the needless suffering caused by these two decisions, it is the fact that there is nothing whatsoever in the Constitution that gives the Supreme Court the power to set America's labor policy.

The problem for Goldwater—and for people who have at times shared similar views—is that Goldwater's concept of the government's proper role rarely, if ever, enjoys anything even approaching majority support from the American electorate. Goldwater lost his race against President Johnson in a landslide. So did Alf Landon after the Liberty League framed his race with Franklin Roosevelt as a battle between the Constitution of Stephen Johnson Field and the Constitution of the United States. This may explain why hardline conservatives have so frequently turned to the courts to implement their policy preferences, but it cannot excuse it. If American government truly derives its legitimacy from the consent of the governed, then an agenda that is so often and so soundly rejected at the polls must not be implemented by the one unelected branch of government when there is no constitutional basis to do so.

At least in the South, however, white supremacists did not need to control the Supreme Court in order to control their state's policies—or the votes that their senators and representatives would cast in Congress. Democracy, it turns out, does not mean much at all if many of the voters cannot vote.

———

FOR EIGHTY-TWO LONG years, from 1875 until 1957, Congress did not pass a single civil rights bill. Indeed, this was true even when such legislation enjoyed majority support. Five civil rights bills passed the House between the end of World War II and 1957, but none of them survived contact with the Senate.[32]

The reason for this inability to legislate was the filibuster, which allowed Southern white supremacists to block any bill they chose, so long as they could convince just a handful of conservatives outside the South to join their obstruction of the legislative process.[33] Moreover, because Southern voting officials ensured that few black voters would actually get to cast meaningful ballots, white supremacist lawmakers faced no consequences for their opposition to civil rights.

The Jim Crow South was largely a collection of one-party states— between 1916 and 1944, for example, the Republican presidential candidate won more than 5 percent of the vote in South Carolina just one time.[34] Thus, the winner of a Democratic primary in the South was virtually guaranteed election, and general elections were largely formalities. For this reason, segregationists could exclude African Americans from the franchise entirely by preventing them from voting in Democratic Party primaries.

In 1923, one state tried to do just that by enacting a law providing that "in no event shall a negro be eligible to participate in a Democratic party primary election held in the State of Texas"— though this first attempt to suppress the black vote did not end well for Texas. The Supreme Court struck down the law in a unanimous opinion proclaiming that "it seems to us hard to imagine a more direct and obvious infringement of the Fourteenth [Amendment]."[35] Even Justice James Clark McReynolds joined this opinion.

This decision, according to the Texas legislature, created "an emergency with a need for immediate action" and the lawmakers quickly replaced the unconstitutional law with a new one providing that "every political party in this State through its State Executive Committee shall have the power to prescribe the qualifications of its own members and shall in its own way determine who shall be qualified to vote or otherwise participate in such political party." Not long thereafter, the state Democratic Party's executive committee enacted a resolution providing that only "white democrats" may participate in their primary.[36]

Though the Court also struck this law down, in 1932, it did so over a dissent from McReynolds and the other members of the Four Horsemen. The Texas law itself, McReynolds claimed, "withholds nothing from any negro." Instead, it merely recognized the Democratic Party's power to "prescribe qualifications for membership." According to McReynolds it was the Party, not the state, that denied voting rights to African Americans. And the Constitution has nothing to say about discrimination by a private organization such as a political party.[37]

Three weeks after the Court's second decision striking down Texas's white-primary scheme, the state's Democrats took matters into their own hands. Acting pursuant to no state law whatsoever, the Party enacted a resolution at its convention providing that only "white citizens" may vote in a Democratic primary.[38] This time, the justices unanimously sided with the segregationists.

Recall that the Fourteenth Amendment provides that "no state" shall "deny to any person within its jurisdiction the equal protection of the laws," and the Fifteenth Amendment provides that "the right of citizens of the United States to vote shall not be denied or abridged by the United States or by any State on account of race, color, or previous condition of servitude." In both cases, the amendments indicate that only government actors—a "state" or the "United States"—are bound by their prohibitions against race discrimination.

Although the two previous white-primary cases struck down a state law that mandated segregation—or at least entangled the state with the process that Texas Democrats used to exclude black voters—this case involved a political party acting on its own. "The qualifications of citizens to participate in party counsels and to vote at party primaries have been declared by the representatives of the party in convention assembled," Justice Owen J. Roberts explained in *Grovey v. Townsend* (1935), "and this action upon its face is not state action."[39] The Texas Democratic Party was not an arm of the government, according to *Grovey*, and therefore it was immune to the Constitution's prohibition on racial voter suppression.

Grovey did not last long. Less than a decade later, the Supreme Court overruled it in the landmark *Smith v. Allwright* (1944) decision.[40] But *Grovey* lasted just long enough to validate a strategy that animated the South's resistance to black voting rights—if the court strikes down one voter suppression practice, just keep coming up with new ones until the courts back off.

Segregationists were nothing if not creative in their efforts to drive African Americans away from the polls. When the Supreme Court said Texas could not disenfranchise black voters directly, they tried to do so indirectly. When that failed, they let party delegates do it for them. And when this tactic failed nearly ten years later, white racists could fall back on poll taxes, or literacy tests, or any of a myriad of other devices intended to keep black voters from the polls. Black voter registration actually did rise in the years following *Smith*, but it rose to only 20 percent of Southern black adults by the year 1952—meaning that at least 4 out of 5 African Americans were still excluded from the polls.[41]

Voter registrars in the South often wielded absolute authority over who could or could not register to vote. As President Johnson told the nation after Selma, "the Negro citizen may go to register only to be told that the day is wrong, or the hour is late, or the official in charge is absent." And should they succeed in speaking to a registrar, a black voter "may be disqualified because he did not spell out his middle name or because he abbreviated a word on the application."[42]

Should they succeed in filling out their application, they may be given a literacy test. A black voter "may be asked to recite the entire Constitution, or explain the most complex provisions of State law. And even a college degree cannot be used to prove that he can read or write."[43]

Nor was this the limit of the obstacles placed before African Americans seeking to vote. Some registrars would only permit voters to register in secret locations at unannounced times, relying on whites to discover where and when to present themselves through word of mouth. Or they would demand that they answer impossible questions such as "how many bubbles are in a bar of soap?" In one Louisiana parish, the registrar refused to register any black voter who couldn't produce three white character witnesses who were personally known to the registrar.[44]

And even if these barriers failed to keep black voters away from the polls, segregationists had yet another tactic at their disposal— terrorism.

In rural Florida, the Klan mailed letters to African Americans warning them that if they cast a vote they would wind up "floating up and down in the river." In Mississippi, the *Jackson Daily News* published the names of voting rights advocates and warned black voters to avoid Democratic primaries "to prevent unhealthy and unhappy results." When Etoy Fletcher, a black veteran, tried to register to vote, the registrar told him that "niggers are not allowed to vote in Rankin County." He was later jumped by four white men who drove him into the woods, beat and flogged him, then warned him that he would be killed if he tried to vote again. In Georgia, the leader of a local NAACP branch was beaten for encouraging African Americans to vote. Two white men who murdered one of those voters were acquitted by an all-white jury.[45]

The courts were powerless to address such terrorism absent aggressive executive action. Even when the Klan's actions were criminalized by federal law, such laws are useless unless federal agents investigate the crimes and prosecutors file the appropriate charges. "The judiciary," as Alexander Hamilton wrote more than two centuries ago, "has no influence over either the sword or the purse." It "may truly be said to have neither force nor will . . . and must ultimately depend upon the aid of the executive arm even for the efficacy of its judgments."[46]

Segregationists, moreover, could often develop new ways of disenfranchising black voters faster than courts could strike the old ways down. When the Supreme Court struck down Texas's white-primary system, white Democrats simply found a new way to reinstate it. When white primaries were outlawed altogether, voter registrars could pick up most of the slack. Even if a judge systematically culled a county's voter suppression tactics, striking down literacy tests and poll taxes and secret voter registration offices, the county could simply enact new policies intended to achieve the same goals.

Nor could courts act on their own. The Constitution does not permit federal courts to take any action whatsoever unless a plaintiff who has experienced a legal injury sues whoever is responsible for that injury.[47] In the Jim Crow South, this meant that courts could not do anything to advance voting rights until a black voter voluntarily agreed to file a lawsuit—an action that could immediately make that voter a target of Klan intimidation or worse.[48]

Meanwhile, the lawyers who brought these suits could also be victims of underhanded tactics. In Alabama, one black attorney who filed a voting rights lawsuit was arrested and then convicted of representing clients without their authorization—after a sheriff intimidated the lawyer's clients into withdrawing that authorization. Upon his conviction, the lawyer was disbarred, thereby ensuring that he wouldn't file any more voting rights cases.[49]

If no voter who was willing to serve as a plaintiff stepped forward right away—or if no attorney was willing or able to file the lawsuit on the voter's behalf—then several elections could take place before any judge had the opportunity to determine whether African Americans were being denied the right to vote. By that point, the officials elected by these tainted elections could have been in office for years.

———

THE VIOLENCE IN Selma that targeted John Lewis and his fellow marchers in 1965 occurred more than twenty years after the Court struck down the white-primary system, and more than a decade after it proclaimed school segregation unconstitutional in *Brown*. Moreover, the events on the Edmund Pettus Bridge were nothing more than the latest in an unbroken string of terrorist attacks on black people that stretched all the way back to Colfax, and before then to the first time a master raised his whip against an African slave.

It was easy for many Americans to ignore this violence when it was largely an abstraction, a sad history people read about in books or in newspapers, if at all. But the events in Selma were made all too real when millions of Americans turned on the evening news to see peaceful protesters being gassed, clubbed, and trampled by white segregationists on horseback. ABC broke into its broadcast of *Judgment at Nuremberg*, a film that incorporates actual footage of Nazi atrocities, to present a breaking news broadcast detailing the events in Selma. When their television screens switched from scenes from Nazi Germany to much more recent footage from Alabama, many viewers believed they were still witnessing scenes from the Third Reich.[50]

The plot of *Judgment at Nuremberg* focuses on the postwar trial of four German judges who acquiesced in the murder of innocents—one of whom is the internationally respected legal scholar Ernst Janning. As the film approaches its climax, a repentant Janning explains how he could send an innocent Jew to his death based on trumped up allegations that the man had sex with an Aryan woman in violation of Nazi Germany's law:

> it was the old, old story of the sacrificial lamb. . . . What difference does it make if a few racial minorities lose their rights? It is only

a passing phase. It is only a stage we are going through. It will be discarded sooner or later. Hitler himself will be discarded—sooner or later.[51]

At the conclusion of his testimony, Janning denounces his three co-defendants—labeling one of them a "decayed, corrupt bigot, obsessed by the evil within himself"—and then he denounces himself as "worse than any of them because he knew what they were, and he went along with them."[52]

Janning might as well have been speaking directly to the millions of Americans who knew about the South's reign of terror but had done nothing to stop it. At the very moment that ABC's viewers were asking how so many of the German people could have stood silently as Hitler rose to power, they were confronted with an opportunity to demonstrate that they would have acted differently.

Demonstrations erupted throughout the country showing solidarity with the men and women beaten in Selma. Hundreds of clergy traveled to Alabama to express their support for civil rights. Seventy million Americans watched a week later when Lyndon Johnson announced his response to a joint session of Congress.[53]

Johnson spoke to a nation enjoying one of the most robust periods of economic growth in its history—just a few months earlier, he had trounced Goldwater in the 1964 presidential election, bolstered by an eye-popping 5.8 percent annual growth rate in the nation's gross domestic product.[54] America emerged from World War II as the wealthiest and most powerful nation in the world. The New Deal rescued countless seniors from the poorhouse. It invigorated long-neglected regions of the nation, and it gave millions of Americans the opportunity to own a home. The children of the Depression knew a level of affluence that would have been unimaginable to their parents.

And yet, Johnson told the nation, all these accomplishments meant nothing so long as American apartheid still exists. "Should we defeat every enemy, should we double our wealth and conquer the stars, and still be unequal" to the problem of black inequality, "then we will have failed as a people and as a nation."[55]

If Southern officials would meet every attempt to enfranchise African Americans with new, more creative obstacles standing between black voters and the polls, then Johnson's solution was to tear down those obstacles before they were even built. The backbone of what became the Voting Rights Act of 1965 was a provision requiring states and localities with a history of excluding voters on the basis of race to "preclear" any new voting rules with federal officials in Washington, DC.[56] Under this provision, any new voting rule enacted in the heart of Jim Crow would be suspended immediately, and would not go into effect until a judge or the Department of Justice reviewed it to ensure that it would not disenfranchise people of color.

The Voting Rights Act eviscerated the South's ability to drive African Americans away from the polls. On the day President Johnson signed this act into law, Mississippi's black voter registration rate hovered below 7 percent. Only two years later, nearly 60 percent of eligible African Americans were registered to vote in Mississippi.[57] Just as the Civil Rights Act achieved what *Brown* could not in the area of public school segregation, the Voting Rights Act flung open the doors of American democracy that judges could only pound on in frustration.

The single most important thing the Supreme Court ever did for civil rights was not *Brown*. It was the Court's decision to do absolutely nothing when first confronted with the Civil Rights Act of 1964 and the Voting Rights Act of 1965. Not long after President Johnson signed the Civil Rights Act into law, a motel in Atlanta and a barbecue restaurant in Birmingham filed a pair of lawsuits objecting to the law on similar grounds to the arguments raised by men like Rehnquist, Bork, and Goldwater. Nevertheless, the justices unanimously upheld the law.[58] Less than two years later, they rejected a similar challenge to the Voting Rights Act.[59]

These three cases were the most important civil rights decisions of their era. By simply getting out of the way and allowing the federal government to do its job, the Warren Court did more to tear down Jim Crow than it could ever have accomplished on its own.

PART III

THE BRIEF RISE AND RAPID FALL OF CONSERVATIVE JUDICIAL RESTRAINT

Chapter 10

THE TRUCE

Two years after President Lyndon Johnson signed the Voting Rights Act, Newark erupted.

On a Wednesday night in July of 1967, two white police officers pulled over a taxi driver named John Smith, later claiming that Smith had "shot around" an intersection and then drove an entire block up the wrong side of the street. Though police reports alleged that Mr. Smith attacked the officers shortly after he was pulled over, Smith himself told a much different story. According to the taxi driver's testimony to a state commission, he never attacked the officers, was arrested with little provocation, and was attacked by one of the cops as the other drove him to the police station.[1]

As they rode together in the police car, Smith testified, the officer turned around, started punching him, and eventually struck Smith so hard in the groin that he was unable to walk from the car to the inside of the police station. Smith said he was then dragged towards the station, where as many as ten cops took him into a room and beat him "for a lengthy period of time." The beating continued after Smith was taken to a cell, where he said that police threw toilet water on him and struck him in the head with a gun butt.[2]

Had Smith been just an ordinary driver, it is possible that he would simply have spent the night in that jail cell, struggling to sleep against the pain caused by injuries that included a broken rib. But the story that police beat a fellow taxi driver without provocation soon began to travel across Newark's taxi radio network. As word spread to the nearby community, the other taxi drivers started shuttling public housing residents to a demonstration outside the police station. When representatives from this demonstration were allowed inside the station to see Mr. Smith, they discovered a bruised man lying on his cell bench with his eyes closed and in apparent physical pain. Smith had not yet received medical attention.[3]

At the urging of the demonstrators, Smith was taken to the hospital and treated for his injuries. The officer in charge of the police precinct also met with several of the protesters. As midnight approached, the protest leaders told the demonstrators to go home and return in the morning for a new demonstration at city hall.[4]

That's when the first Molotov cocktail struck the police station.[5] Six straight days of looting and riots followed.

By 2:20 a.m. on Friday morning, Newark Mayor Hugh Addonizio realized he had lost control of his city. He called the governor to request help from state police and the National Guard. By Saturday, nearly four thousand troops occupied Newark, and they established a perimeter around fourteen square miles of city blocks in an effort to contain the riots. Thousands of poor families, unable to afford freezers and dependent on daily trips to the grocery store to feed themselves, sheltered in their homes and tried to ignore their hunger.[6] By the time the rioters grew quiet, twenty-six people were dead.

In many neighborhoods, the police and guardsmen sent to quell the riot proved more dangerous than the rioters themselves. Black business owners identified their stores by painting the words "Soul Brother" on their windows, in the hopes that this would encourage looters to pass over their businesses. To their horror, several of them later testified, these words seemed to attract unwanted attention from the state police force.

One woman, who lived behind her dry-cleaning shop with her husband, testified that they awoke to the sound of breaking glass and rose to discover state troopers robbing their cash register. When they fled upstairs to avoid a confrontation with the troopers, they saw the police open fire on a nearby candy store.[7]

Another man, who owned a photography studio, saw a man in a state police car shoot out the plate glass window where the business owner had written the words "Soul Brother."

A laundry owner named Bow Woo Wong awoke to discover that someone—not himself—had written "Soul Brother" on the outside of his business. Three bullets decorated Mr. Wong's window.

When a woman went to her own restaurant to investigate its ringing burglar alarm, she was confronted by two carloads of state police. Bullet holes riddled the restaurant. Yet, when she accused the cops of causing this destruction, one officer responded "we will shoot you if you don't get back upstairs."[8]

Meanwhile, on the streets of Newark, trigger-happy guardsmen mistook ordinary noises for sniper fire and began firing back at imaginary enemies. One Newark police officer started firing down an open street when he heard gunshots a block away. The source of the gunshots was another cop who had shot out a street light, believing that darkness would protect him from snipers. Two policemen entered a railroad station at opposite ends of the building, and somehow managed to get in a gun fight with each other.[9]

The children of Eloise Spellman, a forty-one-year-old widow, watched her die when bullets fired by guardsmen and state troopers tore into their home on the tenth floor of a housing project. Police shot a young man named James Rutledge after they caught him rummaging through a closed-down bar, then placed a knife next to the body and claimed that Rutledge tried to attack them. After a horrified state trooper discovered that he or his fellow officers had shot fifty-three-year-old Hattie Gainer, it took three hours for an ambulance to collect her.[10]

A state commission tasked with investigating the causes of the riots found sharp disagreement between Newark's black residents and its dwindling white population. African Americans listed "bad housing," unemployment, and "overcrowding of Negro areas" among the primary causes of the discontent that grew into the riots. Although the commission found no evidence of intentional discrimination, white residents who qualified for public housing were more likely to live in more desirable low-rise developments, while African Americans often wound up in crime-ridden high-rise buildings. Additionally, nearly half of the city's black residents complained of police brutality.[11]

The riots occurred amidst a dramatic shift in Newark's demographics. In the seven years before the riots, sixty thousand white residents left the city. Meanwhile, a similar number of African Americans, mostly from the South, and Hispanic individuals took up residence within Newark's city limits. Yet, although Newark's population remained largely stable during this shift, the new residents were generally less affluent than the people leaving the city— and thus less able to fund the city's operations with their tax dollars. The only way for the city to maintain its same level of services was to raise taxes, but this encouraged yet more affluent residents to flee the city. The result was a death spiral in which white flight begat tax hikes, which begat more white flight.[12]

Another legacy of the city's rapid demographic changes was an almost entirely white police force. Although more than half of Newark's population was black in 1967, only 10 percent of the city's cops were also African American. Moreover, all but 9 of the city's 145 black officers were the lowest possible rank, and fewer than half of the relatively senior officers held command positions.[13]

The state commission's survey found that 70 percent of Newark's black residents believed that police paid more attention to complaints from whites than they did to complaints from African Americans. Many complained that police did not respond at all to calls for assistance, and women complained that police "treat every black woman as if she were a prostitute." Although fears of police brutality were common in Newark's black community, many residents were afraid to register complaints. When victims of brutality did complain, they rarely learned that any action had been taken against the offending officer.[14]

And yet, although Newark's black communities complained about substandard housing, diminishing public services, and a police department that, at best, was inattentive to their needs, the city's white residents blamed the riot on a very different set of causes. "Outside troublemakers," "criminals and hoodlums," and the "search for excitement" were the leading causes of the Newark riots, according to the city's whites. Black residents complained of police brutality; Newark's whites complained that the police were "too soft" on the rioters.[15]

The Newark riot, in other words, exposed very specific kinds of discontent among blacks and whites. African Americans were likely to view the violence in Newark as the result of years of legitimate grievances that had been bottled up and shaken until finally they exploded, whites were far more inclined to dismiss the rioters as "criminals and hoodlums." To many white Americans, Newark, and a similar riot that began in Detroit just a week and a half later, were signs that law and order were breaking down in the United States.[16]

And no one was better poised to exploit this fear than Richard Nixon.

───────────

AS VICE PRESIDENT, Nixon was often a champion of civil rights. Nixon encouraged President Dwight Eisenhower to agree to a meeting with Martin Luther King Jr., and he was a strong supporter of the 1957 Civil Rights Act that broke nearly a century of congressional silence on racial justice. When the Senate voted, at Majority Leader Lyndon Johnson's urging, to effectively neuter much of the act's voter protections by allowing voting rights cases to be heard by hostile Southern juries, Nixon denounced this action as a "vote against the right to vote."[17]

Yet, by 1964, when Barry Goldwater was winning the hearts of Republican loyalists and Johnson was preparing to sign the ban on employment discrimination and whites-only lunch counters, Nixon's rhetoric on civil rights made a significant turn to the right. Speaking in Cincinnati, Nixon previewed the appeal to law and order that would play a starring role in his presidential campaign four years later.

Though Nixon never embraced Goldwater's hardline views—Nixon said that the civil rights bill Goldwater opposed should be a "great step forward in the struggle for equality of opportunity for all Americans"—he tempered his support for civil rights with a direct attack on the tactics that had made major civil rights legislation possible. "The encouragement of disrespect for law through mass demonstrations, boycotts, and violation of property rights," Nixon claimed, "harms rather than helps the cause of civil rights." Though "some justify such tactics on the ground that they may hasten the passage of laws . . . these tactics destroy the will of the people to obey those laws."[18]

Republicans, Nixon urged, "are a Party that was founded on the principle of the rule of law." Indeed, Nixon even recast the history of the GOP's first president to fit his law-and-order narrative—"Abraham Lincoln led the nation to war to maintain the rule of law in our land."[19]

As Nixon reframed the Civil War, the Warren Court was busy transforming much of America's criminal law. Justice Hugo Black's project to ensure that the Bill of Rights limited states' actions as surely as it limited the federal government had obvious implications for criminal justice. Many of the Bill of Rights' protections—from the freedom from "unreasonable searches and seizures" to the right to legal representation to the ban on "cruel and unusual punishments"—apply primarily in the criminal context.

But the Court did more than just formally extend these rights to people facing criminal charges in state courts. A core insight of many of the Warren Court's decisions is that the Bill of Rights must be enforced in a way that cannot easily be evaded by state officials and that applies equally to rich and poor alike. Thus, for example, in *Mapp v. Ohio* (1961),[20] the Court held that state prosecutors may not introduce evidence against a criminal defendant—no matter how serious the crime nor how clearly that evidence establishes the defendant's guilt—if the evidence was discovered in an unlawful search or seizure.[21]

The logic of this rule is that it is sometimes necessary to let the guilty go free in order to protect the innocent from overzealous law enforcement. "Only occasional and more flagrant abuses come to the attention of the courts," Justice Robert H. Jackson once explained, "and then only those where the search and seizure yields incriminating evidence and the defendant is at least sufficiently compromised to be indicted."[22] If police raid an innocent man's or woman's home and uncover no evidence, then there will be no arrest, and no subsequent criminal trial permitting a judge to determine if the raid was unconstitutional. More importantly, there will often be no way to sanction the police officers who authorized this raid, and, thus, nothing deterring them from conducting more illegal raids in the future.

Mapp held that the only way to "compel respect" for the Constitution's ban on unlawful searches and seizures is "by removing the incentive to disregard it." Police conduct illegal searches because they hope to find evidence of criminal activity, so the way to deter such activity is to render the fruit of these searches useless to the prosecution.[23]

Two years later, the Court reached a similar decision in *Gideon v. Wainwright* (1963).[24] Just as *Mapp* rested on the idea that the right to be free from unlawful searches means little unless the police have an incentive to honor that right, *Gideon* held that the Sixth Amendment right to "have the Assistance of Counsel" at a criminal trial was equally meaningless if the defendant cannot afford to hire an attorney. Worse, *Gideon* explained, our entire system of criminal justice is unreliable if indigent defendants don't have the assistance they need to defend themselves in court—"in our adversary system of criminal justice, any person haled into court, who is too poor to hire a lawyer, cannot be assured a fair trial unless counsel is provided for him."[25]

The culmination of this vision, which insisted that constitutional rights must be coupled with remedies sufficiently robust to ensure that the right is applied to everyone, was the Warren Court's decision in *Miranda v. Arizona* (1966).[26]

Miranda, which established the requirement that police warn suspects of their rights to remain silent and to have an attorney,[27] has become so familiar to anyone who has ever watched a police drama that even the conservative Chief Justice William Rehnquist conceded towards the end of his tenure on the Court that it is "part of our national culture."[28] Decades before the *Miranda* warnings became an integral part of every episode of *Law and Order*, however, the Warren Court feared that many suspects would be denied their constitutional rights simply because they did not know that those rights existed in the first place. "For those unaware of" their rights, the Court explained, "the warning is needed simply to make them aware of it."[29]

The backlash to *Miranda* began before it was even decided. Twenty-six state attorneys general filed a brief urging the Court to be cautious before it imposed new constitutional limits on police interrogations. Several of the nation's most respected jurists took the unusual step of publicly urging the Court to turn away from what it appeared ready to do in *Miranda*. Illinois Supreme Court Justice Walter Schaefer warned that the "logical conclusion" of a decision like *Miranda* would be that "no questioning of suspects will be permitted" at all.[30] On the day the Warren Court handed down its *Miranda* opinion, Justice Byron White warned in dissent that "the Court's rule will return a killer, a rapist or other criminal to the streets and to the environment which produced him, to repeat his crime whenever it pleases him."[31] Two years later, Congress passed a law purporting to override *Miranda* in federal prosecutions, although the Court eventually struck that law down.[32]

Miranda, and the Warren Court's record on criminal justice generally, also became a prominent villain in Richard Nixon's appeals to law and order. The *Miranda* decision, according to Nixon, "had the effect of seriously ham stringing the peace forces in our society and strengthening the criminal forces." During his first successful campaign for president, Nixon would rail about three cases where a cab driver, an elderly man, and an elderly woman were murdered by men who later confessed to the crime—but the murderers were "let off" because of "a Supreme Court decision."[33]

In laying out his vision of a more orderly society, Nixon carefully walked a line between Goldwater's radicalism and the too-permissive agenda he attributed to the Supreme Court. "Just three years ago," he began in a 1967 *Reader's Digest* article published in the wake of the Newark and Detroit riots, "this nation seemed to be completing its greatest decade of racial progress and entering one of the most hopeful periods in American history." Nixon then posed a provocative question to men and women who would elect him president a year later: "with this star of racial peace and progress before us, how did it happen that last summer saw the United States blazing in an inferno of urban anarchy?"[34]

Much of the blame for this "anarchy" rested in judges who "have gone too far in weakening the peace forces against the criminal forces." "The first responsibility of government and a primary responsibility of the judicial system," Nixon proclaimed, "is to guarantee to each citizen his primary civil right—the right to be protected from domestic violence." The "system," and, by implication, the Warren Court, "has failed dismally in this responsibility—and it cannot redeem itself by pointing to the conscientious manner in which it treats suspected criminals."[35]

Yet, for all of his appeals to law and order, there was another dimension to Nixon's attacks on the judiciary as well. Nixon did not share Goldwater's belief that the Constitution places strict limits on business regulation, and he certainly did not share the Four Horsemen's belief that it was the role of the Court to impose these limits upon an unwilling nation. Indeed, Nixon did far more than concede Franklin Roosevelt's position that judges have no business setting a nation's economic policy—he embraced this viewpoint as his own. "Some of our judges have gone too far," Nixon warned, "in assuming unto themselves a mandate which is not there . . . to put their social and economic ideas into their decisions."[36]

The antidote to this overreach was a similar remedy to the one Justice Felix Frankfurter once offered to the excesses of the Four Horsemen—judicial deference to the people who were actually elected to make policy. Nixon promised to appoint judges who "would see themselves as the caretakers of the Constitution, not super-legislators with a free hand to impose their social and political viewpoints upon the American people."[37]

The conservative president, in other words, was now driven by a sentiment similar to the one that led Franklin Delano Roosevelt to proclaim that "the Constitution of 1787 did not make our democracy impotent."[38] Just a few years after Goldwater pined for the days when the Supreme Court acted as censors over too-liberal policies, the Warren Court's liberalism had convinced much of the American right that they, too, had something to fear from an activist judiciary. Conservatism no longer belonged to Stephen Johnson Field and James Clark McReynolds. It increasingly belonged to Oliver Wendell Holmes, with his overarching distrust of any judicial action whatsoever.

———

THOUGH NIXON CAMPAIGNED using the rhetoric of judicial restraint, his four appointees to the Supreme Court—Warren Burger, Harry Blackmun, Lewis Powell, and a former Goldwater adviser named William Rehnquist—only achieved a partial rollback of the Court's new role as a force for advancing liberalism.

At the height of the Warren Court, many liberals gazed upon the Supreme Court with the same hunger to see their dreams made real by judicial decree that motivated union busters and Southern cotton mill owners during the *Lochner* Era. One of the most aggressive lawsuits to reach the Court during Earl Warren's final months as chief justice did all but claim that poverty is itself unconstitutional.[39] Though the Warren Court wasn't quite prepared to go this far just months after the American people elected Nixon president—the justices disposed of the case without an opinion[40]—the question of whether the Supreme Court could rescue impoverished children from the consequences of their parents' poverty was very much a live issue during Nixon's first term in office.

In many states, even to this day, public schools are funded, at least in part, through local property taxes. Wealthy communities, with their higher property values and large concentration of affluent residents, can tax their residents at a fairly low rate and still collect a significant amount of revenue to operate public schools for well-to-do children. Meanwhile, poorer districts might charge much higher tax rates and still be unable to raise enough money to fund adequate schools. The result is a separate-but-unequal system in which low-income children face inferior public schools simply because they grew up in the wrong neighborhood.[41]

Though a lawsuit challenging this funding scheme reached the Supreme Court in 1973, the Court upheld the scheme in its 5–4 decision in *San Antonio Independent School District v. Rodriguez*. All four of Nixon's appointees voted with the majority.[42]

Nixon's justices also sided with police over criminal suspects in ways that would come to have profound implications for civil liberties during the so-called War on Terror. Justice Rehnquist's opinion in *New York v. Quarles* (1984) created a "public safety exemption" to the *Miranda* decision permitting police to question a suspect without reading him his rights when such questions are needed to "insure that further danger to the public did not result."[43] Nearly three decades later, *Quarles* formed the basis of the Justice Department's decision not to read Boston Marathon bombing suspect Dzhokhar Tsarnaev his *Miranda* rights once he was captured four days after the bombing.[44]

Similarly, the Court held in *Smith v. Maryland* (1979) that law enforcement has broad latitude to track the phone numbers criminal suspects dial on their telephones, although actually listening to the contents of those calls requires a warrant. People do not have a "reasonable expectation of privacy" in the numbers they dial on the phone, the Court explained, because "telephone users . . . typically know that they must convey numerical information to the phone company; that the phone company has facilities for recording this information; and that the phone company does in fact record this information for a variety of legitimate business purposes." When someone voluntarily conveys this information to their phone company, *Smith* reasoned, they assume "the risk that the information would be divulged to police."[45]

This decision, more than anything else, laid the legal groundwork for the National Security Agency to conduct a massive surveillance program tracking billions of individual phone calls every month.[46]

So Nixon's election, and the four men he placed on the Supreme Court, shut down the most aggressive suits brought by liberals at the end of the Warren era—*Rodriguez*, for example, made it perfectly clear that the Court was not about to declare poverty unconstitutional. The new justices also plotted a course away from the Warren Court's criminal justice decisions that, in Nixon's words, went "too far in weakening the peace forces against the criminal forces."[47]

Yet Nixon's ascendance to power hardly closed the Supreme Court's doors to liberals altogether. Chief Justice Warren Burger, the man Nixon appointed to replace Earl Warren, wrote the very first Supreme Court decision holding that a law violated the Constitution because it treated women differently than men.[48] Five years later, in its landmark *Craig v. Boren* (1976) decision, the Burger Court held that all laws that engage in gender discrimination must be viewed with skepticism by the courts (though it should be noted that both Burger and Rehnquist dissented in *Craig*).[49]

Indeed, if Nixon's plan was to name justices who would reliably please conservative voters, then he failed spectacularly at this task. Three of Nixon's four justices would join a decision that would do more than any other case to fuel conservative outrage at the Supreme Court for at least another four decades—*Roe v. Wade* (1973).[50]

———

THE STRONGEST LEGAL argument supporting the result in *Roe*— that the Constitution establishes a robust right to abortion, at least in the early stages of pregnancy[51]—as well as earlier Court decisions protecting access to contraception,[52] is that reproductive freedom is an essential aspect of women's equality. As future Justice Ruth Bader Ginsburg once explained, *Roe* reshaped the "opportunity women will have to participate as men's full partners in the nation's social, political, and economic life."[53] Without full access to contraception and abortion, women face the constant risk that a pregnancy will disrupt their lives and their careers. For women who cannot afford to raise a child, a pregnancy can set them on the path to a kind of poverty they otherwise never would have known. So a Constitution that guarantees women the "equal protection of the laws" cannot allow government to erect barriers to their advancement by limiting their reproductive freedom.

This argument rests on even stronger legal footing today than it did when *Roe* was decided in 1973. *Roe* reached the Court three years before *Craig* established the modern legal framework protecting women from state-sponsored gender discrimination, when the idea that the Constitution protects women's equality was very much in its infancy. It would have been difficult for lawyers, using only the precedents in place in 1973, to argue that reproductive freedom flowed naturally from a very underdeveloped concept of gender equality under the law.

Since *Craig*, however, the principle that the Constitution protects women's equality has grown even more firmly established than it was in the late 1970s. Laws that discriminate against women are now forbidden by the Supreme Court unless the government has an "exceedingly persuasive justification" for its decision to treat women differently than men.[54] Justice Ginsburg, who was a leading women's rights attorney and a major player in the litigation that culminated with *Craig*, is now a member of the Supreme Court, along with two other women. On the day *Roe* was decided, by contrast, no one who had ever been on the receiving end of misogyny had ever sat on the nation's highest Court.

Indeed, thirty years after *Roe*, at a time when conservative appointments had succeeded in significantly weakening the right to choose an abortion, the Court nonetheless recognized that protecting women's equality means eradicating the view that women exist primarily to be mothers. "Denial or curtailment of women's employment opportunities," the Court explained in a passage quoting Congress's explanation for why it enacted a law providing unpaid leave to workers with a serious illness in the family, "has been traceable directly to the pervasive presumption that women are mothers first, and workers second."[55]

So it is not difficult to imagine a world in which *Roe v. Wade*, or at least, the idea that the Constitution protects women's reproductive choices, had emerged from the same line of Supreme Court cases establishing that the Constitution protects women's equality. What the Court did instead, however, is rely on one of the most open-ended doctrines that has ever made its way into a Supreme Court opinion. The right to choose an abortion, according to *Roe*, can be found "in the concept of personal 'liberty' embodied in the Fourteenth Amendment's Due Process Clause."[56] If that conclusion sounds familiar, that's because *Roe* relies on a similar rationale to the one that the Court relied upon in *Lochner*, which held that the so-called "right to make a contract" is "part of the liberty of the individual protected by the Fourteenth Amendment of the Federal Constitution."[57]

Recall that the Constitution provides that no one may be deprived of "life, liberty, or property, without due process of law," yet it provides virtually no guidance whatsoever on what the word "liberty" means. The fundamental premise of decisions like *Lochner* and *Roe* is that judges—and ultimately the Supreme Court—have the right to decide for themselves what "liberty" means, and to make that decision for the entire nation. The implications of *Roe* as it was written stretch far beyond the question of whether a woman has the right to her own reproductive autonomy, and they reach into the much larger question of whether there are any constraints on how judges interpret the Constitution.

Roe, in other words, placed liberals in the awkward position of defending the very same unchecked approach to judging that left millions of workers virtually powerless against exploitation by their employers—and it also placed conservatives in an equally awkward position. Conservatives had backed a Republican president who campaigned against judges who "put their social and economic ideas into their decisions"—and what that got them was legal abortion in all fifty states.

Less than a decade after Barry Goldwater embraced the same vision of the Constitution that drove the Court to strike down child labor laws, conservatives could no longer see a path forward that ended with the courts implementing their economic agenda. What they needed was a truce.

———

PRESIDENT RONALD REAGAN'S pledge to appoint judges who will show "judicial restraint" was that truce.[58] Judicial restraint meant that judges would not declare the minimum wage unconstitutional or actively engage in union busting, but it also meant that they would not strike down abortion laws. It meant that a president who won two consecutive landslide election victories could carry out his agenda without interference from the unelected branch. In much of his outward rhetoric, at least, Reagan's attitude towards the judiciary appeared very similar to Franklin Roosevelt's.

Below the surface, things were more nuanced. Reagan, for example, briefly attempted to place a judge who later expressed sympathy with *Lochner* and similar decisions on the Supreme Court. Judge Douglas Ginsburg, who Reagan named for the Supreme Court after a failed attempt to elevate Robert Bork, referred to the legal doctrines that defined the *Lochner* Era as the "Constitution-in-exile" in a book review Ginsburg published several years after missing his opportunity to become a justice.[59] Ginsburg's moment as Reagan's choice for the Supreme Court lasted just nine days, however—the judge took himself out of consideration for the high Court after news broke that Ginsburg had previously smoked marijuana.[60]

The Reagan administration may be unique in that it published a lengthy document outlining its vision for the Constitution. This document reveals a vision that, while well to the right of the Warren and Burger Courts, was nonetheless quite moderate in comparison to *Lochner* or the rigid conservative constitutional views espoused by Barry Goldwater.

In 1988, Reagan's Justice Department published its 153-page "Guidelines on Constitutional Litigation," which instructed the Department's attorneys on the administration's vision for the Constitution. More than simply an academic document or a statement of how the Reagan administration hoped the law would unfold in the coming decades, the Guidelines were an explicit directive that Justice Department lawyers should avoid making legal arguments inconsistent with the administration's views. "Proposed departures" from the Guidelines' vision for the Constitution, the document rather ominously warned, "should be considered carefully and discussed with one's supervisor."[61]

There's no question that the vision articulated by the Guidelines is much more conservative than the actual state of the law in 1988. The Guidelines take the view that *Roe* is a "very bad decision" that "is *not* constitutional law and gives almost no sense of an obligation to try to be."[62] Similarly, the Guidelines claim that *Mapp*, which prevents prosecutors from using illegally obtained evidence against a criminal defendant, "lacks a constitutional basis." They are also highly critical of cases enabling victims of discrimination to challenge hiring practices that exclude racial minorities unless there's proof that these practices were designed with racist intent.[63]

Compared to the Four Horsemen's assault on the New Deal or Goldwater's case against the Civil Rights Act, however, the Guidelines were the picture of moderation. The Guidelines did call for Congress's ability to legislate to be narrowed at the margins. After a Reagan White House report denounced a Supreme Court decision holding that state governments must comply with federal minimum-wage law, for example, the Guidelines called for that decision to be read very narrowly.[64] But this was a far cry from the sweeping judicial censorship of workers' rights that occurred during the *Lochner* Era. The Guidelines showed no ambition to declare the minimum wage as a whole unconstitutional, much less to revive the era when prepubescent boys toiled in coal mines.

Significantly, the Guidelines explicitly endorsed the Supreme Court's decision upholding the Voting Rights Act's requirement that states with a history of voter suppression preclear any new voting laws with officials in Washington before those laws could take effect. The Guidelines also name *South Carolina v. Katzenbach* (1966), which upheld the Voting Rights Act, as "consistent" with its vision of the Constitution.[65]

Moreover, the Guidelines explicitly repudiated the very idea that judges can enforce rights not specifically mentioned in the Constitution—a position that would render cases like *Lochner* an impossibility:

Judges are bound by the text of the Constitution and cannot rely on their own notions of desirable public policy to strike down legislative or executive actions. Where the Constitution does not specify the value to be preferred, there is no principled way for courts to discern and provide preferred treatment for such a value. Whether such a value should be accorded protection, and how much protection it ought to receive, are political matters, reserved by the Constitution to the democratic majorities in the states and the political branches of the federal government.[66]

The Guidelines, in other words, set aside the old doctrines that enforced conservative orthodoxy by judicial fiat, in favor of an almost Rooseveltian vision that would largely just get the courts out of the Reagan administration's way. Earl Warren's sixteen years in the Court's center chair, combined with the shock of decisions like *Roe v. Wade*, had convinced the Republican Party that they had something to fear from the judiciary after all.

By the Reagan years, even the men behind Goldwater's opposition to the Civil Rights Act had walked away from many of their most radical claims about the Constitution. In his 1973 confirmation hearings to become Nixon's solicitor general, Robert Bork repudiated his decade-old article claiming that bans on private discrimination are rooted in a "principle of unsurpassed ugliness." Fourteen years later, during his unsuccessful nomination to the Supreme Court, Bork tried to downplay his opposition to the Civil Rights Act as a kind of youthful indiscretion.[67]

"I had come to Yale as an avid free-market type," he told the Senate Judiciary Committee in 1987, "I had gotten into classic economics, which teaches that by and large it's much better to let people arrange their own affairs and their own transactions than to try to govern them by law." As a result, he made the "not uncommon intellectual mistake of trying to apply those principles to social interactions."[68]

Similarly, as Chief Justice of the United States, William Rehnquist sat on three cases in which one of his fellow justices—Justice

Clarence Thomas—embraced an interpretation of the Constitution very similar to the one that drove Goldwater's opposition to the Civil Rights Act.[69] Yet Rehnquist joined none of these opinions, having apparently made peace with the constitutionality of private bans on discrimination.

Indeed, Barry Goldwater himself abandoned his onetime rationale for opposing the Civil Rights Act. Thirty years after he said that he can "find no constitutional basis" for a federal ban on employment discrimination, an elderly Goldwater became honorary co-chair of an effort to enact a federal ban on employment discrimination against gay Americans. Not even Barry Goldwater was still willing to defend Barry Goldwater's previous understanding of the Constitution.[70]

While his party's elders found peace with the fact that they could no longer expect to see a sweeping new conservative vision imposed upon the nation through creative interpretation of the Constitution, a younger but no less ambitious Republican named John Roberts toiled in the bowels of the Reagan White House. There, he too became gripped by distrust of the nation's highest Court. "The generally accepted notion that the court can only hear roughly 150 cases each term," Roberts quipped in a 1983 memo, "gives the same sense of reassurance as the adjournment of the court in July, when we know that the Constitution is safe for the summer."[71]

Twenty-two years later, that same lawyer would have the opportunity to demonstrate his commitment to judicial restraint on the highest possible stage—as Chief Justice of the United States.

He chose a different path.

Chapter 11

RIGGING THE GAME

IT IS EASY, as Franklin Roosevelt and Ronald Reagan both demonstrate, to believe in a limited role for the judiciary when one's political party is at the apex of its popularity. But what happens when that party's political fortunes are most uncertain? The Supreme Court offered a fairly revealing answer to that question on December 12, 2000—the day it effectively declared George W. Bush the next President of the United States.

Bush v. Gore (2000) arose from a nail-bitingly close presidential election. Although Democratic Vice President Al Gore won the national popular vote, initial returns showed Bush with a very small lead—less than eighteen hundred votes out of the nearly six million ballots cast—in the decisive state of Florida. As the number of contested ballots significantly exceeded Bush's margin of victory, the actual winner of Florida's electoral votes, and the winner of the 2000 election as a whole, would turn upon whoever came out on top once the ballots were recounted.[1]

Except that the recount never finished. The five justices who were most inclined to prefer a Republican president to a Democrat shut it down. And they did so in an opinion that explicitly instructed the rest of the nation's judges not to rely upon it as precedent. Probably the most famous, and most widely criticized, line in the *Bush* opinion is the Court's assertion that it was issuing a one-off, good-for-this-ride-only decision that should not be applied to future cases.

According to the five justices who joined the majority opinion, "our consideration" of Florida's attempt to recount the ballots cast in the 2000 presidential election, "is limited to the present circumstances, for the problem of equal protection in election processes generally presents many complexities."[2]

The problem with this one-off approach is that it eliminates one of the most important checks on the Supreme Court's power. When judges have to paint with a broad brush, they must be cautious about how they decide each case for fear that they announce a sweeping new rule that will lead to results that they hate in a future case. But if they are allowed to create narrow, customized rules that insulate each one of their opinions from the next, then that frees them from the consequences of their own decisions. As Justice Antonin Scalia explained in 1989, "when, in writing for the majority of the Court, I adopt a general rule . . . I not only constrain lower courts, I constrain myself as well. If the next case should have such different facts that my political or policy preferences regarding the outcome are quite the opposite, I will be unable to indulge those preferences."[3]

Had the conservative justices who formed the majority in *Bush* been willing to apply their reasoning in other cases, they could actually have done a great deal to ensure fairer elections and greater access to the polls. The crux of the majority's reasoning in *Bush* was that Florida violated the Constitution's promise of "equal protection of the laws" by failing to ensure that every ballot would be treated the same way as every other ballot during the recount. "When the state legislature vests the right to vote for President in its people," the Court explained, "the right to vote as the legislature has prescribed is fundamental; and one source of its fundamental nature lies in the equal weight accorded to each vote and the equal dignity owed to each voter."[4]

Once George W. Bush was declared the winner of the 2000 election, however, and after Bush placed Chief Justice John Roberts and Justice Samuel Alito on the Supreme Court in 2005 and 2006, respectively, the Court's concern for the "equal weight accorded to each vote and the equal dignity owed to each voter" vanished. With

Roberts at its helm, the Court gutted the Voting Rights Act. It welcomed a flood of major campaign donations seeking to reshape American elections. And it aided what may be the most aggressive voter suppression campaign since the Jim Crow era.

In contrast to the *Lochner* Era justices who hobbled democracy by vetoing many progressive laws outright, the Roberts Court is often far more subtle. But the direction of the Roberts Court's election law cases is clear. Time and time again, it has sided against marginalized voters and in favor of wealthy donors seeking to corrupt democracy, and it has done so in ways that advance the partisan preferences of the Court's majority.

———

IN THE EARLY days of 2013, Republicans did not have much to celebrate. President Barack Obama was about to be sworn in for a second term. Republican challenger Mitt Romney was *persona non grata* in Washington after tone-deaf comments—in which he blamed Obama's victory on "gifts" the president supposedly gave to African Americans and Latinos—leaked to the press.[5] Democrats had actually managed to gain two seats in the Senate, despite the fact that they were defending several difficult Senate victories achieved during the Democratic wave election year in 2006.

And, yet, one arm of the Republican Party was absolutely jubilant.

Just over two weeks before Obama's second inaugural, the Republican State Leadership Committee (RSLC) released a memo bragging that they had saved the GOP's House majority from the will of the American people. In 2012, voters actually cast more than 1.3 million more votes for Democratic House candidates than they did for Republicans.[6] And yet Republicans emerged with a significant majority of the seats in Congress.

The RSLC memo credited this outcome to the GOP's efforts to gerrymander key states. "All components of a successful congressional race, including recruitment, message development and resource allocation, rest on the congressional district lines," the memo claimed, "and this was an area where Republicans had an unquestioned advantage." Indeed, because of this advantage "Republicans enjoy a 33-seat margin in the U.S. House seated yesterday in the 113th Congress, having endured Democratic successes atop the ticket and over one million more votes cast for Democratic House candidates than Republicans."[7]

In reality, the reasons why Republican leader John Boehner served a second term as Speaker of the House, even though the American people voted to return Democratic leader Nancy Pelosi to the speaker's chair, are a bit more nuanced. Democratic voters tend to cluster in cities, where they are often packed tight into extremely Democratic congressional districts that elect Democratic members of Congress by enormous margins. Meanwhile, Republican voters tend to be spread out in suburban and rural areas, where Congressional races tend to be tighter. The result is that many Democratic votes are "wasted" simply because they are cast in districts in which the Republican candidate barely has a prayer of winning, while Republican votes are more likely to be cast in races where they can actually make a difference.[8]

Nevertheless, there is no doubt that gerrymandering played a significant role in the GOP's ability to hold onto its majority in 2012, even if it was not the only factor driving this outcome. Indeed, in some states, the effects of gerrymandering were truly absurd. In Ohio, according to the RSLC memo, "Republican redistricting resulted in a net gain for the GOP state House caucus in 2012, and allowed a 12–4 Republican majority to return to the U.S. House of Representatives—despite voters casting only 52 percent of their vote for Republican congressional candidates." In Pennsylvania, voters "reelected a Democratic U.S. Senator by nearly nine points and reelected President Obama by more than five points, but at the same time they added to the Republican ranks in the State House and returned a 13–5 Republican majority to the U.S. House." And in Michigan, a state that President Obama won by nearly ten points, "Republicans at the state level maintained majorities in both chambers of the legislature and voters elected a 9–5 Republican majority to represent them in Congress."[9]

In many states, voters didn't get to choose their own members of Congress. Members of Congress got to choose their own voters.

In case there is any doubt, this kind of gerrymandering is unconstitutional. The First Amendment bans what is known as "viewpoint discrimination." Thus, neither federal nor state governments can apply one set of rules to people who support abortion rights and another set of rules to people who oppose them. Public schools cannot deny facilities to religious clubs if they make them available to secular clubs.[10] And voting officials can't create barriers intended to prevent Democrats from voting while welcoming Republicans to the polls.

But that's a lot like what partisan gerrymandering does. The entire purpose of such gerrymanders is to make one party's voters count as much as possible, while simultaneously minimizing the power of the other party's voters. When state lawmakers in Michigan, Ohio, and Pennsylvania drew district lines designed to elect Republicans to Congress, they gave the voices of Republicans far more force than the voices of Democrats. This practice cannot be squared with the Constitution. As Justice John Paul Stevens once explained, "political affiliation is not an appropriate standard for excluding voters from a congressional district" under the First Amendment.[11]

Yet the Rehnquist and Roberts Courts largely abdicated their responsibility to police the line against partisan gerrymandering. Indeed, in one of the Rehnquist Court's final decisions, *Vieth v. Jubelirer* (2004), a total of four conservative justices joined an opinion by Justice Antonin Scalia suggesting that the courts should abandon altogether any pretenses that they may ever strike down a partisan gerrymander—and effectively allow partisan lawmakers to choose their voters every time it comes time to draw new maps.[12] Though Chief Justice Roberts and Justice Alito did not go quite this far after they were presented with a partisan gerrymandering case in 2006,[13] they have nonetheless been content to allow lawmakers to draw their own district lines.

Scalia's argument against halting partisan gerrymanders is not entirely frivolous—he argues that courts have been unable to come up with a way to easily draw a line between impermissible gerrymanders and constitutionally sound maps that just happen to give an advantage to one party or the other.[14] And certainly Scalia is correct that this is a difficult task. Is a map unconstitutional if 45 percent of a state's voters are Republicans but they only receive 42 percent of the congressional seats? What if they receive 60 percent of the seats? What if they receive none of them?

But the fact that some gerrymandering cases are hard does not change the fact that many of them are easy. In 2012, for example, Michigan's voters cast nearly a quarter of a million more votes for Democratic House members than for Republicans. In total, Democrats received nearly 53 percent of the two parties' votes in Michigan congressional races.[15] And yet, Republicans did not simply win nine of Michigan's fourteen House seats, they then celebrated this achievement with a braggadocious memo touting the success of their gerrymandering project![16]

By refusing to police these unambiguous efforts to defy the First Amendment, the Court sends a clear signal to both parties that they should draw the most misshapen, self-serving districts their increasingly sophisticated computers are capable of generating in order to maximize their own party's success in the next election and minimize the fortunes of the opposition. And because many of the lawmakers who win an election in one year will effectively be able to choose their own voters in the next year, the electorate may find itself powerless to cast a corrupt or incompetent party out of power.

This is exactly the sort of thing a constitution is supposed to prevent. Even in the late 1930s, when the scars of the *Lochner* Era remained fresh and most of the justices were driven by the need for judicial restraint, the Court still warned that judicial intervention might be necessary to combat "legislation which restricts those political processes which can ordinarily be expected to bring about repeal of undesirable legislation."[17]

Government by an entrenched legislature that does not fear being turned out of office due to gerrymandering is no less antidemocratic than the kind of rule by judicial fiat that dominated the *Lochner* Era. Accountability to the voters is the only force that can reliably drive lawmakers to act in the public interest. And cases like *Vieth* strike right at the heart of that accountability. In many districts, they transform elections into nothing more than theater.

————

GERRYMANDERING IS HARDLY the only tactic partisans deployed in recent elections to shape who would have a meaningful opportunity to cast a ballot. Indeed, Republican lawmakers in the so-called swing states that decided the 2012 election were particularly aggressive in finding creative ways to keep voters from the polls.

In the 2012 election, many Florida voters encountered six-hour lines when they arrived at their polling place to cast a ballot. According to one study, in central Florida alone these lines caused approximately forty-nine thousand voters to simply leave the polls without casting their ballots. One man waited two and half hours without voting before he was forced to leave in order to pick up his daughter.[18]

A major contributor to these long lines was a law signed by Republican Governor Rick Scott, which cut the number of early voting days in Florida from fourteen to eight.[19] Many of this law's supporters did not even attempt to hide the logic behind this law. In the words of Florida Republican state Senator Mike Bennett,

> how much more convenient do you want to make [voting]? You want to go to the house? Take the polling booth with us? . . . I wouldn't have any problem making it harder. I would want them to vote as badly as I want to vote. I want the people of the state of Florida to want to vote as bad as that person in Africa who's willing to walk 200 miles. . . . This should not be easy.[20]

A former Florida GOP chairman admitted that Republicans cut early voting days "for one reason and one reason only"—Republicans "firmly believe that early voting is bad for Republican Party candidates." One GOP consultant confessed that the cuts to early voting specifically included the Sunday before Election Day because "that's a big day when the black churches organize themselves" to turn out the vote among their congregations.[21]

Lest there be any doubt, it is indeed true that cutting early voting is an effective way to shift the electorate rightward. The same study that found that tens of thousands of central Florida voters were discouraged by long lines also determined that Obama's margin over Romney would have increased by eleven thousand votes if these voters had cast their ballots.[22] Moreover, early voting is particularly important to low-income voters—a demographic that tends to prefer Democrats to Republicans—because they are more likely to lack the job flexibility necessary to cast their ballot on Election Day. As a federal appeals court laid out in its opinion that struck down an effort to restrict early voting in the swing state of Ohio: "because early voters have disproportionately lower incomes and less education than election day voters, and because all evening and weekend voting hours prior to the final weekend were eliminated . . . 'thousands of voters who would have voted during those three days will not be able to exercise their right to cast a vote in person'" if the new restrictions on early voting were upheld.[23]

Nor are restrictions to early voting the only tactic swing-state Republicans embraced in order to keep Democrats from the polls. Florida, Iowa, and Colorado all attempted to purge voters from their voter rolls—the Florida purge targeted as many as 180,000 voters—based, in part, upon claims that noncitizens might vote unless these purges moved forward.[24] As the 2012 election approached, a spokesperson for Colorado's Republican secretary of state was forced to admit that their purge had uncovered "no confirmed noncitizens."[25] Meanwhile, Florida's purge lists were so riddled with errors that all sixty-seven of the state's local election supervisors refused to participate.[26]

Similarly, a Florida law imposed potentially crippling fines on groups that helped register voters, unless those groups turned in all voter registration forms within forty-eight hours of their completion. Many groups, including the League of Women Voters, decided they could not afford to risk these fines, and they halted registration drives within Florida. A federal judge eventually suspended this law, but only after it had been in effect for nearly a year. According to one report, "the number of new Democrats registering in Florida . . . all but disappeared" while the law was in effect.[27]

The most common new voter suppression laws, however, are strict "voter ID" laws enacted in at least eleven states, which require voters to show a photo ID before they can cast a ballot at the polls.[28] The theory behind these laws is that they are necessary to prevent a very particular kind of voter fraud in which voters show up at polling places pretending to be someone else in order to cast additional ballots. Yet, although this justification may seem intuitive, it has no basis in reality.

Though allegations of voter fraud at the polls are common, they almost always deflate upon further investigation. In 1995, for example, Maryland gubernatorial candidate Ellen Sauerbrey claimed that her opponent, Democrat Parris Glendening, defeated her through a sophisticated voter-fraud campaign. As evidence of a conspiracy, her supporters cited eighty-nine votes that were supposedly cast by dead voters. Yet, an FBI investigation found no evidence whatsoever of votes being cast in the names of dead Marylanders. The closest they came was "one person who had voted then died a week after the election."[29]

A similar investigation in Georgia began with the accusation that over five thousand votes were cast in the name of dead voters over a twenty-year period. Yet the investigation only substantiated one instance of voter fraud, and this single case was later deemed to be an error as well. As it turns out, a man named "Alan J. Mandel" got confused with a man named "Alan J. Mandell." In Michigan, an investigation into 132 votes that were supposedly cast in the names of dead voters revealed that most of those votes were never actually cast in the first place, and most of the remainder involved lawful ballots cast shortly before the voter passed away. And in New York, journalists dug into allegations of widespread voter fraud in 2002 and 2004, but were unable to uncover anything other than clerical errors and mistakes.[30]

A study of Wisconsin ballots cast in the 2004 election revealed only "7 substantiated cases of individuals knowingly casting invalid votes," or 0.0002 percent of the ballots cast in that election. Moreover, all seven of those votes were cast by people with felony convictions who were ineligible to vote—not by someone impersonating another voter at the polls. Accordingly, a voter ID law would have done absolutely nothing to prevent these few, rare cases of illegal voting.[31]

Similarly, a two-year voter fraud investigation led by Iowa's Republican Secretary of State Matt Schultz uncovered exactly zero cases in which a voter showed up at the polls and pretended to be another person. Thus, Schultz was unable to find a single instance of voter fraud that would have been prevented by a voter ID law.[32]

What voter ID laws do accomplish, however, is they discourage many racial minorities, younger voters, and low-income voters from casting a ballot—all of which are groups that tend to prefer Democrats to Republicans. Although slightly more than one out of ten Americans as a whole lack a photo ID, people without ID are not distributed evenly throughout the population. African Americans are more than three times as likely to have no ID as white voters, and Latinos are more than twice as likely not to have ID. Similarly, eligible voters under the age of twenty-four and those making less than $35,000 a year are both significantly more likely than the average American not to have photo identification.[33]

In some cases, voter ID has led to truly absurd results.

In Wisconsin, a Marine Corps veteran named Ricky Tyrone Lewis was denied the ID he needed to comply with the state's law because he was unable to find his birth records. He offered state officials a copy of his honorable discharge papers instead, but to no avail.[34]

Also in Wisconsin, an eighty-four-year-old former elected official who had voted in every election over the past sixty-three years was unable to obtain a voter ID unless she paid the state a fee to obtain her birth certificate—despite the fact that the Constitution forbids states from making "the affluence of the voter or payment of any fee an electoral standard."[35]

In Ohio, even after he produced a photo ID from the Department of Veterans Affairs, eighty-six-year-old World War II veteran Paul Carroll was told he could not vote, because the ID did not include his address.[36]

In Tennessee, ninety-three-year-old Thelma Mitchell was denied a voter ID because she had never received a birth certificate—she was delivered by a midwife in Alabama in 1918, and the state had no record of her birth. When she tried to obtain an ID, a clerk suggested that she could be an "illegal immigrant."[37]

Also in Tennessee, ninety-one-year-old Virginia Lasater abandoned an attempt to obtain an ID because, in her advanced age, she was no longer able to stand for long periods of time. The line to obtain an ID stretched for hours and Lasater had no place to sit.[38]

In Texas, Jessica Cohen lost her license and other identification papers in a burglary. To obtain an ID, she had to pay an unconstitutional fee in order to first obtain a birth certificate.[39]

And finally, a ninety-six-year-old African American woman from Tennessee, Dorothy Cooper, was turned away when she sought a voter ID because she did not have a copy of her marriage license. Cooper later said that she did not have problems voting "during Jim Crow days—only now under voter ID."[40]

Some of these voters were eventually, after much aggravation or after paying unconstitutional fees, able to obtain voter identification. Additionally, it is worth noting that, two years after the two Wisconsin voters were denied ID, the state supreme court changed the state law to ease the process for people without birth certificates.[41]

Nevertheless, it is easy to see how someone confronted with a wall of bureaucracy would simply give up and decide not to vote in the next election. Though estimates vary regarding how many voters will actually be disenfranchised by a strict voter ID requirement, the former *New York Times* data guru Nate Silver estimates that "these laws will prevent something like 2 or 3 percent of registered voters from actually casting a ballot," with far more Democrats being turned away from the polls than Republicans. Indeed, Silver predicted in 2012 that a strict voter ID law "would reduce President Obama's margin against Mitt Romney by a net of 1.2 percentage points." So, in a close election, voter ID could easily steal victory from the hands of a Democratic candidate and hand it to a Republican.[42]

Perhaps this is why, shortly after Pennsylvania enacted a strict voter ID law that was eventually halted by the state courts, the state's Republican House majority leader bragged that the new law "is gonna allow Governor Romney to win the state of Pennsylvania."[43]

———

STATES MUST HAVE some leeway to regulate elections, and these regulations will sometimes limit the choices available to voters. When a state tells a voter to vote at a designated precinct, for example, or when they limit their choices to the names that actually appear on the ballot, it imposes some limits on the voter's freedom. And yet the Constitution permits some of these kinds of restrictions because it would be impossible to administer an election without rules guiding voters and poll workers.[44]

But that doesn't mean that states have carte blanche to enact any voting restriction they choose. The New Deal Court was correct that any law that "restricts those political processes which can ordinarily be expected to bring about repeal of undesirable legislation" should be treated with suspicion,[45] because when lawmakers are allowed to undermine the political process itself, they can quickly render the voters' opinions irrelevant. More recent decisions establish that, when considering a state law that restricts voting, courts must weigh "the extent to which" the state's reasons for enacting the law "make it necessary to burden the plaintiff's rights."[46]

This is why voter ID laws should be struck down. The primary justification offered for these laws, the need to fight voter fraud at the polls, is an almost completely empty justification because such fraud hardly exists. In a nation committed to democracy, imaginary problems cannot excuse disenfranchising real voters.

And yet, the Supreme Court refused to strike down voter ID laws in *Crawford v. Marion County Election Board* (2008). Remarkably, the lead opinion in *Crawford* admitted that the "record contains no evidence of any [in-person voter] fraud actually occurring in Indiana at any time in its history" (the case involved an Indiana voter ID law). Indeed, *Crawford* was only able to cite a single example of such fraud occurring anywhere in the United States at any point within the preceding 140 years![47] But that one example—a single fraudulent vote cast in the name of a Seattle woman who died a few months before election day[48]—outweighed the thousands, perhaps even hundreds of thousands, of voters likely to be disenfranchised by voter ID.

Five years later, the Roberts Court handed down what is probably the biggest blow to voting rights since the Jim Crow era.

Shelby County, Alabama, was, to say the least, a less-than-ideal poster child for a crusade against the Voting Rights Act. The state of Alabama was the site of the original Selma voting rights march that galvanized Congress to enact the act in the first place, and many of its lawmakers still held deeply racist attitudes even after the rest of the county elected its first black president. In 2010, an FBI investigation captured conversations between members of the Alabama legislature who spoke about their desire to kill a referendum on whether the state would legalize electronic bingo because they feared that this referendum might increase black voter turnout if it were on the ballot. During a strategy session with Republican allies, one participant complained that "every black, every illiterate" could be "bused [to the polls] on HUD financed buses" if the referendum were on the ballot (in this context, "HUD" most likely refers to the Department of Housing and Urban Development). A state senator referred to African Americans as "aborigines."[49]

Similarly, in 2008, a city in Shelby County drew a legislative map that gerrymandered its only black councilman out of office. Even after the Justice Department objected to this map under the Voting Rights Act, the city moved forward with an illegal election—which the African American lawmaker lost. Ultimately, DOJ had to bring an enforcement action against the city in order to force it to comply with the law.[50]

And yet, just a few years after this incident, Shelby County's lawyers walked into the Supreme Courtroom and asked the justices to tear the heart out of the Voting Rights Act. Several months later, the Court's five most conservative members complied.

The thrust of Chief Justice Roberts's decision in *Shelby County v. Holder* (2013) is that requiring only some states—the ones with a history of racial voter discrimination—to "preclear" their new voting practices was a "departure from the principle that all States enjoy equal sovereignty." And that the conditions that justified such an alleged departure have changed too much to allow the Voting Rights Act to remain intact. "If it is to divide the States," Roberts lectured Congress, then it "must identify those jurisdictions to be singled out on a basis that makes sense in light of current conditions. It cannot rely simply on the past."[51]

There is no shortage of problems with this decision, but the most significant is that it has absolutely no basis whatsoever in the text of the Constitution. The Fifteenth Amendment provides that "the right of citizens of the United States to vote shall not be denied or abridged by the United States or by any state on account of race, color, or previous condition of servitude," and it gives Congress "power to enforce this article by appropriate legislation." Nothing in the Constitution's text supports the idea that Congress cannot treat states with a history of race discrimination differently than others, or that it must periodically update the list of states subject to the full force of the Voting Rights Act to bring them in line with "current conditions." *Shelby County* has no more basis in the Constitution than *Lochner* did.

(It should also be noted that the Voting Rights Act includes both a "bail in" provision, that allows new states to be subjected to federal supervision if they engage in racial voter discrimination and a "bail out" provision that allows them to be excused from federal supervision if they act in compliance with the law for ten years.[52] So

Congress actually complied with Roberts's fabricated requirement that the Voting Rights Act adapt to changing circumstances.)

Moreover, the scope of Roberts's "principle that all States enjoy equal sovereignty" was explicitly rejected by the Warren Court's original decision upholding the Voting Rights Act several months after President Johnson signed it into law. "The doctrine of the equality of States," the Court explained in 1966, does not bar the Voting Rights Act because "that doctrine applies only to the terms upon which States are admitted to the Union, and not to the remedies for local evils which have subsequently appeared."[53]

But, beyond the cold language of the law, there's a more basic problem with Roberts's decision. It rests on the principle that patients no longer exhibiting symptoms can abruptly stop taking their medicine. Roberts is exactly right that voting conditions for minorities have improved in the South—and the biggest contributor to this fact is the Voting Rights Act itself. As Justice Ginsburg explained in her dissenting opinion, "throwing out preclearance when it has worked and is continuing to work to stop discriminatory changes is like throwing away your umbrella in a rainstorm because you are not getting wet."[54]

Roberts's suggestion that federal supervision was no longer necessary to halt voter suppression in the South was refuted almost as soon as the *Shelby County* decision was announced. Texas waited just two hours to announce that it would move forward with a voter ID law and a legislative map, both of which had been halted under the Voting Rights Act due to their impact on minority voters.[55] By the end of the day, top officials in both Alabama and Mississippi announced that *Shelby County* had paved the way for voter ID in those states as well.[56] *Shelby County* also gave the green light to a strict voter ID law in Virginia as well, although officials in that state were less quick to brag about this fact.[57]

The most ambitious attempt to restrict the franchise, at least in the immediate aftermath of *Shelby County*, came from North Carolina. Less than two months after Roberts effectively killed the requirement that voting laws impacting forty of North Carolina's counties must be precleared, that state's legislature enacted dozens of changes to its election law. Among other things, the new law included a strict voter ID provision. It chopped early voting by a full week. It cut "pre-registration" for sixteen- and seventeen-year-olds that would have enabled them to vote on their eighteenth birthdays. It restricted certain kinds of voter registration drives that tend to serve low-income voters and voters of color. It repealed a public financing system for judicial elections intended to reduce major donors' influence over judges. And it topped all of that off by increasing the amount of money wealthy donors could give to candidates.[58]

Though not all of these provisions would have been blocked under an intact Voting Rights Act—states are permitted to allow wealthy donors to give generously to candidates, for example, regardless of whether this is a good idea—it is difficult to imagine much of this law surviving if not for the Court's decision in *Shelby County*. Voter ID disproportionately disenfranchises voters of color, which is why a federal court halted a similar law in Texas before Roberts gutted the Voting Rights Act.[59] Similarly, there is strong evidence that restrictions on early voting target black voters. In 2008, for example, more than half of early voters in Ohio's largest county were black, despite the fact that African Americans make up just over one-quarter of the population.[60]

Shelby County, in other words, gave states like North Carolina the freedom to experiment with new ways to make it harder to vote that would never have been possible under a fully operational Voting Rights Act, and it did so at the exact same moment that many Republican lawmakers are engaged in what former President Bill Clinton described as the most "determined effort to limit the franchise" since Jim Crow.[61]

———

NOT ALL ELECTIONS can be rigged with the tools this Court has permitted to flourish. Senate and presidential races remain immune to gerrymandering. And even if a state enacts a full array of voter

ID laws and similar voter-suppression provisions, many left-leaning voters will stubbornly insist upon showing up at the polls anyway.

Nevertheless, the wealthiest Americans, thanks in large part to the Roberts Court, now enjoy an unprecedented ability to corrupt elections through the sheer force of their own money. Why bother to rig an election when you can simply buy it?

Consider Sheldon Adelson. Adelson is Bond-villain rich—so rich his net worth exceeds the gross domestic product of nearly two dozen nations put together.[62] And, in the 2012 election cycle, he was also a human ATM for the Republican Party. The casino mogul reportedly spent about $150 million to help elect Republicans in 2012[63]—and that's only a tiny fraction of a fortune estimated at more than $28 billion in 2013.[64]

Adelson is so wealthy that he could spend half a million dollars to elect his preferred candidate in every single US House district, and then do it again, and again, and again for the next 262 years before he ran out of funds. If Adelson wanted, he could drop so much money into a single race that it would be virtually impossible for any candidate to raise enough money to effectively counter the billionaire's views. And Adelson would have to spend so little of his wealth to do so that he would hardly even notice that the money was missing.

And yet, according to the Supreme Court of the United States, there is no chance whatsoever that this kind of lavish spending on political candidates could ever lead those candidates to become corrupted. Indeed, under Roberts's leadership, the Court practically declared that Adelson *should* have more influence than people who cannot afford to spend millions of dollars to elect like-minded politicians. "Favoritism and influence are not . . . avoidable in representative politics," the Court's *Citizens United v. F.E.C.* (2010) proclaims. "It is well understood that a substantial and legitimate reason . . . to make a contribution to . . . one candidate over another is that the candidate will respond by producing those political outcomes the supporter favors."[65]

"Democracy," according to *Citizens United*, "is premised on responsiveness."[66]

Four years later, the Court took this view even further. In *Mc-Cutcheon v. F.E.C.* (2014) the conservative justices effectively legalized various money-laundering schemes allowing donors to launder seven-figure donations to the most contentious races in the country.[67] The basis for this decision was these five justices' very narrow conception of what constitutes political corruption. In *McCutcheon,* Chief Justice Roberts wrote that campaign finance laws may only address one kind of corruption— "dollars for political favors." Campaign finance laws, according to Roberts's opinion in *McCutcheon,* "may not seek to limit the appearance of mere influence or access."[68] The implication is that lawmakers can literally sell their time to donors at an hourly rate, just so long as they do not explicitly promise to cast a certain vote in exchange for cash.

Indeed, if it were up to Roberts, wealthy donors would have broad latitude to—in Justice Anthony Kennedy's words—"[choose] the judge" in their own cases.[69] In *Caperton v. A.T. Massey Coal* (2009), Roberts authored a dissent backing a wealthy coal baron who almost literally bought a seat on the West Virginia Supreme Court while a major verdict was pending against the coal baron's company.

In 2002, a West Virginia jury awarded a $50 million verdict against the A.T. Massey Coal Company—a company that later became infamous after an explosion in one of its coal mines killed twenty-nine mine workers.[70] In West Virginia, justices of the state's Supreme Court of Appeals are elected to twelve-year terms. While the jury's $50 million verdict was awaiting an appeal to the state supreme court, Massey's CEO spent $3 million, most of which was given to a group named "And For The Sake Of The Kids." This group ran ads claiming that one of the sitting West Virginia Supreme Court justices had unleashed a convicted child rapist on the public, and supported the incumbent's opponent, attorney Brent Benjamin. After Benjamin won the election, he cast the deciding vote to toss out the verdict against Massey.[71]

Although a bare majority of the US Supreme Court held that Benjamin should have recused himself from this case, Roberts was incredulous at this outcome. "Why is the Court so convinced that this is an extreme case" warranting the Court's intervention, he demanded. Indeed, Roberts, in an opinion joined by three of his colleagues, suggested that any amount of money given to elect anyone to the bench would be acceptable, so long as that money was not donated directly to the candidate's campaign. "This point cannot be emphasized strongly enough," Roberts insisted. "Other than a $1,000 direct contribution from Blankenship, Justice Benjamin and his campaign had no control over how this money was spent."

So long as the money was funneled to some group other than the judge's own campaign, wealthy individuals should be free to buy up judgeships on the courts that are likely to hear their cases someday.

———

ROBERTS'S DISTINCTION BETWEEN money given directly to candidates and money given to so-called independent groups seeking to shape the outcome of an election is rooted in the original sin of American campaign-finance law—the Court's decision in *Buckley v. Valeo* (1976)—which created a very similar distinction.

Buckley involved a comprehensive package of campaign-finance reforms enacted due to widespread fears that politics had become a pay-to-play operation. In 1964, the year Lyndon Johnson defeated Barry Goldwater, 64 percent of the nation believed that the government is "run for the benefit of all the people." This number declined in Johnson's second term and it absolutely collapsed after Nixon entered the White House. By 1974, just 21 percent of Americans believed that government was on their side—nearly 70 percent agreed that it is "pretty much run by a few big interests."[72]

No doubt much of this collapse was due to corruption scandals within the Nixon White House itself. A Senate investigation discovered that the dairy industry pledged $2 million to President Nixon's reelection campaign to gain a meeting with administration officials regarding price supports for that industry. Eventually, industry representatives scored a meeting with Nixon himself—and not long after that meeting the president overruled his secretary of agriculture's decision not to increase the price supports the industry craved.[73]

Many ambassadorships also appeared to be available to the highest bidder. The Senate investigation "identified over $1.8 million in Presidential campaign contributions as ascribable, in whole or in part, to 31 persons holding ambassadorial appointments from President Nixon, and stated that six other large contributors, accounting for $3 million, appear to have been actively seeking such appointment at the time of their contributions." A top Nixon fundraiser pled guilty to federal corruption charges after promising a donor the job of ambassador to Trinidad—in return for $100,000 in campaign donations to be split between Nixon's campaign and various senate candidates selected by the White House.[74]

Nor were these corruption scandals limited to the White House. One oil executive testified that campaign donations were perceived by businessmen as a "calling card, something that would get us in the door and make our point of view heard" by members of Congress. The former chair of American Airlines claimed that many companies made illegal contributions "in response to pressure for fear of a competitive disadvantage that might result" if they did not make these donations.[75]

To eliminate, or at least, to roll back this kind of corruption, Congress enacted a wide-ranging package of reforms that included a cap of $1,000 per election on donations to any individual candidate. To ensure that donors did not evade this cap by paying for campaign ads themselves or donating to organizations that supported the candidate's campaign, the law also limited "independent expenditures by individuals and groups 'relative to a clearly identified candidate'" to $1,000 per year.[76]

Yet the Court treated the first kind of contributions—contributions directly to a candidate—as completely different from the second kind—so-called "independent expenditures" to groups seeking to influence the election.

As the justices correctly realized, campaign-finance laws present difficult questions under the First Amendment. Money spent on campaign ads and other campaign activities fund the kind of "discussion of public issues and debate on the qualifications of candidates [that] are integral to the operation of the system of government established by our Constitution." So if campaign-finance laws unfairly hobble candidates' abilities to convey their messages to the electorate, "the ability of the citizenry to make informed choices among candidates for office" will suffer.[77]

But victorious candidates go on to wield great power, and that power can be used to sell ambassadorships in Trinidad or to punish airlines that do not donate to your campaign—unless the law does something to stop them. "To the extent that large contributions are given to secure a political quid pro quo from current and potential office holders, the integrity of our system of representative democracy is undermined," the Court concluded in *Buckley*, and this concern was sufficient to overcome fears that a cap on campaign donations would limit candidates' abilities to broadcast their messages.[78]

Just as important, *Buckley* recognized that, in order to regulate campaign donations, there does not need to be an actual quid pro quo arrangement—that is, an explicit deal in which a candidate agrees to trade political favors in return for donations. "Of almost equal concern as the danger" of such an explicit deal "is the impact of the appearance of corruption stemming from public awareness of the opportunities for abuse inherent in a regime of large individual financial contributions." Massive donations create the appearance that politicians are on the take. Voters quite sensibly wonder why a man like Sheldon Adelson would spend tens of millions of dollars unless he expected to get something in return. And if politicians fixate on the interests of wealthy individuals and corporations, then voters may decide that it is no longer worth participating in democracy because the game is rigged in someone else's favor. Avoiding "the appearance of improper influence" is essential "if confidence in the system of representative Government is not to be eroded to a disastrous extent."[79]

The original sin of *Buckley*, however, was not recognizing that spending by men like Adelson can be just as corrupting regardless of whether or not it passes through a candidate's campaign before it funds a campaign ad. Though there is some complexity to the Court's analysis of this question, it rested in large part upon the belief that "the absence of prearrangement and coordination of an expenditure with the candidate . . . alleviates the danger that expenditures will be given as a quid pro quo for improper commitments from the candidate."[80]

Although this conclusion may be true at the relatively low levels of spending enforced by the statute in *Buckley*—it is unlikely that an elected official will rush to do favors for someone who made only a few thousand dollars' worth of contributions to groups that ran ads supporting the official in the last election—the same cannot be said when a donor spends hundreds of thousands or millions of dollars to elect a candidate. In 2012, Republican presidential candidate Mitt Romney met twice with Sheldon Adelson: once in a private meeting at Adelson's offices in Las Vegas and again at a high-dollar fundraiser in Jerusalem.[81] It is unlikely that Romney did so because he wanted to learn how to run a casino.

And even if meetings of this sort were entirely innocent, that does not alleviate the appearance of corruption created when wealthy donors pay millions of dollars to influence elections. After all, *Buckley* recognized that the mere appearance of corruption is "of almost equal concern" as under-the-table dealings between politicians and donors.

There can be no reasonable doubt that increased spending by wealthy donors fosters an appearance of corruption. After *Citizens United* made it even easier for interest groups to channel their money into campaign ads, a poll determined that 69 percent of Americans believe that "new rules that let corporations, unions and people give unlimited money to" groups seeking to influence elections "will lead to corruption." Only 15 percent disagreed with this conclusion.[82]

To put that number in perspective, a different poll found that 34 percent of Americans believe in ghosts, 23 percent believe they have actually seen a ghost or have "been in one's presence," and 19 percent believe in "spells or witchcraft."[83] There appear to be more Americans who believe in wizards and witches than there are who believe that unlimited election spending does not lead to corruption. It just happens that five of these rare individuals sit on the Supreme Court.

———

ALTHOUGH ADELSON-LIKE spending was technically legal before *Citizens United*, which held that corporations and unions have the same right to spend on elections that actual people do, there were some obstacles that held back the flood of election spending that followed that decision. Before *Citizens United*, for example, the legality of organizations similar to the now ubiquitous "Super PACs"— groups that bundle many donations together in order to pay for campaign ads—was uncertain. Thus, if someone like Adelson wanted to purchase a campaign ad, the only legally surefooted way to do so was to disclose that the ad was "Paid for by Sheldon Adelson."[84] As a practical matter, these obstacles deterred quite a bit of election spending. Between 2008, the last presidential election year before *Citizens United*, and 2012, the first presidential election after the decision, spending by non-campaign groups rose 245 percent in the presidential election, by 662 percent in House races, and by 1,338 percent in Senate races.[85]

Citizens United also has profound partisan implications. In 2010, the first election cycle following that decision, conservative groups outspent liberal groups nearly 2 to 1. In the 2012 election cycle, more than 70 percent of the over one billion dollars in spending by Super PACs and similar organizations came from conservative groups (although, in fairness, part of this skew can be chalked up to the fact that Democrats did not have a contested presidential primary in 2012).[86]

Notably, all five of the justices who formed the *Citizens United*'s majority were appointed by Republican presidents, while three of the four justices in dissent were appointed by Democrats. After Justice John Paul Stevens—a Gerald Ford appointee who dissented in

Citizens United—retired from the Court, a similar campaign-finance case reached the justices. All five of the Court's Republicans voted to reaffirm *Citizens United*; all four of its Democrats voted to "reconsider" it.[87]

Of course, the obvious rejoinder to this concern that *Citizens United* benefited one political party at the expense of the other is that Sheldon Adelson spent lavishly to elect candidates like Mitt Romney, but Barack Obama still defeated Romney in 2012. Nevertheless, this rejoinder ignores two crucial facts about the impact of campaign spending.

The first is that President Obama was, in the words of one anti-Obama campaign ad, "the biggest celebrity in the world."[88] Most voters have very well-formed opinions about an incumbent President of the United States, and that opinion is unlikely to be changed because they watch an ad—or even a barrage of ads—funded by groups that oppose the president.

The same cannot be said, however, about state representatives, judges, city council members, and other, far more obscure officials. Most Americans cannot name a single member of their state supreme court, for example—indeed, a 2010 poll found that only 28 percent of Americans could name the Chief Justice of the United States.[89] This is why a $3 million infusion of cash by a wealthy coal baron into a state supreme court race can be so impactful. Many voters are unlikely to know much at all about the candidates beyond what they learn from campaign ads.

Additionally, even when campaign spending doesn't succeed in changing the result of an election, it may be very effective in changing the way elected officials actually govern. One study found that elected state supreme court justices who receive almost no money from business interest groups vote "in favor of business about 46.2 percent of the time," while justices who receive half or more of their contributions from business groups "vote in favor of business interests almost two-thirds of the time." Moreover, this effect is strongest among Democratic justices. That is, Democrats who receive a large amount of money from business interests are significantly more likely to side with those interests than other Democrats, while the disparity among Republican justices is less pronounced.[90]

One explanation for this phenomenon is that Republican justices who are already inclined to support business interests will continue to do so after they receive a campaign donation, but Democrats who might otherwise have sided against a donor's interests may be moved to change their mind by enough campaign cash—or by the fact that they need to interact with a large number of wealthy, business-minded donors in order to secure those donations. As the study's author writes, "because Republican justices typically already favor business interests more than Democratic justices, additional business contributions may have a smaller effect on Republican justices' voting."[91]

Big campaign donations, in other words, may not simply help elect Republicans. They may also cause Democrats to govern like Republicans.

———

THERE IS NO direct evidence that the justices behind decisions like *Bush, Shelby County, Citizens United, Vieth, Crawford,* and *McCutcheon* are motivated solely by partisanship. With one exception—Justice Stevens voted with the conservatives in the *Crawford* voter ID case—these cases were all 5–4 decisions drawn along familiar ideological lines. But that does not change the fact that these cases have consistently favored one political party over the other, and it is the party that controls a majority of the seats on the Supreme Court.

Whatever the Court's motivation in reaching these decisions, however, they are a significant departure from the post–New Deal consensus in favor of democracy, and of the Court's one-time recognition that laws that restrict the political process itself should be viewed with suspicion.[92] Indeed, in many cases, the Roberts Court isn't simply refusing to remove barriers in the way of the democratic process, it is actively constructing new ones.

Chapter 12

THE FINAL WORD

TARDIVE DYSKINESIA IS a horrific disease that causes patients literally to lose control of their own bodies. In some cases, patients' limbs flail about so violently that they have trouble walking. In others, the patients may struggle to eat or speak because they are unable to stop loudly smacking their mouths and tongues. A federal court described the symptoms of tardive dyskinesia as "grotesque." One woman with this disease repeatedly checked herself into the hospital because she was terrified that she would bite off her own tongue.[1]

In 2001, Gladys Mensing went to her doctor seeking treatment for stomach problems, and she was prescribed the drug metoclopramide, which she took for four years. Although the warning label for this drug warned that it could cause tardive dyskinesia, it claimed that the risk of this or similar disorders was "comparatively rare."[2] So when Mensing decided to take the drug, she had no reason to believe that she was likely to be disabled by it several years later.

In reality, however, patients who developed neurological problems after taking metoclopramide were not in the least bit rare. Though the drug's label disclosed that only about one in five hundred patients experience these problems after short-term use, it did not reveal the full extent of the danger faced by the one-third of metoclopramide users who take it for multiple years.[3] According to one study, more than a quarter of people who take the drug for several years develop tardive dyskinesia. One of them was Mensing.[4]

And yet, the Supreme Court's five most conservative members held that the company that failed to warn Mensing of the grave danger she faced if she took their drug was immune to her lawsuit against them.

The Court's opinion in *PLIVA v. Mensing* (2011) is difficult to summarize in a few sentences—or even in a few paragraphs—but the crux of it hinges upon the complex obligations federal law imposes on drug manufacturers to warn patients about the dangers inherent in their drugs. Before a drug maker can bring a new drug to market, it must prove the drug's safety and effectiveness, and the drug's label must provide adequate warnings of any potential dangers. If a generic drug maker later wants to copy this drug, however, it has somewhat different obligations. Once the Food and Drug Administration (FDA) determines that a brand-name drug has an adequate label, generic drug companies who copy that drug are obligated to use exactly the same label. Thus, so long as the brand-name drug company keeps its label up to date with new information about the risks of taking its drug, generic versions of that medication will also provide the same warnings.[5]

Justice Clarence Thomas's majority opinion argued, in essence, that this placed the generic drug company that makes metoclopramide in an impossible bind. Although Minnesota law obligated the company to give Mensing better information than it did, federal law also required that same company to use a label identical to a different, inadequate label. It was impossible, Thomas reasoned, for the company to comply with both federal and state law, so Mensing's state lawsuit had to give way to the federal rule.[6]

Yet, as Justice Sonia Sotomayor explained in dissent, this characterization of the law was not entirely accurate. Warning labels are not carved in stone. If a responsible drug company learns that its drug presents previously unknown dangers, it has a moral obligation to inform the FDA of this fact—indeed, according to the FDA itself, it has a legal obligation to do so as well.[7] And once the FDA knows about these previously unknown risks, it can ensure that the label is changed. A generic drug company, Sotomayor argued, must make sure that the FDA is aware that a drug's label is inadequate—and give the FDA an opportunity to see that the label is changed—before the company can claim that it is impossible for it to comply with state law.[8]

This one case, with its tragic facts and arcane legal analysis, is, in many ways, a microcosm of the modern Supreme Court. Though the Rehnquist and Roberts Courts at times invoked their power to interpret the Constitution in order to reshape the law—as the Roberts Court did by striking down campaign-finance laws in *Citizens United* and much of the Voting Rights Act in *Shelby County*—modern-day judicial conservatives are much less likely to rely on ideological interpretations of the Constitution than their predecessors in the *Lochner* Era. Outside of its election law cases, an area where the Roberts Court is particularly aggressive, there are far fewer recent examples of the justices reaching constitutional decisions that just happen to align with their ideological views than there were a century ago. When the Rehnquist Court had the opportunity to overrule *Miranda*, it explicitly declined to do so.[9] Twelve years later, when Chief Justice Roberts had the chance to repeal the Affordable Care Act, he (mostly) refused to do so.[10]

Yet the fact that contemporary judicial conservatives have not handed down a latter-day *Lochner v. New York* does not mean that they've failed to make an ideological mark on the law. In many cases, it simply means they are more subtle than their forebears. While justices like Field, Fuller, Brewer, and Sutherland read doubtful restrictions on government into the vaguest phrases of the Constitution, modern-day conservatives often prefer a different tactic. By reading civil rights laws narrowly, or by placing procedural barriers between workers and the courthouse door, or by shunting consumers into tribunals that are stacked in favor of the companies they are suing, the Court can undermine progressive legislation just as surely as if they had declared it unconstitutional.

Moreover, as Congress grows more and more dysfunctional, the distinction between a Supreme Court decision reinterpreting the

Constitution and another decision that achieves the same result by rethinking an ordinary statute matters less and less. Traditionally, the Court's constitutional precedents were understood to be particularly difficult to displace, because, in Professor William Eskridge's words, "the difficulty of amending the Constitution makes the Court the only effective resort for changing obsolete constitutional doctrine."[11] Court decisions interpreting acts of Congress, by contrast, could always be overruled by a new act of Congress.

In an age when Congress and the president can barely agree upon whether or not to shut down the government,[12] however, the idea that Congress will get its act together long enough to overrule a Supreme Court decision is largely a pipe dream. The justices are no longer simply the final word on the Constitution, they are typically the final word on everything that comes before them.

ARGUABLY, THE MOST famous victim of workplace discrimination in America is Lilly Ledbetter, a former supervisor in a Goodyear Tire and Rubber plant. Ledbetter worked for Goodyear for nearly two decades in a role dominated by male employees. Despite exemplary performance reviews, Ledbetter earned nearly $7,000 per year less than the lowest-paid man with the same role in the company—her highest paid male counterpart earned more than $18,000 more than she did.[13]

Under federal law, many victims of discrimination face a very brief deadline. They must take action against their employee within 180 days "after the alleged unlawful employment practice occurred" or else they can lose their right to challenge this discrimination forever.[14] Yet there is an important fail-safe protecting people who, like Ledbetter, may face many years of pay discrimination. As a unanimous Supreme Court explained in a 1986 race discrimination case, "each week's paycheck that delivers less to [an African American] than to a similarly situated white is a wrong actionable" under federal law. Thus, the 180-day clock starts anew each time a worker receives a discriminatory paycheck, and this rule applies equally in race and gender cases because both are banned by the same federal law.[15]

Or, at least, this fail-safe existed until Justice Samuel Alito got his hands on it in *Ledbetter v. Goodyear Tire* (2007). Because many employers offer annual raises as a percentage of the employee's current salary, persons who are paid lower salaries early in their careers due to pay discrimination can wind up earning far less than their colleagues years or decades after that single act of unequal treatment. Yet Alito's opinion for the Court held that a woman in Ledbetter's position must challenge the decision to pay her less than her male colleagues almost immediately after it happens.[16]

According to Justice Ruth Bader Ginsburg's dissent, Alito's opinion lacked even a basic understanding of the "realities of the workplace." Pay disparities "are often hidden from sight." "It is not unusual," Ginsburg continued, "for management to decline to publish employee pay levels, or for employees to keep private their own salaries."[17] Women in Ledbetter's position are unlikely to discover that they are victims of discrimination within just six short months.

Moreover, even when a woman learns that she is paid less than her male colleagues, she may not recognize this disparity as pay discrimination: "pay disparities often occur, as they did in Ledbetter's case, in small increments; cause to suspect that discrimination is at work develops only over time." And if the employee suspects foul play, she may not want to risk her career over what initially appears to be just a little bit of money. "Small initial discrepancies may not be seen as meet for a federal case," Ginsburg warned, "particularly when the employee, trying to succeed in a nontraditional environment, is averse to making waves."[18]

Of course the epilogue to the *Ledbetter* case is that Congress overruled Alito's opinion less than two years later, in the very first bill President Obama signed into law. Yet, the tale of how this bill became law says as much about the much more frequent finality of Supreme Court decisions as it does about elected officials' power to undo what the Supreme Court has done.

Just over two weeks after the Court's decision, House Democrats announced their plans to introduce legislation correcting Alito's decision, and Ledbetter herself testified to a House committee in favor of the law not long thereafter—although the bill stalled due to President George W. Bush's opposition and that of his fellow Republicans.[19] Ledbetter would go on to speak at the Democratic National Convention in 2008 (and in 2012), and she starred in an Obama campaign ad attacking GOP candidate John McCain for opposing the Democratic bill.

After Democrats won one of the most lopsided electoral victories in decades—regaining control of the White House and capturing supermajorities in both houses of Congress—the Lilly Ledbetter Fair Pay Act did become law, but it did so with only sixty-one votes in the Senate. If just two fewer senators had voted for the law, it would not have had the sixty votes needed to overcome a Republican filibuster.

Alito's *Ledbetter* decision, in other words, fell victim to a perfect storm. Justice Ginsburg authored a particularly persuasive dissent explaining, in terms that non-lawyers could easily understand, why Alito's opinion was unjust. Overturning *Ledbetter* became a driving cause for Democratic politicians shortly before a wave election gave those Democrats unusually large majorities in Congress. And Lilly Ledbetter herself is an especially telegenic figure who played a significant role in the campaign strategy of future President Obama.

And yet, with so much in its favor, the Lilly Ledbetter Fair Pay Act barely made it through Congress. Few laws seeking to correct erroneous Supreme Court decisions do anymore. Between 1975 and 1990, according to one study, Congress overrode an average of 12 Supreme Court decisions during each two-year term. Between 2001 and 2012, that number fell to 2.7 decisions overruled every two years.[20]

Unlike Lilly Ledbetter, Jack Gross did not get to speak at the Democratic National Convention. After thirty-two years with his company, FBL Financial Group, Gross claims that he was demoted, at least in part, because of his age—Gross was fifty-four years old.

Typically, federal law permits what are known as "mixed-motive" lawsuits when workers believe they are victims of discrimination. Under the standard that should prevail in age-discrimination cases, when workers can prove that illegal discrimination "played a motivating part in an employment decision," they win their lawsuit unless their employer can prove that "it would have made the same decision even if it had not taken [an illegal consideration] into account."[21]

These lawsuits serve a very important purpose. There's nothing illegal about firing an incompetent, obnoxious, or even a poorly dressed worker who happens to be a woman, a racial minority, or above a certain age. It is illegal, however, to fire someone *because of* their race, their gender, or because they are over the age of forty. Thus, employment discrimination cases often turn on a supervisor's secret motives—motives that a judge or jury will have a difficult time discovering unless they are capable of reading minds. Mixed-motive lawsuits help force supervisors to disclose their secret motives, at least after the plaintiff has demonstrated that discrimination played some part in the way he or she was treated, because the employer needs to either explain their reasons for acting against an employee or lose the case. Thus, such lawsuits can rescue the victims of discrimination from the impossible task of having to prove that their bosses were thinking only of prejudice at particular moments in time.

Except that, in *Gross v. FBL Financial Services* (2009), the five conservative justices eliminated mixed-motive lawsuits in age-discrimination cases—despite the fact that the federal law banning age discrimination uses language that the Court has long understood to permit these kinds of cases.[22] Although a bipartisan bill, the Protecting Older Workers Against Discrimination Act,[23] would overrule the Court's decision in *Gross*, as of this writing that bill has gone nowhere in Congress.

Not long after *Gross*, the Supreme Court handed down another decision that placed similar obstacles in front of workers whose employers retaliate against them after they complain that their boss violated their civil rights.[24]

The very same day, the Court made it significantly harder to prevent sexual or racial harassment in a case brought by a kitchen worker who claimed that she was harassed at work for being black. Although federal law provides fairly robust protection to workers harassed by their supervisor, the Court's 5–4 decision in *Vance v. Ball State University* (2013) defined the term "supervisor" very narrowly. Under Justice Alito's opinion in *Vance*, a worker's boss counts as a "supervisor" only if the boss has the power to hire, fire, reassign, or otherwise cause a significant change in the worker's job responsibilities or compensation.[25]

Alito's opinion in *Vance*, however, suffers from the exact same problem as his opinion in *Ledbetter*; it shows no understanding of the "realities of the workplace," where workers' day-to-day lives are frequently directed by people with no immediate authority to fire, demote, or take similar action against them. In one case described in Justice Ginsburg's dissent, an African American woman's boss—the man who assigned her work, controlled her schedule, and directed her workday—repeatedly commented on her "fantastic ass," "luscious lips," and "beautiful eyes," at times using racial slurs as well. At one point, her boss "pulled her on his lap, touched her buttocks, and tried to kiss her while others looked on." And, yet, this woman's boss does not count as her "supervisor" under Justice Alito's standard.[26]

In another case, a newly hired female truck driver was assigned to a "lead driver" whose job was to evaluate her job performance. This lead driver then "forced her into unwanted sex with him, an outrage to which she submitted, believing it necessary to gain a passing grade."[27] And, yet, this man does not count as her "supervisor" under Alito's standard, either.

Neither of these women was invited to speak at the Democratic National Convention, and Congress has done nothing to overrule Alito's opinion in *Vance*.

Ultimately, however, cases like *Ledbetter* and *Vance* are small potatoes compared to another line of decisions that have rendered the courts inaccessible to countless Americans. As it turns out, even if Congress is capable of enacting the most robust protections for workers and consumers, these protections mean very little if they cannot be enforced by courts in the first place.

———

IN FEBRUARY 2005, Anastasiya Komarova received an ominous phone call demanding that she pay a debt that she did not owe. The caller, who contacted Komarova at the Northern California day spa where she worked, claimed that she and her husband, Christopher Propper, had defaulted on their credit card and that she owed nearly $8,000.[28]

In reality, this was the first time Komarova had ever heard of this debt—or of anyone named Christopher Propper, for that matter. Indeed, Komarova, who immigrated to the United States from Russia in 1995, did not have any credit cards at all when the account the debt collector referred to was opened.[29] What she did have, however, was a very similar name to a Southern California woman named "Anastasia Komarova." That woman's fiancé—not Anastasiya-with-a-y—had opened up a joint credit account with his future wife. And, the real debtor's very similar name was enough to force Anastasiya to spend more than a year of her life fighting to keep a debt collector's hands off of money that it had no right to take.[30]

The debt collector was able to stake a claim to Anastasiya's money thanks to an obscure clause buried in many credit card agreements. Anastasia-without-a-y's credit card agreement included a forced-arbitration clause, which provided that if any dispute arose between the credit card company and a cardholder, that dispute would be resolved by a privatized arbitration system rather than by a real judge or jury.[31] Many businesses will outright refuse to deal with anyone who does not agree to forced arbitration. Others simply bury the forced-arbitration clause in a lengthy contract riddled with cryptic language, betting on the fact that most consumers do not consult an attorney before they sign something as ordinary as a credit card agreement.

Yet MBNA, the credit card company at the heart of this case, did more than simply insert a forced-arbitration clause into their agreement, they also called for a very specific arbitration company the National Arbitration Forum (NAF)—to provide the arbitrators. NAF, according to a lawsuit filed by the San Francisco City Attorney's office, was an "arbitration mill" that "churn[s] out arbitration awards in favor of debt collectors and against California consumers." Indeed, when a business sought a judgment against a consumer from the NAF, "the NAF arbitrator decided in favor of the business entity and against the consumer 100% of the time."[32]

In 2011, NAF settled this case, agreeing to shut down its consumer arbitration business altogether in the state of California.[33] Two years earlier, it agreed to a similar settlement with the state of Minnesota.[34]

Yet, in the years before these settlements, NAF arbitrators decided thousands of cases, often providing little more than the most cursory review of each case before issuing an order against the consumer. One NAF arbitrator signed sixty-eight arbitration decisions in the same day, awarding the debt collector every single penny they requested in each case. Another NAF arbitrator, Harvard law professor Elizabeth Bartholet, claims that NAF removed her from several cases after she ruled against a credit card company in a single case.[35] So when the debt collector that targeted Anastasiya filed a claim with the NAF, the arbitrator did not even give the case enough attention to discover that the collector had the wrong woman. Instead, they issued the collector an award of $11,214.33—more than $3,000 more than the real debtor actually owed on her credit card.[36]

And yet, despite the fact that there are so few safeguards against abusive arbitration that the NAF was essentially able to sell rubber stamp arbitration awards to debt collectors for many years, the Supreme Court is one of forced arbitration's greatest boosters.

———

IN 1925, CONGRESS enacted the Federal Arbitration Act (FAA), which had the modest goal of allowing businesses to agree to resolve their disputes with other businesses through arbitration rather than through more costly litigation.[37] In this context, arbitration is entirely appropriate. When sophisticated businesspeople sit down across a negotiating table, they can hammer out an agreement that is fair to both parties and that ensures that the arbitrators called upon to resolve any future disputes will be objective and evenhanded. The problem arises when businesses sneak forced-arbitration clauses into contracts when they know full well that the person on the other side of the agreement has no idea what they are signing away—or when they muscle people into forced arbitration by refusing to do business with them unless they sign away their right to sue in a real court.

Beginning in the 1980s, however, the Supreme Court handed down a series of decisions that paved the way for abusive arbitration. In 1983, for example, the Court declared that "any doubts concerning the scope of arbitrable issues should be resolved in favor of arbitration."[38] One year later, the Court held that state courts, and not just federal courts, are required to enforce forced-arbitration agreements—despite the fact that the drafter of the FAA explicitly denied that the law provided a "federal bludgeon to force an individual State into an unwilling submission to arbitration enforcement."[39]

What's interesting about these early arbitration cases, however, is that the justices did not appear to understand the practical implications of their decisions, as the Court's liberals often voted to expand arbitration while its conservatives often voted the other way. The 1983 arbitration decision, for example, was authored by the crusading liberal Justice William J. Brennan, with Justice William Rehnquist authoring the dissent. Rehnquist also joined the dissent in the decision that forced states into "unwilling submission to arbitration enforcement."

By the recent turn of the century, however, the justices were aligning along familiar ideological lines—and often doing considerable violence to the plain language of the law in the process. The FAA explicitly exempts "workers engaged in foreign or interstate commerce" from its provisions protecting arbitration agreements.[40] Yet five conservative justices held in *Circuit City v. Adams* (2001) that forced-arbitration clauses may be imposed on most workers engaged in foreign or interstate commerce.[41] The upshot of this decision is that most employers can now order their workers to sign a forced-arbitration agreement, under pain of immediate termination if they refuse to do so.

Similarly, in *AT&T v. Concepcion* (2011), the Supreme Court held that businesses can use the FAA to pressure workers and consumers into signing away their rights to bring class action lawsuits, even though the FAA says nothing whatsoever about class actions.[42]

Ironically, the fact that very little was at stake for the plaintiffs in *Concepcion*—the case involved a dispute over $30.22—demonstrates just how harmful this decision will be for consumers. If a company cheats a customer out of $300,000, that customer has a big financial stake in winning a lawsuit against the company, and can probably find a lawyer willing to take the case on a contingency fee basis, meaning that the lawyer will be paid a share of their client's winnings. But if the same company cheats 10,000 people out of $30 each, the company is just as well off as if they'd taken all that money from one person, but hardly any of the potential plaintiffs is likely to file a lawsuit. As one federal judge explained in a similar case, "the realistic alternative to a class action is not 17 million individual suits, but zero individual suits, as only a lunatic or a fanatic sues for $30."[43]

Class actions allow all of the thousands (or even millions) of people with $30 claims to join together under the same lawsuit—and to use the potential that, together, they could win a top-dollar lawsuit to attract an excellent attorney. By effectively neutralizing class actions against any company clever enough to insert a no-class-action clause into its customer agreements, the Supreme Court gave unscrupulous businesses a license to cheat their customers so long as they do so a few dollars at a time.

Admittedly, there is still one important limit on forced arbitration: people cannot be forced into arbitration unless they agree to contracts containing forced-arbitration clauses. Indeed, for this reason, the debt collector that targeted Anastasiya Komarova ultimately had no case against her—although it took about a year of harassment during which Komarova received approximately three calls a week before the collector figured it was the wrong person at the other end of the line.[44]

But avoiding forced-arbitration clauses is much harder than it sounds. These clauses are now all but ubiquitous in many of the most common consumer and employment agreements. One study examined contracts from the banking, cable, credit, brokerage, and cell phone industries, and discovered that nearly 77 percent of them contained a forced-arbitration clause. Meanwhile, 93 percent of the (admittedly very few) employment contracts examined by this study contained a similar clause.[45]

In fairness, there are some signs that at least one industry is moving away from forced arbitration, despite the Supreme Court's efforts to enshrine it into law. In 2009, several major banks announced that they would no longer use forced-arbitration clauses in credit card agreements after consumer groups and state regulators shined light on the kind of abusive practices that targeted Komarova.[46] Nevertheless, the upshot of the Court's forced-arbitration cases is that the decision to employ them or not to employ them rests almost entirely with individual companies. And these companies can deny services or employment altogether to those who refuse to relinquish their ability to assert their rights in court.

Forced arbitration, in other words, could potentially do just as much to undermine the rights of ordinary Americans as any decision handed down in the *Lochner* Era. What use is a minimum-wage law or a right to be free from discrimination if all of the judges who would enforce those rights are replaced by "arbitration mills" that exist solely to rule against workers and consumers?

———

ONE COMMON THEME in many of the Roberts Court's interpretations of federal law—from *Mensing* to *Ledbetter* to *Concepcion*—is that wealthy corporate parties tend to do very well, and workers and consumers fare very poorly. An advocacy group known as the

Constitutional Accountability Center (CAC) maintains an annual tally of how often the justices side with the United States Chamber of Commerce in cases in which the Chamber files a brief. Because the Chamber is both a leading corporate interest group and an unusually active Supreme Court litigant—in the Court's 2013 term, for example, the Chamber filed a brief in more than one in five of the cases decided by the justices[47]—CAC believes that the Chamber's win rate before the justices is a good proxy for how likely the Court is to side with big business.

The data is striking. Between 2006, when Alito joined the Court and became the fifth member of its current majority bloc, and the day the justices began their summer recess in June of 2014, the Roberts Court sided with the Chamber in 70 percent of cases.[48] That compares with a 56 percent win rate for the Chamber under Chief Justice Rehnquist and a 43 percent win rate under the Nixon-appointed Chief Justice Warren Burger. Justice Alito, the most consequential recent Supreme Court appointee because he replaced the much more moderate Justice Sandra Day O'Connor and shifted the Court sharply to the right, is also the member of the Court who is most likely to side with the Chamber. He votes with America's leading advocacy group for big business 76 percent of the time.[49]

Of course, the interests of big businesses are often at odds with those of their employees and consumers. When well-moneyed companies win in court, they frequently do so at the expense of laws intended to protect Americans who are far less wealthy and powerful.

Few cases presented the tension between the interests of an employer and the rights of its employees more clearly than the Court's decision in *Burwell v. Hobby Lobby* (2014). *Hobby Lobby* involved federal regulations that establish a minimum level of coverage that employers must offer if they provide health benefits to their employees—including a requirement that these health plans cover birth control. The owners of Hobby Lobby, a nationwide chain of crafting stores, objected to several forms of birth control on religious grounds—and they claimed that these objections trump their legal obligation to provide contraceptive coverage to their employees.[50]

Before *Hobby Lobby*, this wasn't even a particularly difficult legal question. In *United States v. Lee* (1982), a case interpreting the scope of the First Amendment's guarantee that the government will make no law "prohibiting the free exercise" of religion, the Court established that business owners cannot cite their religious beliefs in order to avoid compliance with the same law that applies to their competitors. "When followers of a particular sect enter into commercial activity as a matter of choice," the Court held in *Lee*, "the limits they accept on their own conduct as a matter of conscience and faith are not to be superimposed on the statutory schemes which are binding on others in that activity." So Hobby Lobby's owners had no right to wield their own religious beliefs to ignore their legal obligations to their employees. Granting overbroad exemptions to employers with religious objections to the law, the Court explained in *Lee*, "operates to impose the employer's religious faith on the employees."[51]

Admittedly, American religious liberty law saw a number of twists and turns between *Lee* and *Hobby Lobby*. Justice Antonin Scalia's opinion for the Court in *Employment Div. v. Smith* (1990)—a case holding that two members of a Native American faith did not have the constitutional right to use the illegal drug peyote in a religious ceremony—drastically reduced the scope of religious objectors' rights not to comply with the law, even in cases where permitting the religious objection would do nothing to harm third parties.[52] This unpopular decision inspired the Religious Freedom Restoration Act of 1993 (RFRA), which was enacted to overrule *Smith* and restore the law as it existed the day before *Smith* was decided.[53] (Although, it should be noted that RFRA only applies to lawsuits challenging federal laws. *Smith* still controls religious liberty lawsuits challenging state laws.)[54]

Alito's opinion in *Hobby Lobby*, however, went far beyond the narrow purpose Congress had in mind when it enacted RFRA. It held, for the first time in the Court's history, that a for-profit corporation can raise a successful religious objection to a federal law.[55] And it erased the balance struck by the Court's opinion in *Lee*, which prevented religious business owners from "impos[ing] the employer's religious faith on the employees."[56] The upshot is that the rights of

Hobby Lobby and its billionaire owners now trump the rights of its wage employees.

It remains to be seen just how far the Roberts Court is willing to allow religious objectors to go in seeking exemptions from the law. In the past, however, such objectors have been quite aggressive in citing their religious beliefs to justify abhorrent practices. In 1959, for example, a Virginia judge wrote in an opinion upholding that state's ban on racial marriage equality that

> Almighty God created the races white, black, yellow, malay and red, and he placed them on separate continents. And but for the interference with his arrangement there would be no cause for such marriages. The fact that he separated the races shows that he did not intend for the races to mix.[57]

A year later, Mississippi politician Ross Barnett won his state's governorship after making a similar claim that "the good Lord was the original segregationist." Several decades earlier, Georgia Governor Allen Candler defended unequal public schooling for African American students on the grounds that "God made them negroes and we cannot by education make them white folks."[58]

Women have similarly been victims of discrimination justified by religious faith. In the 1980s, a private religious school called Fremont Christian denied health benefits to most of the married women in their employ—although they provided such benefits to all male employees and to unmarried women—because of the school's religious belief that "in any marriage, the husband is the head of the household and is required to provide for that household." Fremont even claimed that they should be exempted from federal civil rights law banning gender discrimination because their faith gave them license not to follow this law—though a federal appeals court disagreed in 1986.[59]

More recently, gay men and lesbians have become the targets of claims that discrimination should be allowed so long as it is rooted in religious belief. In 2013, for example, the New Mexico Supreme

Court rejected a claim by a professional photographer who claimed that her religion entitled her to deny services to a lesbian couple in violation of a state anti-discrimination law.[60]

Although Justice Alito's opinion in *Hobby Lobby* explicitly states that religious objectors may not evade "prohibitions on racial discrimination,"[61] it rather pointedly does not say that laws prohibiting discrimination against women or gay people can be enforced against business owners who claim that their sexism or anti-gay views are rooted in religious faith. The implication is that Alito would allow discrimination on the basis of anything other than race to continue, so long as it is justified by a business owner's religious belief—though it is worth noting that Justice Anthony Kennedy, who provided the key fifth vote in *Hobby Lobby*, authored a concurring opinion hinting that he is less willing to tolerate discrimination rooted in religious belief.[62]

Regardless of how far the Roberts Court is willing to take *Hobby Lobby*, however, the Court's opinion fundamentally changes the relationship between workers and employers with religious objections to the law. For the first time in American history, the Court held that a for-profit employer may cite its owners' religious beliefs in order to diminish the rights of its employees. And it did so by ignoring the limited goals Congress intended to accomplish when it enacted RFRA. Congress, of course, could overrule *Hobby Lobby* by passing a new law restoring RFRA's original purpose, but that would require a functioning Congress that is committed to the idea that the rights of workers should not be negated by the personal views of their employers.

Until such a Congress arrives, *Hobby Lobby* will remain untouchable, just as cases like *Vance*, *Mensing*, and *Concepcion* remain impervious to the will of a higher power. The Roberts Court will have free rein to rework the balance of power between big businesses and ordinary Americans, and no one will be able to stop them.

Chapter 13

THE CONSTITUTION HAS ALWAYS BEEN AT WAR WITH EURASIA

Tʜᴇ ʟᴀsᴛ ᴛʜɪɴɢ Christina remembered was letting two men buy her a drink at a Fort Lauderdale bar. Then she woke up hours later on a roadside, with injuries to her genitals suggesting that she was raped. Though she had no memory of how she left the bar or wound up cut and bruised on the side of a road, it was soon obvious that she'd been drugged.[1]

Months later, Christina learned that her rape was a preexisting condition.

After she woke up with signs of a sexual assault, Christina's doctor prescribed her a month's worth of anti-AIDS medication as a precaution in case her assailants were HIV positive. Several months after she took these drugs, when she lost her health insurance and needed to find a new plan, she discovered that no insurance company would cover her. Though Christina never developed an HIV infection, insurers saw that she'd once taken anti-AIDS drugs—and that marked her as someone who might have an expensive medical condition the insurance companies did not want to pay for.[2]

Christina's experience was not particularly unusual. Before the Affordable Care Act banned the practice, numerous insurers denied care to women infected with a sexually transmitted disease by their rapist or to rape survivors with post-traumatic stress disorder.³ Eight states permitted insurers to deny coverage to a woman because she'd experienced domestic violence.⁴

And these coverage denials were hardly limited to victims of violence. Before Obamacare, insurance companies refused to cover Americans for conditions as severe as cancer or as routine as hay fever. Women who became pregnant could immediately lose their ability to obtain insurance, as could college athletes in excellent physical condition who experienced an injury.⁵ Moreover, for the millions of Americans unable to obtain insurance prior to the Affordable Care Act, every trip to the doctor was a flirtation with bankruptcy. According to a 2007 study, nearly two-thirds of all bankruptcies in the United States had a "medical cause."⁶

Worse, in the world before Obamacare, many Americans simply watched their bodies fall into ruin because they were unable to afford care. George, a teenaged diabetic in Buffalo, had a factory job that offered him no insurance and too little money to pay for the insulin, syringes, and testing materials he needed to manage his condition. Unable to control his blood sugar levels, he went blind at age twenty. One year later he died of multiple organ failure.⁷

George's sister Tina worked a waitressing job that also left her uninsured. At twenty-four she had a baby, only to watch that child die five months later due to complications from gestational diabetes. A year later, Tina had a fatal heart attack.

If George and Tina had been insured, their fates almost certainly would have been different. "I had to face their mother at the funerals knowing if they had gotten good care for diabetes, we could have prevented all their end organ disease," their doctor later explained to a reporter. "George would not have gone blind. The baby would have lived. Neither would have had heart or kidney problems."⁸

In Kansas City, a well-regarded gynecologist and Vietnam veteran named Joseph started experiencing involuntary twitches. Eventually, they became so bad that he lost his medical practice—and with it his house, his car, and his health insurance. For eleven years, he was unable to afford the $200 blood test that would have diagnosed his condition as Huntington's disease. He frequently skipped meals in order to pay for medication. Joseph's story ended less tragically than George's or Tina's—he eventually found a clinic willing to diagnose his condition and provide him with care—but he watched his life slip into ruin for more than a decade before that happened.[9]

In rural Idaho, a twenty-eight-year-old mother developed a rare bacterial infection in her heart. Because her convenience store job did not provide her with insurance, she delayed care long enough that a mass formed in her heart, entered an artery, and traveled to her brain, killing her. In a particularly cruel twist, the convenience store promoted her to assistant manager shortly before her death—a promotion that came with health insurance. She left behind two small children.[10]

Beth lost her health insurance after her husband crushed his right leg in a motorcycle accident, causing him to lose his job. A diabetic with a heart condition, Beth stopped seeing her specialist, stopped taking one of her insulin drugs, and started rationing her heart medication in order to save money to pay for her husband's care. Before she found care at a free clinic, Beth's health deteriorated to the point that she was unable to get out of bed.[11]

In Jamestown, New York, a small town a little more than an hour south of Buffalo, an unemployed carpenter arrived at the hospital with bloody urine and sky-high blood sugar due to his untreated diabetes. When the hospital diagnosed him with cancer, he refused surgery because he had no way to pay for it—though he changed his mind six months later after the cancer grew worse.

In the final months of his life, he lost his ability to work after he accidentally cut off his own thumb. He faced regular calls from a collection agency seeking payment for the cancer surgery. His toes had to be amputated due to his unchecked diabetes. His vision grew worse and one of his kidneys failed. After he developed cancer in his bladder, he lost that organ as well. Though he eventually qualified for Medicaid, that was after his family discovered him lying on the floor from a stroke brought on by his diabetes. He died in a nursing home, sharing a room with four other men.[12]

A sixty-four-year-old Idaho woman developed a prolapsed uterus, a weakening in the pelvic muscles that held her womb in place. Although her uterus was literally hanging outside her vagina, the woman delayed surgery for a year so that this expensive procedure would be covered by Medicare.[13]

A young boy developed a tooth infection that spread to his heart, eventually causing permanent damage, because his mother did not make enough money as a janitor to pay for his care.[14]

A Chicago electrician blinded by his diabetes had no way to pay for his medications, so he was forced to go back to work despite the fact that he could not see the electric wires he worked with—he'd feel his way along them to figure out what he was doing.[15]

Doctors often based treatment decisions for their uninsured patients on which drug company had recently provided them with free samples of their product. "You change medication every time a patient comes in and switch them to whatever free samples you happen to have that day," according to a physician in an inner-city health clinic. Another doctor relied on free samples to treat a schizophrenic woman with thoughts of suicide. The woman's husband was on ten different medications, and would beg for samples of each one.[16]

This is what health care looked like in the United States of America—the richest nation the world has ever known—before President Barack Obama signed the Affordable Care Act. Hard-working Americans died because their jobs did not provide them with health benefits. Mothers prayed helplessly over sick children who were unable to receive the most basic care. Senior citizens counted the days until they qualified for Medicare and could finally receive treatment for long-neglected conditions. Rape survivors were treated like pariahs by the insurance industry.

According to one study published by six Harvard physicians, nearly 45,000 American adults died in 2005 because they lacked health insurance. That's more than one death every twelve minutes.[17]

And yet, just seven minutes after Obama signed the Affordable Care Act into law in March of 2010, a group of thirteen state attorneys general filed a lawsuit asking the courts to return America to the days when patients had to beg their doctors for free samples of lifesaving drugs.[18]

———

AMONG LEGAL EXPERTS, this lawsuit was widely viewed as a joke. Charles Fried, who served as Solicitor General of the United States under Ronald Reagan, told Fox News that he "would be happy to come on this program and eat a hat which I bought in Australia last month made of kangaroo skin," if the Supreme Court struck down the law.[19]

Judge Laurence Silberman, a prominent conservative who received the Presidential Medal of Freedom from George W. Bush, wrote in an opinion upholding the law that the lawsuit asked the courts to impose a rule that had no basis "in either the text of the Constitution or Supreme Court precedent."[20]

Judge J. Harvie Wilkinson, one of a handful of judges President Bush interviewed for the seat on the Supreme Court that eventually went to Chief Justice John Roberts, said in the *New York Times* that the case against Obamacare would "imbue judges with unprecedented powers to topple an exhaustively debated and duly enacted federal law." The notion that judges could strike down "commercial regulation on ill-defined and subjective bases is a prescription for economic chaos," Wilkinson warned. And it was a notion that "the framers, in a simpler time, had the good sense to head off."[21]

Even many of the lawyers closest to the legal attacks on the Affordable Care Act secretly believed that they had a weak case. David Rivkin, one of the lead trial attorneys challenging the law, later admitted that many of his "colleagues were privately skeptical" that he could win. Randy Barnett, a libertarian law professor recruited by the challengers to give scholarly legitimacy to their lawsuit, also harbored hidden misgivings. After reading a pair of op-eds Rivkin coauthored laying out his legal case, Barnett concluded that "if those

were the best arguments that the law is unconstitutional, then I figured it must be constitutional."[22]

Shortly before the justices heard oral arguments on the health
care lawsuit, the American Bar Association polled "a select group of
academics, journalists and lawyers who regularly follow and/or comment on the Supreme Court," seeking their predictions on how the
Court was likely to decide the case. Eighty-five percent predicted
that the law would be upheld.[23]

And, yet, with only the most tenuous legal arguments on their
side, the Affordable Care Act's opponents came within a hair of
convincing the Supreme Court to repeal it. Four justices voted to
wipe the law off the books in its entirety,[24] and the fifth, Chief Justice Roberts, reportedly flipped his vote sometime after the case was
argued—he'd initially voted to strike down the bulk of the law.[25]

The remarkable thing about the Obamacare litigation isn't the
fact that Roberts changed his vote, and it certainly isn't the fact that
a legal argument that was widely perceived as absurd by the legal
community ultimately did not carry the day. The remarkable thing
about the Obamacare litigation is that the justices took it so seriously
despite the fact that it had no basis "in either the text of the Constitution or Supreme Court precedent."

With the possible exception of Justice Clarence Thomas, the four
justices who voted to strike down the Affordable Care Act had not
previously staked out positions as radical as their predecessors from
the *Lochner* Era. Only Thomas for example, had indicated that he
would return to the days when federal child labor laws were considered unconstitutional.[26]

Nevertheless, in what the Supreme Court eventually labeled *National Federation of Independent Business ("NFIB") v. Sebelius* (2012),
four justices wholeheartedly accepted the methodology of cases like
Lochner. In voting to strike down Obamacare, these justices implicitly
called for the Court to embrace Professor Christopher Tiedeman's
century-old warnings against the "absolutism of a democratic majority," and they adopted Tiedeman's remedy against this absolutism:

to strike down laws enacted by the people's democratically elected leaders "even though these acts do not violate any specific or special provision of the Constitution."[27]

———

ON THE DAY the Obamacare lawsuits were filed, health reform's defenders had very good reasons to believe that the suits would be swiftly rebuked by the courts. Among other things, they had a 2005 opinion written by one of the most conservative justices on the Supreme Court that left little doubt that the Affordable Care Act is constitutional.

What the law's opponents had on their side was a single unpopular provision of a complicated law with many interlocking parts. They believed that, by tearing out this one provision, they could bring down the entire edifice of Obamacare along with it.

The Affordable Care Act's "individual mandate," the provision requiring most Americans either to obtain health insurance or to pay somewhat higher income taxes, was far and away the least beloved provision of the law, but it was also the keystone that held much of it together. Congress does not enact unpopular legal provisions lightly, and they had a very good reason for writing this particular one into this particular law—without the individual mandate, much of the Affordable Care Act would have been completely unworkable.

Though Christina's experience with the insurance companies that labeled her rape a preexisting condition was unnecessarily cruel, health insurers did not always deny coverage to people with such conditions for idle reasons. The purpose of health insurance is to allow many people to pool their money together so that any one of them who experiences unexpected health bills in the future can draw upon the money in that pool to pay for those bills. But if people who are already sick are allowed into an insurance pool they have not previously paid into, then they are likely to drain all the money out of it—leaving nothing left for the people who have responsibly paid their premiums all along. Before Obamacare, insurance companies would prevent this from happening by refusing to cover many people who were already sick.

The problem of providing insurance to people with preexisting conditions is not easy to fix. Seven states tried to solve it by simply prohibiting insurers from denying coverage to people with those conditions, and the results were disastrous.[28] In Kentucky, nearly all of the state's individual insurance providers fled the state after it banned discrimination against people with preexisting conditions.[29] In New Jersey, many premiums rose more than 350 percent.[30] In the state of Washington, there were entire counties where it was impossible for individuals to buy health insurance at any price.[31]

The reason for these catastrophes is a problem known as "adverse selection." If someone is sick and uninsured, they want to buy health insurance right away so that it will cover their expensive medical bills. But if someone is healthy, they are much less likely to see the need for insurance. Thus, if a state prohibits insurers from denying coverage to sick people, those insurers will be deluged with new customers with expensive medical bills—forcing the insurers to raise their premiums to cover these new costs. Once premiums go up, however, many healthy people will decide that the cost of their insurance isn't worth it—further depleting the money in the insurance pool as more and more premium-paying customers drop out. The result is a death spiral in which higher premiums beget fewer healthy customers, which beget higher premiums, which beget fewer healthy customers.[32]

The individual mandate is the solution to this dilemma. By imposing a tax penalty on healthy people who fail to purchase insurance, an individual mandate brings healthy people into the insurance pools, and it can even reverse a death spiral that has already begun. In 2006, when Massachusetts Governor Mitt Romney signed a health reform bill adding an individual mandate to that state's law—Massachusetts already banned insurers from denying coverage to people with preexisting conditions—the average premium for individual health insurance fell 40 percent in less than three years.[33]

All of this doesn't just make the individual mandate a good idea, it makes it constitutional as well. The Supreme Court held in 1944 that Congress's power to regulate commerce includes the power to regulate the insurance industry.[34] More than six decades later, Justice Antonin Scalia explained that "where Congress has the authority to enact a regulation of interstate commerce, 'it possesses every power needed to make that regulation effective.'"[35] Thus, because the individual mandate is needed to make the Affordable Care Act's protections for people with preexisting conditions work effectively, it is clearly constitutional under Justice Scalia's rule.

The Affordable Care Act's defenders did not need to rely on a fairly recent opinion by Justice Scalia to defend the law, however. In *Gibbons v. Ogden* (1824), the very first Supreme Court decision interpreting Congress's power to "regulate commerce . . . among the several states," Chief Justice John Marshall wrote that there is "no sort of trade" that the words "regulate commerce" do not apply to. Moreover, Marshall explained, once Congress enjoys the power to regulate something, it may do so however it chooses so long as it does not violate some other provision of the Constitution, such as the right to free speech or the right to be free from unlawful searches or seizures. Congress's power to regulate interstate commerce is "plenary," meaning that it is unqualified or absolute.[36]

So the federal government has the power to regulate the national marketplace for health care, and it may choose how it wants to shape this regulation. If Congress wants to provide a financial incentive for people without health insurance to buy into an insurance pool— rather than leaving them to pay for their health care some other way when they inevitably become ill—then that is a decision the Constitution leaves to the people's elected representatives. And it is not the job of the courts to second-guess this decision.

Indeed, the justices who voted to strike down the Affordable Care Act made the exact same mistake that Chief Justice Melville Fuller made when he briefly neutered America's antitrust law, or that Justice William Day made when he struck down federal child-labor laws. They based their decision on "a distinction which was novel when made and unsupported by any provision of the Constitution."[37]

Fuller and Day relied on an extra-constitutional distinction between laws regulating "transportation" and those regulating "manufacturing." Similarly, Obamacare's opponents relied on a distinction between laws that regulate "activity" and laws that compel passive individuals to take a particular action. Permitting Congress to pressure people to act when they'd rather do nothing, the four dissenting justices claimed in the *NFIB* case, "gives such an expansive meaning to the Commerce Clause that *all* private conduct (including failure to act) becomes subject to federal control, effectively destroying the Constitution's division of government powers."[38]

If that argument sounds familiar, it's because it is. Indeed, it is the exact argument Justice Day made in *Dagenhart* when he claimed that, if the Supreme Court upheld a child labor law, "all freedom of commerce will be at an end, and the power of the States over local matters may be eliminated, and thus our system of government [will] be practically destroyed."[39]

More important, it is also a false argument. A pair of cases decided by the Rehnquist Court establishes that Congress has broad authority over the nation's economy, but far less authority over non-economic matters.[40] Thus, the Affordable Care Act—which comprehensively regulates the nation's health care market—is constitutional, while federal laws banning murder, rape, assault, battery, truancy, or child abuse would all be unconstitutional because they do not regulate the economy. Non-economic matters such as these can be regulated only by the states.

Obamacare's opponents both on the Supreme Court and off repeatedly warned that, if the individual mandate were upheld, then any number of absurd laws would follow. If the federal government can induce people to buy health insurance, they argued, then Congress could use the same power to force people to buy broccoli.[41]

The fact that one can imagine a slippery slope, however, does not mean that they will inevitably wind up at the bottom of it.[42] Indeed, if the fact that a judge can envision a slippery slope were sufficient reason to declare a law unconstitutional, then it's likely that all laws would have to be struck down. If Congress has the power to ban products like heroin and machine guns, it could also use that power to ban apple pie and ice cream! If Congress has the power to enact a ten-dollar minimum wage, it could use that power to enact a million-dollar minimum wage! If Congress can levy a 25 percent income tax, it could use that power to levy a 99.99 percent income tax! If Congress can ban child labor, it could ban all labor!

Moreover, there is something fundamentally aristocratic about the idea that judges must shrink federal authority in order to ward off the most horrible theoretical law those judges can possibly imagine. As Chief Justice Marshall explained in his opinion laying out the broad reach of Congress's authority to regulate commerce, "the wisdom and the discretion of Congress, their identity with the people, and the influence which their constituents possess at elections . . . are the restraints on which the people must often rely solely, in all representative governments."[43] The premise of any democracy is that the people must be trusted to make decisions for themselves, even if a small group of men with lifetime tenure believe that those people will come to regret their decision.

If the Affordable Care Act—or any other law, for that matter— turns out to be a bad idea, the Constitution provides a very simple remedy. It's called an election. As Chief Justice Roberts wrote in his opinion upholding most of the law,

> members of this Court are vested with the authority to interpret the law; we possess neither the expertise nor the prerogative to make policy judgments. Those decisions are entrusted to our Nation's elected leaders, who can be thrown out of office if the people disagree with them. It is not our job to protect the people from the consequences of their political choices.[44]

The case against Obamacare was nothing less than an effort to steal away the right to self-governance that our Constitution gives to the American people and redistribute it to five men on the Supreme

Court. And it came within an inch of succeeding. Four of those five men wholeheartedly embraced this effort. And the fifth, Roberts, accepted most of the plaintiffs' arguments, including their narrow reading of Congress's authority to regulate commerce.

An argument with no basis "in either the text of the Constitution or Supreme Court precedent"[45] received five votes on the Supreme Court of the United States—and this result should scare anyone who fears unchecked government power far more than any law enacted by Congress. If elected officials enact absurd laws banning apple pie or forcing people to buy broccoli, they are unlikely to remain in office much longer. Each election gives the voters an opportunity to punish lawmakers who write their most arbitrary whims into the law.

The same cannot be said of the justices of the Supreme Court, however, who answer to no higher authority and who serve for life. The only check on the justices' power is their obedience to the text of the Constitution and their unwillingness to write their own preferences into the law. If the justices stray from constitutional text and their own precedents, then they abandon any limits on their own behavior. If the Supreme Court had the power to strike down the Affordable Care Act, based on an argument with no basis in the Constitution, then there is nothing preventing the justices themselves from banning apple pie or forcing people to buy broccoli.

And unlike members of Congress, the justices cannot be voted out of office. When they behave arbitrarily, they face no consequences whatsoever.

————

THE LEGAL CASE against Obamacare was more than simply an indictment of the Supreme Court. It offered a direct window into how easily partisans can be convinced that something is unconstitutional simply because they want it to be.

The idea of an individual mandate originated in a 1989 report published by the conservative Heritage Foundation. Although Heritage's health plan was far less generous than the law President Obama would sign more than two decades later,[46] it contained an explicit call for a mandate requiring "all households to obtain adequate insurance." Every household, Heritage explained, "has the obligation, to the extent it is able, to avoid placing demands on society by protecting itself."[47]

In the late 1980s and early 1990s, the idea of an individual mandate appealed to conservative intellectuals because it maintained the central role private insurers play in the American health care system, rather than relying upon a government takeover of the health insurance industry. Milton Friedman, the Nobel Prize–winning conservative economist, called for Medicare and Medicaid to be replaced "with a requirement that every U.S. family unit have a major medical insurance policy."[48] Two years after Heritage released its plan, a team of health policy experts led by University of Pennsylvania economist Mark Pauly suggested "mandatory basic coverage" as a conservative alternative to "national health insurance" proposals favored by liberals. "Our strategy," Pauly and his coauthors explained, "is to design a scheme that limits governmental rules and incentives to the extent necessary to achieve the objectives."[49] Twenty years later, Pauly told the *Washington Post*'s Ezra Klein that the purpose of his plan was to convince the George H.W. Bush administration to adopt a "market-oriented" alternative to a government-run health plan.[50]

Although Pauly did not convince President Bush to embrace his plan, in 1993, Republican Senator John Chafee and twenty-one mostly Republican co-sponsors proposed the "Health Equity and Access Reform Today Act," which included an individual mandate. Five senators who voted against the Affordable Care Act—Robert Bennett, Kit Bond, Chuck Grassley, Orrin Hatch, and Richard Lugar—were among this bill's co-sponsors.[51] Former Speaker Newt Gingrich would later explain that Republicans viewed the individual mandate as a more moderate approach than the health plan offered by the Clinton administration—"virtually every conservative saw the mandate as a less dangerous future than what [First Lady] Hillary [Rodham Clinton] was trying to do."[52] (Hillary Clinton chaired the task force charged with devising the Clinton administration's health care plan.)

And then there was Mitt Romney, who signed an individual mandate into law as Massachusetts governor. In 2005, Romney labeled the Massachusetts health plan "the ultimate conservative idea" because it required people to take "responsibility for their own care."[53] Six months after President Obama took office, Romney offered the Massachusetts plan as a model for national health reform. "Using tax penalties" such as an individual mandate, Romney explained, "encourages 'free riders' to take responsibility for themselves rather than pass their medical costs on to others."[54] Less than two years later, however, Romney promised to "repeal Obamacare," claiming that it "is bad law constitutionally, it's bad policy, it's bad for American families."[55]

Romney also claimed that the health care law was "one reason why President Obama will be a one-term president."[56]

Gingrich, for his part, claimed that he'd been "wrong" to support an individual mandate before President Obama signed one into law.[57] Likewise, Senator Grassley was one of the five senators who'd supported the mandate when it was a Republican proposal in 1993 and he told Fox News during the early stages of the debate over Obamacare that "there is a bipartisan consensus to have individual mandates."[58] Nevertheless, he later joined forty-two of his fellow Senate Republicans in an amicus brief claiming that the individual mandate "is foreclosed by the structure and purposes of our Constitution as well as [the Supreme Court's] precedents."[59] Senators Hatch and Lugar, both of whom had also co-sponsored the Republican proposal for an individual mandate in 1993, joined Grassley in signing this brief, arguing that the individual mandate was unconstitutional (Bennett and Bond were no longer senators when the amicus brief was filed).

Heritage, for its part, filed an amicus brief of its own claiming that "Heritage's legal scholars have been consistent in explaining that the type of mandate in the [Affordable Care Act] is unconstitutional." Notably, however, the think tank that invented the individual mandate was unable to cite a single example of a Heritage legal scholar arguing that such a mandate is unconstitutional before Barack Obama became president of the United States.[60]

It is tempting to write these contradictions off as hypocrisy, and even to question whether Romney, Grassley, and others were being dishonest when their reading of the Constitution fell so easily in line with their partisan preferences. But it is likely that something much more disturbing occurred. The human brain has a remarkable capacity for what is known as "motivated reasoning." That is, when someone is confronted with information that they do not want to be true, their brain frequently rationalizes that information away so that it does not threaten their preexisting beliefs.

According to one study, when strong partisans encounter facts that threaten their political beliefs, the rational centers of their brains may never consider those facts at all. At the height of the 2004 presidential election, a team of neuroscience researchers conducted brain scans of committed Republicans presented with unflattering information about President George W. Bush and of committed Democrats presented with similarly unflattering information about Democratic candidate John Kerry. What they found is that the areas of the brain associated with calm, reasoned thinking showed little activity when partisans encountered facts that paint their preferred candidate in a bad light.[61]

Instead of processing such information rationally, partisans' brains actually use a reward and punishment system to prevent them from changing their strongly held beliefs. Once partisans are confronted with unwelcome facts about a favored candidate, the centers of their brains associated with emotional distress kick into gear, and they remain active until the brain finds a way to rationalize away the unwanted facts. Moreover, when the brain succeeds in rationalizing away the unwanted facts, the distress centers of the brain turn off and the centers associated with positive feelings turn on.[62] As one of the researchers behind this study later explained, these positive emotional centers "overlap substantially with those activated when drug addicts get their 'fix.'"[63]

Hardcore partisans, in other words, are almost literally addicted to their own beliefs.

Motivated reasoning is such a powerful force that it can even triumph over a person's ability to solve objective, purely analytic problems such as a math equation. Another study involved a group of test subjects who were screened to determine that they were good at math. These subjects were presented one of two different datasets. The first dataset, when analyzed correctly, suggested that banning guns increases crime; the other dataset, when properly analyzed, led to the opposite conclusion. In each case, however, the data was presented in such a way that the correct answer was counter-intuitive. That is, regardless of how they felt about gun regulation, if test subjects merely glanced at the numbers without taking the time to figure out the correct mathematical process, they were likely to reach the wrong answers.[64]

Nevertheless, the study found that liberals were much more likely to solve this math problem correctly when it led to the conclusion they wanted—that fewer guns lead to less crime. And conservatives were also much more likely to reach the correct answer when it supported their desired belief that gun bans increase crime.[65]

Studies such as these have profound implications for the legitimacy of judicial review. If partisans cannot solve a math problem that calls into doubt their beliefs about guns, how can we trust a Supreme Court justice to "solve" a much more challenging legal problem in which the political stakes are much greater and the "correct" answer may not be so clear cut? Worse, if our brains are wired to reward orthodoxy and punish deviations, how can judges be convinced to change their minds if they have initial, strongly partisan reactions to particular cases? The terrifying implication of these motivated reasoning studies is not just that judges will often place their partisan views before the law; it is that they will truly believe that they have reached the correct result when they do so.

It's important not to overstate this point. Judges like J. Harvie Wilkinson and Laurence Silberman determined that the Affordable Care Act is constitutional, despite their conservative politics. Judge Jeffrey Sutton, a George W. Bush appointee who was a leading conservative litigator before joining the bench, also rejected a challenge to Obamacare, although on somewhat more nuanced grounds.[66] Chief Justice Roberts ultimately voted to uphold the bulk of the law as well, although on the unexpected grounds that the individual mandate is a valid exercise of Congress's power to levy taxes.[67] On the Democratic side of the ledger, Clinton-appointed Justice Stephen Breyer and Obama-appointed Justice Elena Kagan joined Roberts in holding that states could opt out of the provisions of the Affordable Care Act expanding the Medicaid program to millions of poor and near-poor Americans[68]—a decision that rendered nearly six million Americans ineligible for Medicaid coverage in the early months of Obamacare's implementation.[69] So it is not the case that all judges will simply vote their partisan preferences all of the time.

But the case against the individual mandate, at the very least, was also an easy case. It was rooted in a legal argument that was widely viewed as unlikely to succeed by legal experts, and it was dismissed— even mocked—by legal luminaries such as Ronald Reagan's former solicitor general. Roberts, Wilkinson, Silberman, and Sutton may be Republicans, but they are also highly intelligent lawyers who learned to sniff out overreaching advocacy long before they became judges. That odor may have simply overpowered their partisan instincts here.

Another explanation for why some Republican judges voted to uphold the individual mandate is that their partisanship may have been counterbalanced by some other, equally powerful motivator. Silberman and Sutton, for example, both considered the constitutionality of Obamacare as lower court judges who risk the shame of being overruled by a higher court if they allow their partisan views to overcome their ability to apply the law objectively—so they have a built-in motivation to fully consider arguments that they might initially view with skepticism.

Recall that the study demonstrating that partisanship interferes with our ability to do math was designed around a problem in which the correct answer was counter-intuitive. One explanation for that study's result is that partisans who see an intuitive answer that aligns with their politics will end their analysis at that point, while partisans who encounter an answer that seems right at first glance but that also runs counter to their beliefs are more likely to put in the extra work necessary to determine whether that answer is actually correct. As the science journalist Chris Mooney wrote, when mathematically skilled individuals "sense an apparently wrong answer that offends their political sensibilities, [they] are both motivated and equipped to dig deeper, think harder, and even start performing some calculations—which in this case would have led to a more accurate response."[70]

But a lower-court judge who fears that he could be reversed by a higher authority may be similarly motivated to "dig deeper" and "think harder" about whether the result they want in a politically charged case is actually the correct answer. Judges who develop reputations for being reversed frequently by higher courts will lose credibility with their judicial superiors and become even more likely to be reversed in future cases. Their desire to preserve their reputations—and, with it, their ability to influence more powerful jurists—may be enough to convince such judges to "think harder" about a case that they initially were inclined to view a particular way. The judges' need to protect their professional credibility may be enough to overcome motivated reasoning.

Indeed, Judge Sutton's own opinion considering the Affordable Care Act suggests that he set aside his own first impression of the case in order to reject this challenge to the law. Though he acknowledged a "lingering intuition—shared by most Americans, I suspect—that Congress should not be able to compel citizens to buy products they do not want," Judge Sutton ultimately concluded that "not every intrusive law is an unconstitutionally intrusive law." "Even the most powerful intuition about the meaning of the Constitution must be matched with a textual and enforceable theory of constitutional limits," Sutton wrote. "Sometimes an intuition is just an intuition."[71]

It is less clear why Roberts, who answers to no one other than himself, ultimately voted counter to his partisan preference—although we do know that he initially voted to strike the individual mandate and then changed his mind after giving the case a second look. Perhaps he feared that a partisan vote in this most politically charged case would deal a fatal blow to the legitimacy of his Court. Perhaps, as former acting Solicitor General Walter Dellinger argued, Roberts understood that the Affordable Care Act was the market-driven alternative to a government-run health plan—and he didn't "want to say that the market alternatives are ruled out and you can only use monolithic government alternatives."[72] Or perhaps, as *Slate*'s Dahlia Lithwick suggested, Roberts remembered that he didn't come to Washington to reignite the *Lochner* Era.[73] Indeed, he spent many of his earliest years in Washington working for a Reagan administration that sought a truce with the judiciary built upon the rhetoric of judicial restraint.

For the four Republican justices who voted to remove Obamacare from the books in its entirety, however, that truce is dead. They did not simply embrace a tenuous legal argument, they embraced a tenuous legal argument that ran headlong into one of Justice Scalia's own opinions. And they voted to enact their political party's number-one policy priority in the process.

If the justices cannot be relied upon to set their partisan views aside in an easy case such as this one, how can they be trusted to interpret a Constitution that is absolutely riddled with vague and open-ended phrases? What are the "privileges or immunities of citizens of the United States"?[74] What makes a search or seizure "unreasonable"?[75] Which punishments are "cruel and unusual"?[76] If the government wants to deny someone "liberty," how much "process" is "due"?[77] What is a "public use" of private property?[78] How should the United States guarantee a "republican form of government"?[79] What is the "general welfare of the United States"?[80] Which laws are "necessary and proper" for carrying into effect Congress's enumerated powers?[81]

Many of these questions perplexed the very men who wrote these phrases into the Constitution. And yet we trust a Court with nine unelected judges and a terrible track record to issue binding pronouncements about what that Constitution means. This is the same Court that decided *Dred Scott* and *Cruikshank*. The same Court that invalidated the minimum wage and child labor laws. The same Court that held that a woman could be sterilized against her will. The same Court that upheld Japanese internment and that opened the doors to segregation. The same Court that gave us *Citizens United* and *Bush v.*

Gore. And the same Court that nearly stripped health care from millions of Americans.

We placed our Constitution in the hands of John Archibald Campbell, and we placed it in the hands of Stephen Johnson Field—and we gave them the ability to read whatever they chose into our founding document.

Their successors enjoy that very same power to this day.

EPILOGUE
The Gathering Storm

THE SUPREME COURT of the United States has not served America well. And there are no obvious solutions that will ensure that its future does not resemble its past. Even if it were desirable to eliminate the Court, doing so would require a constitutional amendment. Article III of the Constitution provides that "the judicial power of the United States, shall be vested in one Supreme Court." And, as early twentieth-century opponents of child labor learned, amending the Constitution is nearly impossible if any influential political faction opposes the amendment. It is very likely, to say the least, that an amendment fundamentally transforming the judicial branch of government would experience considerable opposition.

One alternative to a constitutional amendment would be to take a page out of Franklin Roosevelt's playbook and revive his court-packing plan. Court-packing, or a similar plan to undermine the Court's independence, would eviscerate the Court's credibility as a fair arbiter of American law. After all, why should anyone trust the decisions of the Supreme Court to be rooted in neutral principles of law when its membership is easily manipulated by whichever political party last won a decisive election? Court-packing could also be done without a constitutional amendment, as ordinary legislation can expand the size of the Court.

But the fact that court-packing would avoid the onerous constitutional amendment process hardly means that a court-packing
bill would actually survive a congressional vote. In 1937, Roosevelt
enjoyed a rare mandate that few presidents can claim at any point
during their time in the White House. Yet FDR, fresh off a landslide reelection, experienced swift and bipartisan opposition to his
court-packing plan. Future presidents are unlikely to succeed where
he failed.

Lest there be any doubt, however, eliminating the Supreme
Court—or effectively destroying its moral standing through a proposal such as court-packing—would not be desirable. Congress can
pass a Civil Rights Act, but courts are needed to apply it in individual cases. Congress can ban child labor, but courts are needed
to sanction the individual employers who defy the ban. And while
many cases that created doubtful rights, such as *Lochner*'s freedom
to contract, imposed needless suffering on a generation of American
workers, the core rights protected by the Constitution—the right to
free speech, the right to a fair trial, the right to be free from unjust
discrimination, and so forth—are essential freedoms that belong to
all of humanity. As the darker moments of American history demonstrate, these rights will not always be respected by elected lawmakers
acting without supervision.

Similarly, unless there is a single high court at the apex of the
judiciary, local judges may refuse to enforce constitutional rights that
are unpopular in their home states. In the wake of *Brown v. Board
of Education*, for example, Senate Judiciary Committee Chair James
Eastland, a senator from Mississippi and an arch-segregationist, manipulated his committee's procedures to give home-state senators an
effective veto over anyone nominated to federal judgeships in their
states—thus giving senators who opposed *Brown* the power to veto
judges who supported public school integration.[1] Absent a higher
judicial authority in the nation's capital, much of the enforcement
of *Brown* and the civil rights legislation that eventually tore down
Jim Crow would have been left to the judges appointed to the bench
under Eastland's regime. Many of them would simply have declared

the Civil Rights Act unconstitutional, confident in the knowledge that they would not be overruled.

Indeed, in one of the first Civil Rights Act cases to reach the Supreme Court, a federal district court in Alabama did strike down the law, holding that "if Congress has the naked power to do what it has attempted in [the Civil Rights Act], there is no facet of human behavior which it may not control . . . and rights of the individual to liberty and property are in dire peril."[2] Nearly half a century later, a federal judge used that exact reasoning to strike down the entire Affordable Care Act, reasoning that if Congress had the power to enact Obamacare, then "it is not hyperbolizing to suggest that Congress could do almost anything it wanted."[3] If there had not been further review by higher judicial authorities, these decisions would have remained good law—or, at least, they would have remained good law within the jurisdictions of the courts that decided them. America would have become an atomized nation, where federal law meant one thing in Michigan and another thing entirely in Florida.

Another way of reining in the Supreme Court would be to ensure that the law was very precisely drafted, leaving fewer ambiguities that the justices could resolve in favor of their preferred outcome. Eliminating every single ambiguous phrase in the federal law would be a daunting task, however, if it is even possible. It would be difficult for lawmakers to anticipate every instance in which a law might apply in the future, and to write specific instructions explaining how that case should be handled when it does finally arise many years later. Moreover, even if Congress could draft every single statute with such painstaking precision, that is still no guarantee that the justices will follow those instructions. Recall the Court's *Circuit City* decision, which held that the Federal Arbitration Act applies to most workers engaged in foreign or interstate commerce despite the fact that the FAA explicitly exempts "workers engaged in foreign or interstate commerce."[4]

Additionally, many of the most ambiguous passages in federal law are provisions of the Constitution itself. To reach the *Lochner* decision, for example, the majority opinion relied on the Constitution's promise that no state may "deprive any person of life, liberty, or property without due process of law."[5] This is also the same constitutional provision the Court relied upon nearly three generations later in *Roe v. Wade*. Thus, even if the public agreed in principle that a constitutional amendment was necessary to prevent the Court from reviving decisions like *Lochner*, any actual attempt to do so is likely to run headlong into America's intractable abortion debate. One powerful faction would demand that any amendment must include language explicitly protecting a woman's right to choose an abortion, while another, equally powerful faction would demand that the amendment include language explicitly *denying* that the Constitution protects a woman's right to choose an abortion (indeed, many opponents of abortion might insist that the Constitution ban the practice altogether). Since accommodating either faction would transform the proposed amendment into something half the nation's lawmakers would vigorously oppose, the amendment would almost certainly die in Congress.

A final proposal would be to change the way judges are appointed to federal courts, including the Supreme Court, to weed out judicial nominees who are committed partisans likely to fall victim to motivated reasoning. Several states choose their judges in ways that are intended to minimize the influence of partisan officials. In Alaska, for example, the governor is required to fill judicial vacancies by selecting from a list of candidates provided by a "judicial council," and the majority of the seats on this council are held by nonpartisan officials.[6]

Notably, this process led to a rare moment of consensus between President Obama and former Alaska Governor Sarah Palin. In 2009, Palin selected a state judge named Morgan Christen from the list of candidates the judicial council provided her for an open seat on the Alaska Supreme Court. The governor stated at the time that she has "every confidence that Judge Christen has the experience, intellect, wisdom and character to be an outstanding Supreme Court justice."[7] Two years later, Obama offered a similar assessment of Christen when he nominated her to a vacant seat on a federal appeals court.[8]

There is at least one precedent for a similar judicial selection process to Alaska's at the federal level. In 1977, President Jimmy Carter created the "United States Circuit Judge Nominating Commission," which consisted of thirteen panels that would recommend potential nominees for federal appellate judgeships.[9] If a president wished to create a similar commission to ensure that all federal judges and justices will be recommended by a nonpartisan body, they would have the power to do so.

The problem with this solution, however, is that, barring a constitutional amendment, nothing prevents a future president from dismantling any such commission, just as President Ronald Reagan ended Carter's commission shortly after taking office.[10] Presidents of either party would be foolish to delegate their ability to name judges to a nonpartisan commission when they know full well that the other party is unlikely to do the same when they occupy the White House.

In the end, the only practical solution to bad Supreme Court justices is good Supreme Court justices. And the only way to ensure that new justices will not repeat the Supreme Court's past is to elect presidents who are committed to a very different future.

There is reason to be hopeful that such a future is possible. The liberalism of the Warren Court was an accident, made possible by the fact that President Dwight Eisenhower did not realize how Chief Justice Earl Warren and Justice William Brennan would conduct themselves on the Court, among other things. Today, however, it is much easier to imagine a president intentionally nominating judges who show appropriate judicial restraint in the vast majority of cases while simultaneously respecting values such as equality, open debate, and respect for the rights of the accused that are actually written into the Constitution.

The character of the legal profession, and especially of the elite lawyers who are typically tapped to fill federal judicial vacancies, is also quite different than it was more than a century ago. Liberals in the Roosevelt era and conservatives in the Nixon and Reagan eras have both taken their turn railing against activist judges who thwart the will of the people. The norm of judicial deference to elected officials that emerged during the New Deal is now the status quo. And the same resistance to change that once cut in favor of striking down economic legislation now cuts against it.

Similar norms have developed against laws that ban dissent, or laws that sanction official racism, or laws that would bring back the sham trials that characterized Southern justice for much of the Jim Crow era. Americans, and the American legal profession, expect the rights that are explicitly written into the Constitution to be enforced, even if we cannot always agree about what the scope of those rights should be.

So there is a possible future in which newly appointed justices repudiate the excesses of the Roberts Court and embrace the Court's important but limited role as protector of genuine constitutional rights.

————

THERE IS, HOWEVER, another possible future that looks a whole lot like the Supreme Court's past. As of this writing, four members of the Court—Justices Antonin Scalia, Anthony Kennedy, Ruth Bader Ginsburg, and Stephen Breyer—are in their late seventies or early eighties. The next President of the United States is likely to replace some of them, or perhaps all four.

From the Roosevelt era through the Reagan-era truce, there was a widespread consensus in favor of judicial restraint on most issues that come before the Supreme Court. That consensus has broken down. Given the almost mythological significance that Republican lawmakers bestow upon their opposition to the Affordable Care Act, it is unlikely that anyone nominated to the Supreme Court by a Republican president will believe that Obamacare is constitutional. If Ginsburg or Breyer is replaced by such a nominee, tens of millions of Americans could lose their health care just months later.

The Court's fairly recent decisions advancing gay rights could also be overruled if its membership shifts even slightly to the right. *United States v. Windsor* (2013), which struck down the so-called Defense of

Marriage Act's ban on federal recognition of same-sex marriages, was a 5–4 decision.[11] Similarly, although six justices joined the Court's decision eliminating bans on gay (and many other forms of) sex in *Lawrence v. Texas* (2003),[12] the sixth vote was Justice Sandra Day O'Connor, who has since been replaced by arch-conservative Justice Samuel Alito. If one more vote flips, the Court could give the green light to laws criminalizing sex between consenting adults.

Indeed, although gay rights is one of the few areas in which the Roberts Court has actually moved the law to the left, the courts have hardly been a refuge for sexual minorities for most of American history. For many years, the federal government treated gay people as if they were deviants unable to control their basest urges. In 1965, for example—the same year that President Lyndon Johnson signed the Voting Rights Act—an early gay rights group known as the Mattachine Society of Washington petitioned the United States Civil Service Commission to rescind a policy that declared openly gay people "unsuitable for Federal employment." The Commission did not simply reject the Mattachine Society's plea, it explained that it would leave this policy in place because of

> the revulsion of other employees by homosexual conduct and the consequent disruption of service efficiency, the apprehension caused other employees of homosexual advances, solicitations or assaults, the unavoidable subjection of the sexual deviate to erotic stimulation through on-the-job use of the common toilet, shower and living facilities, the offense to members of the public who are required to deal with a known or admitted sexual deviate to transact Government business, the hazard that the prestige and authority of a Government position will be used to foster homosexual activity, particularly among the youth, and the use of Government funds and authority in furtherance of conduct offensive both to the mores and the law of our society.[13]

These were not the words of some aberrant anti-gay group; it was an official statement of policy by the government of the United

States of America. And the federal government was hardly alone in this position. As the Commission noted in its response to the Mattachine Society, "homosexual conduct, including that between consenting adults in private, is a crime in every jurisdiction, except under specified conditions, in Illinois."[14]

For many decades, the Court showed no interest whatsoever in prohibiting this kind of discrimination against gay people. When an early gay rights case, brought by two Minnesota men seeking the right to marry, reached the Supreme Court in 1972, the justices dismissed their case with a single sentence—the appeal was "dismissed for want of substantial federal question."[15] (At the time, this was a common formulation the justices used to dispose of cases they deemed unworthy of their time.)[16] Fourteen years later, in *Bowers v. Hardwick* (1986), the justices held that there was no "constitutional right of homosexuals to engage in acts of sodomy,"[17] a decision that was eventually overruled in *Lawrence*.

So the Court's solicitude for gay rights is a very recent development, and it hangs by the thread of a single justice's vote. Supporters of gay rights rely on the Supreme Court to remain their ally at great peril.

For many leading Republicans, however, reversing the Roberts Court's few flirtations with liberalism is the least of their agenda. Though not every Republican lawmaker finds inspiration in the Constitution of Stephen Johnson Field, many of them do. House Judiciary Chair Bob Goodlatte has said that Medicare, Medicaid, and Social Security are all unconstitutional.[18] Senator Mike Lee of Utah has, at various times, claimed that child labor laws, food stamps, the Food and Drug Administration, federal disaster relief, Medicaid, income assistance for the poor, Medicare, and Social Security all violate the Constitution.[19] The day after President Barack Obama signed the Affordable Care Act, then-governor of Virginia Bob McDonnell signed legislation purporting to nullify Obamacare—in direct violation of the Constitution.[20] Since then, other governors have signed unconstitutional legislation purporting to nullify federal gun laws[21] and, oddly enough, federal lightbulb regulation.[22] Senator

Rand Paul of Kentucky not only spoke out against the Civil Rights Act in 2010—using arguments similar to the ones Barry Goldwater raised against the Act in 1964[23]—he also called *Lochner* "a wonderful decision."[24]

If someone sharing these views is elected president in 2016, they could name as many as four new justices to the Supreme Court. Along with the presumed vote of Justice Clarence Thomas—who, in a 1995 opinion, endorsed the same narrow view of federal power that drove the Court to strike down child labor laws in *Dagenhart*[25]—that would add up to enough votes on the Court to rethink nearly eight decades of constitutional law. The Affordable Care Act, the Civil Rights Act, the right to join a union, the minimum wage, and even federal child labor laws could all be on the chopping block.

If the narrow vision of federal power that prevailed prior to the Great Depression had served America well, then such an effort to turn back the clock would make sense. Likewise, if the terrible consequences flowing from a more robust welfare and regulatory state that was predicted by groups like the Liberty League had actually manifested, then it might make sense to rethink the last several generations of American constitutional law. But these consequences have not come about. To the contrary, America thrived in the decades following the end of the *Lochner* Era.

In 1928, the year before the Depression began, the average American earned about ten thousand dollars annually in modern dollars.[26] Today, they earn nearly three times as much.[27] In 1940, just three years after the justices took the brakes off of the New Deal, only 5 percent of the population over the age of twenty-five held a bachelor's degree or higher. By 2009, that number rose to 30 percent.[28] Social Security lifts an estimated twenty-two million Americans out of poverty today. Indeed, without this crown jewel of the New Deal, over 44 percent of American seniors would have incomes below the poverty line.[29]

If the average worker did not earn three times as much today as they did on the eve of the Great Depression, or if America had not grown into a nation of scholars, or if a strong federal government had not torn down a brutal system of Southern apartheid, then it would make sense to consider whether the post–New Deal Supreme Court has allowed our nation to stray down a dangerous path.

But the reality is that, in the years since Roosevelt won his battle with the Four Horsemen, the United States became the mightiest nation in the history of politics and the wealthiest nation in the history of money. Our children do not labor in cotton mills. Our grandparents do not suffer in poorhouses.

Two visions of the Constitution have struggled for dominance in the United States ever since Hamilton clashed with Jefferson over the constitutionality of the First Bank of the United States. In one, the United States should be governed by the men and women who are elected to govern, and, while the Constitution does place explicit limits on government that must be policed by the Supreme Court, it is not the job of the Court to micromanage decisions that belong to the people's elected representatives.

In the other vision, the primary purpose of the Constitution is to restrain government action, even if lawmakers could easily act to prevent human suffering. As Senator Lee said in a 2010 lecture in which he argued that federal child labor laws are unconstitutional, the Constitution "was designed to be a little bit harsh."[30]

Both visions have, at times, been ascendant. So we know what kind of country America became when the Supreme Court cast a skeptical eye on democracy, and we know about the power and affluence we achieved after the Supreme Court allowed the American people to govern themselves. The men and women who would exchange self-governance for an aggressive Supreme Court, in other words, must answer a difficult question similar to one that Justice O'Connor asked in a somewhat different context:

Why would we trade a system that served us so well for one that served our great-grandparents so poorly?[31]

Acknowledgments

THERE IS SOMETHING intoxicating about reading a judicial opinion. Most writers write to persuade. Or they write to inform. Or they write to entertain. Judges, however are not ordinary writers. Judges are sorcerers. They write and the world changes. An innocent man is given his life back. A worker is given back his or her livelihood. A president is forced to reveal his or her darkest secrets.

Like countless other young lawyers who came of age studying the works of wizards like Earl Warren, Bill Brennan, and Thurgood Marshall, I left law school enthralled by this power. A lawyer argues a case. A judge writes words. And then the arc of the moral universe bends a little more towards justice.

The inspiration for this book, and the much more jaded view of the Supreme Court that it presents, was a work assignment that landed in my lap despite the fact that I was far too young and inexperienced for it. The Affordable Care Act had just become law and conservative activists and Republican state officials were lining up to bring lawsuits challenging it, most of them rooted in the same legal argument Judge Laurence Silberman would later dismiss as having no basis "in either the text of the Constitution or Supreme Court precedent." And someone had asked Neera Tanden, then the chief operating officer of the Center for American Progress and later its president, if she could find someone to write a brief on behalf of various patient groups in support of the law.

I remember that a colleague—I can't remember who—forwarded me an email indicating that Neera was looking for someone who could work on the brief. And I remember sticking my head in Neera's office and asking her about the project. I did not expect to walk out of her office with instructions to churn out a first draft of the brief within the next thirty-six hours.

At the time, I was just a few years out of law school. I also questioned whether this brief would really matter. Like so many other constitutional lawyers with far more knowledge and experience than I had, I'd read the relevant Supreme Court precedents and determined that the legal attack on Obamacare had no chance of succeeding. I still remember what I told Neera after she gave me my marching orders: "I'll get right on it, but do you really think it's necessary?"

Over the course of the next two years I learned that precedents cannot always be trusted. I learned that judges wield a dangerous magic. And that this magic can just as easily be used to tear down progress as it can be used to build it up. But, most importantly, I learned what it was like to be on the receiving end of arbitrary power. If the case against the Affordable Care Act had been rooted in prior decisions, or if it had some basis in constitutional text, then I would have been saddened but not shocked if we had lost the case. But the Supreme Court came within one vote of stripping potentially life-saving health care from millions of Americans, and it did so based on nothing that I could recognize as law.

I will always be grateful to Neera for trusting me to defend this law, for allowing me to grow more and more involved with the legal, political, and media strategies involved in Obamacare's defense, and for trusting me with these tasks when I was just beginning my career. Thanks also to Tony Carrk, who demonstrated a superhuman ability to track down obscure health statistics when I was crashing on a deadline at two in the morning; to Si Lazarus and Rochelle Bobroff, my co-counsel on what wound up being the most significant brief I worked on during this litigation; and especially to Lori Lodes, who taught me more about how to sell an idea to people who are barely listening than anyone else I will probably ever know.

Though I owe the inspiration for this book to Neera and the project she gave me, I owe my career to Faiz Shakir. Faiz grew Think-Progress from a handful of young people writing about politics into one of the paragons of America's progressive media. Somewhere along the way, he decided that the best use for my talents was to have me write about the Supreme Court for his publication's audience. Faiz rescued me from obscurity. And he gave me the platform I needed to secure a book deal. I cannot imagine what I would be doing with my life right now if I had never met Faiz.

ThinkProgress's founder (and Faiz's successor), Judd Legum, is a visionary editor who gives me the freedom to write what I want to write, and who trusts me when I say that people will actually want to read about how arcane legal doctrines shape their lives. Judd also gave me the time I needed to finish this book. Without his generosity, it would be nothing more than an idea.

Hiring Nicole Flatow is the single best professional decision I have made in my entire career. Nicole is my partner at ThinkProgress Justice and brings a degree of compassion for the mistreated and the falsely accused that I envy and admire. Nicole also carried a heavy load back at the office while I was at home working on this book. Her work ethic and sound judgment are the reason I felt free to step out of the office to write my manuscript.

This book benefited immensely from conversations with journalists and scholars such as Adam Winkler, Dahlia Lithwick, Garrett Epps, Kent Greenfield, Pam Karlan, and others whom I am being very neglectful by forgetting to mention here. Thanks also to law professors such as Jeff Powell, Jed Purdy, Neil Siegel, Stuart Benjamin, Chris Schroeder, William Van Alstyne, and especially Erwin Chemerinsky, who all showed considerable patience with me when I was their student, and my understanding of the Constitution was far less developed than I led myself to believe. Special thanks to Mike Sacks for his helpful comments on my manuscript, and to my close libertarian friend Josh Blackman, who warned me about how this book would be criticized. I can't say that I took every piece of advice that Josh gave me. But at least I'll know where the arrows are coming from.

I will always be grateful to Judge Eric Clay, who gave me a clerkship and who showed far more concern for justice than most of the justices in this book. Judge Clay showed me how a court operates and, often, how it should operate.

And finally, to Holley. You nursed me when I was sick and listened to me when I was furious about something some obscure judge had done. You hauled metric tons of books from your library to our home. You tolerate the fact that I always come to bed late. And you never fail to remind me that my cooking fills the living room with aggressive, pungent odors. I love you dearly. And I look forward to having more time to spend with you now that this book is done.

Notes

INTRODUCTION

1. Charles Lane, *The Day Freedom Died: The Colfax Massacre, the Supreme Court and the Betrayal of Reconstruction* (New York: Henry Holt, 2009), 103–109.

2. Ibid., 260.

3. 92 US 542, 559 (1876).

4. 60 U.S. (19 How.) 393, 407, 412 (1857).

5. President Abraham Lincoln, The Emancipation Proclamation (January 1, 1863), available at http://www.archives.gov/exhibits/featured_documents /emancipation_proclamation/transcript.html.

6. Akhil Reed Amar, "The Bill of Rights and the Fourteenth Amendment," 101 *Yale L.J.* 1193, 1235 (1992).

7. Korematsu v. United States, 323 U.S. 214 (1944).

8. Buck v. Bell, 274 U.S. 200 (1927).

9. Hammer v. Dagenhart, 247 U.S. 251 (1918); Irene M. Ashby, "Child Labor in Southern Cotton Mills," *The World's Work*, Vol. 2, 1290, 1291, 1294 (1901).

10. Adkins v. Children's Hospital, 261 U.S. 525, 552–553 (1923); Adair v. United States, 208 U.S. 161, 175 (1908).

11. Citizens United v. FEC, 128 S. Ct. 1471 (2008).

12. Shelby County (Ala.) v. Holder, 133 S. Ct. 2612 (2013).

13. Espionage Act, § 3, 40 Stat. 553–554 (1917).

14. Schenck v. United States, 249 U.S. 47, 52 (1919).

15. *The Federalist* No. 78 (Alexander Hamilton).

CHAPTER 1: HOW THE CIVIL WAR WAS UNDONE

1. Ronald M. Labbé and Jonathan Lurie, *The Slaughterhouse Cases: Regulation, Reconstruction, and the Fourteenth Amendment* (Lawrence: University Press of Kansas, 2003), 34.

2. Ibid., 35.

3. Ibid., 23.

4. Herbert Hovenkamp, "Technology, Politics, and Regulated Monopoly: An American Historical Perspective," 62 *Tex. L. Rev.* 1263, 1298 (1984).

5. Labbé and Lurie, *Slaughterhouse Cases*, 40.

6. Hovenkamp, "Technology, Politics," 1299–1300.

7. Labbé and Lurie, *Slaughterhouse Cases*, 64.

8. Hovenkamp, "Technology, Politics," 1298–1300.

9. Louisiana Constitution, Art. 2 (1868).

10. Labbé and Lurie, *Slaughterhouse Cases*, 70.

11. Slaughter-House Cases, 83 U.S. (16 Wall.) 36, 59 (1873).

12. Ibid., 59–60.

13. Michael A. Ross, "Obstructing Reconstruction: John Archibald Campbell and the Legal Campaign against Louisiana's Republican Government, 1868–1873," 49 *Civil War History* 235, 241 (2003).

14. Jonathan Lurie, "Ex-Justice Campbell: The Case of the Creative Advocate," 30 *J. of Sup. Ct. Hist.* 17, 18 (2005).

15. Ibid., 20.

16. Ibid.

17. Ross, "Obstructing Reconstruction," 242.

18. Ibid., 249.

19. Labbé and Lurie, *Slaughterhouse Cases*, 194.

20. *Judge Field: Sound in Doctrine, Brave in Deed* 4 (1880), available at http://archive.org/details/judgefieldsoundi00np.

21. Paul Kens, *Justice Stephen Field: Shaping Liberty from the Gold Rush to the Gilded Age* (Lawrence: University Press of Kansas, 1997), 155.

22. Munn v. Illinois, 94 US 113, 148 (1887) (Field, J., dissenting).

23. Ex parte Garland, 71 U.S. 333, 376 (1887).

24. Ibid., 382–399 (Miller, J., dissenting).

25. *Judge Field*, 5–7.

26. Plessy v. Ferguson, 163 U.S. 537, 548 (1896).

27. Virginia v. Rives, 100 U.S. 313, 335 (1880) (Field, J., concurring in the judgment).

28. Kens, *Justice Stephen Field*, 13.

29. Ibid., 132–137; John Hoyt Williams, *A Great and Shining Road: The Epic Story of the Transcontinental Railroad* (New York: Times Books, 1988), 114.

30. Kens, *Justice Stephen Field*, 134.

31. Hon. Creed Haymond et al., *The Social, Moral and Political Effect of Chinese Immigration. Policy and Means of Exclusion: Memorial of the Senate of California to the Congress of the United States, and an Address to the People of the United States* (1877), 7; available at http://archive.org/stream/chineseimmigrati01slsn#page/n135/mode/2up.

32. Chinese Exclusion Act of 1882, ch. 126, 22 Stat. 58 (1882) (repealed 1943).

33. The Chinese Exclusion Case, 130 U.S. 581, 603–606 (1889).

34. Slaughter-House Cases, 83 (16 Wall.) U.S. 36, 92–93 (1873) (Field, J., dissenting).

35. Michael A. Ross, "Hill-Country Doctor: The Early Life and Career of Supreme Court Justice Samuel F. Miller in Kentucky, 1816–1849," 71 *Filson Club Hist. Q.* 430, 432–436 (1997).

36. William Lloyd Garrison, "To The Public," *The Liberator* (Jan. 1, 1831), 1.

37. Ross, "Hill-Country Doctor," 442.

38. Ibid., 445, 461.

39. Ibid., 446–449.

40. Slaughter-House Cases, 83 (16 Wall.) U.S. 36, 71–72 (1873).

41. Ibid., 64.

42. Ibid., 78.

43. Ibid., 96 (Field, J., dissenting).

44. Charles Lane, *The Day Freedom Died: The Colfax Massacre, the Supreme Court and the Betrayal of Reconstruction* (New York: Henry Holt, 2009), 64.

45. Ibid., 65–66.

46. Eric Foner, *Reconstruction: America's Unfinished Revolution, 1863–1877* (New York: Harper Perennial, 2002), 550.

47. Lane, *Day Freedom Died*, 70.

48. Ibid., 70–72.

49. Ibid., 91–92.

50. Ibid., 93.

51. Ibid., 97–102.

52. Ibid., 102–105.

53. United States v. Cruikshank, 92 U.S. 542, 548 (1876).

54. Ibid., 552.

55. Ibid., 553.

56. Ibid., 556.

57. Foner, *Reconstruction*, 550–551.

58. Charles L. Sanders, "The President Who Hurt Negroes Most," *Ebony* (May 1964), 112.

59. Foner, *Reconstruction*, 580–581.

CHAPTER 2: THE BARON OUTSIDE CHICAGO

1. Quoted in John Hoyt Williams, *A Great and Shining Road: The Epic Story of the Transcontinental Railroad* (New York: Times Books, 1988), 9.

2. Horace Greeley, *An Overland Journey from New York to San Francisco in the Summer of 1859* (New York: C. M. Saxton, Barker, & Co., 1860), 272.

3. Williams, *Great and Shining Road*, 10.

4. Ibid., 8–9.

5. Stanley Buder, *Pullman: An Experiment in Industrial Order and Community Planning, 1880–1930* (New York: Oxford University Press, 1967), 21–22.

6. Tom Jackson et al., "The Wealthiest Americans Ever," *NYTimes* (July 15, 2007), available at http://www.nytimes.com/ref/business/20070715_GILDED_GRAPHIC.html.

7. Kenneth D. Ackerman, *The Gold Ring: Jim Fisk, Jay Gould, and Black Friday, 1869* (Falls Church, VA: Viral History Press, 2012), 189–204.

8. Toledo, A. A. & N.M. Ry. Co. v. Pennsylvania Co., 54 F. 730, 739 (N.D. Ohio 1893).

9. *See, for example,* Waterhouse v. Comer, 55 F. 149, 154 (C.C.W.D. Ga. 1893): "All those who combine and conspire with employees to thus quit, or, as officials of labor organizations, issue printed orders to quit, or to strike, with an intent to embarrass the court in administering the property, render themselves liable for contempt of court."

10. William E. Forbath, *Law and the Shaping of the American Labor Movement* (Cambridge: Harvard University Press, 1991), 89.

11. John P. Frey, *The Labor Injunction: An Exposition of Government by Judicial Conscience and Its Menace* (Cincinnati, OH: Equity Publishing Company, 1923), iii (introduction by Samuel Gompers).

12. Buder, *Pullman*, 4.

13. US Bureau of the Census, *Population of 100 Largest Urban Places: 1850* (June 15, 1998), available at http://www.census.gov/population/www/documentation/twps0027/tab08.txt; US Bureau of the Census, *Population of 100 Largest Urban Places: 1860* (June 15, 1998), available at http://www.census.gov/population/www/documentation/twps0027/tab09.txt.

14. Buder, *Pullman*, 4–5.

15. Ibid., 5.

16. Frederick Clifton Pierce, *Field Genealogy: Being the Record of All the Field Family in America, Whose Ancestors Were in This Country Prior to 1700*, Volume 2, (Chicago: W. B. Conkey Company, 1901), 674.

17. Buder, *Pullman*, 8.

18. David Ray Papke, *The Pullman Case: The Clash of Labor and Capital in Industrial America* (Lawrence: University Press of Kansas, 1999), 4; Liston Edgington Leyendecker, *Palace Car Prince: A Biography of George Mortimer Pullman* (Boulder: University Press of Colorado, 1992), 37.

19. Leyendecker, *Palace Car Prince*, 38–40.

20. Ibid., 78.

21. Buder, *Pullman*, 21–23.

22. Ibid., 29.

23. Ibid.

24. Ibid., 19.

25. Beth Tompkins Bates, *Pullman Porters and the Rise of Protest Politics in Black America, 1925–1945* (Chapel Hill: University of North Carolina Press, 2000), 21.

26. Buder, *Pullman*, 17–18.

27. Leyendecker, *Palace Car Prince*, 165.

28. Buder, *Pullman*, 32–33.

29. Richard Theodore Ely, "Pullman: A Social Study," 70 *Harper's New Monthly Magazine* 453, 456–457 (Feb. 1885).

30. Ibid.; Leyendecker, *Palace Car Prince*, 169.

31. Papke, *Pullman Case*, 18.

32. Leyendecker, *Palace Car Prince*, 169.

33. *See* Buder, *Pullman*, 71, 76; Papke, *Pullman Case*, 11; Ely, "Pullman: A Social Study," 460.

34. Ely, "Pullman: A Social Study," 465.

35. Papke, *Pullman Case*, 8.

36. Ibid., 9.

37. Ibid., 9–10.

38. Melvyn Dubofsky, *Industrialism and the American Worker: 1865–1920*, 3rd edition (Wheeling, IL: Harlan Davidson, 1996), 65–69.

39. United States Strike Commission, *Report on the Chicago Strike of June–July, 1894*, (Washington, DC: Government Printing Office, 1895), xxiii–xxiv (hereinafter "Strike Report").

40. *See* Richard White, *Railroaded: The Transcontinentals and the Making of Modern America* (New York: W. W. Norton, 2012), 475–482.

41. Christina Romer, "Spurious Volatility in Historical Unemployment Data," 94 *J. of Political Econ.* 1, 31 (1986).

42. Strike Report, xxi: "For the year ending July 31, 1893, the dividends were $2,520,000, and the wages $7,223,719.51. For the year ending July 31, 1894, the dividends were $2,880,000, and the wages $4,471,701.39."

43. Ibid., xxxiv.

44. Ibid., xxxii, 572.

45. W. F. Burns, *The Pullman Boycott: A Complete History of the Great R. R. Strike* (St. Paul, MN: McGill Printing Co., 1894), 18–19.

46. Strike Report, xxiv.

47. Ibid., xxxv.

48. Papke, *Pullman Case*, 24.

49. Strike Report, 425–426.

50. Ibid., 417.

51. Ibid., xxxvii, 424.

52. Ibid., 537, xxxv.

53. Ibid., 621–622.

54. Ibid., xxxviii.

55. Ibid., xxxviii.

56. Ibid., xxxviii–xxxix.

57. Ibid., 131.

58. Papke, *Pullman Case*, 23–25.

59. Strike Report, 132.

60. Ibid., 135.

61. Ibid., xxix; *see* Papke, *Pullman Case*, 27: "The managers' group in 1892 had established a wage scale for the Chicago switchmen, and they had also proposed elaborate wage schedules that the member railroads might use on their entire lines."

62. Papke, *Pullman Case*, 28.

63. Strike Report, xliv–xlv.

64. Papke, *Pullman Case*, 29–30.

65. Ibid., 32.

66. Ibid., 30.

67. Strike Report, xlv–xlvi.

68. Papke, *Pullman Case*, 33.

69. Strike Report, xlv.

70. Ibid., 421–422.

71. Papke, *Pullman Case*, 40–41.

72. Ibid., 41.

73. Ibid., 41–42.

74. Letter from Grover Cleveland, President of the United States, to John P. Altgeld, Governor, Ill. (July 5, 1894), in *The Daily News Almanac and Political Register for 1895* (2d ed. 1895), 83; available at http://hdl.handle.net/2027/mdp.39015026439961?urlappend=%3Bseq=90.85.

75. Papke, *Pullman Case*, 45.

76. Eugene V. Debs, "How I Became a Socialist," *New York Comrade* (April 1902).

77. Papke, *Pullman Case*, 50.

78. Debs, "How I Became," 75.

79. Papke, *Pullman Case*, 62.

80. United States v. Sing Tuck, 194 U.S. 161, 182 (1904) (Brewer, J., dissenting).

81. J. Gordon Hylton, "The Judge Who Abstained in Plessy v. Ferguson: Justice David Brewer and the Problem of Race," 61 *Miss. L.J.* 315, 316, 324 (1991).

82. Ibid., 342–343.

83. Tarrance v. Florida, 188 U.S. 519, 524 (1902).

84. Jones v. Montague, 194 U.S. 147, 152–153 (1904).

85. Hylton, "Judge Who Abstained," 361.

86. Knowlton v. Moore, 178 U.S. 41, 110 (1900) (Brewer, J., dissenting); Magoun v. Illinois Trust & Sav. Bank, 170 U.S. 283, 301 (1898) (Brewer, J., dissenting).

87. Knoxville Iron Co. v. Harbison, 183 U.S. 13, 17–18 (1901); Ibid., 22 (Brewer, J., dissenting).

88. McLean v. Arkansas, 211 U.S. 539, 550 (1909); Ibid., 551 (Brewer, J., dissenting).

89. Brass v. North Dakota, 153 U.S. 391, 405 (1894) (Brewer, J., dissenting); Budd v. New York, 143 U.S. 517, 551 (1892) (Brewer, J., dissenting).

90. Budd, 143 U.S. at 551.

91. Forbath, *Law and American Labor*, 65.

92. Ibid., 65–66.

93. In re Debs, 158 U.S. 564, 592 (1895).

94. Papke, *Pullman Case*, 35.

95. Debs, 158 U.S. at 600.

96. Ibid., 591.

CHAPTER 3: THE TWO CONSTITUTIONS

1. *See* United States v. E.C. Knight Co., 156 U.S. 1 (1895).

2. Carl B. Swisher, *American Constitutional Development* (Boston: Houghton Mifflin, 1943), 420–421.

3. Henry Demarest Lloyd, "Lords of Industry," 138 *N. Am. Rev.* 535 (1884), available at http://xroads.virginia.edu/~DRBR/1884hdlloyd.html.

4. Ibid.

5. Tom Jackson et al., "The Wealthiest Americans Ever," *NYTimes* (July 15, 2007), at http://www.nytimes.com/ref/business/20070715_GILDED _GRAPHIC.html.

6. *See, for example,* Scofield v. Ry. Co., 43 Ohio St. 571, 597 (Ohio) ("The defendant contracted with the Standard Oil Company that in consideration of the promise of the company to ship all their product of petroleum over the defendant's railroad, it undertook to ship the same at an average rate of about ten cents per barrel below its published rates.")

7. Henry Demarest Lloyd, "The Story of a Great Monopoly," *The Atlantic* (Mar. 1, 1881), available at http://www.theatlantic.com/magazine/archive/1881 /03/the-story-of-a-great-monopoly/306019/?single_page=true (hereinafter "Great Monopoly").

8. Ibid.

9. Interstate Commerce Act, ch. 104, § 2, 24 Stat. 379 (1887).

10. *See, for example,* Lloyd, "Great Monopoly"; Lloyd, "Lords"; *see also* Swisher, *American Constitutional Development*, 421 (explaining Lloyd's influence in generating anti-monopoly sentiment).

11. Swisher, *American Constitutional Development*, 422.

12. Democratic Party Platform (June 5, 1888), available at http://www .presidency.ucsb.edu/ws/?pid=29584; *see also* William Letwin, *Law and Economic Policy in America: The Evolution of the Sherman Antitrust Act* (New York: Random House, 1965), 86 (quoting same).

13. Letwin, *Law and Economic Policy,* 86–87.

14. Ibid., 87.

15. Swisher, *American Constitutional Development*, 428.

16. Keith E. Whittington, "Congress Before the Lochner Court," 85 *B.U.L. Rev.* 821, 846–47 (2005).

17. Willard L. King, *Melville Weston Fuller: Chief Justice of the United States, 1888–1910* (New York: Macmillan, 1950), 1, 30–32.

18. Salmon L. Chase et al., "Appeal of the Independent Democrats (Jan. 19, 1854)," in Oliver Joseph Thatcher, *The Library of Original Sources: 1833–1865*, Volume 9 (New York: University Research Extension, 1907), 147.

19. James W. Ely, Jr., *The Chief Justiceship of Melville W. Fuller* (Columbia: University of South Carolina Press, 1995), 6.

20. King, *Melville Weston Fuller*, 41–42.

21. Ibid., 42.

22. Ibid., 44–45.

23. Ely, *Chief Justiceship*, 7–8.

24. Ibid., 9.

25. King, *Melville Weston Fuller*, 99–100.

26. Ibid., 93.

27. *Judge Field: Sound in Doctrine, Brave in Deed* (1880), 4; available at http://archive.org/details/judgefieldsoundi00np.

28. *See* Alexander Hamilton, "Alexander Hamilton's Final Version of the Report on the Subject of Manufactures," in Harold C. Syrett ed., *The Papers of Alexander Hamilton*, Volume 10: *December 1791–January 1792* (New York: Columbia University Press, 1966), 230, 303; Alexander Hamilton, "Final Version of an Opinion on the Constitutionality of an Act To Establish a Bank," in Harold C. Syrett ed., *The Papers of Alexander Hamilton*, Volume 8: *February–July 1791* (New York: Columbia University Press, 1966), 97, 102–107.

29. For a more detailed discussion of these two early visions of the Constitution, see Ian Millhiser, "Worse Than Lochner," 29 *Yale L. & Pol'y Rev. Inter Alia* 50, 61–65 (2011), available at http://yalelawandpolicy.org/sites/default /files/YLPRIA29_Millhiser.pdf.

30. Ibid., 63–64.

31. Articles of Confederation, arts. II & III.

32. Akhil Reed Amar, *America's Constitution: A Biography* (New York: Random House, 2005), 25–28.

33. Letter to Joseph Jones, May 31, 1780, in John C. Fitzpatrick, ed., *The Writings of George Washington from the Original Manuscript Sources*, Volume 18 (Wash-

ington, DC: Government Printing Office, 1931–1944), 453. The author is grateful to Elizabeth Wydra for pointing him to Washington's writings on the need for a strong central government. *See, for example,* Elizabeth B. Wydra, "Constitutional Fairy Tales and the Affordable Care Act," *Politico* (Feb. 5, 2012), available at http://www.politico.com/news/stories/0212/72470.html#ixzz2cilT8dkf.

34. Fitzpatrick, *George Washington*, 490 (Letter to Alexander Hamilton, March 4, 1783).

35. Fitzpatrick, *George Washington*, 505 (Letter to Alexander Hamilton, March 31, 1783).

36. Jack M. Balkin, *Living Originalism* (Cambridge, MA: Belknap Press, 2011), 144.

37. 22 U.S. (9 Wheat.) 1, 193 (1824).

38. Ibid., 209.

39. Ibid., 194.

40. Ibid., 189.

41. Balkin, *Living Originalism*, 149.

42. United States v. E.C. Knight, 156 U.S. 1, 9 (1895).

43. Ibid., 16.

44. Ibid., 17.

45. 157 U.S. 429 (1895).

46. Donald Grier Stephenson, Jr., *Campaigns and the Court: The U.S. Supreme Court in Presidential Elections* (New York: Columbia University Press, 1999), 121.

47. Pollock, 157 U.S., 558–572.

48. Ibid., 567.

49. Ibid., 572.

50. Ibid., 571.

51. Ibid.

52. Pollock, 157 U.S., 568.

53. Ibid., 569.

54. Ibid., 574.

55. Ibid., 607 (Field, J., concurring in part and concurring in the judgment).

56. Hylton v. United States, 3 U.S. 171 (1796).

57. Springer v. United States, 102 U.S. 586, 602 (1881).

58. Calvin H. Johnson, "Apportionment of Direct Taxes: The Foul-Up in the Core of the Constitution," 7 *William & Mary Bill of Rights J.* 1, 21 (1998).

59. Calvin H. Johnson, "Fixing the Constitutional Absurdity of the Apportionment of Direct Tax," 21 *Const. Commentary* 295, 344–346 (2004); Erik M. Jensen, "The Taxing Power, the Sixteenth Amendment, and the Meaning of 'Incomes,'" 33 *Ariz. St. L.J.* 1057, 1110–1114 (2001).

60. William Howard Taft, "Message Concerning Tax on Net Income of Corporations," in William Howard Taft, *Presidential Addresses and State Papers* (New York: Doubleday, Page, 1910), 166, 167.

61. 175 U.S. 211, 240 (1899).

62. Adair v. United States, 208 U.S. 161, 178 (1908).

63. Carter v. Carter Coal Co., 298 U.S. 238, 303–305 (1936).

64. Coronado Coal Co. v. United Mine Workers, 268 U.S. 295, 310 (1925).

CHAPTER 4: THE PRICE OF A COKE

1. Francis H. Nichols, "Children of the Coal Shadow," 20 *McClure's Magazine* 435, 435, 437–439 (1903).

2. Ibid., 438.

3. Ibid.

4. John Spargo, *The Bitter Cry of the Children* (New York: Macmillan, 1906), 164.

5. Ibid.; Nichols, "Children of the Coal Shadow," 438.

6. Spargo, *Bitter Cry*, 166.

7. Ibid., 163, 165.

8. Alan Derickson, *Black Lung: Anatomy of a Public Health Disaster* (Ithaca, NY: Cornell University Press, 1998), 4–6.

9. Nichols, "Children of the Coal Shadow," 440.

10. Kellogg Durland, "Child Labor in Pennsylvania," *The Outlook* (May 9, 1903), 126.

11. Spargo, *Bitter Cry*, 156–159.

12. Ibid.

13. Lewis W. Hine, "Baltimore to Biloxi and Back: The Child's Burden in Oyster and Shrimp Canneries," 30 *The Survey* 167, 168–169 (1913).

14. Ibid., 170.

15. Ibid., 171.

16. Florence Kelly and Alzina P. Stevens, "Wage-Earning Children," in Jane Addams et al., *Hull-House Maps and Papers. A Presentation of Nationalities and Wages in a Congested District of Chicago, Together with Comments and Essays on Problems Growing out of the Social Conditions* (New York, T. Y. Crowell, 1895), 49, 66–67.

17. Ibid., 58.

18. Spargo, *Bitter Cry*, 177–178.

19. Ibid., 178–179.

20. Inland Steel Co. v. Yedinak, 172 Ind. 423, 425–426 (1909).

21. Irene M. Ashby, "Child Labor in Southern Cotton Mills," in 2 *The World's Work* 1290, 1291, 1294 (1901).

22. Ibid., 1291–1293.

23. Ibid., 1295.

24. Robert H. Bremner et al., *Children and Youth in America: A Documentary History*, Volume 2 (Cambridge, MA: Harvard University Press, 1971), 616.

25. Ibid.

26. Spargo, *Bitter Cry*, 149.

27. Marie Van Vorst, *The Cry of the Children: A Study of Child-Labor* (New York: Moffat, Yard, 1908), 48, 110.

28. Ashby, "Child Labor," 1293.

29. Ibid.

30. Albert J. Beveridge, "Child Labor and the Nation," 29 *Annals of the Am. Academy of Political and Social Science* 115, 118 (1907).

31. Nichols, "Children of the Coal Shadow," 439; Spargo, *Bitter Cry*, 143.

32. Beveridge, "Child Labor and the Nation," 118.

33. Ibid., chapter 2, n. 36, and accompanying text.

34. 41 *Cong. Rec.* 1552–1557, 1792–1826, 1867–1883.

35. Ibid., 1824 (statement of Senator Bacon).

36. Stephen B. Wood, *Constitutional Politics in the Progressive Era: Child Labor and the Law* (Chicago: University of Chicago Press, 1968), 18–19.

37. Walter I. Trattner, *Crusade for the Children: A History of the National Child Labor Committee and Child Labor Reform in America* (Chicago: Quadrangle Books, 1970), 89, 120.

38. William Howard Taft, *Popular Government: Its Essence, Its Permanence and Its Perils* (New Haven, CT: Yale University Press, 1913), 143.

39. Woodrow Wilson, *Constitutional Government in the United States* (New York: Columbia University Press, 1908), 170–171.

40. Wood, *Constitutional Politics*, 66–67.

41. Ibid., 40–41.

42. United States v. E.C. Knight, 156 U.S. 1, 9 (1895).

43. 188 U.S. 321, 354 (1903).

44. Hipolite Egg Co. v. United States, 220 U.S. 45, 57–58 (1911).

45. Hoke vs. United States, 227 U.S. 308, 320–321 (1913).

46. Wood, *Constitutional Politics*, 57, 77.

47. Hammer v. Dagenhart, 247 U.S. 251, 268 n. 1 (1918).

48. Wood, *Constitutional Politics*, 81–82, n. 6.

49. Ibid., 43–45, 84.

50. "John G. Johnson, Noted Lawyer, Dies," *N.Y. Times* (Apr. 14, 1917), available at http://query.nytimes.com/mem/archive-free/pdf?res=F30714FD3E5E11738DDDAC0994DC405B878DF1D3 (hereinafter "Johnson Obit").

51. Benjamin R. Twiss, *Lawyers and the Constitution: How Laissez Faire Came to the Supreme Court* (Princeton: Princeton University Press, 1942), 208.

52. Ibid.; Wood, *Constitutional Politics*, 84–85.

53. Johnson Obit.

54. Wood, *Constitutional Politics*, 88.

55. Ibid., 91–93.

56. Lowell Mellett, "The Sequel to the Dagenhart Case," 6 *The American Child* 3, 3 (1924).

57. Ibid., 105.

58. Coppage v. Kansas, 236 U.S. 1, 16 (1915).

59. Wood, *Constitutional Politics*, 156.

60. Alfred H. Knight, *Utter Justice: Verbal Glimpses into Fifteen Hundred Years of Our Legal History* (New York: iUniverse, 2008), 97.

61. John Knox, *The Forgotten Memoir of John Knox: A Year in the Life of a Supreme Court Clerk in FDR's Washington* (Chicago: University of Chicago Press, 2002), 113, 141 (Dennis J. Hutchinson and David J. Garrow, eds.).

62. Jeff Shesol, *Supreme Power: Franklin Roosevelt vs. The Supreme Court* (New York: W. W. Norton, 2010), 6.

63. Knox, *Forgotten Memoir*, 74.

64. Ibid., 9–10.

65. Ibid., 24.

66. Knight, *Utter Justice*, 97.

67. Ibid.; Knox, *Forgotten Memoir*, xix.

68. Knox, *Forgotten Memoir*, xix; Louise Weinberg, "The McReynolds Mystery Solved," 89 *Denv. U.L. Rev.* 133, 141–142 (2011).

69. Weinberg, "McReynolds Mystery," 141.

70. Ibid., 142.

71. Michael J. Klarman, "A Celebration of Justice Ruth Bader Ginsburg: Social Reform Litigation and Its Challenges," 32 *Harv. J.L. & Gender* 251, 267 (2009).

72. Knox, *Forgotten Memoir*, 51.

73. Albert P. Blaustein and Roy M. Mersky, "Rating Supreme Court Justices," 58 *A.B.A. J.* 1183, 1187 (1972).

74. *See* Weinberg, "McReynolds Mystery," 142, n. 60.

75. Hammer v. Dagenhart, 247 U.S. 251, 272 (1918).

76. Gibbons v. Ogden, 22 U.S. (1 Wheat.) 1, 196–197 (1824).

77. United States v. Darby, 312 U.S. 100, 116 (1941).

78. Dagenhart, 247 U.S. at 276.

79. Mellett, "Sequel to Dagenhart," 3.

80. Ibid.

CHAPTER 5: YOU LOAD SIXTEEN TONS
AND WHAT DO YOU GET?

1. The title of this chapter is a lyric from *Sixteen Tons*, sung by Tennessee Ernie Ford, a song about a coal miner trapped in debt by low wages paid in scrip.

2. Irene M. Ashby, "Child Labor in Southern Cotton Mills," in 2 *The World's Work* 1290, 1291–1292 (1901).

3. W.J. Cash, *The Mind of the South* (New York: Vintage, 1991), 200–201.

4. Ibid., 200.

5. Alexander Keyssar, *Out of Work: The First Century of Unemployment in Massachusetts* (New York: Cambridge University Press, 1986), 45, 50.

6. Mark Aldrich, *Safety First: Technology, Labor, and Business in the Building of American Work Safety, 1870–1939* (Baltimore, MD: Johns Hopkins University Press, 1997), 80.

7. Ibid., 81.

8. Hardy Green, *The Company Town: The Industrial Edens and Satanic Mills That Shaped the American Economy* (New York: Basic Books, 2010), 73.

9. Aldrich, *Safety First*, 53.

10. Harry Caudill, *Night Comes to the Cumberlands: A Biography of a Depressed Area* (Boston: Little, Brown, 1963), 120.

11. Aldrich, *Safety First*, 41–42, 53–55.

12. Ibid., 53–55; Caudill, *Night Comes*, 119.

13. Green, *Company Town*, 58, 66.

14. John W. Hevener, *Which Side Are You On? The Harlan County Coal Miners, 1931–39* (Champaign: University of Illinois Press, 2002), 16–18.

15. Green, *Company Town*, 59.

16. Clayton D. Laurie, "The United States Army and the Return to Normalcy in Labor Dispute Interventions: The Case of the West Virginia Coal Mine Wars, 1920–1921," 50 *W. Va. Hist.* 1 (1991), available at http://www .wvculture.org/history/journal_wvh/wvh50–1.html.

17. Ill. Steel Co. v. Zolnowski, 118 Ill. App. 209, 212–214 (Ill. App. Ct. 1st Dist. 1905); William Hard, *Injured in the Course of Duty* (New York: Ridgway Company, 1910), 40–41.

18. Zolnowski, 118 Ill. App. at 214–216.

19. Crystal Eastman, *Work-Accidents and the Law* (New York: Charities Publication Committee, 1910), 121–122.

20. Zolnowski, 118 Ill. App. at 215.

21. Robert Asher, "The Limits of Big Business Paternalism: Relief for Injured Workers in the Years before Workmen's Compensation," in David Rosner and Gerald Markowitz, eds., *Dying for Work: Workers' Safety and Health in Twentieth-Century America* (Bloomington: Indiana University Press, 1987), 19.

22. Aldrich, *Safety First*, 104–105.

23. State ex rel. Zillmer v. Kreutzberg, 114 Wis. 530, 547 (Wis. 1902).

24. In re Preston, 63 Ohio St. 428, 439 (Ohio 1900).

25. State v. Loomis, 115 Mo. 307, 320 (Mo. 1893).

26. In re Morgan, 26 Colo 415, 451 (Colo. 1899) (quoting Leep v. Railway Co., 58 Ark. 407, 421 (Ark. 1894).

27. Zillmer, 114 Wis., 532.

28. Ibid., 540–542.

29. Ibid., 536, 538–540, quoting Christopher G. Tiedeman, *A Treatise on State and Federal Control of Persons and Property in the United States Considered*

from Both a Civil and Criminal Standpoint, Volume 2 (St. Louis: F. H. Thomas Law Book Co., 1900), § 204.

30. Christopher G. Tiedeman, *A Treatise on State and Federal Control of Persons and Property in the United States Considered from Both a Civil and Criminal Standpoint,* Volume 1 (St. Louis: F. H. Thomas Law Book Co., 1900), ix.

31. *Slaughterhouse Cases,* 83 U.S. 36, 110 & n. 39 (Field, J., dissenting); *see also* Paul Kens, *Lochner v. New York: Economic Regulation on Trial* (Lawrence: University Press of Kansas, 1998), 118.

32. Christopher G. Tiedeman, *The Unwritten Constitution of the United States: A Philosophical Inquiry into the Fundamentals of American Constitutional Law* (New York: G. P. Putnam's Sons, 1890), 80–81.

33. Kens, *Lochner v. New York,* 6.

34. Ibid., 6–7.

35. Ibid., 8.

36. International Association of Factory Inspectors, Ninth Annual Convention of the International Association of Factory Inspectors of North America Held at Providence RI.

37. Ibid., 17; Kens, *Lochner v. New York,* 8–9.

38. Inspectors, 14–16.

39. Kens, *Lochner v. New York,* 13.

40. Ibid., 13, 17.

41. Session Laws of New York, 1895, vol. 1, ch. 518, §2–6.

42. Ibid., § 1.

43. James W. Ely, Jr., "Rufus W. Peckham and Economic Liberty," 62 *Vand. L. Rev.* 591, 593 (2009).

44. Giles v. Harris, 189 U.S. 475 (1903).

45. Cumming v. Richmond County Board of Education, 175 U.S. 528, 543–545 (1899).

46. People v. King, 110 N.Y. 418 (N.Y. 1888).

47. Hickey v. Taaffe, 105 N.Y. 26, 35–36 (1887).

48. Ely, "Rufus W. Peckham," 594, 604.

49. Holden v. Hardy, 169 U.S. 366, 395–396 (1898).

50. Talcott v. Buffalo, 125 N.Y. 280, 289–290 (1891).

51. Kens, *Lochner v. New York,* 132.

52. Lochner v. New York, 198 U.S. 45, 53 (1905).

53. Ibid., 57.

54. Ibid., 53.

55. Ibid., 70–71 (Harlan, J., dissenting).

56. Ibid., 59.

57. Alexis de Tocqueville, *Democracy in America and Two Essays on America* (London: Penguin Books, 2003), 313.

58. Ibid.

59. Russell G. Pearce, "Lawyers as America's Governing Class: The Formation and Dissolution of the Original Understanding of the American Lawyer's

Role," 8 *U. Chi. L. Sch. Roundtable* 381, 392, 396–397 (2001); John Austin Matzko, *The Early Years of the American Bar Association, 1878–1928* (unpublished dissertation on file with author, 1984), 16, 32–33.

60. Pearce, "Lawyers," 399.

61. Benjamin R. Twiss, *Lawyers and the Constitution: How Laissez Faire Came to the Supreme Court* (Princeton, NJ: Princeton University Press, 1942), 145–146.

62. Matzko, *Early Years*, 193–194.

63. Ibid., 194.

64. Ibid., 208.

65. Edmund Burke, *Reflections on the Revolution in France* (Oxford, UK: Oxford University Press, 1993), 61.

66. This formulation was originally drafted by *National Review* founder William F. Buckley, who wrote that his publication "stands athwart history, yelling Stop, at a time when no one is inclined to do so, or to have much patience with those who so urge it." William F. Buckley, Jr., "Our Mission Statement," *National Review* (Nov. 19, 1955), available at http://www.nationalreview.com /articles/223549/our-mission-statement/william-f-buckley-jr.

67. David E. Bernstein, *Rehabilitating Lochner: Defending Individual Rights Against Progressive Reform* (Chicago: University of Chicago Press, 2011), 3.

68. Muller v. Oregon, 208 U.S. 412, 416–417, 423 (1908).

69. Ibid., 421–423.

70. Lochner, 198 U.S. at 56.

71. Coppage v. Kansas, 236 U.S. 1, 14 (1915).

72. Muller, 208 U.S. 326–327.

73. Bunting v. Oregon, 243 U.S. 426, 438–439 (1917).

74. Adkins v. Children's Hosp., 261 U.S. 525, 552–553 (1923).

75. Tiedeman, *Treatise on State and Federal Control,* 81.

76. Adair v. United States, 208 U.S. 161, 175 (1908).

77. Ibid., 174.

CHAPTER 6: MEN FEARED WITCHES AND BURNT WOMEN

1. Buck v. Bell, 274 U.S. 200, 207 (1927).

2. Paul A. Lombardo, *Three Generations, No Imbeciles: Eugenics, the Supreme Court, and Buck v. Bell* (Baltimore, MD: Johns Hopkins University Press, 2010), 134.

3. Ibid., 103.

4. Edwin Black, *War Against the Weak: Eugenics and America's Campaign to Create a Master Race* (New York: Four Walls Eight Windows, 2008), 40.

5. Ibid.

6. Lombardo, *Three Generations*, 140.

7. Act of Mar. 20, 1924, ch. 394, 1924 Va. Acts 569.

8. Black, *War Against the Weak*, 42.

9. Lombardo, *Three Generations*, 111.

10. Joseph S. DeJarnette, "Mendel's Law: A Plea for a Better Race of Men," available at http://www.dnalc.org/view/11212-Mendel-s-Law-Poem-by-Joseph-DeJarnette-MD-witness-in-Buck-vs-Bell-case.html.

11. Lombardo, *Three Generations*, 115.

12. 274 U.S. 207.

13. *See* Henry Herbert Goddard, *The Kallikak Family: A Study in the Heredity of Feeble-Mindedness* (New York: Macmillan, 1913), 68–69. ("All this degeneracy has come as the result of the defective mentality and bad blood having been brought into the normal family of good blood.")

14. For additional discussion of the origins of eugenics, see Black, *War Against the Weak*, 9–12.

15. Goddard, *The Kallikak Family*, 17–18, 36.

16. Ibid., 30.

17. Ibid., 18–19.

18. Ibid., 53.

19. Ibid., 9.

20. State ex rel. Zillmer v. Kreutzberg, 114 Wis. 530, 538 (Wis. 1902).

21. Herbert Spencer, *Social Statics, or The Conditions Essential to Human Happiness Specified and the First of Them Developed* (New York: D. Appleton & Co., 1883), 412–414.

22. Ibid., 415.

23. Ibid., 413–416.

24. Richard Hofstadter, *Social Darwinism in American Thought* (Boston: Beacon Press, reprint ed. 1992), 34–35.

25. Ibid., 48.

26. Spencer, *Social Statics*, 24.

27. Barry Werth, *Banquet at Delmonico's: Great Minds, the Gilded Age, and the Triumph of Evolution in America* (New York: Random House, 2009), xxv.

28. Francis Galton, *Probability, the Foundation of Eugenics* (Oxford, UK: Clarendon Press, 1907), 5.

29. Black, *War Against the Weak*, 11–12.

30. Ibid., 12.

31. Act of Mar. 20, 1924, ch. 394, 1924 Va. Acts 569.

32. Robert M. Mennel and Christine L. Compston, eds., *Holmes and Frankfurter: Their Correspondence, 1912–1934* (Lebanon, NH: University Press of New England, 1996), 19.

33. Jeffrey Rosen, *The Supreme Court: The Personalities and Rivalries that Defined America* (New York: Times Books, 2007), 108.

34. Lochner v. New York, 198 U.S. 45, 75–76 (Holmes, J., dissenting).

35. Rosen, *Supreme Court*, 89.

36. Ibid., 88.

37. Black, *War Against the Weak*, 44.

38. Ibid., 43.

39. Rosen, *Supreme Court*, 84.

40. Ibid., 84–86.

41. Ibid., 87.

42. Pete Daniel, "Up From Slavery and Down to Peonage: The Alonza Bailey Case," 57 *J. of Am. Hist.* 654, 655 (1970).

43. Ibid., 657–658.

44. Bailey v. Alabama, 219 U.S. 219, 243 (1911).

45. Ibid., 246 (Holmes, J., dissenting).

46. *See* Victoria Nourse, "*Buck v. Bell:* A Constitutional Tragedy from a Lost World," 39 *Pepp. L. Rev.* 101, 113 (2011).

47. David Upham, "Pope Pius XI's Extraordinary—But Undeserved—Praise of the American Supreme Court," 14 *Rutgers J. Law & Relig.* 25, 59 (2012).

48. Lombardo, *Three Generations*, 154.

49. Irving Fisher and Eugene Lyman Fisk, *How to Live: Rules for Healthful Living Based on Modern Science* (New York: Funk and Wagnalls, second edition, 1915), 14, 44, 323.

50. Jeff Shesol, *Supreme Power: Franklin Roosevelt vs. the Supreme Court* (New York: W. W. Norton, 2009), 66.

51. Paul Kens, *Lochner v. New York: Economic Regulation on Trial* (Lawrence: University Press of Kansas, 1998), 172.

52. Adkins v. Children's Hosp., 261 U.S. 525, 546 (1923).

53. Shesol, *Supreme Power*, 67–68.

54. Home Bldg. & Loan Asso. v. Blaisdell, 290 U.S. 398, 454, 472 (1934) (Sutherland, J., dissenting).

55. 65th Cong., 1st Sess., in 55 Cong. Rec. S 214 (Apr. 4, 1917).

56. Geoffrey R. Stone, *Perilous Times: Free Speech in Wartime from the Sedition Act of 1798 to the War on Terrorism* (New York: W. W. Norton, 2004), 136–137.

57. *See* ibid., 170–171; Schenck v. United States, 249 U.S. 47, 49 (1919); Espionage Act, § 3, 40 Stat. 553–554 (1917).

58. Stone, *Perilous Times*, 153.

59. Ibid., 156.

60. Ibid., 171–173.

61. Schenck, 249 U.S. 49–50.

62. Leaflet distributed by the Socialist Party to conscripts (Aug. 20, 1917), available at http://www.english.illinois.edu/-people-/faculty/debaron/380/380 reading/schenckpamphlet.html.

63. Schenck, 249 U.S. 52–53.

64. Frohwerk v. United States, 249 U.S. 204, 207–209 (1919).

65. Thomas Healey, *The Great Dissent: How Oliver Wendell Holmes Changed His Mind—and Changed the History of Free Speech in America* (New York: Metropolitan Books, 2013), 85.

66. J. Robert Constantine, ed., *Gentle Rebel: Letters of Eugene V. Debs* (Champaign: University of Illinois Press, 1995), 123.

67. Ibid., 120.

68. Healey, *Great Dissent*, 86–87.

69. Eugene V. Debs, *Eugene V. Debs Speaks* (Atlanta, GA: Pathfinder Press, 1994), 239.

70. Ibid., 239, 248.

71. Healey, *Great Dissent*, 89.

72. Debs v. United States, 249 U.S. 211, 216–217 (1919).

73. Stone, *Perilous Times*, 201–203.

74. Abrams v. United States, 250 U.S. 616, 628 (1919) (Holmes, J., dissenting).

75. Ibid., 630 (Holmes, J., dissenting).

76. Whitney v. California, 274 U.S. 357, 376 (1927) (Brandeis, J., concurring).

CHAPTER 7: THE BOTTOM FALLS OUT

1. David M. Kennedy, *Freedom from Fear: The American People in Depression and War, 1929–1945* (Oxford, UK: Oxford University Press, 1999), 162–166.

2. Ibid., 164.

3. Lorena Hickok et al., *One Third of a Nation: Lorena Hickok Reports on the Great Depression* (Champaign: University of Illinois Press, 1983), xi.

4. Ibid.

5. Ibid.

6. Kennedy, *Freedom from Fear*, 165.

7. Ibid., 169.

8. Ibid.; Hickok, *One Third of a Nation*, 20.

9. *Old-Age Pensions: Hearing on H.R. 20002 before the House Committee on Labor*, 64th Cong., 2d Sess. 3 (1917) (statement of Rep. Sherwood).

10. Nancy J. Altman, *The Battle for Social Security* (Hoboken: John Wiley & Sons, 2005), 6–7.

11. Ibid., 7.

12. New York Commission on Old Age Security, *Old Age Security: Report of the New York State Commission* (Albany: J. B. Lyon, 1930), 80–81 (hereinafter "New York Report").

13. Ibid., 81.

14. Altman, *Battle for Social Security*, 6–7.

15. New York Report, 395–397.

16. Ibid., 396–402.

17. Abraham Epstein, *Facing Old Age: A Study of Old Age Dependency in the United States and Old Age Pensions* (New York: Alfred A. Knopf, 1922), 54.

18. Ibid., 53.

19. Kennedy, *Freedom from Fear*, 131–132.

20. Ibid., 134–136.

21. Ibid., 136.

22. Ben S. Bernanke, "The Macroeconomics of the Great Depression: A Comparative Approach," 27 *J. Money, Credit & Banking* 1, 4 (1995).

23. A. L. A. Schechter Poultry Corp. v. United States, 295 U.S. 495, 542–543 (1935).

24. Kennedy, *Freedom from Fear*, 137–146.

25. Gov. Franklin D. Roosevelt, Address at Oglethorpe University in Atlanta, Georgia (May 22, 1932), available at http://www.presidency.ucsb.edu/ws/?pid=88410.

26. President Herbert Hoover, *The Consequences of the Proposed New Deal*, Address at Madison Square Garden, New York (October 21, 1932), available at http://publicpolicy.pepperdine.edu/faculty-research/new-deal/hoover-speeches/hh102132.htm.

27. Kennedy, *Freedom from Fear*, 297.

28. National Labor Relations Act ("NLRA") § 1, 29 U.S.C. § 151 (2013).

29. Coppage v. Kansas, 236 U.S. 1 (1915); Adair v. United States, 208 U.S. 161 (1908).

30. NLRA §§ 7 & 8.

31. Railroad Retirement Bd. v. Alton R. Co., 295 U.S. 330 (1935); Altman, *Battle for Social Security*, 73.

32. 247 U.S. 251, 271–272 (1918).

33. Alton R., 295 U.S. 362.

34. Frederick Rudolph, "The American Liberty League, 1934–1940," 56 *Am. Hist. Rev.* 19, 19 (1950).

35. Ibid.

36. Jeff Shesol, *Supreme Power: Franklin Roosevelt vs. the Supreme Court* (New York: W. W. Norton, 2009), 111.

37. Kim Phillips-Fein, *Invisible Hands: The Businessmen's Crusade Against the New Deal* (New York: W. W. Norton, 2010), 5.

38. Ibid., 10.

39. Arthur Krock, "American Liberty League Soon to Begin Activities," *N.Y. Times* (Nov. 9, 1934), available at http://select.nytimes.com/gst/abstract.html?res=F50D16FF3558177A93C2A8178AD95F408385F9.

40. Shesol, *Supreme Power*, 108.

41. Alfred E. Smith, "The Facts in the Case," Speech to the American Liberty League Dinner (Jan. 25, 1936), available at http://kdl.kyvl.org/catalog/xt7wwp9t2q46_94_1?.

42. Associated Press v. National Labor Relations Bd., 301 U.S. 103 (1937).

43. Sydnor Thompson, "John W. Davis and His Role in the Public School Segregation Cases—A Personal Memoir," 52 *Wash. & Lee L. Rev.* 1679, 1682 (1995).

44. Ibid., 1693, n. 47.

45. John W. Davis, *The Constitution: What It Means to the Man in the Street* (American Liberty League, Feb. 1936), 8; available at http://kdl.kyvl.org/catalog /xt7wwp9t2q46_97_1?.

46. John W. Davis, "The Redistribution of Power," Speech Before the New York Bar Association (Jan. 24, 1936), available at http://kdl.kyvl.org/catalog /xt7wwp9t2q46_90_1?.

47. Ibid.

48. American Liberty League, *Economic Planning—Mistaken But Not New* (Nov. 1935), 4–5; available at http://kdl.kyvl.org/catalog/xt7wwp9t2q46_72_1?.

49. William R. Perkins, "A Rising or a Setting Sun," Speech to The Sphex Club, Lynchburg, VA (Sep. 1936), available at http://kdl.kyvl.org/catalog/xt7 wwp9t2q46_132_1?.

50. Walter E. Spahr, "The People's Money," Speech to a round table discussion of "The Constitution and the New Deal" at the University of Virginia (Jul. 10, 1935), available at http://kdl.kyvl.org/catalog/xt7wwp9t2q46_48_1?.

51. Forney Johnson, "The Economic Necessity in the Southern States for a Return to the Constitution," Speech over the Dixie Network of the Columbia Broadcasting System (Oct. 29, 1935), available at http://kdl.kyvl.org/catalog /xt7wwp9t2q46_70_1?.

52. Ibid.

53. William Edward Leuchtenburg, *The FDR Years: On Roosevelt and His Legacy* (New York: Columbia University Press, 1997), 115–116.

54. Edwin Walter Kemmerer, *Our Growing National Debt and Inflation.* Radio address (Nov. 1935), available at http://kdl.kyvl.org/catalog/xt7wwp9t2q 46_73_1?.

55. "Maine Elects to Go with Rest of Nation," *N.Y. Times* (Sept. 10, 1957), available at http://select.nytimes.com/gst/abstract.html?res=F60611F6385 A177B93C2A81782D85F438585F9.

56. President Franklin D. Roosevelt, *Second Inaugural Address* (Jan. 20, 1937), available at http://historymatters.gmu.edu/d/5105/.

57. John C. Fitzpatrick, ed., *The Writings of George Washington from the Original Manuscript Sources, 1745–1799*, Volume 18 (Washington, DC: Government Printing Office, 1931), 490 (Letter to Alexander Hamilton, March 4, 1783).

58. Pollock v. Farmers' Loan & Trust Co., 157 U.S. 429 (1895).

59. Gerard N. Magliocca, "Court-Packing and the Child Labor Amendment," 27 *Const. Commentary* 101, 104, 113 (2011).

60. Ibid., 113–117.

61. Sanford Levinson, *Our Undemocratic Constitution: Where the Constitution Goes Wrong (And How We The People Can Correct It)* (Oxford: Oxford University Press, 2006), 160.

62. Ibid.

63. Magliocca, "Court-Packing," 116.

64. Ibid., 122–123.

65. Kennedy, *Freedom from Fear*, 330.

66. Joshua Glick, "Comment, On the Road: The Supreme Court and the History of Circuit Riding," 24 *Cardozo L. Rev.* 1753, 1756, 1802 (2003).

67. Ibid., 1813.

68. Timothy Huebner, "The First Court-Packing Plan," *SCOTUSblog* (Jul. 3, 2013), at http://www.scotusblog.com/2013/07/the-first-court-packing-plan/.

69. Shesol, *Supreme Power*, 251–252.

70. President Franklin D. Roosevelt, *Press Conference* (Feb. 5, 1937), available at http://www.presidency.ucsb.edu/ws/?pid=15359.

71. Shesol, *Supreme Power*, 291.

72. Kennedy, *Freedom from Fear*, 331.

73. Eric Schickler et al., *The Oxford Handbook of the American Congress* (Oxford: Oxford University Press, 2011), vii.

74. Shesol, *Supreme Power*, 310.

75. Ibid.

76. Ta-Nehisi Coates, "The Case for Reparations," *The Atlantic* (May 21, 2014), at http://www.theatlantic.com/features/archive/2014/05/the-case-for-reparations/361631/.

77. Shesol, *Supreme Power*, 311.

78. Ibid., 313–316.

79. Ibid., 295.

80. John Anthony Maltese, *The Selling of Supreme Court Nominees* (Baltimore, MD: Johns Hopkins University Press, 1998), 56–61.

81. Briggs v. Elliott, 103 F. Supp. 920, 923 (E.D. S.C. 1952).

82. Briggs v. Elliott, 132 F. Supp. 776, 777 (E.D. S.C. 1955).

83. Railroad Retirement Bd. v. Alton R. Co., 295 U.S. 330 (1935).

84. United States v. Butler, 297 U.S. 1 (1936).

85. Morehead v. New York ex rel. Tipaldo, 298 U.S. 587, 610–612 (1936).

86. West Coast Hotel Co. v. Parrish, 300 U.S. 379, 391, 398–399 (1937).

87. NLRB v. Jones & Laughlin Steel Corp., 301 U.S. 1, 33–34 (1937).

88. States v. E.C. Knight, 156 U.S. 1, 16 (1895).

89. Jones & Laughlin Steel, 301 U.S. 41–42.

90. NLRB v. Friedman-Harry Marks Clothing Co., 301 U.S. 58, 99 (1937) (McReynolds, J., dissenting).

91. Helvering v. Davis, 301 U.S. 619 (1937); Steward Machine Co. v. Davis, 301 U.S. 548 (1937).

92. John Knox, *The Forgotten Memoir of John Knox: A Year in the Life of a Supreme Court Clerk in FDR's Washington* (Chicago: University of Chicago Press, 2002), 247.

93. Letter from Justice Willis Van Devanter to President Franklin D. Roosevelt (May 18, 1937), available at http://3197d6d14b5f19f2f440–5e13d29c 4c016cf96cbbfd197c579b45.r81.cf1.rackcdn.com/collection/papers/1930 /1937_0518_VanDevanterRetirement.pdf.

CHAPTER 8: THE BIGGEST DAMNED-FOOL
MISTAKE I EVER MADE

1. George B. Tindall, "The Question of Race in the South Carolina Constitutional Convention of 1895," 37 *J. of Negro Hist.* 277, 286 (1952).

2. George B. Tindall, *The Emergence of the New South, 1913–1945* (Baton Rouge: University of Louisiana Press, 1967), 170.

3. David Robertson, *Sly and Able: A Political Biography of James F. Byrnes* (New York: Norton, 1994), 85–86.

4. Ibid., 60–63.

5. John Y. Simon, ed., *The Papers of Ulysses S. Grant*, Volume 27 (Carbondale: Southern Illinois University, 2005), 199 (Letter to Daniel H. Chamberlain, Jul. 26, 1876).

6. Robertson, *Sly and Able*, 48–49.

7. Ibid., 50.

8. Tindall, *New South*, 277.

9. Ibid., 57.

10. "Byrnes Lashes Out at G.O.P. in Saluda Meeting," *Florence, S.C. Morning News* (Jun. 11, 1936), 4.

11. Robertson, *Sly and Able*, 5.

12. Sydnor Thompson, "John W. Davis and His Role in the Public School Segregation Cases—A Personal Memoir," 52 *Wash. & Lee L. Rev.* 1679, 1693 & n. 47 (1995).

13. *Brown v. Board of Education of Topeka*, 347 U.S. 483, 495 (1954).

14. Acting Solicitor General Neal Katyal, "Confession of Error: The Solicitor General's Mistakes During the Japanese-American Internment Cases," *The Justice Blog* (May 20, 2011), at http://blogs.justice.gov/main/archives/1346.

15. Ibid.; *see also* Korematsu v. United States, 584 F. Supp. 1406, 1414–1417 (N. D. Ca. 1984) (explaining how the Justice Department covered up evidence undermining the case for Japanese internments).

16. Korematsu v. United States, 323 U.S. 214, 218, 223–224 (1944).

17. Ibid., 233 (Murphy, J., dissenting).

18. Noah Feldman, *Scorpions: The Battles and Triumphs of FDR's Great Supreme Court Justices* (New York: Hachette, 2010), 51.

19. Ibid., 57.

20. Ibid.

21. Ibid., 58.

22. Ibid., 141.

23. John Gould Fletcher, "Is This the Voice of the South?" *The Nation* (Dec. 27, 1933), 137.

24. Powell v. Alabama, 287 U.S. 45, 50–51 (1932).

25. Ibid., 51.

26. Ibid., 50–56.

27. Michael J. Klarman, *From Jim Crow to Civil Rights: The Supreme Court and the Struggle for Racial Equality* (Oxford: Oxford University Press, 2006), 119.

28. Bettis v. State, 164 Ark. 17, 19 (Ark. 1924).

29. Klarman, *Jim Crow*, 119.

30. Powell, 287 U.S. 71.

31. Strauder v. West Virginia, 100 U.S. 303, 309–310 (1880).

32. Norris v. Alabama, 294 U.S. 587, 589 (1935).

33. *See* Batson v. Kentucky, 476 U.S. 79 (1986).

34. Brown v. Mississippi, 297 U.S. 278, 281–282 (1936).

35. Adamson v. California, 332 U.S. 46, 89 (1947) (Black, J., dissenting).

36. Ibid., 83–84 (Black, J., dissenting).

37. Feldman, *Scorpions*, 375, 381; Klarman, *Jim Crow*, 294.

38. Klarman, *Jim Crow*, 294.

39. Mark Tushnet, "What Really Happened in *Brown v. Board of Education*," 91 *Colum. L. Rev.* 1867, 1881 (1991).

40. Ibid.; Klarman, *Jim Crow*, 300–301.

41. Klarman, *Jim Crow*, 297.

42. Stephen M. Feldman, *Free Expression and Democracy in America: A History* (Chicago: University of Chicago Press, 2008), 285–286.

43. *See* Felix Frankfurter, "The Case of Sacco and Vanzetti," *The Atlantic* (Mar. 1, 1927), available at http://www.theatlantic.com/magazine/archive /1927/03/the-case-of-sacco-and-vanzetti/306625/?single_page=true.

44. Klarman, *Jim Crow*, 303.

45. Robert H. Jackson Center, *William T. Coleman (2005) on Felix Frankfurter* (May 18, 2005), at https://www.youtube.com/watch?v=8K8cM3pYPp8.

46. Feldman, *Scorpions*, 30.

47. Minersville School Dist. v. Gobitis, 310 U.S. 586, 592, n.1 (1940).

48. Ibid., 598.

49. Feldman, *Scorpions*, 185.

50. W. Va. State Bd. of Educ. v. Barnette, 319 U.S. 624, 646–647 (1943) (Frankfurter, J., dissenting).

51. Baker v. Carr, 369 U.S. 186, 272–276 (1962) (Frankfurter, J., dissenting).

52. Ibid., 270 (Frankfurter, J., dissenting).

53. Klarman, *Jim Crow*, 303.

54. Adam Liptak, "New Look at an Old Memo Casts More Doubt on Rehnquist," *N.Y. Times* (Mar. 19, 2012), at http://www.nytimes.com/2012/03/20/us /new-look-at-an-old-memo-casts-more-doubt-on-rehnquist.html?_r=0.

55. Memorandum from William H. Rehnquist to Justice Robert H. Jackson, *A Random Thought on the Segregation Cases* 2 (Dec. 1952), available at 117 *Cong. Rec.* 45, 440–441 (1971).

56. Klarman, *Jim Crow*, 305.

57. Ibid., 306–307.

58. Feldman, *Scorpions*, 397–398.

59. *See* G. Edward White, *Earl Warren: A Public Life* (Oxford: Oxford University Press, 1982), 138–140 (detailing the effort to enact a "fair play" resolution that effectively scuttled Senator Robert Taft's bid for the GOP presidential nomination).

60. Klarman, *Jim Crow*, 302.

61. Feldman, *Scorpions*, 399, 402; Norman I. Silber, *With All Deliberate Speed: The Life of Philip Elman: An Oral History Memoir* (Ann Arbor: University of Michigan Press, 2004), 198–199.

62. Klarman, *Jim Crow*, 302; Feldman, *Scorpions*, 402.

63. Brown v. Bd. of Educ., 349 U.S. 294, 756–757 (1955) ("Brown II").

64. Klarman, *Jim Crow*, 318–319.

65. "Declaration of Constitutional Principles," 102 *Cong. Rec.* 4460, 4515–4516 (1956) (statement of Sen. Walter F. George, widely known as "The Southern Manifesto").

66. James v. Almond, 170 F. Supp. 331, 335 (E.D. Va. 1959).

67. Peter Applebome, "Orval Faubus, Segregation's Champion, Dies at 84," *N.Y. Times* (Dec. 15, 1994), available at http://www.nytimes.com/learning/general/specials/littlerock/faubus.html.

68. Klarman, *Jim Crow*, 359.

69. Griffin v. County School Board, 377 U.S. 218, 229 (1964).

70. Charles J. Ogletree, *All Deliberate Speed: Reflections on the First Half-Century of* Brown v. Board of Education (New York: W. W. Norton, 2004), 3.

71. Alden Whitman, "Earl Warren, 83, Who Led High Court in Time of Vast Social Change, Is Dead," *N.Y. Times* (Jul. 10, 1974), available at http://www.nytimes.com/learning/general/onthisday/bday/0319.html.

72. *See, for example,* Brandenburg v. Ohio, 395 U.S. 444 (1969); New York Times Co. v. Sullivan, 376 U.S. 254 (1964).

73. Katz v. United States, 389 U.S. 347 (1967).

74. Reynolds v. Sims, 377 U.S. 533, 558 (1964).

75. Seth Stern and Stephen Wermiel, *Justice Brennan: Liberal Champion* (New York: Houghton Mifflin Harcourt, 2010), 139.

CHAPTER 9: SHOULD WE DOUBLE OUR
WEALTH AND CONQUER THE STARS

1. Sally Belfrage, *Freedom Summer: A Civil Rights Worker's Personal Account of the Historic Mississippi Summer Project of 1964* (New York: Viking, 1965), 17.

2. Ibid.

3. Ibid., 16.

4. Ibid., 10.

5. Ibid., 26.

6. John Lewis, *Walking with the Wind: A Memoir of the Movement* (Orlando, FL: Harcourt Brace, 1998), 127.

7. Ibid.

8. Ibid., 128.

9. Ibid., 326.

10. Ibid., 327–329.

11. Michael J. Klarman, *From Jim Crow to Civil Rights: The Supreme Court and the Struggle for Racial Equality* (Oxford: Oxford University Press, 2006), 363.

12. Ibid., 362–363.

13. *Lyndon Johnson: 1965: Containing the Public Messages, Speeches, and Statements of the President*, Book 1, (Washington, DC: Office of the Federal Register, National Archives and Records Service, General Services Administration, 1966), 282 (hereinafter "LBJ").

14. Williamson v. Lee Optical of Oklahoma, Inc., 348 U.S. 483, 488 (1955) (internal quotation marks omitted).

15. Memorandum from William H. Rehnquist to Justice Robert H. Jackson, *A Random Thought on the Segregation Cases* 2 (Dec. 1952), available at 117 *Cong. Rec.* 45, 440–441 (1971) (hereinafter "Rehnquist Memo").

16. John A. Jenkins, *The Partisan: The Life of William Rehnquist* (New York: PublicAffairs, 2012), 69.

17. Rehnquist Memo, 45, 441.

18. William H. Rehnquist, Letter to the Editor, "Public Accommodations Law Passage Is Called 'Mistake,'" *Ariz. Republic*, (June 4, 1964), reprinted in Nominations of William H. Rehnquist of Arizona, and Lewis F. Powell, Jr., of Virginia, to be Associate Justices of the Supreme Court of the United States: Hearing Before the S. Comm. on the Judiciary, 92d Cong. 307 (1971).

19. Ibid.

20. Adair v. United States, 208 U.S. 161, 174 (1908).

21. Dennis McLellan, "Denison Kitchel, 94; Ran Goldwater's Presidential Bid," *Los Angeles Times* (Oct. 24, 2002), available at http://articles.latimes.com/2002/oct/24/local/me-kitchel24.

22. Rick Perlstein, *Before the Storm: Barry Goldwater and the Unmaking of the American Consensus* (New York: Nation Books, 2009), 169.

23. Ibid., 363.

24. Ibid.

25. Hedley Donovan, "The Difficulty of 'Being Fair' to Goldwater," *Life* (Sep. 18, 1964), 93, 94.

26. Perlstein, *Before the Storm*, 363.

27. Robert Bork, "Civil Rights—A Challenge," *The New Republic* (Aug. 31, 1965), 21, 22.

28. 103 *Cong. Rec.* 13421 (Jun. 18, 1964) (statement of Senator Goldwater).

29. Ibid.

30. "Freedom of Association Cuts Two Ways—Barry," *Associated Press* (Oct. 19, 1964).

31. 247 U.S. 251, 276 (1918).

32. Robert A. Caro, *Master of the Senate: The Years of Lyndon Johnson* (New York: Vintage, 2003), 851–852.

33. Ibid., 852–853.

34. Klarman, *Jim Crow*, 201.

35. Nixon v. Herndon, 273 U.S. 536, 540–541 (1927).

36. Nixon v. Condon, 286 U.S.73, 81–82 (1932).

37. Ibid., 94 (McReynolds, J., dissenting).

38. Grovey v. Townsend, 295 U.S. 45, 47 (1935).

39. Ibid., 48.

40. 321 U.S. 649, 666 (1944).

41. Klarman, *Jim Crow*, 236.

42. LBJ, 282.

43. Ibid.

44. Klarman, *Jim Crow*, 244, 246.

45. Ibid., 250.

46. *The Federalist No. 78* (Alexander Hamilton).

47. *See* Lujan v. Defenders of Wildlife, 504 U.S. 555, 560–561 (1992).

48. Klarman, *Jim Crow*, 252.

49. Ibid.

50. Barbara Harris Combs, *From Selma to Montgomery: The Long March to Freedom* (New York: Routledge, 2013), 40; Klarman, *Jim Crow*, 440.

51. *Judgment at Nuremberg* (United Artists, 1961).

52. Ibid.

53. Klarman, *Jim Crow*, 440.

54. Office of Management and Budget, *Fiscal Year 2013 Budget of the U.S. Government* (Washington, DC: US Government Printing Office, 2012), 327.

55. LBJ, 281.

56. 42 U.S.C. § 1973c(a).

57. Michael J. Pitts, "The Voting Rights Act and the Era of Maintenance," 59 *Ala. L. Rev.* 903, 904 (2008).

58. Katzenbach v. McClung, 379 U.S. 294 (1964); Heart of Atlanta Motel v. United States, 379 U.S. 241 (1964).

59. South Carolina v. Katzenbach, 383 U.S. 301 (1966).

CHAPTER 10: THE TRUCE

1. New Jersey Governor's Select Commission on Civil Disorder, *Report for Action* (Trenton, NJ: State of New Jersey, 1968), 105 (hereinafter "Riot Report").

2. Ibid., 106.

3. Ibid., 107–108; Kevin Mumford, *Newark: A History of Race, Rights, and Riots in America* (New York: NYU Press, 2008), 98.

4. Riot Report, 107–108.

5. Ibid., 108.

6. Ibid., 118–123.

7. Ibid., 120.

8. Ibid., 120–121.

9. Ibid., 136, 149.

10. Rick Perlstein, *Nixonland: The Rise of a President and the Fracturing of America* (New York: Scribner, 2008), 192–193.

11. Riot Report, 3, 22, 57.

12. Ibid., 47–48, 66.

13. Ibid., 28–30.

14. Ibid., 35–36.

15. Ibid., 3.

16. Perlstein, *Nixonland*, 194–195.

17. Taylor Branch, *Parting the Waters: America in the King Years, 1954–63* (New York: Simon and Schuster, 1988), 220–221.

18. Richard Nixon, "The Irresponsible Tactics of Some of the Extreme Civil Rights Leaders" (Feb. 12, 1964) in Rick Perlstein, ed., *Richard Nixon: Speeches, Writings, Documents* (Princeton: Princeton University Press, 2010), 111–115.

19. Ibid., 113.

20. 367 U.S. 643 (1961).

21. Ibid., 656.

22. Brinegar v. United States, 338 U.S. 160, 181 (1949) (Jackson, J., dissenting).

23. Mapp, 367 U.S. 656.

24. 372 U.S. 335 (1963).

25. Ibid., 344.

26. 384 U.S. 436 (1966).

27. Ibid., 468–475.

28. Dickerson v. United States, 530 U.S. 428, 443 (2000).

29. Miranda, 384 U.S. at 468.

30. Yale Kamisar, "The Warren Court and Criminal Justice: A Quarter-Century Retrospective," 31 *Tulsa L. J.* 1, 8–10 (1995).

31. Miranda, 384 U.S. at 542 (White, J., dissenting).

32. 18 U.S.C. § 3501; Dickerson, 530 U.S. 431–432.

33. Yale Kamisar, "The Rise, Decline, and Fall (?) of *Miranda*," 87 *Wash. L. Rev.* 965, 974 (2012).

34. Richard Nixon, "What Has Happened to America?" *Readers Digest* (Oct. 1967) in Perlstein, *Richard Nixon*, 119–121.

35. Ibid., 121–123.

36. Christopher E. Smith and Thomas R. Hensley, "Unfilled Aspirations: The Court-Packing Efforts of Presidents Reagan and Bush," 57 *Alb. L. Rev.* 1111, 1115 (1994).

37. Ed Cray, *Chief Justice: A Biography of Earl Warren* (New York: Simon and Schuster, 2008), 497.

38. President Franklin D. Roosevelt, *Second Inaugural Address* (Jan. 20, 1937), available at http://historymatters.gmu.edu/d/5105/.

39. *See* Frank I. Michelman, "Foreward: On Protecting the Poor Through the Fourteenth Amendment," 83 *Harv. L. Rev.* 7, 48 (1969) (describing the theory behind this lawsuit as so sweeping that it could require that "each person, upon completion of his education, would be equally well prepared to play the game of Life").

40. McInnis v. Ogilvie, 394 U.S. 322 (1969).

41. New America Foundation, *School Finance: Federal, State and Local K–12 School Finance* (Jun. 30, 2013), available at http://febp.newamerica.net /background-analysis/school-finance; Michelman, "Foreward," 48.

42. 411 U.S. 1, 6 (1973).

43. 467 U.S. 649, 657 (1984).

44. Ian Millhiser, "What You Need To Know About Why The Boston Bombing Suspect Hasn't Been Read His Miranda Rights," *ThinkProgress* (Apr. 19, 2013), at http://thinkprogress.org/justice/2013/04/19/1898851/what-you -need-to-know-about-why-the-boston-bombing-suspect-hasnt-been-read -his-miranda-rights/.

45. Smith v. Maryland, 442 U.S. 735, 743–744 (1979).

46. Ian Millhiser, "This Is the Most Important Paragraph in the Court Decision Against the NSA," *ThinkProgress* (Dec. 16, 2013), at http://thinkprogress .org/justice/2013/12/16/3072731/important-paragraph-court-decision-nsa/; Eric Pfeiffer, "NSA Spied on 124.8 Billion Phone Calls in Just One Month: Watchdog," (Oct. 23, 2013), at http://news.yahoo.com/nsa-spied-on-124–8-billion -phone-calls-in-just-one-month—watchdog-group-claims-213633988.html.

47. Nixon, "What Has Happened?" 121–123.

48. Reed v. Reed, 404 U.S. 71, 77 (1971).

49. 429 U.S. 190, 197 (1976).

50. 410 U.S. 113 (1973).

51. Ibid., 164.

52. *For example:* Eisenstadt v. Baird, 405 U.S. 438 (1972); Griswold v. Connecticut, 381 U.S. 479 (1965).

53. Ruth Bader Ginsburg, "Some Thoughts on Autonomy and Equality in Relation to *Roe v. Wade*," 63 *N.C. L. Rev.* 375, 375 (1985).

54. United States v. Virginia, 518 U.S. 515, 524 (1996).

55. Nevada Dept. of Human Resources v. Hibbs, 538 U.S. 721, 736 (2003).

56. Roe, 410 U.S. at 129; *see also* Ibid., 153 ("This right of privacy, whether it be founded in the Fourteenth Amendment's concept of personal liberty and restrictions upon state action, as we feel it is").

57. Lochner v. New York, 198 U.S. 45, 53 (1905).

58. Bernard Weinraub, "Reagan Says He'll Use Vacancies to Discourage Judicial Activism," *N.Y. Times* (Oct. 22, 1985), available at http://www.nytimes.com/1985/10/22/world/reagan-says-he-ll-use-vacancies-to-discourage-judicial-activism.html.

59. Douglas H. Ginsburg, "Delegation Running Riot," 1995 *Regulation*, 83, 84 (1995).

60. Steven V. Roberts, "Ginsburg Withdraws Name As Supreme Court Nominee, Citing Marijuana 'Clamor,'" *N.Y. Times* (Nov. 8, 1987), available at http://www.nytimes.com/1987/11/08/us/ginsburg-withdraws-name-as-supreme-court-nominee-citing-marijuana-clamor.html.

61. Office of Legal Policy, US Department of Justice, Guidelines on Constitution Litigation 1 (1988) (hereinafter "Guidelines"). For an in-depth discussion on the Guidelines' impact on at least some areas of constitutional law, see generally Dawn E. Johnsen, "Ronald Reagan and the Rehnquist Court on Congressional Power: Presidential Influences on Constitutional Change," 78 *Ind. L. J.* 363 (2003).

62. Guidelines, 82–83 (quoting John H. Ely, "The Wages of Crying Wolf: A Comment on *Roe v. Wade*," 82 *Yale L.J.* 920, 947 [1973]).

63. Ibid., 87, 92–97.

64. Ibid., 54–56; Johnsen, "Ronald Reagan," 394–395.

65. Guidelines, 58.

66. Ibid., 79.

67. "Excerpts from Questioning of Judge Bork by Senate Committee Chairman," *N.Y. Times* (Sep. 16, 1987), at http://www.nytimes.com/1987/09/16/us/excerpts-from-questioning-of-judge-bork-by-senate-committee-chairman.html?pagewanted=all.

68. Ibid.

69. *See* Gonzales v. Raich, 545 U.S. 1, 58 (2005) (Thomas, J. dissenting) ("Commerce, or trade, stood in contrast to productive activities like manufacturing and agriculture."); United States v. Morrison, 529 U.S. 598, 627 (Thomas, J., concurring) (2000) ("The very notion of a 'substantial effects' test under the Commerce Clause is inconsistent with the original understanding of Congress' powers and with this Court's early Commerce Clause cases."); United States v. Lopez, 514 U.S. 549, 588 (1995) (Thomas, J., concurring) ("The term 'commerce' was used in contradistinction to productive activities such as manufacturing and agriculture").

70. Lloyd Grove, "Barry Goldwater's Left Turn," *Wash. Post* (Jul. 28, 1994), at http://www.washingtonpost.com/wp-srv/politics/daily/may98/goldwater072894.htm.

71. John M. Broder and Carolyn Marshall, "White House Memos Offer Opinions on Supreme Court," *N.Y. Times* (Jul. 30, 2005), available at http://www.nytimes.com/2005/07/30/politics/politicsspecial1/30judge.html.

CHAPTER 11: RIGGING THE GAME

1. Bush v. Gore, 531 U.S. 98, 100–101 (2000).

2. Ibid., 109.

3. Antonin Scalia, "The Rule of Law as a Law of Rules," 56 *U. Chi. L. Rev.* 1175, 1179 (1989); *see also* Alan M. Dershowitz, *Supreme Injustice: How the High Court Hijacked Election 2000* (New York: Oxford University Press, 2001), 123 (quoting same).

4. Bush, 531 U.S. 104.

5. Igor Volsky, "Romney Says Obama Only Won Because He Gave 'Big Gifts' To Blacks and Latinos," *ThinkProgress* (Nov. 14, 2012), at http://think progress.org/election/2012/11/14/1193471/romney-says-obama-only -won-because-he-gave-big-gifts-to-blacks-and-latinos/.

6. Ian Millhiser, "Thanks To Gerrymandering, Democrats Would Need to Win the Popular Vote by Over 7 Percent to Take Back the House," *ThinkProgress* (Jan. 2, 2013), at http://thinkprogress.org/justice/2013/01/02/1382471 /thanks-to-gerrymandering-democrats-would-need-to-win-the-popular -vote-by-over-7-percent-to-take-back-the-house/.

7. Republican State Leadership Committee, *REDMAP 2012 Summary Report* (Jan. 4, 2013), available at http://www.rslc.com/redmap_2012_summary _report (hereinafter "RSLC Memo").

8. Ruy Teixeira, "Why Democrats Win The Presidency But Lose The House," *ThinkProgress* (May 29, 2013), at http://thinkprogress.org/justice /2013/05/29/2058001/why-democrats-win-the-presidency-but-lose-the -house/.

9. RSLC Memo.

10. Lamb's Chapel v. Ctr. Moriches Union Free Sch. Dist., 508 U.S. 384, 392–395 (1993).

11. Vieth v. Jubelirer, 541 U.S. 267, 324–325 (2004) (Stevens, J., dissenting).

12. 541 U.S. 267, 305–306 (2004) (plurality opinion).

13. League of United Latin Am. Citizens v. Perry, 548 U.S. 399, 492–493 (2006) (Roberts, C.J., concurring in part, concurring in the judgment in part, and dissenting in part).

14. Ibid., 305 ("Neither Article I, § 2, nor the Equal Protection Clause, nor . . . Article I, § 4, provides a judicially enforceable limit on the political considerations that the States and Congress may take into account when districting").

15. David Wasserman, "2012 National House Popular Vote Tracker," available at https://docs.google.com/spreadsheet/ccc?key=0AjYj9mXElO_QdH ZCbzJocGtxYkR6OTdZbzZwRUFvS3c#gid=0 (last visited on March 4, 2014).

16. RSLC Memo.

17. United States v. Carolene Products Co., 304 U.S. 144, 153 n. 4 (1938).

18. Ian Millhiser, "Study: Rick Scott's Long Voting Lines Cost Obama a Net 11,000 Votes in Central Florida," *ThinkProgress* (Jan. 2, 2013), at http:// thinkprogress.org/justice/2013/01/02/1382841/study-rick-scotts-long-voting -lines-cost-obama-a-net-11000-votes-in-central-florida/; Judd Legum, "After Republicans Restrict Early Voting Hours, Floridians Wait More Than 6 Hours To Vote," *ThinkProgress* (Nov. 4, 2012), at http://thinkprogress.org/election /2012/11/04/1135571/after-republicans-restrict-early-voting-hours-floridians -wait-more-than-6-hours-to-vote/.

19. Aviva Shen, "Florida Governor Signs Election Reform Bill Reversing His Own Voter Suppression Laws," *ThinkProgress* (May 23, 2013), at http:// thinkprogress.org/justice/2013/05/23/2052401/florida-governor-signs -election-reform-bill-reversing-his-own-voter-suppression-laws/.

20. Dara Kam, "Elections Overhaul En Route to Governor," *The Palm Beach Post* (May 5, 2011), at http://www.postonpolitics.com/2011/05/elections -overhaul-en-route-to-governor.

21. Dara Kam and John Lantigua, "Former Florida GOP Leaders Say Voter Suppression Was Reason They Pushed New Election Law," *The Palm Beach Post* (Nov. 25, 2012), at http://www.palmbeachpost.com/news/news/state- regional-govt-politics/early-voting-curbs-called-power-play/nTFDy/.

22. Millhiser, "Rick Scott."

23. Obama for America v. Husted, 697 F. 3d 423, 431–432 (6th Cir. 2012). The author of this book clerked for Judge Eric Clay, who authored the opinion in Obama for America, in 2007–2008.

24. Aviva Shen, "Top Iowa Republican Poised to Begin New Voter Purge," *ThinkProgress* (Sep. 6, 2012), at http://thinkprogress.org/justice/2013/09 /06/2581791/voting-advocates-ask-judge-stop-iowa-voter-purge/; Judd Legum and Ian Millhiser, "Exclusive: Florida Congressman Demands Gov. Rick Scott 'Immediately Suspend' Voter Purge," *ThinkProgress* (May 23, 2012), at http://thinkprogress.org/justice/2012/05/23/489511/exclusive-florida -congressman-demands-gov-rick-scott-immediately-suspend-voter-purge.

25. Aviva Shen, "Voter Purges in Florida and Colorado Find Almost 'No Confirmed Noncitizens,'" *ThinkProgress* (Sep. 7, 2012), at http://thinkprogress .org/justice/2012/09/07/812871/voter-purges-in-florida-and-colorado-find -almost-no-confirmed-noncitizens/.

26. Judd Legum, "All 67 Florida Election Supervisors Suspend Governor Rick Scott's Voter Purge," *ThinkProgress* (Jun. 2, 2012), at http://thinkprogress .org/justice/2012/06/02/494088/all-67-florida-election-supervisors-suspend -governor-rick-scotts-voter-purge/.

27. Matt Dixon, "Democratic Registration All but Dries Up Since New Florida Laws," *Florida Times-Union* (August 27, 2012), at http://members .jacksonville.com/news/florida/2012–08–27/story/democratic-registration-all

-dries-new-florida-laws; Scott Keyes, "Breaking: Federal Judge Blocks Florida Voter Suppression Law," *ThinkProgress* (May 31, 2012), at http://thinkprogress .org/justice/2012/05/31/493196/judge-blocks-florida-voter-law/.

28. National Conference of State Legislatures, *Voter Identification Requirements* (Oct. 17, 2013), at http://www.ncsl.org/research/elections-and-campaigns /voter-id.aspx#State_Reqs.

29. Marcia Myers, "Election Theft Ruled Out," *The Baltimore Sun* (Aug. 24, 1995), at http://articles.baltimoresun.com/1995–08–24/news/1995236093 _1_voting-machines-vote-fraud-criminal-conspiracy.

30. Justin Levitt, *The Truth About Voter Fraud* (New York: NYU, Brennan Center for Justice, 2007), 14–15.

31. Ibid., 31.

32. Josh Israel, "Iowa's Republican Secretary of State Just Proved That Voter ID Laws Are Unnecessary," *ThinkProgress* (May 9, 2014), at http://thinkprogress .org/justice/2014/05/09/3436160/iowa-matt-schultz-no-voter-id-fraud/.

33. Hamed Aleaziz, Dave Gilson, and Jaeah Lee, "UFO Sightings Are More Common Than Voter Fraud," *Mother Jones* (Jul./Aug. 2012), at http:// www.motherjones.com/politics/2012/07/voter-id-laws-charts-maps.

34. Scott Keyes et al., "Voter Suppression 101: How Conservatives Are Conspiring to Disenfranchise Millions of Americans," *Center for American Progress* (Apr. 2012), 8.

35. Ibid..; Harper v. Virginia State Bd. of Elections, 383 U.S. 663, 666 (1966).

36. Keyes, "Voter Suppression 101," 7.

37. Ibid.

38. Ibid., 9.

39. Ibid.

40. Ibid., 8.

41. Milwaukee Branch of the NAACP v. Walker, 2014 WI 98, at *31–34 (2014).

42. Nate Silver, "Measuring the Effects of Voter Identification Laws," *N.Y. Times* (Jul. 15, 2012), at http://fivethirtyeight.blogs.nytimes.com/2012/07 /15/measuring-the-effects-of-voter-identification-laws/?_php=true&_type =blogs&_r=0.

43. Annie-Rose Strasser, "Pennsylvania Republican: Voter ID Laws Are 'Gonna Allow Governor Romney To Win,'" *ThinkProgress* (Jun. 25, 2012), at http://thinkprogress.org/election/2012/06/25/505953/pennsylvania -republican-voter-id-laws-are-gonna-allow-governor-romney-to-win/.

44. *See* Burdick v. Takushi, 504 U.S. 428, 433–434 (1992) ("To subject every voting regulation to strict scrutiny and to require that the regulation be narrowly tailored to advance a compelling state interest, as petitioner suggests, would tie the hands of States seeking to assure that elections are operated equitably and efficiently").

45. Carolene Products, 304 U.S, 152 n. 4.

46. Burdick, 504 U.S. 434 (quoting Tashjian v. Republican Party of Conn., 479 U.S. 208, 213–214 [1986]).

47. Crawford v. Marion County Election Bd., 128 S. Ct. 1610, 1619 & n. 11 & 12 (2008) (Opinion of Stevens, J.).

48. Phuong Cat Le and Michelle Nicolosi, "Dead Voted in Governor's Race," *Seattle Post-Intelligencer* (Jan. 7, 2005), at http://www.seattlepi.com/local /article/Dead-voted-in-governor-s-race-1163612.php#page-1.

49. Shelby County v. Holder, 133 S. Ct. 2612, 2645–2647 (2013) (Ginsburg, J., dissenting).

50. Ibid., 2646 (Ginsburg, J., dissenting).

51. Ibid., 2618, 2629.

52. Ibid., 2644 (Ginsburg, J., dissenting).

53. South Carolina v. Katzenbach, 383 U.S. 301, 328–329 (1966).

54. Shelby County, 133 S. Ct. at 2650 (Ginsburg, J., dissenting).

55. Aviva Shen, "Two Hours After the Supreme Court Gutted the Voting Rights Act, Texas AG Suppresses Minority Voters," *ThinkProgress* (Jun. 25, 2013), at http://thinkprogress.org/justice/2013/06/25/2212281/two-hours -after-the-supreme-court-gutted-the-voting-rights-act-texas-ag-suppresses -minority-voters/.

56. Kim Chandler, "Alabama Photo Voter ID Law to Be Used in 2014, State Officials Say," *AL.com* (June 25, 2013), at http://blog.al.com/wire /2013/06/alabama_photo_voter_id_law_to.html; "Voting Rights Act Ruling Clears Path for Mississippi Voter ID Use in 2014 (updated)," *Associated Press* (Jun. 25, 2013) at http://blog.gulflive.com/mississippi-press-news/2013/06 /voting_rights_act_ruling_clear.html.

57. Kara Brandeisky and Mike Tigas, "Everything That's Happened Since Supreme Court Ruled on Voting Rights Act," *ProPublica*, (Nov. 1, 2013), at http://www.propublica.org/article/voting-rights-by-state-map.

58. NC Session Law 2013–381; *see also* Scott Keyes, "North Carolina on Cusp of Passing Worst Voter Suppression Bill in the Nation," *ThinkProgress* (Jul. 23, 2013), at http://thinkprogress.org/justice/2013/07/23/2340941/nc -voter-suppression/.

59. Texas v. Holder, 888 F. Supp. 2d 113, 115 (D.D.C. 2012).

60. Norman Robbins and Mark Salling, "Racial and Ethnic Proportions of Early In-Person Voters in Cuyahoga County, General Election 2008, and Implications for 2012," pages 1 and 4, available at http://nova-ohio.org/Racial% 20and%20ethnic%20proportions%20of%20early%20in-person%20voting.pdf.

61. Ian Millhiser, "Bill Clinton: GOP War on Voting Is Most Determined Disenfranchisement Effort Since Jim Crow," *ThinkProgress* (Jul. 7, 2011), at http://thinkprogress.org/justice/2011/07/07/262400/clinton-war-on-voting -jim-crow/.

62. Ian Millhiser, "GOP Casino Baron Sheldon Adelson Pledges $500,000 to Buy a Single House Seat," *ThinkProgress* (Aug. 27, 2012), at http://think

progress.org/justice/2012/08/27/750111/gop-casino-baron-sheldon
-adelson-pledges-500000-to-buy-a-single-house-seat/.

63. Peter H. Stone, "Sheldon Adelson Spent Far More on Campaign Than Previously Known," *Huffington Post* (Dec. 3, 2012), at http://www.huffington post.com/2012/12/03/sheldon-adelson-2012-election_n_2223589.html.

64. "Forbes 400: #11 Sheldon Adelson," *Forbes* (Sep. 2013), at http://www .forbes.com/profile/sheldon-adelson/.

65. Citizens United v. FEC, 558 U.S. 310, 359 (2010) (quoting McConnell v. FEC, 540 U.S. 93, 297 [2003] [opinion of Kennedy, J.]).

66. Ibid.

67. For a fuller description of the money-laundering schemes authorized by McCutcheon case, see Ian Millhiser, "How the Supreme Court Just Legalized Money Laundering by Rich Campaign Donors," *ThinkProgress* (Apr. 2, 2014), at http://thinkprogress.org/justice/2014/04/02/3422036/how-the-supreme -court-just-legalized-money-laundering-by-rich-campaign-donors/.

68. McCutcheon v. FEC, 134 S. Ct. 1434, 1441, 1451 (2014) (plurality opinion of Roberts, C.J.).

69. Caperton v. A. T. Massey Coal Co., 556 U.S. 868, 886 (2009).

70. Ibid., 872; Ian Urbina, "No Survivors Found After West Virginia Mine Disaster," *N.Y. Times* (Apr. 9, 2010), available at http://www.nytimes.com /2010/04/10/us/10westvirginia.html.

71. Caperton, 556 U.S. 872–875.

72. Buckley v. Valeo, 519 F.2d 821, 839 & n.34 (D.C. Cir. 1975).

73. Ibid., 839, n.36.

74. Ibid., 839, n.38.

75. Ibid., 839, n.37.

76. Buckley v. Valeo, 424 U.S. 1, 7 (1976).

77. Ibid., 14–15.

78. Ibid., 26–27.

79. Ibid. (quoting United States Civ. Serv. Comm'n v. Nat'l Ass'n of Letter Carriers, 413 U.S. 548, 565 [1973]).

80. Ibid., 47.

81. Lisa Lerer, "Romney Closing Doors at Israeli Fundraiser with Sheldon Adelson," *Bloomberg* (Jul. 28, 2012), at http://go.bloomberg.com/political -capital/2012–07–28/romney-closing-doors-at-israeli-fundraiser-with-sheldon -adelson/; Laura Strickler, "Romney to Meet with Sheldon Adelson on Tues-day," *CBS News* (May 29, 2012), at http://www.cbsnews.com/news/romney -to-meet-with-sheldon-adelson-on-tuesday/.

82. Ian Millhiser, "More Americans Believe in Witchcraft Than Agree with Citizens United," *ThinkProgress* (Apr. 24, 2012), at http://thinkprogress.org /justice/2012/04/24/470450/more-americans-believe-in-witchcraft-than -agree-with-citizens-united.

83. Ibid.

84. Richard L. Hasen, "The Numbers Don't Lie," *Slate* (Mar. 9, 2012), at http://www.slate.com/articles/news_and_politics/politics/2012/03/the _supreme_court_s_citizens_united_decision_has_led_to_an_explosion_of _campaign_spending_.html;

85. Daniel H. Lowenstein, Richard L. Hasen, and Daniel P. Tokaji, *Election Law: Cases and Materials*, 5th ed. (Durham, NC: Carolina Academic Press, 2013), 44–45.

86. Center for Responsive Politics, "Total Outside Spending by Election Cycle, Excluding Party Committees," *Open Secrets*, at http://www.opensecrets .org/outsidespending/cycle_tots.php (last visited Mar. 4, 2014).

87. Am. Tradition P'ship v. Bullock, 132 S. Ct. 2490 (2012).

88. Michael Falcone, "Obama Gets 'Celebrity Treatment' in New McCain Ad," *N.Y. Times* (Jul. 30, 2008), at http://thecaucus.blogs.nytimes.com/2008 /07/30/obama-gets-celebrity-treatment-in-new-mccain-ad/?_php=true& _type=blogs&_r=0.

89. Pew Research Center, "Chief Justice Thurgood Marshall" (Aug. 10, 2010), at http://www.pewresearch.org/daily-number/chief-justice-thurgood -marshall/.

90. Joanna Shepherd, "Justice at Risk: An Empirical Analysis of Campaign Contributions and Judicial Decisions," *American Constitution Society* (Jun. 2013), available at http://www.acslaw.org/ACS%20Justice%20at%20Risk%20%28 FINAL%29%206_10_13.pdf.

91. Ibid.

92. Carolene Products, 304 U.S.152 n. 4.

CHAPTER 12: THE FINAL WORD

1. McNeil v. Wyeth, 462 F.3d 364, 366 (5th Cir. 2006); R. Yassa, "Functional impairment in tardive dyskinesia: medical and psychosocial dimensions," 80 *Acta Psychiatrica Scandinavica* 65, 66 (1989).

2. McNeil, 462 F.3d 366.

3. Ibid., 369–370.

4. PLIVA, Inc. v. Mensing, 131 S. Ct. 2567, 2572 (2011).

5. Ibid., 2574–2575.

6. Ibid., 2577–2578.

7. Ibid., 2576–2577.

8. Ibid., 2588–2589 (Sotomayor, J., dissenting).

9. Dickerson v. United States, 530 U.S. 428, 444 (2000).

10. Nat'l Fed'n of Indep. Bus. v. Sebelius, 132 S. Ct. 2566, 2594 (2012).

11. William N. Eskridge, Jr., "Overruling Statutory Precedents," 76 *Geo. L. J.* 1361, 1362 (1988).

12. For a more detailed explanation of the flawed constitutional structure that led to the government shutdown in 2013, see Ian Millhiser, "Don't Like the Shutdown? Blame the Constitution," *ThinkProgress* (Sep. 30, 2013), at http://thinkprogress.org/justice/2013/09/30/2644771/shutdown-constitution/.

13. Ledbetter v. Goodyear Tire & Rubber Co., Inc., 127 S. Ct. 2162, 2178 (2007) (Ginsburg, J., dissenting).

14. Ibid., 2178.

15. Bazemore v. Friday, 478 U.S. 385, 395 (1986) (unanimous concurring opinion of Brennan, J.).

16. Ledbetter, 127 S. Ct. at 2177.

17. Ibid., 2182 (Ginsburg, J., dissenting).

18. Ibid., 2178 (Ginsburg, J., dissenting).

19. Sheryl Gay Stolberg, "Obama Signs Equal-Pay Legislation," *N.Y. Times* (Jan. 29, 2009), at http://www.nytimes.com/2009/01/30/us/politics/30 ledbetter-web.html; Jesse J. Holland, "House Dems Target Court's Pay Ruling," *Associated Press* (Jun. 12, 2007), at http://usatoday30.usatoday.com/news /washington/2007–06–12–2953732132_x.htm; Jesse Lee, "Lilly Ledbetter to Testify Before Education & Labor Committee," *The Gavel* (Jun. 5, 2007), at http://thegavel.democraticleader.house.gov/?p=450.

20. Adam Liptak, "In Congress's Paralysis, a Mightier Supreme Court," *N.Y. Times* (Aug. 20, 2012), at http://www.nytimes.com/2012/08/21/us /politics/supreme-court-gains-power-from-paralysis-of-congress.html.

21. Gross v. FBL Financial Services, Inc., 129 S. Ct. 2343, 2346–2347, 2349 (2009).

22. Ibid., 2353–2354 (Steven, J., dissenting).

23. H.R. 2852, 113th Cong., 1st Sess. (2013); S. 1391, 113th Cong., 1st Sess. (2013).

24. Univ. of Tex. Southwestern Med. Ctr. v. Nassar, 133 S. Ct. 2517 (2013).

25. 133 S. Ct. 2434, 2443 (2013).

26. Ibid., 2459 (Ginsburg, J., dissenting).

27. Ibid., 2460 (Ginsburg, J., dissenting).

28. Komarova v. National Credit Acceptance, Inc., 175 Cal. App. 4th 324, 331 (Ct. of App. of Ca., 1st Dist. 2009).

29. Jim Avila, "Taking on Credit Card Companies; Are Cards Stacked Against Consumers?" *Good Morning America* (May 29, 2008).

30. Komarova, 175 Cal. App. 4th at 330–335.

31. Ibid., 331.

32. People v. National Arbitration Forum, Inc., No. CGC-08–473569 (Sup. Ct. of Ca., filed Aug. 22, 2008), *Complaint for Injunctive Relief and Civil Penalties for Violations of Business and Professions Code Section 17200.*

33. National Arbitration Forum, No. CGC-08–473569, *Injunction Findings of Fact, and Order for Entry of Judgment Pursuant to Stipulation* (Sup. Ct. of Ca., Oct. 18, 2011).

34. Robert Berner, "Big Arbitration Firm Pulls Out of Credit Card Business," *Bloomberg* (Jul. 19, 2009), at http://www.businessweek.com/investing /wall_street_news_blog/archives/2009/07/big_arbitration.html.

35. John O'Donnell, "The Arbitration Trap: How Credit Card Companies Ensnare Consumers," *Public Citizen* (Sep. 2007), available at https://www .citizen.org/documents/Final_wcover.pdf.

36. Komarova, 175 Cal. App. 4th at 331.

37. Gilmer v. Interstate/Johnson Lane Corp., 500 U.S. 20, 38–39 (1991) (Stevens, J., dissenting).

38. Moses H. Cone Mem'l Hosp. v. Mercury Constr. Corp., 460 U.S. 1, 24–25 (1983).

39. Southland Corp. v. Keating, 465 U.S. 1, 14–16 (1984); Ibid., 26–27 (O'Connor, J., dissenting).

40. 9 U.S.C. § 1.

41. 532 U.S. 105, 115–116 (2001); Ibid., 136 (Souter, J., dissenting).

42. 131 S. Ct. 1740, 1751–1753 (2011).

43. Ibid., 1761 (quoting Carnegie v. Household Int'l, Inc., 376 F.3d 656, 661 [7th Cir. 2004]).

44. Komarova, 175 Cal. App. 4th at 333–334.

45. Theodore Eisenberg et al., "Arbitration's Summer Soldiers: An Empirical Study of Arbitration Clauses in Consumer and Nonconsumer Contracts," 41 *U. Mich. J.L. Reform* 871, 883–884 (2008).

46. Kathy Chu, "Bank of America Ends Arbitration of Credit Card Disputes," *USA Today* (Aug. 13, 2009), at http://usatoday30.usatoday.com/money /industries/banking/2009–08–13-bank-of-america-no-arbitration_N.htm? csp=34.

47. Tom Donnelly, "The U.S. Chamber of Commerce Continues Its Winning Ways," *Constitutional Accountability Center* (Jun. 30, 2014), at http://theus constitution.org/text-history/2753/us-chamber-commerce-continues-its -winning-ways; Kedar Bhatia, "Final Stat Pack for October Term 2013 and Key Takeaways," *SCOTUSblog* (Jun. 30, 2014), at http://www.scotusblog.com /2014/06/final-stat-pack-for-october-term-2013-and-key-takeaways-2/.

48. Donnelly, "Chamber of Commerce," 47.

49. Ian Millhiser, "The Most Partisan Supreme Court Justice of All," *Think Progress* (Jul. 2, 2014), at http://thinkprogress.org/justice/2014/07/02/34 55366/the-most-partisan-justice/.

50. Burwell v. Hobby Lobby, Nos. 13–354 & 13–356, 2014 U.S. LEXIS 4505 at *22–24 & *33–34 (Mar. 25, 2014).

51. United States v. Lee, 455 U.S. 252, 261 (1982).

52. *See* Employment Div. v. Smith, 494 U.S. 872, 879 (1990) ("the right of free exercise does not relieve an individual of the obligation to comply with a valid and neutral law of general applicability on the ground that the law proscribes [or prescribes] conduct that his religion prescribes [or proscribes]").

53. *See* 42 U.S.C § 2000bb ("The purposes of this chapter are . . . to restore the compelling interest test as set forth in Sherbert v. Verner, 374 U.S. 398 (1963) and Wisconsin v. Yoder, 406 U.S. 205 (1972) and to guarantee its application in all cases where free exercise of religion is substantially burdened. . . ."); Hobby Lobby, 2014 U.S. LEXIS 4505 at *110–111 (Ginsburg, J., dissenting).

54. City of Boerne v. Flores, 521 U.S. 507, 533–534 (1997).

55. *See* Hobby Lobby, 2014 U.S. LEXIS 4505 at *118 (Ginsburg, J., dissenting) ("Until this litigation, no decision of this Court recognized a for-profit corporation's qualification for a religious exemption from a generally applicable law, whether under the Free Exercise Clause or RFRA.").

56. Ibid., *148–150 (Ginsburg, J, dissenting).

57. Loving v. Virginia, 388 U.S. 1, 3 (1967).

58. Ian Millhiser, "When 'Religious Liberty' Was Used to Justify Racism Instead of Homophobia," *ThinkProgress* (Feb. 26, 2014), at http://thinkprogress .org/justice/2014/02/26/3333161/religious-libert y-racist-anti-gay/.

59. EEOC v. Fremont Christian School, 781 F.2d 1362, 1364, 1368–1369 (9th Cir. 1986).

60. Elane Photography, LLC v. Willock, 309 P. 3d 53, 76 (N.M. 2013).

61. Hobby Lobby, 2014 U.S. LEXIS 4505 at *87.

62. *See* Ibid., *96–97 (Kennedy, J, concurring) ("Among the reasons the United States is so open, so tolerant, and so free is that no person may be restricted or demeaned by government in exercising his or her religion. Yet neither may that same exercise unduly restrict other persons, such as employees, in protecting their own interests, interests the law deems compelling").

CHAPTER 13: THE CONSTITUTION HAS
ALWAYS BEEN AT WAR WITH EURASIA

1. Danielle Ivory, "Rape Victim's Choice: Risk AIDS or Health Insurance?" *Huffington Post* (Mar. 18, 2010), at http://www.huffingtonpost.com/2009/10 /21/insurance-companies-rape-_n_328708.html.

2. Ibid.

3. Ibid.

4. Les Blumenthal, "Domestic Violence as Pre-Existing Condition? 8 States Still Allow It," *McClatchy Newspapers* (Oct. 4, 2009), at http://www .mcclatchydc.com/2009/10/04/76477/domestic-violence-as-pre-existing.html.

5. Karen Pollitz et al., "How Accessible Is Individual Health Insurance for Consumers in Less-Than-Perfect Health?" *Henry J. Kaiser Family Foundation* (June 2001), 7, 9, 19 n. 27; available at http://kaiserfamilyfoundation.files .wordpress.com/2013/01/how-accessible-is-individual-health-insurance-for -consumer-in-less-than-perfect-health-report.pdf.

6. David U. Himmelstein et al., "Medical Bankruptcy in the United States, 2007: Results of a National Study," 122 *Am. J. of Med.* 741, 742 (2007).

7. Howard Bell, "Case Study: The Uninsured, True Stories of Unnecessary Sickness, Death and Humiliation," 49 *The New Physician* (Sep. 2000), available at http://www.amsa.org/programs/barriers/case.pdf.

8. Ibid.

9. Ed Pilkington, "Dying for Affordable Healthcare—The Uninsured Speak," *The Guardian* (Aug. 21, 2009), at http://www.theguardian.com/society /2009/aug/21/healthcare-provision-us-uk.

10. Bell, "Uninsured."

11. Ibid.

12. Ibid.

13. Ibid.

14. Ibid.

15. Ibid.

16. Ibid.

17. Andrew P. Wilper et al., "Health Insurance and Mortality in US Adults," 99 *Amer. J. of Pub. Health* 2289, 2295 (2009).

18. "13 Attorneys General Sue Over Health Care Overhaul," *Associated Press* (Mar. 23, 2010), at http://usatoday30.usatoday.com/news/nation/2010–03 –23-attorneys-general-health-suit_N.htm.

19. Igor Volsky, "Reagan's Solicitor General Promises To 'Eat A Hat Made Of Kangaroo Skin' If Courts Repeal Health Law," *ThinkProgress* (Apr. 15, 2010), at http://thinkprogress.org/health/2010/04/15/171390/fried-unconstitutional/.

20. Seven-Sky v. Holder, 661 F. 3d 1, 18 (D.C. Cir. 2011).

21. J. Harvie Wilkinson III, "Cry the Beloved Constitution," *N.Y. Times* (Mar. 11, 2012), at http://www.nytimes.com/2012/03/12/opinion/cry-the -beloved-constitution.html.

22. Josh Blackman, *Unprecedented: The Constitutional Challenge to Obamacare* (New York: PublicAffairs, 2013), 37, 43–44.

23. Jon Healey, "Legal Experts Predict a Supreme Court Win for 'Obama-care,'" *L.A. Times* (Mar. 13, 2012), at http://opinion.latimes.com/opinionla /2012/03/poll-of-legal-experts-predicts-a-win-for-obamacare.html.

24. Nat'l Fed'n of Indep. Bus. v. Sebelius, 132 S. Ct. 2566, 2677 (2012) (joint dissenting opinion).

25. Jan Crawford, "Roberts Switched Views to Uphold Health Care Law," *CBS News* (Jul. 2, 2012), at http://www.cbsnews.com/news/roberts-switched -views-to-uphold-health-care-law/.

26. United States v. Lopez, 514 U.S. 549, 586–588 (1995) (Thomas, J., concurring) (suggesting that the Court should return to the *Lochner* Era view that Congress's power to regulate commerce does not include the power to regulate "agriculture" or "manufacturing").

27. Christopher G. Tiedeman, *The Unwritten Constitution of the United States: A Philosophical Inquiry into the Fundamentals of American Constitutional Law* (New York: G. P. Putnam's Sons, 1890), 80–81.

28. NFIB, 132 S. Ct. 2614 (Ginsburg, J., dissenting).

29. Adele M. Kirk, "Riding the Bull: Experience with Individual Market Reform in Washington, Kentucky and Massachusetts," 25 *J. Heath Politics, Pol'y & L.* 133, 152 (2000).

30. Alan C. Monheit et al., "Community Rating and Sustainable Individual Health Insurance Markets in New Jersey," 23.4 *Health Affairs* 167, 169–170 (2004).

31. Maine Bureau of Insurance, *White Paper: Maine's Individual Health Insurance Market* (Jan. 22, 2001), 8.

32. NFIB, 132 S. Ct. at 2585.

33. Jonathan Gruber, Massachusetts Institute of Technology, *The Senate Bill Lowers Non-Group Premiums: Updated for New CBO Estimates* 1 (2009), available at http://www.politico.com/static/PPM145_final_try.html.

34. United States v. South-Eastern Underwriters Ass'n, 322 U.S. 533, 553 (1944).

35. Gonzales v. Raich, 545 U.S. 1, 36 (2005) (Scalia, J., concurring in the judgment).

36. Gibbons v. Ogden, 22 U.S. (9 Wheat.) 1, 193–194, 196 (1824).

37. United States v. Darby, 312 U.S. 100, 116 (1941).

38. 132 S. Ct. at 2649 (joint dissenting opinion).

39. Hammer v. Dagenhart, 247 U.S. 251, 276 (1918).

40. See United States v. Morrison, 529 U.S. 578, 611 (2000) ("*Lopez*'s review of Commerce Clause case law demonstrates that in those cases where we have sustained federal regulation of intrastate activity based upon the activity's substantial effects on interstate commerce, the activity in question has been some sort of economic endeavor.").

41. NFIB, 132 S. Ct. at 2650 (joint dissenting opinion).

42. *See* Ibid., 2625 (Ginsburg, J., concurring in part, concurring in the judgment in part, and dissenting in part) ("When contemplated in its extreme, almost any power looks dangerous").

43. Gibbons, 22 U.S (9 Wheat.) at 197.

44. NFIB, 132 S. Ct. at 2579.

45. Seven-Sky, 661 F. 3d at 18.

46. For a fuller discussion of the differences between Heritage's plan and the Affordable Care Act, see Scott Lemieux, "The ACA v. the Heritage Plan: A Comparison in Chart Form," *Lawyers, Guns & Money* (Dec. 6, 2013), at http://www.lawyersgunsmoneyblog.com/2013/12/the-aca-v-the-heritage-plan-a-comparison-in-chart-form.

47. Stuart M. Butler, *Assuring Affordable Health Care for All Americans*, 218 The Heritage Lectures 6 (1989).

48. Blackman, *Unprecedented*, 7.

49. Mark V. Pauly et al., "A Plan for 'Responsible National Health Insurance,'" 10 *Health Affairs*, 5, 6, 10 (1991).

50. Ezra Klein, "An Interview with Mark Pauly, Father of the Individual Mandate," *Wash. Post* (Feb. 1, 2011).

51. Health Equity and Access Reform Today Act of 1993 (S. 1757, Nov. 11, 1993), available at http://thomas.loc.gov/cgi-bin/bdquery/z?d103:SN01 770:; "Summary of a 1993 Republican Health Reform Plan," *Kaiser Health News* (Feb. 23, 2010), at http://www.kaiserhealthnews.org/Stories/2010 /February/23/GOP-1993-health-reform-bill.aspx.

52. Blackman, *Unprecedented*, 8.

53. Scott S. Greenberger, "Romney Eyes Penalties for Those Lacking Insurance," *Boston Globe* (Jun. 22, 2005), at http://www.bostonglobe.com/lifestyle /health-wellness/2005/06/22/romney-eyes-penalties-for-those-lacking -insurance/nq24PsjA5kWOfZpNfZhWoJ/story.html.

54. Mitt Romney, "Mr. President, What's the Rush?" *USA Today* (Jul. 30, 2009), available at http://usatoday30.usatoday.com/printedition/news/2009 0730/column30_st.art.htm.

55. Glen Johnson, "Romney Addresses Health Care, Not Authenticity," *Boston Globe* (Mar. 7, 2011), at http://www.boston.com/news/politics/political intelligence/2011/03/romney_addresse_1.html.

56. Ibid.

57. Blackman, *Unprecedented*, 11.

58. "Transcript: Sens. Dodd, Grassley on 'FNS,'" *Fox News* (Jun. 14, 2009), available at http://www.foxnews.com/story/2009/06/14/transcript-sens-dodd -grassley-on-fns/.

59. Br. of Members of the United States Senate as *Amici Curiae* in Support of Respondents on the Minimum Coverage Provision Issue at 5, Dep't of Health & Human Servs. v. Florida (2012) (No. 11–398).

60. Br. of Amicus Curiae The Heritage Foundation in Support of Plaintffs-Appellees at 6, Florida v. Dep't of Health & Human Servs, 648 F.3d 1235 (11th Cir. 2011) (Nos. 11–11021 & 11–067); *see also* Ibid., 14 (admitting that "Heritage's first serious legal analysis of the [Affordable Care Act] was not published until late 2009").

61. Drew Westen et al., "Neural Bases of Motivated Reasoning: An fMRI Study of Emotional Constraints on Partisan Political Judgment in the 2004 U.S. Presidential Election," 18 *J. of Cognitive Neuroscience* 1947, 1947–1949 (2006).

62. Ibid., 1955–1956.

63. Drew Westen, *The Political Brain: The Role of Emotion in Deciding the Fate of the Nation* (New York: PublicAffairs, 2008), xiv.

64. Dan M. Kahan et al., "Motivated Numeracy and Enlightened Self-Government," 7–10 (Sep. 2013), available at https://papers.ssrn.com/sol3 /papers.cfm?abstract_id=2319992.

65. Ibid., 18.

66. Thomas More Law Center v. Obama, 651 F. 3d 529, 565–566 (6th Cir. 2011) (Sutton, J., concurring in part).

67. Nat'l Fed'n of Indep. Bus. v. Sebelius, 132 S. Ct. 2566, 2594 (2012).

68. Ibid., 2607.

69. Sy Mukherjee, "Study: GOP Obstruction Is Leaving Nearly 6 Million Americans Without Medicaid Coverage," *ThinkProgress* (Feb. 11, 2014), at http://thinkprogress.org/health/2014/02/11/3279551/urban-institute -medicaid-expansion/.

70. Chris Mooney, "Science Confirms: Politics Wrecks Your Ability to Do Math," *Mother Jones* (Sep. 4, 2013), at http://www.motherjones.com/politics /2013/09/new-study-politics-makes-you-innumerate.

71. Thomas More, 651 F. 3d, 564–565.

72. Ian Millhiser, "Why Roberts Will Vote to Uphold the Affordable Care Act," *ThinkProgress* (Feb. 16, 2011), at http://thinkprogress.org/health/2011 /02/16/171940/roberts-aca/.

73. Dahlia Lithwick, "It's Not About the Law, Stupid," *Slate* (Mar. 22, 2012), at http://www.slate.com/articles/news_and_politics/jurisprudence/2012 /03/the_supreme_court_is_more_concerned_with_the_politics_of_the_health _care_debate_than_the_law_.html.

74. US Const., Amend. XIV, Sec. 1.

75. Ibid., Amend. IV.

76. Ibid., Amend. VIII.

77. Ibid., Amend. V and XIV, Sec 1.

78. Ibid., Amend. V.

79. Ibid., Art. IV, Sec. 4.

80. Ibid., Art. I, Sec. 8.

81. Ibid.

EPILOGUE: THE GATHERING STORM

1. Ian Millhiser, "The Imaginary Rule That Keeps Obama's Judges From Being Confirmed," *ThinkProgress* (Apr. 17, 2014), at http://thinkprogress.org /justice/2014/04/17/3427259/blue-slip/.

2. McClung v. Katzenbach, 233 F. Supp. 815, 825 (N.D. Ala. 1964).

3. Florida v. U.S. Dep't of Health & Human Servs., 780 F. Supp. 2d 1256, 1286 (N.D. Fla. 2011).

4. 9 U.S.C. § 1; Circuit City v. Adams, 532 U.S. 105, 115–116 (2001); Ibid., 136 (Souter, J., dissenting).

5. Lochner v. New York, 198 U.S. 45, 53 (1905).

6. Alaska Const. Art. IV; §§ 5 & 8; for an extended discussion of Alaska's merit selection process, and of the Carter merit selection commission discussed

below, see Erwin Chemerinsky, *The Case Against the Supreme Court* (New York: Viking, 2014), 298–300.

7. Lisa Demer, "Palin Bucks Pressure in Supreme Court Appointment," *Anchorage Daily News* (Mar. 4, 2009), at http://www.adn.com/2009/03/04/711378/palin-bucks-pressure-in-supreme.html.

8. "President Obama Nominates Justice Morgan Christen for the United States Court of Appeals," *The White House* (May 18, 2011), at http://www.whitehouse.gov/the-press-office/2011/05/18/president-obama-nominates-justice-morgan-christen-united-states-court-ap.

9. Exec. Order No. 11,972, 42 Fed. Reg. 9659 (Feb. 17, 1977).

10. Ian Millhiser, "How an Absurd Senate Rule Kept a Powerful Judgeship Open for 1000 Days and Counting," *ThinkProgress* (May 28, 2013), at http://thinkprogress.org/justice/2013/05/28/2064261/how-an-absurd-senate-rule-kept-a-powerful-judgeship-open-for-1000-days-and-counting/.

11. 133 S. Ct. 2675 (2013).

12. 539 U.S. 558 (2003).

13. Letter from John W. Macy, Chairman, Civil Service Commission, to the Mattachine Society of Washington at 2 (Feb. 25, 1966), available at http://rainbowhistory.omeka.net/items/show/4937951.

14. Ibid.

15. Baker v. Nelson, 409 U.S. 810 (1972).

16. *See* Lyle Denniston, "Gay Marriage and *Baker v. Nelson*," *SCOTUSblog* (Jul. 4, 2012), at http://www.scotusblog.com/2012/07/gay-marriage-and-baker-v-nelson/.

17. 478 U.S. 186, 191 (1986).

18. Ian Millhiser, "Incoming House Judiciary Chair Said That Medicare and Social Security Are Unconstitutional," *ThinkProgress* (Nov. 13, 2012), at http://thinkprogress.org/justice/2012/11/13/1180421/incoming-house-judiciary-chair-said-that-medicare-and-social-security-are-unconstitutional/.

19. Ian Millhiser, "Mike Lee Suggests FEMA, Federal Poverty and Food Safety Programs Are All Unconstitutional," *ThinkProgress* (Jan. 19, 2011), at http://thinkprogress.org/politics/2011/01/19/139683/mike-lees-katrina/.

20. Virginia ex rel. Cuccinelli v. Sebelius, 656 F. 3d 253, 267, 270 (4th Cir. 2011).

21. K.S.A. § 50–1204(a) (2013) ("A personal firearm, a firearm accessory or ammunition that is manufactured commercially or privately and owned in Kansas and that remains within the borders of Kansas is not subject to any federal law, treaty, federal regulation, or federal executive action").

22. Tex. Bus. & Com. Code § 2004.003 (2013).

23. Ian Millhiser, "Tea Party Activists Aren't Gearing Up for 2016—They Want to Refight 1964," *ThinkProgress* (Mar. 10, 2014), at http://thinkprogress.org/justice/2014/03/10/3381721/conservative-actvists-at-cpac-arent-gearing-up-for-2016-they-want-to-refight-the-1964-election/.

24. Ian Millhiser, "Rand Paul Praises Horrendous Supreme Court Decision, Would Let Employers Ruthlessly Exploit Workers," *ThinkProgress* (Mar. 7, 2013), at http://thinkprogress.org/justice/2013/03/07/1684111/rand-paul-all -laws-protecting-workers-are-constitutionally-suspect/.

25. *See* United States v. Lopez, 514 U.S. 549, 586 (1995) (Thomas, J., concurring) (arguing that, in the Constitution, "the term 'commerce' was used in contradistinction to productive activities such as manufacturing and agriculture").

26. Morris A. Copeland, "The National Income and Its Distribution," in *Nat'l Bureau of Econ. Research, Recent Changes in the United States* (Cambridge, MA: National Bureau of Economic Research, 1929), 757.

27. United States Census Bureau, *State & County Quickfacts* (Jun. 27, 2013), available at http://quickfacts.census.gov/qfd/states/00000.html.

28. Camille L. Ryan and Julie Siebens, *Educational Attainment in the United States: 2009* (Washington, DC: United States Census Bureau, 2012), 4; available at https://www.census.gov/prod/2012pubs/p20–566.pdf.

29. Paul N. Van de Water et al., "Social Security Keeps 22 Million Americans Out Of Poverty: A State-By-State Analysis," Center on Budget and Policy Priorities (Oct. 25, 2013), available at http://www.cbpp.org/cms/?fa=view &id=4037.

30. Ian Millhiser, "Sen. Mike Lee Calls Child Labor Laws Unconstitutional," *ThinkProgress* (Jan. 14, 2011).

31. *See* McCreary County v. ACLU, 545 U.S. 844, 882 (2005) (O'Connor, J., concurring). O'Connor originally posed a similar question in the context of religion—"Those who would renegotiate the boundaries between church and state must therefore answer a difficult question: Why would we trade a system that has served us so well for one that has served others so poorly?"

Index

Abolitionism, Holmes's view of, 116
Abortion rights, 206–210, 278
Adair v. United States, 105–106
Addonizio, Hugh, 196
Addyston Pipe & Steel Co. v. United States, 61–62
Adelson, Sheldon, 229, 236
Adkins v. Children's Hospital, 104, 119
Adulterated foods, 74
Affordable Care Act
  Commerce Clause, 264
  conditions before the enactment of, 255–258
  constitutional remedies for, 265
  freedom of commerce, 80
  importance of a Supreme Court, 277
  individual mandate, 261–263, 266–269
  partisanship determining constitutionality of, 266–274
  repeal efforts, 240, 259–261, 282
  rightward shift of the Court threatening, 280
African Americans
  Brewer's opinions on race, 40–42
  Civil Rights Act, 178
  desegregation of Southern schools, 153
  election manipulation in Florida, 220
  Frankfurter's clerk, 168
  Hamburg, South Carolina massacre, 159

  Holmes's view of Reconstruction, 116
  Knights of Labor, 29–30
  Louisiana legislature, 5–6
  McReynolds's shabby treatment of, 77–78
  Newark riots, 195–199
  Peckham's dismissive treatment of, 95
  Plessy v. Ferguson, 9, 39, 41, 95, 167, 170, 179–180
  Pullman railroad employees, 25–26
  right-wing Southern politics, 158–159
  Scottsboro Boys, 163–166
  Southern states' peonage system, 116–117
  voter suppression tactics, 52–53, 151, 185–190, 192, 220–225
  workplace discrimination, 241–242
  See also Brown v. Board of Education; Racism
Age discrimination, 243–244
AIDS/HIV, 255–256
Alaska: judicial appointment methods, 278–279
Alito, Samuel
  Court siding with the Chamber of Commerce, 251
  gutting the Voting Rights Act, 214–215
  Hobby Lobby, 252–254
  partisan gerrymandering, 217

Alito, Samuel (*continued*)
  racial and sexual harassment in the
    workplace, 245
  rightward shift of the Court, 281
  workplace discrimination, 242–243
Amendment process
  eliminating the Court, 275
  income tax, 146–147
  reviving Lochner, 278
  unpredictable results of, 147
  See also specific amendments
American Bar Association (ABA),
  100–101, 260
American Civil Liberties Union
  (ACLU), 167
American Federation of Labor (AFL),
  21, 30
American Legion, 141
American Liberty League, 140–144,
  180
American Protective League, 121
American Railway Union (ARU), 30,
  32, 34–35, 37–38, 42–43, 50
American Sugar Refining Company,
  57–58, 61–62
Antisemitism, 78
Antitrust law, 21, 48–50, 56–57,
  61–62, 263–264
Apartheid, Southern, ix–x, xv. *See also*
  Segregation
Appointment method for judges,
  278–279
Arbitration, forced, 246–250
Articles of Confederation, 54–56
AT&T v. Concepcion, 249, 254

Bacon, Augustus, 72
Bailey, Josiah, 151–152
Bakeries, 92–94, 97–98. *See also*
  Lochner v. New York
Baldwin, Simeon, 100
Bank failures during the Great
  Depression, 134
Bankruptcy, medical causes of,
  256–258
Barnett, Randy, 259–260

Barnett, Ross, 253
Bartholet, Elizabeth, 247
Bellamy, Edward, 42
Benjamin, Brent, 230–231
Bennett, Mike, 219, 268
Bennett, Robert, 267
Bernanke, Ben, 135
Beveridge, Albert, 71–74
Bill of Rights, xi, 165
Bingham, John, xii, 13, 16
Birth control, 251–252
Black, Hugo, 162–163, 165–166, 173
Black lung disease, 65
Blackmun, Harry, 204
Blaine, James, 49–50
Boehner, John, 216
Bond, Kit, 267–268
Bork, Robert, 182–183, 209, 211
Bowers v. Hardwick, 282
Boycotts, 21–22, 34–36
Boyd, James Edmund, 76
Brandeis, Louis, 78, 125–126,
  152, 154
Brennan, William, 175, 247
Brewer, David Josiah
  business monopolies, 45
  child labor regulation, 72
  Debs decision, 40–41
  dissatisfaction with modern
    lawyers, 100
  maximum hours law, 96
  progressive views, 41–42
  Pullman strike, 44
  skepticism of government, 42–43
  women's inferiority, 103–104
Breyer, Stephen, 280
Broadhead, James, 100–101
Brotherhood of Locomotive Firemen,
  29–30
Brown v. Board of Education
  Black's opinion despite racist past,
    166–167
  Byrnes's segregationist views, 161
  Davis's arguments in, 142
  Frankfurter's opinion, 170
  implementation order, 172–174

importance of a Supreme Court, 276–277

Parker's narrow interpretation of, 153

Rehnquist's skepticism of, 179–180

Southern resistance, 178–179

Warren's opinion, 171–172

Bryan, William Jennings, 50

Buchanan, James, 52

Buck, Carrie, 107–110, 112–113, 117

Buck v. Bell, 107–110, 117–118

Buckley v. Valeo, 231, 233–234

Burger, Warren, 204

Burke, Edmund, 102

Burton, Harold, 166–167

Burwell v. Hobby Lobby, 251–254

Bush, George H.W., 267

Bush, George W., 213–215, 243, 269

Bush v. Gore, 213–215

Butler, Benjamin, 4, 49

Butler, Pierce, 118

Byrnes, Jimmy, 158–161, 174

Campaign spending, 215, 228–237

Campbell, John Archibald
antigovernment and pro-segregationist views, 6–7, 12–14

Fourteenth Amendment justification for segregation, xv, 89–90

Justice Black and, 163

Slaughterhouse Cases, 11

Candler, Allen, 253

Canneries, 67–68

Caperton v. A.T. Massey Coal, 230–231

Cardozo, Benjamin, 78

Carlisle, John, 50

Carpenter, Ruly, 139–140

Carpet factories, 68

Carpetbaggers, ix

Carroll, Paul, 223

Carter, Jimmy, 279

Catholic Church: opposition to Child Labor Amendment, 147

Censorship, xiii, 119–120, 123–126

Central Pacific Railroad, 9–11

Chafee, John, 267

Chafin, Don, 86–87

Chamber of Commerce, 251

Champion v. Ames, 74

Chase, Samuel, 59

Chicago, Illinois, 22–23

Chicago World's Fair (1893), 34

Child labor
canneries, 67–68

coal mining, 63–66

cotton mills in the South, 69–71, 82–83

Fourteenth Amendment, xiii

glass factories, 66–67

illness associated with, 68

steam boiler operation, 84

Child Labor Amendment (1924), 147–148

Child labor regulation
Adkins v. Children's Hospital affecting women's and children's wages, 105

Alabama, 71

Beveridge's push for federal legislation, 72–74

constitutionality of, 79, 263–264

federal regulation, 71–72

Keating-Owen Act, 75–76

states' ratification of an amendment permitting, 147–148

Children
caring for parents, 131–132

civil rights volunteers, 176–177

eugenics, 107–111

Gobitis case, 168–169

Great Depression, 130

Chinese Exclusion Act (1882), 10–11, 40

Chinese immigrants, 9–11, 40

Cholera, 12

Christen, Morgan, 278

Cigar factories, 68

Circuit City v. Adams, 248–249, 277

Circuits, judicial, 149

Citizens United v. F.E.C., 229–230, 234–237, 240

Citizenship rights, xi–xii

Civil Rights Act (1964)
  constitutionality of, 106
  Court rejecting challenges to, 192
  Goldwater's opposition, 181–184,
    211
  private discrimination and official
    racism, 182–183
  Rand Paul's opposition to, 283
  role in school desegregation, 178
  state courts striking down, 277
Civil rights and the civil rights
    movement
  Court undermining progressive
    legislation, 240–241
  Nixon's rightward shift on, 199–200,
    202–203
  placing states' rights ahead of,
    183–184
  Selma, Alabama violence, 177–178
  suppressing black voters in the
    South, 185–190, 192
  volunteer preparation, 176–177
  Warren Court's expansion on,
    200–202
Civil Service Commission, US,
    281–282
Civil War
  Campbell's legal career, 6–7
  eugenics and slavery, 112
  Holmes's service in, 115–116
  Kansas-Nebraska Act, 51
  Nixon's civil rights frame, 200
Clark, Champ, 120
Clark, David, 74–75, 80
Clark, Tom, 167
Class action lawsuits, 249
Clay, Cassius M., 11–12
Cleveland, Grover, 30, 36–38, 48–50,
    53–54, 58–59, 96
Clifford, Nathan, x–xi
Clinton, Hillary Rodham, 267
Coal mining
  campaign spending, 230–231
  child labor, 63–65
  dangers on the job, 84–86
  girls' and women's work, 65–66

  labor control and disputes, 86–87
  legal failure to protect workers, 91
Cohen, Jessica, 223
Coleman, William T., 168
Colfax Massacre, ix, x, 13–16,
    159, 165
Collective bargaining, 137, 155–156
Colorado mining towns, 86
Commerce, regulation of, 56–58,
    73–74, 79, 263–264
Common law doctrines, 88–89
Company store, 89
Concentration camps, xiii, 161–162
Congress, US
  anti-Chinese legislation, 10
  Articles of Confederation, 55–56
  bank failures, 134–135
  Civil Rights Act, 178
  civil rights bills from 1875 to 1957,
    185
  commerce regulation, 56–57,
    264–265
  constitutional remedies for
    unpopular legislation, 265–266
  Court reinterpreting legislation, 277
  interstate transportation of goods,
    138
  Keating-Owen Act, 79
  Ledbetter v. Goodyear Tire, 242–243
  overriding the Court, 240–241,
    243, 254
  Reagan's Guidelines on
    Constitutional Litigation, 210
  Republican House majority despite
    Democratic victories, 215–217
  Roosevelt's Court-packing plan, 151
  setting limits on the power of, 80
  setting the size of the Court,
    149–150
  Wilson's declaration of war,
    120–121
Conscription, 120–122, 158
Conservatism
  American Liberty League, 140–141
  Buck v. Bell, 117–119
  judicial restraint and, 279

legitimacy of American government, 184–185
opposition to the Fourteenth Amendment, 147
traditionalism breeding, 99–100
Constitutional Accountability Center (CAC), 251
Coolidge, Calvin, 142
Cooper, Dorothy, 223
Corporate interests, Court support for, 250–251
Corruption, 21–232
Cotton mills, 69–71, 74–76, 82–83, 147–148
Court-packing plan, Roosevelt's, 150–152, 156, 275–276
Craig v. Boren, 206–207
Crawford v. Marion County Election Board, 225
Credit card companies, 246–249
Cruikshank, Bill, 16–18
Cumming v. Richmond County Board of Education, 95
Cummings, Homer, 150

Dagenhart. See Hammer v. Dagenhart
Dagenhart, Reuben, 76, 81–82
Darrow, Clarence, 40
Darwin, Charles, 109, 111
Davis, Jefferson, xv, 6
Davis, John W., 142–143, 160
Day, William Rufus, 77, 263–264
Debs, 45, 58
Debs, Eugene
imprisonment of, 44, 122
Justice Brewer's opinion, 42–43
Pullman strike, 28–30, 34–40
socialism and pacifism, 123–124
Debt collection, 246–247, 249–250
Declaration of Independence, 89–90
Defense of Marriage Act, 280
Dellinger, Walter, 272–273
Democracy
constitutional legitimacy for voting against civil rights, 184
Roberts Court election law cases, 215

threatening gradualism, 102
Tiedeman's fear of, 99
traditionalism breeding conservatism, 99–100
Democracy in America (Tocqueville), 100
Democratic Party
Affordable Care Act, 266–274
antitrust sentiment, 48–49
consequences of gerrymandering, 215–217
election fraud in Louisiana, 14–15
suppression of black voters in the South, 185–190
viewpoint discrimination through gerrymandering, 216–218
voter manipulation in Florida, 220
white supremacists' efforts to gain control, 14
Demographics of voting, 215–217, 220. *See also* Gerrymandering
Direct taxes, 59–61
Disabled individuals, 107–109
Discrimination
age discrimination, 243–244
employment discrimination against gays, 212, 281–282
employment discrimination against women, 241–243
preexisting medical conditions, 262
private discrimination, 181–182, 211–212
religious justification for, 252–254
viewpoint discrimination, 217, 219
voter suppression tactics, 220, 222
Voting Rights Act "bail in" and "bail out" provisions, 226–227
Discrimination, private, 180–183
Dissent, laws against, 280
Douglas, Stephen, 50, 52
Douglas, William O., 166–167
Draft, 120–122, 158
Dred Scott v. Sandford, x, 6, 41
Drug manufacturers, 239–240
Du Pont, Irénée, 140–141, 143–144

Due process, xi–xii. *See also* Fourteenth
    Amendment rights
DuPont company, 139–141

Early voting days, 219–220, 228
Economic issues
    American Liberty league attacking
        New Deal programs, 144–145
    congressional and Court jurisdiction
        over, 264
    Emergency Banking Relief Act,
        134–135
Education
    Dagenhart's lack of, 81
    property taxes funding, 204–205
    Pullman's focus on, 26–27
    religious justification for
        segregation, 253
    See also Brown v. Board of Education
Eisenhower, Dwight D., xiv, 171,
    174, 199
Elderly population, effect of the Great
    Depression on, 131–132
Election fraud
    gerrymandering contributing to,
        225–226
    Grant Parish voter suppression,
        14–15
    lack of evidence, 221–222
    voter suppression, 52–53, 151,
        185–190, 192, 215–218,
        220–225, 228–229
Elections
    campaign spending, 215, 228–237
    discriminatory practices, 225–227
    viewpoint discrimination through
        gerrymandering, 216–219
    voter suppression in
        Reconstructionist South,
        14–15
    voter suppression in the 2012
        election, 219–224
    voter suppression in the South,
        225–228
    voter suppression tactics, 221–228
    See also Gerrymandering

Electoral mandate of legislators and
    justices, 184–185
Emancipation Proclamation,
    challenging the constitutionality
    of, 53
Emergency Banking Relief Act (1933),
    135
Employment discrimination, 212,
    241–244, 281–282
Employment Div. v. Smith, 252
Equal protection clause, xii, 9, 41–42,
    186, 207, 214
Erie Canal, 22
Eugenics, 107–115, 117–119
Executive Committee of Southern
    Cotton Manufacturers, 75

Faubus, Orval, 173
FBL Financial Group, 243–244
Federal Arbitration Act (FAA),
    247–249, 277
Federal government
    barriers to worker safety measures, 89
    child labor regulation, 71–72
    collusion over the Pullman strike,
        36–39
    discord in Washington's cabinet,
        54–55
    Washington's vision of a robust
        national government, 146–147
Federal Reserve, 134–135
Field, Benjamin, 23–24
Field, Marshall, 25–26
Field, Stephen Johnson
    antigovernment views, 7–11, 42
    Fourteenth Amendment protecting
        "right of free labor," 91
    Fuller's views coinciding with, 54
    income tax, 60
    Lincoln's appointment, 149
    Lochner v. New York, 96
    popularity among Republicans, 282
    Pullman's connection to, 23–24
Fifteenth Amendment rights
    racist election regulations, 226
    Reconstruction Amendments, xi

First Amendment rights
American Liberty League, 141
banning viewpoint discrimination,
217
campaign-finance laws, 233
Gobitis case, 168–169
government censorship, xiii,
123–126
Lochner, 119–120
religious beliefs in the workplace,
252
United States v. Cruikshank, 17–18
Fletcher, Etoy, 188
Fletcher, John Gould, 163
Florida
Bush v. Gore, 213–215
voter suppression in the 2012
elections, 219–221
Food and Drug Administration
(FDA), 239–240
Four Horsemen, 118, 136, 148,
150–153, 156, 186, 284
Fourteenth Amendment rights
Holmes's view of social Darwinism
and eugenics, 114–115
justifying oppressive labor
practices, 97
provisions of, xi
Reconstruction Amendments, xii
reproductive freedom, 208
right of free labor, 91
shielding southern whites' rights,
12–13
Frankfurter, Felix
antidote to judicial excesses, 203
Brown v. Board of Education,
169–171
constitutionality of segregation in
the schools, 167–168
Gobitis case, 168–169
Holmes and, 114
Free soilers, 51
Free speech. *See* First Amendment
rights
Fremont Christian school, 253
Fried, Charles, 259

Friedman, Milton, 267
Fuller, Melville
antitrust law, 263–264
child labor regulation, 72, 74
direct and indirect taxation, 60
income tax, 146–147
Lochner v. New York, 94–95
political stance, 50–54
regulation of commerce, 57–58
Sugar Trust Case, 57–59
tariff reform, 58–59
Wisconsin workers' right to
organize, 89

Gainer, Hattie, 197
Galton, Francis, 112–113, 117
Garfield, James, 75
Gas lighting, 96
Gay rights
employment discrimination, 212
marriage equality, 253, 279–280
potential for overruling gay rights
decisions, 280–282
religious justification for
discrimination, 253–254
Gender discrimination, 207
General Managers' Association,
35–37, 43
Georgia: voter fraud allegations,
221–222
German Americans: WWI
conscription, 120–121
Gerrymandering
affecting black voters and politicians,
225–226
Illinois, 52–53
Republicans' congressional victory,
215–217
Senate and presidential races,
228–229
viewpoint discrimination,
216–219
Gibbons v. Ogden, 56–57, 263
Gideon v. Wainwright, 201
Gingrich, Newt, 267–268
Ginsburg, Douglas, 209

Ginsburg, Ruth Bader
  Ledbetter v. Goodyear Tire, 242–243
  racial and sexual harassment in the
    workplace, 245
  replacement of, 280
  Roe v. Wade, 206
  Voting Rights Act, 227
Glass factories, 66–67
Glendening, Parris, 221
Goldwater, Barry
  Civil Rights Act, 181–184
  employment discrimination against
    gays, 212
  Johnson's election victory, 191
  Nixon's civil rights shift, 199–200
Gompers, Samuel, 21
Goodyear Tire and Rubber, 241–243
Gore, Al, 213–215
Gould, Jay, 20, 30, 49
Gradualism, 100–102
Grain warehouse case, 8, 42
Grant, Ulysses S., x, 17–18, 20, 25
Grassley, Chuck, 267–268
Great American Desert, 19–20
Great Depression
  bank failures, 134
  effect on Pullman Company
    workers, 30–33
  stock market crash of 1929,
    129–130
Greeley, Horace, 19–20
Greenback Party, 49
Gregory, James, 65
Gregory, Thomas, 121
Griggs, John, 101
Gross, Jack, 243–244
Gross v. FBL Financial Services,
  243–244
Grovey v. Townsend, 187
Guidelines on Constitutional Litigation,
  209–211
Gun laws, 282–283

Hamburg, South Carolina massacre,
  159
Hamilton, Alexander, xiv, 54–55, 189

Hammer v. Dagenhart, 77, 79–81,
  116, 138, 183–184, 264
Harlan, John Jr., 39
Harlan, John Marshall, 40, 58,
  98–99, 114
Harrison, Benjamin, 49–50
Hatch, Orrin, 267–268
Hayes, Rutherford B., 18
Health and safety
  carpet and furniture factories, 68
  coal mining, 64–66, 84–86
  common law doctrines, 88–89
  cotton mill workers in the South,
    69–71, 83
  courts' refusal to protect workers, 95
  Illinois Steel disaster, 87–88
  lack of compensation for fatalities,
    87–88
  legal failure to protect workers,
    89–91
  lunch counter sit-in, 177
  maximum-hours law, 94, 96,
    104–105, 159–160, 162
  New York City bakeries, 92–94,
    97–98
  police brutality, 195–196
  poorhouses, 132–133
  See also *Lochner v. New York*
Health Equity and Access Reform
  Today Act, 267
Healthcare
  failing health and death through
    lack of, 256–258
  Hobby Lobby's control of
    reproductive rights, 251–252,
    254
  rape as a preexisting condition,
    255–256, 261
  religious beliefs denying health care,
    253
Heritage Foundation, 266–268
Hickok, Lorena, 129–131
Hobby Lobby, 251–252, 254
Holmes, Oliver Wendell
  censorship, 124–126
  character and views of, 113–114

eugenics, 118
  Frankfurter's admiration for, 168
  imprisonment of Eugene Debs,
    122–124
  Lochner opinion, 114–115
  war wounds, 115–116
  WWI cases of sedition over
    conscription, 121–122
Homelessness during the Great
  Depression, 132–133
Hoover, Herbert, 134, 136, 174
Housing
  cotton mill towns in the South,
    71, 82
  discrimination in Newark,
    197–198
  New York City bakeries, 93–94
  poorhouses, 132
  Pullman, Illinois, 26–28, 31–32
Houston, Charles Hamilton, 78
How to Live (Taft), 118
Hughes, Charles Evans, 154–156

Ideology
  arbitration enforcement, 247–248
  interpreting the law based on, 240
  primary purpose of the Constitution,
    284
Illegal search, 200–201
Illinois Steel Company, 87–88
Income tax, 59–61, 146–147
Indentured servitude, 116–117,
    121–122
Individual mandate of Obamacare,
    261–263, 266–269
Inequality
  income inequality of Pullman
    workers, 26, 31, 33–35
  property taxes funding education,
    204–205
  workplace discrimination, 241–246
Internment of Japanese Americans,
    161–162
Interstate Commerce Act (1887), 48
Interstate transportation of goods, 138
Iredell, James, 59

Jackson, Robert H., 167, 170–171,
    179, 201
Janning, Ernst, 190–191
Japanese Americans, 161
Jay, John, 149
Jefferson, Thomas, 54
Jehovah's Witnesses, 168–169
Jim Crow segregation. *See Brown v.
  Board of Education;* Civil rights
  and the civil rights movement;
  Segregation
Johnson, Andrew, 149
Johnson, Hiram, 152
Johnson, John G., 75–76
Johnson, Lyndon
  black voter suppression in the South,
    178–179, 187–188, 192
  Civil Rights Act, 106, 191–192
  landslide victory, 184
  Nixon's civil rights stance, 199
  popular perception of government,
    231–232
Judgment at Nuremberg (film), 190–191
Judicial restraint
  Bush v. Gore, 213–214
  judicial intervention replacing,
    218–219
  Nixon appointees, 204–205
  Reagan appointees, 209
  replacing respect for constitutional
    rights, 279
  Roberts's view of, 212, 273
Judicial review, 270
Jury discrimination, 165
Justice Department, US, 178, 226

"Kallikak, Martin" (pseudonym), 110
Kansas-Nebraska Act (1854), 51–52
Keating-Owen Act (1916), 74–76, 79
Kellogg, William Pitt, 14–15, 17
Kennedy, Anthony, 230, 254, 280
Kennedy, John F., 181
Kerry, John, 269
King, Martin Luther, Jr., 199
Kitchel, Denison, 181–182
Knights of Labor, 29–30

Komarova, Anastasiya, 246–247, 249–250
Korematsu v. United States, 162
Ku Klux Klan, 141, 153, 162–163, 188–189

La Follette, Robert, 123
Labor force
  antitrust law, 62
  discarding the elderly during the Depression, 131–132
  lack of safety for factory workers, 83–84, 87–88
  New York City bakeries, 92–94, 97–98
  Pullman Strike, 32–39
  Pullman's grip on railroad workers, 25–28
  See also Child labor; Child labor; Cotton mills; Working conditions
Labor regulation
  Chinese Exclusion Act, 10–11
  Holmes's *Lochner* opinion, 114
  poor decisions by the Court, xiii
  railroad workers, 21
  See also Child labor regulation
Labor unions. *See* Union labor
Landon, Alf, 144–145, 184
Lasater, Virginia, 223
Lawrence v. Texas, 281–282
Ledbetter, Lilly, 241–243
Ledbetter v. Goodyear Tire, 241–243, 245
Lee, Robert E., ix–x
Lewis, John, 177–178
Lewis, Ricky Tyrone, 222
Liberty League. *See* American Liberty League
Liberty of contract doctrine, 102–105, 137, 153
Life Extension Institute, 118
Lilly Ledbetter Fair Pay Act, 243
Lincoln, Abraham
  Douglas's election challenge, 52–53
  Emancipation Proclamation, x
  Field's appointment, 9

Fuller's political connection, 50–51
Miller's appointment, 12
Pacific Railroad Act, 19–20
Peckham's antipathy to, 95
Literacy tests for black voters, 188
Lithwick, Dahlia, 273
Lloyd, Henry Demarest, 48
Lochner, Joseph, 94–95
Lochner v. New York
  censorship, 119–120
  constitutional basis for, 277–278
  Holmes's opinion, 114–115
  liberty of contract doctrine, 102–104, 153
  Peckham's opinion, 94–95, 97
  private discrimination, 181
  Rand Paul's support of, 283
  Reagan's view of the Court, 209
  revival of, 118–119
  skepticism of government, 99, 102
  unconstitutionality of the decision, 184
  worker safety regulation, 97–99
Looking Backward (Bellamy), 42
Lottery tickets, 74
Lugar, Richard, 267–268
Lunch counter sit-in, 177
Lynchings, 164–165

Manderson, Charles, 101
Mapp v. Ohio, 200–201, 210
Marriage equality, 253, 279–280
Marshall, John, 56–58, 72, 79, 263, 265
Marshall, Thurgood, 78
Marxism, 42, 122
Mattachine Society of Washington, 281–282
Maximum-hours law, 94, 96, 104–105, 159–160, 162
McCutcheon v. F.E.C., 230
McDonnell, Bob, 282
McEnery, John, 14–15
McReynolds, James
  Buck v. Bell, 117–118
  character of, 77–78

child labor regulation, 79
freedom of contract, 154–155
National Labor Relations Act, 156
Roosevelt's Court-packing plan, 150
suppressing black voters in the
  South, 186
Medicaid, 267
Medicare, 267
Mendel, Gregor, 109
Mensing, Gladys, 238–239, 254
Meredith, James, 181
Metoclopramide, 238–239
Miles, Nelson, 36–38
Military forces
  Brown implementation, 173
  Newark riots, 195–199
  Pullman labor strike, 36–37
Miller, Samuel Freeman, 11–13, 116
Minersville School District v. Gobitis,
  168–169
Minimum-wage laws, 153–155
Mining industry, 96. *See also* Coal
  mining
Minton, Sherman, 166–167, 174
Miranda v. Arizona, 201–203, 205, 240
Missouri Compromise, 51–52
Mitchell, Thelma, 223
Mixed-motive lawsuits, 244
Monopolies, 45–50, 57
Mooney, Chris, 272
Morehead v. Tipaldo, 153–154
Moses, Bob, 176
Muller v. Oregon, 103, 105

Nash, Christopher Columbus, 14–16
National Arbitration Forum (NAF),
  247
National Association for the
  Advancement of Colored People
  (NAACP), 152–153, 167–168,
  178
National Child Labor Committee, 73
National Guard: Newark riots,
  195–198
National Labor Relations Act (1935),
  136–139, 142–143

*National Labor Relations Board v. Jones
  & Laughlin Steel,* 155–156
National Security Agency, 205
Native Americans, 252
Nazi Germany, 190–191
Negligence, law of, 88–89
Nelson, Levi, 16
New Deal
  American Liberty league attacking,
    140–145
  Black's efforts to preempt, 162
  conservatives' hostility towards,
    140–141
  election regulation, 224–225
  Four Horsemen's determination to
    thwart, 118
  Southern lawmakers' struggle for
    power, 151
New Orleans, Louisiana, 3–5, 11
New York City bakeries, 92–94,
  97–98
New York v. Quarles, 205
Newark, New Jersey, 195–199
NFIB v. Sebelius, 260–261
Nicotine poisoning, 68
Nine-justice Court, 149–150
Nixon, Richard
  campaign spending, 231–232
  civil rights, 199–204
  constitutionality of poverty, 206
  equal funding for education,
    204–205
  Miranda and criminal justice,
    202–203
Nuisance law, 43

Obama, Barack, 215–216, 220, 236,
  243
O'Connor, Sandra Day, 251, 281
O'Hare, Kate Richards, 124
Oil industry, 47–48
Olney, Richard, 36–38, 50
On the Origin of Species (Darwin), 109
One-party South, 151, 185–190, 192
Organized labor. *See* Union labor
Oxford, Mississippi, 181

Pacific Railroad Act (1862), 19–20
Palin, Sarah, 278
Parker, Harry, 77–78
Parker, John J., 152–153, 174
Partisanship
  determining constitutionality,
    266–274
  influencing the Court, 275, 278,
    280–281
  overcoming rationality, 269–272
  view of Affordable Care Act,
    269–274
Paul, Rand, 282–283
Pauly, Mark, 267
Peckham, Rufus Wheeler
  antipathy to African Americans,
    95–96
  disdain for worker safety, 98–99
  Holmes's *Lochner* opinion, 114
  Lochner decision, 94–95, 97
  maximum-hours law, 96
Pellagra, 83
Pelosi, Nancy, 216
Pension system, 131–132, 138, 153. *See
  also* Social Security Act
Peonage system, Southern, 116–117
Peyote use, 252
Phoenix, Arizona anti-discrimination
  ordinance, 180–181
Pipe-makers case, 61–62
Pitney, Mahlon, 77
Pittsburgh Coal Company, 86
Pledge of Allegiance, 168–169
Plessy v. Ferguson, 9, 39, 41, 95, 167,
  170, 179–180
PLIVA v. Mensing, 239, 254
Police brutality, 195–197
Police forces, Miranda rights and,
  201–202
Political participation, Chinese
  residents' exclusion from, 10
Pollock v. Farmers' Loan & Trust, 58–61
Poor, Henry Varnum, 19
Poorhouses, 132–134
Poverty
  cotton mill workers in the South, 83

failing health and death through lack
  of healthcare, 256–258
Great Depression, 129–131
long-term benefits of the New Deal,
  283–284
opposition to the New Deal, 119
unconstitutionality of, 204–206
Powell, Lewis, 204
Preexisting medical conditions,
  255–256, 261–262
Price discrimination, 48
Privacy, reasonable expectation of,
  205–206
Private discrimination, 181–182,
  211–212
Privileges and immunities, xi–xii, 7.
  See also Fourteenth Amendment
  rights
Property rights law, 43, 180–181,
  183–184
Propper, Christopher, 246
Prostitutes, 74
Protecting Older Workers Against
  Discrimination Act, 244
Public safety exemption for *Miranda*,
  205
Pullman, George, 22–28, 30–39
Pullman Palace Car Company, 24–28,
  36–39, 42–43

Racial equality
  Reconstructionist-era Court's lack of
    interest in, 9
Racism
  American Liberty League, 144
  civil rights era violence, 177–178
  internment of Japanese Americans,
    161–162
  Jimmy Byrnes's right-wing politics,
    158–159
  laws sanctioning, 280
  Newark police force, 198–199
  racial harassment in the workplace,
    245–246
  Rehnquist's view of *Brown* and
    Plessy, 179–181

religious exemptions from the law,
253
Southern resistance to *Brown,*
178–179
Tillman's bigoted populism,
159–160
United States v. Cruikshank and
Dred Scott, x
See also African Americans
*Railroad Retirement Board v. Alton
Railroad,* 138, 153
Railroads
Chinese Exclusion Act, 40
effect on corporate behavior, 45–50
labor-management conflict, 62
Pacific Railroad Act, 19–20
pension law, 138, 153
Pullman labor strike, 22–30, 32–39,
42–44
sleeping cars, 23–28
Standard Oil relationship with,
47–48
workers' lack of legal protections, 21
Rape
as a preexisting medical condition,
255–256, 258, 261
convictions, 163–164
Raskob, John J., 139
Reagan, Ronald, 182, 209–211, 279
Reconstruction
Campbell's white supremacist
views, 7
Colfax Massacre, ix–x
comparing the New Deal to, 144
end of, 18
Field's lack of interest in, 9
Fourteenth Amendment, xi
Slaughterhouse Cases, 3–11, 13, 16,
91, 116
Southern states' peonage system,
116–117
white supremacists' efforts to control
Louisiana, 13–14
Reconstruction Amendments, xi,
12–13
Redistricting. *See* Gerrymandering

Reed, Stanley, 167, 172
Rehnquist, William
appointment to the Court, 204
arbitration enforcement, 247
Brown v. Board of Education, 170,
179, 181–182
Civil Rights Act, 182, 211–212
Miranda decision, 201–202, 205,
240
partisan gerrymandering, 217
private discrimination, 180–181
public safety exemption for *Miranda,*
205
Religion
eugenics and, 118
free exercise in the workplace, 252
religious exemptions from the law,
252–253
Religious Freedom Restoration Act
(RFRA, 1993), 252, 254
Reproductive freedom, 206–210,
251–252, 278. *See also*
Sterilization, compulsory
Republican Party
Affordable Care Act, 266–274
anti-monopoly platform, 49
Bush v. Gore, 213–214
campaign contributions, 229
election manipulation in Florida,
219–220
election manipulation in Louisiana,
14–15
House majority despite Democratic
victories, 215–217
Nixon's civil rights frame, 200
Reagan's *Guidelines* for the judiciary,
211
reversing the Roberts Court
decisions, 282–283
viewpoint discrimination through
gerrymandering, 216–218
voter suppression, 151, 185–190,
192, 215–218, 220–225, 228–229
workplace discrimination case, 243
Republican State Leadership
Committee (RSLC), 215–216

Retirement
  of the Four Horsemen, 148–149
  poverty during the Great
    Depression, 131–134
  Roosevelt's vision of, 149
  Van Devanter's retirement from
    the Court, 157
  See also Social Security Act
Revolutionary War, 110
Rivkin, David, 259–260
Roberts, John, ix(quote)
  Affordable Care Act, 260, 270–271
  campaign finance laws, 230–231
  election regulation, 226
  gutting the Voting Rights Act,
    214–215, 217
  skepticism about the Court, 212
  Social Security Act, 156–157
  voting counter to partisan
    preferences, 272–273
Roberts, Owen J., 152–153, 187
Roberts Court
  campaign spending, 229
  favoring wealthy donors, 215,
    250–251
  gay rights, 281
  ideological views and, 240
  partisan gerrymandering, 217–218
  religious exemptions from the law,
    253–254
  thwarting democracy, 237–238
  Voting Rights Act, 225
Rockefeller, John D., 47–48, 60
Roe v. Wade, 206–211, 278
Romney, Mitt, 215, 220, 234, 262,
  268–269
Roosevelt, Franklin
  American Liberty league attacking
    New Deal, 140–145
  bank failures, 134
  Byrnes's appointments, 160–161
  conflict with the business
    community, 139–141
  Court-packing plan, 150–152, 156,
    275–276
  economic overreach, 203–204

Emergency Banking Relief Act, 135
  McReynolds and, 77–78
  policy vision and conflict with the
    Court, 135–136
  political appointees, 161–162
  Reagan's attitude towards the
    judiciary, 209
  reelection, 145–146
  restoring a robust national
    government, 148–149
  Social Security, 156
  workers' right to unionize, 136–139
Roosevelt, Theodore, 73, 77
Rutledge, James, 197

Sacco, Nicola, 167
Safety. *See* Health and safety
*San Antonio Independent School District
  v. Rodriguez*, 205
Sanitation in New York City bakeries,
  92–94
Sauerbrey, Ellen, 221
Scalia, Antonin
  checks on Court power, 214
  interstate commerce regulation, 263
  partisan gerrymandering, 217–218
  religious objectors' compliance with
    the law, 252
  replacement of, 280
Schaefer, Walter, 202
Schenck, Charles, 121–122
Schultz, Matt, 222
Schurz, Carl, 112
Scott, Rick, 219
Scottsboro Boys, 163–166
Scrip, paying workers with, 42, 89, 91
Search and seizure laws, 200–201
Sedgwick, Theodore, 59
Sedition, 120–121
Segregation
  Adair and *Lochner* in light of, 106
  Colfax Massacre, ix
  Courts paving the way for, xiii
  Davis's advocacy for, 142
  Justice Black's decision on, 166–167
  Parker's interpretation of *Brown*, 153

religious justification, 253
suppressing black voters, 185–190,
192
See also Brown v. Board of Education
Selma, Alabama, 177–178, 190–191,
225–226
Sexual harassment, 245–246
Sexually transmitted diseases (STDs),
255–256
Shelby County v. Holder, 226–228, 240
Sherman Antitrust Act (1890), 21, 43,
50, 57–58, 61
Sherwood, Isaac, 131
Shrimp picking, 67–68
Silberman, Laurence, 259, 270
Silk mills, 65–66
Silver, Nate, 223–224
Sixteenth Amendment rights, 61,
146–147
Skating rink, discrimination at, 95
Skepticism
Brewer's skepticism of governance,
42
democracy threatening gradualism
and liberty, 101–102
Field's, xv
Holmes's view of the truth, 115
Peckham's *Lochner* opinion, 99
Skilled labor, 83
Slaughterhouse Cases, 3–11, 13, 16,
91, 116
Slavery, 11–12, 94–95
Smith, Adam, 91
Smith, Al, 141–142
Smith, John, 195–196
Smith v. Allwright, 187
Smith v. Maryland, 205
Social Darwinism, 109, 114, 117
Social Security Act
African Americans' exclusion from,
151–152
American Liberty league attacking,
144–145
as socialist policy, 143
constitutionality of the railroad
pension system, 138–139

Court's affirmation of, 156
long-term benefits, 283–284
Social Statics (Spencer), 111
Socialism
American Liberty League attack on
Roosevelt, 142–144
state courts' opposition to labor
protection, 89
opposition to the Fourteenth
Amendment, 147
perception of the New Deal,
140–141
Socialist Party, 121–124
Sodomy laws, 281–282
Sotomayor, Sonia, 239–240
South Carolina v. Katzenbach, 210
Southern Manifesto, 173
Spellman, Eloise, 197
Spencer, Herbert, 90, 111–113, 119
Standard Oil Company, 47–48
Stanford, Leland, 20
State elections, 216–217
States' rights
Child Labor Amendment
ratification, 147
dismantling Affordable Care, 259,
261
drug manufacturers' responsibilities,
239
expansion of civil rights in state
courts, 200–202
Frankfurter's defense of, 169–170
judicial appointment methods,
278–279
Keating-Owen child labor act, 75
Lochner decision, 97–98
Massachusetts individual mandate
healthcare plan, 268
need for a Supreme Court, 276
racist business practices, 183–184
Reconstruction Amendments, xi
universal application of the Bill of
Rights, 165–166
voter suppression tactics, 185–187,
221–228
Voting Rights Act, 192, 227

Sterilization, compulsory, xiii, 107–109, 112–113, 119
Stevens, John Paul, 217, 235–237
Stock market crash, 129–130
Strikebreakers, 86
Strikes, labor
  New York City bakeries, 93–94
  Pullman labor, 29–30, 32–39, 42–44
  railroad workers' lack of legal protections, 21–22
Strong, William, 8
Suffrage. *See* Voting rights for African Americans
Sugar trust, 57–58
Sugar Trust Case, 57–58, 61–62, 72–75, 79
Summers, Hatton, 150–151
Sutherland, George, 117–119
Sutton, Jeffrey, 270, 272
Sweatshops, xiii

Taft, William Howard, 21, 61, 73, 77–79, 117–118
Tardive dyskinesia, 238–239
Tariff reform bill, 50
Taxation
  anti-Chinese laws, 10
  black families paying for white schools, 95
  direct tax, 59–60
  equal funding for education, 204–205
  Massachusetts healthcare plan, 268
  tariff reform bill, 50, 58–59
Tennessee districting, 169–170
Tennessee Valley Authority (TVA), 151
Terrorism
  Colfax Massacre, ix, x, 13–16, 159, 165
  Jim Crow segregation, 178–179, 188, 190–191
  Selma, Alabama, 190–191
  suppressing black voters, 188–190
  War on Terror, 205

Textile workers, 83
Thirteenth Amendment rights
  Reconstruction Amendments, xi
  Southern states' peonage system, 116–117
  WWI anti-conscription activism, 121–122
Thomas, Clarence
  Affordable Care Act, 260
  Civil Rights Act, 211–212
  drug manufacturers' responsibilities, 239
  rightward shift of the Court, 283
Tiedeman, Christopher, 90–92, 96, 99–100, 102, 260–261
Tilden, Samuel, 18
Tillman, "Pitchfork Ben," 158–160
Tocqueville, Alexis de, 99–100
Trumbull, Lyman, 39–40
Trusts, 45–50, 57–58
Tuberculosis, 66
Twentieth Amendment, 134

Unemployment during the Great Depression, 129–130
Union busters, 86
Union labor
  American Railway Union, 30, 32
  collective bargaining as fundamental right, 155–156
  Debs's socialism and pacifism, 122–123
  employers' right to forbid employees joining unions, 105–106
  judges' perceptions as dangerous, 42–43
  Kentucky labor dispute, 86
  National Labor Relations Act, 136–139
  Pullman Strike, 36–39
  railroad workers, 21–22, 29–30
  strikes and boycotts, 21–22
  Wisconsin opinion protecting business owners from, 89–90
United States Circuit Judge Nominating Commission, 279

United States v. Cruikshank, x, 16–18, 164–165
United States v. Lee, 252
United States v. Windsor, 280–281

Van Devanter, Willis, 77, 117–118, 157
Vance v. Ball State University, 245, 254
Vanderbilt, Cornelius, 20, 47, 49
Vanzetti, Bartolomeo, 167
Vieth v. Jubelirer, 217, 219
Viewpoint discrimination, 217, 219
Vinson, Fred, 167, 171, 174
Voter ID laws, 221–225, 228
Voter purging, 230–231
Voter suppression, 52–53, 151, 185–190, 192, 215–218, 220–225, 228–229
Voting Rights Act (1965), 192, 210, 214–215, 225–228
Voting rights for African Americans, xi, xiii, 14–15, 41, 185–190, 192

Wages and salaries
    Adkins v. Children's Hospital affecting women and children, 105
    children in glass factories, 67
    compensation for injuries and fatalities, 88–89
    cotton mills in the South, 70, 82
    General Managers' Association cuts in railroad wages, 35
    Great Depression, 130–131
    long-term benefits of the New Deal, 283–284
    minimum-wage laws, 153–154
    mining communities, 65–66
    paying in scrip, 42
    progressive Northern states, 83
    Pullman's wage cuts, 43
    shrimp picking, 68
    voter suppression tactics, 222
    workplace discrimination against women, 241–246
Wagner, Robert, 136
Walker, Edwin, 38

War on Terror, 205
Warmoth, Henry Clay, 5, 14
Warren Court
    advancing liberalism, 204
    anomalous nature of, 279
    Brown v. Board of Education, 171–173, 179, 192
    civil rights expansion, 200–204
    constitutional transformation, 174–175
    constitutional transformation under, 174–175
    embracing democracy, 179–180
    Miranda v. Arizona, 201–202
    Nixon's attacks on, 202–203, 206
    state sovereignty over the Voting Rights Act, 227
Washington, Booker T., 116
Washington, George, 54–56, 146
Wertz, Edwin, 124
West Coast Hotel v. Parrish, 154
Westward expansion, 19–20
Wheeler, Burton, 152
White, Byron, 202
White, Edward Douglas, 77
White League, 17
White supremacists
    businesses' immunity to regulation, 7–11
    Colfax Massacre, 15–16
    efforts to control Louisiana, 13–14
    Reconstruction Amendments protecting whites' rights, 12–13
    Reconstruction-era Southern states, 7
    Tillman's South Carolina, 158–159
Wickes, Thomas, 33, 35
Wilkinson, J. Harvie, 259, 270
Williams, Hosea, 177–178
Wilson, Woodrow, 73–75, 78–79, 120–121, 123–125, 140
Wisconsin
    ballots, 222
    labor laws, 97
    workers' right to organize, 89–90

Women and girls
  Buck v. Bell, 107–109
  coal mining communities, 65–66
  cotton mill labor, 83
  denial of healthcare coverage, 253,
    255–258, 261
  imprisonment of antiwar protesters,
    124
  "liberty of contract" doctrine, 103
  McReynold's hostility towards, 78
  minimum-wage laws, 154–155
  perceived inferiority, 104–105
  rape as a preexisting medical
    condition, 261
  religious justification for denying
    healthcare benefits, 253
  Roe v. Wade, 206–208, 210, 278
  workplace discrimination, 241–243
Wong, Bow Woo, 197
Work week limits, 94, 96, 104–105,
  159–160, 162
Working conditions
  age discrimination, 243–244
  courts accommodating factory
    owners, 88–90

  discriminating against gays in the
    workplace, 281–282
  discriminating against women in the
    workplace, 241–243
  employers' failure to offer healthcare
    coverage, 255–258
  factories and coal mines,
    84–85
  forced-arbitration agreements, 249
  Goodyear's workplace
    discrimination, 241–243
  Hobby Lobby's control of
    reproductive rights, 251–252
  legal failure to protect workers,
    89–91
  New York City bakeries, 92–94, 97
  racial and sexual harassment in the
    workplace, 245–246
World War I, xiii, 120–124, 140
World War II internment of Japanese
    Americans, 161–162
World's Fair, 34, 37

Zillmer v. Kreutzberg, 90
Zolnowski, John, 87–88

Ian Millhiser is a senior fellow at the Center for American Progress and the editor of ThinkProgress Justice. He received his J.D. from Duke University and clerked for Judge Eric L. Clay of the United States Court of Appeals for the Sixth Circuit. His writings have appeared in a diversity of legal and  mainstream publications, including the *New York Times*, the *Los Angeles Times*, *U.S. News & World Report*, *Slate*, the *Guardian*, the *Nation*, the *American Prospect*, the *Yale Law and Policy Review,* and the *Duke Law Journal*. He lives in Arlington, Virginia, and asks his friends in DC not to judge him harshly for that fact.

The Nation Institute

we have only so much space in our freezers, it's more competitive than ever, and all that—but I doubt if you'll find those answers very satisfying."

"No, you're right," I said. "It's a tough industry, to say the least. But that's true of a lot of products, and a lot of industries. Frankly, I still can't figure it out. I think we have a terrific product. And we're constantly coming up with new flavors and combinations. We've had huge success with our pink peppermint coconut swirl, for example. I can't understand why you buy other brands, and ignore ours."

At that moment Monica brought our lattes to the table. Mike thanked her, then took a sip of his before turning back to me.

"I think I can help you there," he said, reflecting on what I'd asked. "But let me ask you a few questions first."

"Sure," I said. I felt I knew our product cold—no pun intended—and could handle anything he threw my way.

"You're convinced your ice cream is of high quality. Is that because your quality engineers have tested it against all the others?"

"Of course," I said. "Well, most of them," I admitted. "We may not be the top of the line, but our quality is far higher than most brands. And we usually are able to use natural ingredients."

"My guess is, however, you're using your own criteria in judging that quality. When we look at your ingredients and fat percentage, and the percentage of natural ingredients that you use versus additives, compared to other brands, you actually come out far down the list. My guess is that you use natural ingredients when it's cost effective to do so, and compromise if the cost of ingredients is too high. Am I right?"

My sheepish silence confirmed his suspicions.

"Do your people talk to the store buyers, or to the customers, about what they're looking for in an ice cream?"

I had no answer for that one, either. The fact was, we usually didn't. If he had pressed me, I would have been forced to admit that we really weren't trying to make the very best ice cream on the market. We just couldn't find a way to make a better grade of ice cream without jacking up our prices beyond what the market would bear. Instead, we relied on our ability to constantly come up with new flavors and snazzy packaging, leading the pack in a few offerings. And it usually worked, at least for a time.

The problem was, each competitor watched our sales like a hawk. Within a few months of our launching new flavors, they would imitate the ones that really took off and ignore our new ice creams and other desserts that didn't catch on. Except that they would make their ice cream better, or at a lower price. We could hold our lead for only a quarter or two before watching competitors take it over.

I knew all this—and realized that Mike probably did,

too. My continued silence told him just where we stood. Just like that, he had shifted me from offense to defense.

"I have to ask," Mike went on, "is *quality* really the driving force behind your brand? Does it really shape everything you do?"

I could only bite my lip, embarrassed.

"I think the reason you're so upset that we don't buy your ice cream," he continued, in a surprisingly direct manner, "is not because you feel our *customers* are missing out on how wonderful your ice cream is, but because *you* are missing out on selling to more customers. You're amazed that we don't agree with your criteria, or your results.

"Pete, if I may," he said, speaking softly. "You're a bright guy, a decent guy from a good family. I'm sure you spend a lot of time at your factory worrying over how to improve the quality of your ice cream, and increase your factory's productivity so that you can reduce costs and offer more competitive prices. You clearly have pride in what you do.

"But you don't seem to know where to begin in thinking about what quality is, and how you can improve it. You're dying to make this sale. I understand that. But your people have never asked us what we want, or what our customers want. You haven't asked me how you could help Natural Foods, or our guests. Your focus is on selling your ice cream, and not much else.

"I'm not surprised," Mike said. "What you do at Dairy

Cream is similar to what so many companies in our country do. Let me tell you something that Glen Goodwell explained to me years ago, when he was first creating Natural Foods. When it comes to innovation—coming up with great new products or technology or ideas—American companies are the best in the world, hands down. Innovation is part of our DNA. That's not true in other countries. But when it comes to quality, to the constant, continual daily efforts to improve a product or service, to really ensure that it meets exacting standards every time, and thereby builds lasting loyalty, we falter.

"It's like the story of the tortoise and the hare—and we're the hare, leading the race with our innovations. But eventually the tortoise catches up, just as your competitors catch up to your new flavors and pass you by with constant, incremental improvements, simply because they make quality the priority in everything they do.

Quality is just not part of our DNA.

"The fact is, as Glen pointed out to me, quality is just not part of our DNA. And it *is* part of the DNA of companies in Japan, and has gradually become part of the makeup of Korean companies. As a result, we're constantly creating new products, and new markets, only to lose them to other companies. American companies find themselves on a treadmill, constantly having to come up with new innovations in order to stay ahead of our competition. Did you know that America created the global positioning system in car? We invented the transistor, the computer chip, the airplane—so much of the stuff that is a part of our lives. And yet we lose most of those markets as fast as we create them.

"To bring this back to earth, you guys at Dairy Cream are constantly outsmarting your competitors by coming out with snazzy new ice cream flavors. But because you don't make the effort to find out what we, the customers, want in terms of quality, your competitors end up eating your lunch."

I felt humiliated. I could tell I was near tears—unbelievably, to me, for I am a pretty stoic guy. I only hoped he'd stop.

"I'm sorry," he said. "But I'm a lot older and hopefully a little wiser. I've already made the mistakes you're making now. At Natural Foods, *quality* is at the heart of everything we do. We're the exception in our niche—where everyone else seems intent on chasing the latest trend—and that's why we've been so tremendously successful."

"Mike," I finally said, the knot in my stomach urging me to come clean. "I need help. The fact is, we're in trouble. If

I can't help us find a way to increase revenues and profits—and soon!—Malcolm Jones, our owner, has threatened to fire the current management team or sell off the whole company. Either way, I'm out of a job, and our scores of employees are out of work. Malcolm has charged me with shaking things up, and I don't know what to do—I just don't know how to turn things around at Dairy Cream. I've got a wife and two kids. I'm embarrassed to ask this of you, when I haven't seen you in so long—but I need your help. You seem to have found a way to do this. Tell me what I can do to make *quality* part of our culture, too."

Mike looked at me thoughtfully. Then he nodded his head. "If you're looking for help selling your ice cream, we might as well go to the source. Natural Foods is built on the idea of excellence, and excellence starts with helping others as much as you can—every day. Excellence isn't a task or chore we perform to sell something. It's a passion to help others that restores us in the process. Until you understand that, you'll never change your thinking, or increase your sales. The first step, my friend, is to start talking to and taking care of the people who have taken care of you. Let me ask you something. You've been worried about how things have been going for a while, right?"

I nodded, numbly.

"One place to start—have you talked about your concerns with your closest adviser and consumer—your wife?"

I shook my head, suddenly embarrassed again.

He looked at his watch. "Listen, I've got to tackle a few things here this afternoon. But I've got some time in the morning. Why don't you drop by before we open, at, say, seven, and I'll give you a few pointers on how to get started. Improving quality won't happen overnight—it'll take work. But I think I can give you some suggestions on how to get the ball rolling—and get your owner off your back."

I didn't sell any ice cream that day, but that no longer seemed quite so important.

CHAPTER TWO

Learning to Listen

Although I went home that day with more questions than answers, at least I had the sense that the questions were leading me in the right direction.

That night, after Jean and I put the kids to bed, I had a long talk with her about what was going on at work. When I told her about Malcolm's ultimatums and the fact that it was up to me to turn things around, Jean was stunned.

"Why didn't you tell me this earlier?" she asked, obviously hurt.

"I didn't want to worry you unnecessarily," I admitted. "But I was wrong to keep it to myself. I'm sorry." Over the next hour before we went to bed, we talked about the factory, and both of our fears. After her initial anger over how much I'd been keeping from her, she was incredibly helpful and supportive, offering to shoulder even more of the burden at home with the kids while I struggled to find answers at work. I was surprised at how good it felt simply to share my fears and concerns, and not keep them hidden from those I cared about. After all, they were equally affected.

The next morning I woke up eager to talk again with Mike. I wore a crisp shirt, a new tie, and newly shined shoes. For some reason, I sensed that Mike would notice the details and see them as the sign of respect I intended.

I drove up to Natural Foods with a completely different mind-set than the one I'd had the day before. Rather than a purchase order, I was looking for advice and, hopefully, answers.

I found Mike waiting for me at the front entrance. Before long we were seated at the same table we'd sat at the day before.

A different waitress arrived to take our orders. "Café latte, Mike?"

"Absolutely, Amy, thank you. Pete, what would you like?"

"The same."

"Two, please."

Mike seemed genuinely pleased to see me. "You look better, more relaxed," he said in his typically direct manner.

"I feel a lot better."

"You told your wife about your troubles at the factory?"

I laughed. "How could I not, after our conversation yesterday?"

"And how did she respond?"

"Well, she was surprised about the situation at Dairy Cream, of course. But very supportive, which felt awfully good."

"Good," Mike said. "Good for both of you."

"When I left your store yesterday, I felt embarrassed," I admitted. "I was willing to put aside a half day to sell a crate of ice cream to a relative stranger, but I hadn't been willing to spend a half hour telling my wife what's been bothering me at work. What I don't understand yet, though, is the connection between my talking to my wife, and quality."

Mike paused. "Think about what you did. You showed respect for the relationship you and your wife have had over the years. You took the time to express your feelings to her, so that she would know what was bothering you. You asked her for her opinions, you showed you cared for her and trusted her."

"Yes," I said. "And believe me, I'm glad I did. But what's that have to do with selling ice cream?"

"It all comes down to taking care of those who matter to you. Because business, any business, is about people—the people you work with, and the customers you sell to. Let me explain it this way," Mike said. "When I wake up in the morning, I don't say to myself: 'How can we make our numbers today at Natural Foods?' I say, 'What can we do for the people who've done so much for us?' Sometimes, when our numbers are a bit down near the end of the month and I feel myself and our teammates starting to press, I tell them, 'Let's not worry about it. If we're going to miss our target, we might as well have fun doing it, and earn some points in the process with our customers. Let's go out and have some fun!' And the first time we took that approach, the darnedest thing happened: We had a blast, and our numbers went up. We beat our goals! We've done it a few times since, and it's worked every time. My point is this: Profits are the result, the *by-product* of great service, great quality, great teamwork—*not an end in themselves.*"

"But how is this connected to quality?" I asked.

Profits are the result, the *by-product* of great service.

Amy returned with our coffee. Mike paused. "Thank you, Amy. These look great." I took a sip; it was delicious, as advertised.

"Fun and money," Mike repeated. "How are they connected? Excellent question. And it speaks to the foundation you need to build to begin making quality part of everything you do." He took another sip. "Pete, what's your favorite hobby?"

"Golf," I offered.

"How often do you play?"

"Every other Saturday—just enough to ruin my entire summer."

"You and me both, brother," he said, laughing. "And when you're playing golf, are you thinking about anything else?"

"Not if I can help it!" I said.

"In other words, you're entirely focused on what you're doing. So let me ask you, what do you like about it?"

"A beautiful Saturday morning, hanging out with my friends, enjoying the outdoors, a little friendly competition. What's not to like?"

"You clearly are passionate about it," Mike said. "That's great. Because without passion, *nothing* is fun. Doesn't matter if your hobby is playing golf or collecting stamps, gardening or restoring classic cars. If you don't put much of yourself into it, you can't get much out of it."

"Amen," I said.

"What I've noticed about people is that they almost always work harder at their *hobbies* than at their *jobs*. They spend all kinds of time and effort and energy on something that *costs* them money—just because they love it! You probably spend a few minutes most days at the office or in your car thinking about your last round, or the lesson you just took, or some new technique you read about, or the new course you're looking forward to playing on vacation."

I laughed. "Guilty as charged."

"Let me tell you a secret: Your employees do the same thing. They put their hobbies ahead of their work."

"Well, is that a problem?" I asked, suddenly defensive about the people who worked under me. "I mean, if it doesn't affect their work?"

"Not at all," Mike replied. "But my point is this: If you want to turn your place around, you need to get your people to invest themselves in their *work* the way they do with their hobbies. How do you do that? It has to start at the top, with you."

I couldn't help but be struck by how true Mike's observation sounded. It made complete sense. I needed to find a way to make our employees as committed to their jobs as they were to their hobbies.

"All right," I said to my newfound mentor. "So before I create a culture of quality at Dairy Cream, I need to find a way to better motivate our workforce. But how do I do that?"

"The first step," Mike said, "is to turn what you do every day out of *necessity* into something you want to do, something you *love* to do.

"Here's something that has always been useful to me," Mike said, pulling a small laminated card out of his wallet. It contained some verse from a poem by Robert Frost called "Two Tramps in Mud Time," stating that the narrator's goal in life was "to unite" his avocation and vocation, as his "two eyes make one in sight."

"We've all met people performing seemingly thankless jobs who seem to be having a blast," Mike continued. "Like the guy who delivers our mail in my neighborhood,

Turn what you do every day out of necessity into something you love to do.

who always seems to have a smile and a friendly greeting. Our old mail carrier seemed to hate his work, and it showed. Our new mail carrier is a godsend! One day I asked him how he managed to always be so upbeat. He told me, 'Hey, everyone needs their mail delivered. When most people miss a day of work, no one notices. But if the mail wasn't delivered one day, *everyone* would notice! The fact is, we're important. We help people with their day-to-day lives. And because I know I'm helping people, and making a difference, I can't help but enjoy what I'm doing.' "

"All right," I conceded. "But the importance of every job isn't always that obvious."

"Trust me," Mike said, "if you have a job, you're needed—or else your job wouldn't exist! It doesn't matter whether you are a plant manager or a janitor. But people have to *see* how valuable their jobs are to those around them. Do you think Amy grew up dreaming of serving coffee in a café? Did Jenny, the woman you met yesterday, set her sights on working at an information stand? Somehow, I don't think so. But the way they throw themselves into their work, you'd think they did. And why do they do that? Because we make it clear how important they are, to our customers and to Natural Foods. We value their input and opinions. We make them responsible and encourage their contributions. And because of that, their jobs really *are* fun! Finding ways to foster that kind of motivation is part of our mission at Natural Foods. On paper, their jobs aren't glamorous. But you can make any job fun, and fulfilling—*if you show them how they are contributing!*"

INTERNAL CUSTOMERS SERVED HERE

"Right now morale at Dairy Cream is pretty low," I admitted, "about as low as our revenues were last quarter. People are grumbling about the plant, their coworkers, their supervisors, the other departments."

Mike grimaced. "Those are real problems, Pete, I'm not going to lie to you. What do you think the cause—or causes—might be?"

"The causes?" I asked.

"People don't start disliking their jobs and coworkers for no reason. Is there anything specific they're complaining about?"

"Everything, and nothing, it seems to me. I guess they feel like there is nothing they can do to maybe make a difference," I admitted, surprised by my sudden insight. "How do you ensure your employees take care of your customers?" I asked.

Mike smiled sympathetically. "Okay," he said. "Lesson number one: Every company has *two kinds* of customers, those *outside* the company, and those *inside* the company. And your *first* customers are your internal ones—your employees or coworkers. If you don't take care of your employees, you can't expect them to take care of your customers outside of the company.

"In my experience, every company finds its own ways

to ensure that employees take care of the company's customers the way managers want them to. At Natural Foods, to a surprising degree," Mike said, "*I* don't make sure of it, *our employees* do. We have over two hundred team members in this store alone. There is simply no way I could play policeman for every worker if they're determined to undermine our business. Instead, we utilize a friendly form of peer pressure to get everyone going in the same direction. Our team members encourage each other in a way that lets everyone knows they're part of and accountable to the team. Trust me, it's much better to have them all urging each other on instead of me trying to cheer the whole team on by myself."

"So how do you accomplish that?"

"Tell you what—why don't we ask them?" Mike said, turning to Amy. "Amy, can you join us for a few minutes?"

"Sure," she said. "Just let me tie up a few loose ends and I'll be right over."

A minute later Amy was back.

"Don't you have customers to cash out?" I asked her, looking around the café.

"My colleague Jerry said he'd do it for me."

"But doesn't that cut into your tips?" I asked, concerned that by spending time to talk to us, Amy was going to lose money.

"Not the way we handle it," Amy said. "All the money

on our team—the café team—is divided equally among us, based on our hours."

"But what if a coworker doesn't pull his or her weight? Doesn't that hurt everyone else?"

"It could," she said, "in another café. But it's almost impossible here. First, we have the power to review each other's work and pay. And second, we pick our team-mates."

I was incredulous. "You do?"

Amy and Mike both laughed. "Want to take this one, Mike?"

"No, Amy, it's probably better coming from you."

"Well," she said, "at Natural Foods, when we need to hire someone, we put our entire team—on the café team, we have about thirty-five full-timers—to work on it. We screen the applicants, interview the finalists, then pick one new candidate, by majority vote, for a one-month trial. After that month, we vote again. So being an employee's cousin might help you get an interview, but it won't get you the job if you can't cut it, because no one wants someone on the team who's not going to carry their weight, and cost them money. And after you hire them, it's pretty hard to complain about a teammate when you helped to pick him!"

"So each employee feels a sense of ownership over their workplace, and the people they work with," I said.

"Exactly," Mike said. "Each team—the produce team, the deli team, the bakery team—has a lot of power to make their own decisions."

"Let me give you an example," Amy chimed in. "Most café customers finish their shopping, then sit down for a cup of coffee or a snack. But we noticed some of our customers walking back into the store to get a few more things—pay for them—and return to their tables to eat. So someone had the bright idea to allow the café staff to become 'runners' for the café customers. It increased our sales more than 20 percent in the first month alone. Turns out a lot of customers were tempted to buy more things, but didn't feel like getting up and leaving their bags. But with us to help, they said, sure! And we can do it more quickly because we know where everything is."

"When you have that kind of teamwork and autonomy," Mike said, "you become engaged in your work, and it becomes fun.

"The point is," he went on, "if you give your employees responsibility, and treat them as the important parts of your business that they are—they respond. Give them the right tools and training, encouragement and compensation, give them the opportunity to be heard, and they'll be more engaged in their work and more invested in your business. We've found that when you set up the right systems, your teammates push each other far harder than you could ever push them. And the better we treat our employees, the better they treat our customers. It never happens any other way. This, Pete, is the *foundation* for quality. This is the kind of environment in which quality can take root and flourish. And quality is everything."

The better you treat your employees, the better they treat your customers.

The urge to get back to my own factory so I could put some of Mike's ideas to work was overwhelming. I thanked Mike for his advice and insights, and Amy for her time—and for the latte. "Would you mind telling me more about how you create a culture of quality another time?"

"Sure," Mike said, laughing. "Give me a call later in the week. And let me know how things go," he said as I hurried out the door.

I returned to our factory with more energy and enthusiasm than I could ever remember feeling before. As I drew near the plant, a few things suddenly became obvious to me: I noticed, as if for the first time, that we had no sign

with our company's name. There was no indication anywhere on the grounds even of what we manufactured.
When I walked through the plant doors, a low hum of
mediocrity seemed to fill the air. It hit me like an offensive
odor after spending the morning at Natural Foods.

Our second shift was preparing to clock in. I asked
them to meet with me for a few minutes in the lunchroom
before they started work. Since I offered them overtime,
they quickly agreed. I decided to meet with the earlier shift
when they got off work fifteen minutes later. I gathered all
the office workers I could as well, leaving a skeleton crew
to answer the phones.

Since I had only a few minutes, I got right to the point.
"I've decided to put my cards on the table," I told them.
That seemed to get their attention immediately. "We're up
against it. I've been told that either we start selling more ice
cream or Dairy Cream is going to be sold. If that happens,
who knows when our last payday might be. And that includes me."

That wiped the nonchalant expressions off their faces.
Several leaned forward in their seats.

"When did you find this out?" one of our mixers asked.

"Couple of weeks back," I said. "I wasn't sure whether
to tell you or not. But I realized we're all in this together.
We're going to sink or swim as a team, like it or not."

The questions started flowing: How much more ice

cream do we need to sell? When would the decision be made? Why was it their fault if the ice cream doesn't sell?

When their questions were exhausted, I explained that I wasn't sure how much more we needed to sell, or by when. That was for Mr. Jones to decide. "But," I added, "why leave any of this to chance? We all have bills to pay and families to feed. Yes, it's our sales reps' job to sell our product, but it's our job to give them the best possible product to sell.

"Right now I want to figure out where we stand, in *your* view, and what we can do to make Dairy Cream a better company. First, what do you think of the job we're doing now?"

There was a lot of mumbling. I heard "Could be better, I suppose" and "Haven't really thought about it"—before I cut through the din. "How many people think we make the best ice cream on the market?"

Not a hand went up.

"How many people love working here?"

Again, eyes shifted around the room, but no hands.

"All right," I said. Before, I would have gotten angry at their honesty, but I remembered something Mike had told me: All information was good information. "We've identified two of our biggest problems: We don't make the best ice cream, and people don't love working here. Now, how can we fix that?"

There was a pause. No one dared speak.

I tried again. "What can we do to make our product better? How can we make this company a better place to work?" Again, no takers. I reached into my back pocket, pulled out my wallet, and said, "A hundred bucks for the best idea."

"Well," said Julie, a serious young woman, "we could use more light. It's too dark in parts of the plant; you can't always see what you're doing, or judge the texture of the ice cream."

"All right," I said. The Old Me would have complained about the cost and said we have enough lighting. But they worked the machines, not me. "Good," I said. "Can someone write these down?" Julie volunteered.

"Less baggy lab coats," another said. "Sometimes they get caught in the machines."

"A nicer lunchroom, so we don't mind working extra shifts."

"Good," I said, "Keep 'em coming!"

And so they did, listing several ideas I had never given much thought to, from fixing the pockmarked condition of the parking lot to improving the quality of the fruit we added to our specialty ice creams.

"These are great ideas, folks," I said, looking at Julie's list. "We can't do them all at once, of course . . . "

"Of course," snickered Kevin, the company cynic, getting a few laughs.

"But I'm going to see what I can do immediately."

"So who gets the hundred?" Kevin asked. I had forgotten about the money.

"You all do. Take it and get yourselves a nice lunch."

Kevin picked up the crisp bill I placed on the table. "Ah, there really *is* a free lunch, then!"

CHAPTER THREE

The Secret of LEO

In the days after my meeting with our employees, I had time to sort out just what had happened to change my thinking.

Without saying so, Mike had challenged me to reconsider how I managed the people under me. As much as I tried to deny it, I had to admit that Mike was right: I was in the habit of simply deciding what people should do instead of listening to what they had to say, and then meeting their needs.

This was not a small thing, I realized. It was key to making quality part of the way we worked. Like a lot of managers, according to Mike, I blamed my company's lack of focus on the quality of our workforce or our aging equipment. But quality, I realized, starts with strong leadership. It starts with me listening more closely to our workers, and to our customers. And I recognized that what was true for me at work was true at home as well. I love my wife and kids, but did I listen to what they had to say? Did I make a habit of *asking* them what was important to them rather than assuming our views were the same? Just in the past two days, Jean had noticed the difference in how I listened to her, and the kids, at dinner, and in the way I helped them with their homework. As at the factory, already my new attitude was paying dividends.

I wanted to talk with Mike about how my thinking had changed—and find out what I needed to do next. But with everything I had to do as a result of the ideas our workers had given me, I had to wait until the following Monday to see him again.

"So," Mike said, diving right in when we sat down together. "What's new?"

I told him about my meeting with the Dairy Cream employees, and the ideas they had given me to improve our ice cream and our working conditions. "They were reluctant to open up at first. But after getting their feet wet, it was as if a dam had burst. Same with the other shift. I got a lot of good ideas about things we can do to improve conditions at the plant."

Mike smiled. "I'm pleased. Give yourself some credit, Pete. Not many managers would have the courage to open up the floor like that to their employees."

"Hey, desperate times require desperate measures!"

"Perhaps. But remember, what you did last week you can do anytime, whether you're desperate or not," Mike said. "In fact, the more often you listen to your employees, the less desperate you will be. The same is true of your customers.

"You have tilled the soil, to prepare it for the seed of quality, by reaching out to your employees. The next thing you need to do as a manager," Mike said, smiling, "is to focus on *what* you do, not just the results."

"What do you mean?"

"As I said at our last conversation, when I focus solely on results, on store profits, we don't do as well. But when I focus on helping people, we excel.

Focus on *what* you do, not just the results.

"Let me explain it in golfing terms. Someone once asked Jack Nicklaus, one of the greatest golfers of all time, how often he looked at the leaderboard to see his score and those of his opponents during a tournament. He replied that he *never* looked at the scoreboard until the final day of a tournament. Why? Because if you think about your *score,* you'll lose your focus on how you *achieve* a good score— by playing well. Whereas if you focus on the things you need to do to *get* a good score—swinging smoothly, paying attention to the wind and the slope of the green and the pin placement—the score will take care of itself."

Mike took a sip from his latte, letting his words sink in.

"And that's how I feel about our business," he said. "If we just keep taking care of our people—our internal customers—and do the things we need to do to satisfy our external customers, from stocking the foods they want to making their experience in our stores the best we can possibly make it, the profits seem to take care of themselves. But the second we start focusing solely on profits, we lose track of our customers' needs, and the profits disappear."

"Okay," I said. "I guess that makes sense. I need to focus on what we're doing to get the results, not just the results themselves. My high school basketball coach used to tell us not to worry about the scoreboard. Just play well, and the scoreboard would keep track of the points for us."

"Exactly," Mike said.

"But how does one create a culture of excellence?"

"Quality is the result of both 'people power' and what the quality gurus call 'process power'—in other words, the people who work for you as well as how you do things in running your business. The foundation for excellence is laid by creating a motivated team. And, as you know, that can happen only when you value your team—everyone from the CEO to the store manager to the accountant to the assembly line worker. Once you've established a motivated, engaged workforce—the people power part—you are ready to focus on the 'how' of how you do things. At Natural Foods, we use LEO to help lead the way."

"Leo?" I asked, confused. "Who's Leo?"

Mike laughed. "LEO isn't a person. It's an acronym that Glen Goodwell came up with. It stands for *Listen, Enrich,* and *Optimize.* It has to do with *listening* to your customers, *enriching* the products or services you offer, and *optimizing* the customer experience. It is part of the language we all use, from Glen Goodwell to Amy in the café. You've already learned about listening to your internal customers. Well, you need to listen to your *external* customers in the same way."

"Jeez," I said doubtfully. "This may be a great approach for a retail or service company, but we're an ice cream manufacturer. We sell ice cream to retail stores. We don't have traditional customers."

"Wrong!" Mike said. "That is one of the *biggest* mistakes companies make, that taking care of customers is not their domain. Let me tell you something: If you *sell* something, you have customers. And if you have customers, you're in service. And if you plan to *stay* in business, your most important job is to *take care* of those customers! For example, if Dairy Cream wants Natural Foods to be a future customer, you would do well to listen closely to what we want."

If you sell something, you have customers.

"Okay," I said, reflecting on Mike's point. "But there must be more to Natural Foods' success than that."

"Of course," Mike said. "After all, I've only begun to tell you about LEO. But the second I forget those first, basic principles, nothing else I do really matters."

"All right. So let me see if I've got it so far: First, I need to motivate our workforce by showing them how important they are.

"Second, if we're in business, we're in service."

"Right," Mike said, pleased.

"Okay," I said. "So, tell me about LEO."

"In golf," Mike said, "to strike the ball well, you need to focus on your swing. What's the first step in breaking down your swing?"

"Your stance, your grip."

"Right. If you aren't holding the club right or if your feet aren't positioned properly, you don't have much chance of hitting the ball well. With LEO, the first step is to *listen*. Listen to your clients or customers, both your *internal* and your *external* customers. Find out what they need, what they want. In business, if you don't listen well, you have little chance of doing anything else well that matters. Every company *says* it listens, but few really do. Too often, they end up with Deejay Syndrome."

I laughed. "Deejay Syndrome? What's that?"

"I was a deejay in college, believe it or not. Back when everything was on 'albums.' You know," he said with a twinkle in his eye, "those big black vinyl discs you played on a turntable."

Listen to your clients or customers.

"Ohhhh yeah," I laughed, playing along.

"Anyway," Mike continued, "as a deejay, I'd play all the songs I liked, assuming everyone else would like them, too, if they had any taste. My boss, who'd worked at a major radio station in the city, told me that was the biggest and

most common mistake of deejays—and also the biggest rat-
ings killer. He told me it wasn't my job to make people like
my music. It's my job to play the music *they* wanted. And
you find that out only by asking them. That's how we invented the call-in request lines. Tell us what you want, and
we'll play it.

"When it comes to Natural Foods," Mike said, "we not
only try to find out what our customers want in terms of
variety, and brands—we try to give them just about *anything* they ask for. It's so rare for a customer to ask for anything that when they do, we knock ourselves out to fulfill
their request. And that should hold true for every company, whether it's a commercial business selling to other
businesses or a company that makes sporting apparel for
weekend warriors."

"But don't your efforts to give customers what they
want confuse your message? Natural Foods is known for
carrying healthy, wholesome food, no preservatives, no additives, isn't it? You have terrific produce and prepared
foods," I said. "Yet you sell steak, pork, and pigs' knuckles,
not to mention beer. Doesn't that confuse your message?"

"Yes, our focus *is* on healthy, natural foods. And our
standards are uncompromising," Mike said. "And that's
exactly what makes us different from most stores, who sell
everything under the sun. When you walk into your average store, if you're looking for natural products, you have

to do a lot of label-checking. When you walk into our store, you can pick up anything off our shelves. Because that's all we sell. It pays to be known for something, and stick to it.

"But that doesn't mean our customers have to subscribe to *everything* that our managers, or our CEO, believe is healthy. What our customers *can* believe is that all our products are high quality, fresh, and made from natural food, whether prepared in our own kitchens, bakeries, and manufacturing plants or in the facilities of the companies we carry.

"Our CEO and founder, Glen Goodwell, is a vegetarian. But Goodwell knew that if he sold only the food he wanted to eat, he'd be out of business before long. Instead, he asked his customers at the first co-op he opened decades ago what *they* wanted. He watched what sold the fastest, and he provided more of that. A lot of us don't eat half the stuff we sell, starting with, for my part, bulgur wheat. But it's not our job to make sure everyone eats what we eat, just as it's not a music store clerk's job to push only the music he or she listens to. What we agree upon is a shared appreciation for the healthiest food available. Within that framework, our mission is to give our customers what they want. Do you know who our ideal customer is?" Mike asked.

"I guess not."

Mike said, smiling, "Anyone who wants to buy our products. Anyone! When FedEx was founded, the company's CEO named it FedEx because he assumed the only people who would need their service would be federal reserve banks. He didn't envision high school seniors sending off their college applications the day before the deadline, or lawyers sending out urgent contracts, or moms sending care packages to their sons overseas. But it wasn't FedEx's job to decide who their customer was supposed to be—only to determine what service the company was offering."

"Does that explain the signs I see around here for your tailgate specials?" I asked.

Quality is defined by the customer.

"Absolutely! When we started Natural Foods, we *never imagined* that we'd be a hit with the football tailgate crowd. But it turns out they love delicious, fresh food, and we do whatever we can to keep them coming back. The bottom line is: Quality is defined by the customer. And you can get their definition only by listening to them."

"So point number one," I said, "is listen to what your customers want instead of just giving them what you *think* they want?"

"Bingo," Mike said, grinning. "But there's a little more to satisfying your customers than just that. You see, most customers have several different needs.

"The first is the most *basic*—providing the bare minimum the customer expects so he goes away without complaining. These needs are so fundamental that customers don't even ask for them—they simply expect them to be there. With cars, we expect them to start up every time and run reliably. With hotels, we expect a safe, clean, comfortable room to be ready for us, as promised by the reservation we've made. For us, our store has to be well stocked with the foods our customers expect to find here; it has to be clean and well organized, with helpful employees. At Dairy Cream, your ice cream has to come in a certain number of flavors, be of a certain consistency and quality, and be well packaged with a lid on it.

"The second need has to do with *performance*. When a customer requests a certain product or service, it must do what it is expected to do. It must perform as promised. If a car buyer requests that his dealer install a GPS system or DVD player, the system or player must not just play, but provide useful navigational maps or superb sound. A car that achieves strong performance offers good handling, or superior pickup or acceleration, a particularly quiet ride, or luxurious appointments. A store like ours provides the right variety of selection, convenience, and service. If it does not, our customers will be disappointed and ultimately we will lose them. If we promise to offer a wide variety of high-quality natural foods, and our quality or selection is only average, or a customer finds that the food they've purchased is filled with artificial flavors and sweeteners, they will be disappointed and leave. And they may not come back.

"The third customer need is what we think of as *excitement*—giving customers that extra something that gets their attention, that *delights* them, and makes your product or service stand out. For us, as a retail store, that means making sure the service our staff provides is as exceptional as the food we carry. We have plenty of teammates to help people, and they are able to explain everything in the store and do so accurately and enthusiastically. We look for ways to make every aspect of our customers' experience a positive one, from the moment they enter the store to the moment they leave the checkout counter. Sounds simple, but you'd be amazed at how few businesses work to provide that for their customers. For a car manufacturer, achieving excitement might mean creating a new hybrid SUV that reduces gasoline consumption, or a stylish new model that appeals to younger buyers. At Dairy Cream, you might introduce a new, full-flavor diet ice cream for the baby boomer generation, or a new ice cream dessert to add to your product line. Without these, the customer may not complain, or necessarily be disappointed. But with these, from free coffee at a convenience store to free headphones on an airline flight, from the dazzling capabilities of a new product like the iPod to GM's creation of the OnStar communication system to assist motorists who need help, you can provide a way to dramatically increase a customer's delight—and loyalty.

"What Glen Goodwell found is that most companies in America are better at delivering 'excitement'—the flash and sizzle—than they are at providing the customer's 'basic' needs," Mike said.

Most companies in America are better at delivering "excitement" than they are at providing customers' "basic" needs.

"Why is that?"

"Well, it's not only customers who get excited about the icing on the cake. Employees and companies get more excited about delivering it, too. It's fun to make the flashy play. Everyone loves to hit home runs. There isn't as much excitement in successfully fielding a ground ball. Yet if you can't make the routine plays, the occasional home run isn't going to help you."

"Good point," I acknowledged, taking another sip of my latte.

"Let me tell you about something that happened to me last month. I was flying home from a business meeting at our national headquarters. I was sitting in economy class, just a couple rows behind first class. An older gentleman, seventy-five or so, was sitting in the aisle seat in the first row. The last passengers had just boarded, when this gentleman asked the flight attendant for a glass of water. She tells him, 'I'm sorry, sir, but you're not in first class. Preflight beverage service is available only for first-class customers.' "

"You're kidding me," I exclaimed. "For a glass of *water*?"

"Yup," Mike said. "A younger guy sitting across the aisle, hearing this, asks the flight attendant, 'You mean you can't get this man a glass of water?'

" 'No, sir,' the attendant said, sticking to her guns. 'It's restricted to first-class passengers.' She couldn't or wouldn't make any judgments for herself; all she could do was parrot the airline policy. Well, this guy got up, walked to the galley area where the flight attendants keep the drinks, and got a

• • •

I left my meeting with Mike with a lot to think about. Replaying Mike's discussion about listening to the customer, I realized we needed to do just that at Dairy Cream. I needed to know more of what our accounts thought of our ice cream, and our packaging, our pricing, and promotion efforts—the delis, convenience stores, grocery chains, and concessionaires who stocked our ice cream—as well as what the end users, the people who *ate* our ice cream, thought.

The first thing I did in the intervening days was to convene a meeting of our sales force. Rather than ask them to sell more ice cream, however—the kind of tough-love motivational speech I know they expected—I asked them to *talk* to their accounts. Find out what our customers felt we were doing right—and doing *wrong*. How did we stack up against other ice cream makers on quality, on price, on promotions and giveaways? What did they feel we could do to help them sell more of our brand? We spent over an hour going over a list I'd prepared of the kinds of questions they should ask. But I encouraged them to not stop there, but engage in a genuine, ongoing dialogue with our accounts, asking for their input and advice on how we could help them.

Next, with the reluctant acquiescence of our owner, Malcolm Jones, I hired a marketing company to conduct several focus groups of ordinary consumers, to find out what they thought of our ice cream and what they wanted to see more of.

small bottle of water, a plastic cup, some ice, and a cocktail napkin, and delivered it to the older man across the aisle. 'Here you go, sir. I hope this does the trick.'

"By this time, *everyone* is watching this drama unfold. When the younger man served the older man his water, the economy class erupted in cheers."

"Good for him," I said, surprised at how upset I felt about the incident. "What did the flight attendant do?"

"She stayed out of sight until the plane took off. Then she emerged as if nothing had happened. But her brittle expression betrayed her feelings; underneath, she was seething. It was pretty clear to all of us that she wasn't the least bit sorry about her refusal to help the old man. The message she conveyed was that she couldn't care less about him, or any of us. She was just irritated at having been shown up in front of the rest of the passengers. She didn't have a clue about the first rule of business, that business is first and foremost about the customer! She probably never will. She's a perfect example of someone who is customer tone-deaf. And that is true of a lot of businesses as well; they don't listen to their customers."

"What a story," I said. "But it does raise a question. What if everyone on the plane started asking for water?"

"Good point," Mike said. "Here's how we tell our people at Natural Foods to handle the 'exceptions.' First, help the customer out if you can. But when you do, let them know you're doing something special: We might tell them, 'Normally, only our first-class customers get drinks before takeoff, but for you, I'll make an exception.' This lets all the others know that not everyone can have water, and it lets the customer know they're being given special attention. None of us on that flight would have minded that we didn't get a preflight glass of water. We would have been thrilled just to see the attendant help this older passenger.

"Think what that glass of water cost the airline," Mike said. "A nickel? Ten cents? And what did it cost them *not* to give it to him? How many people on that flight have re-told that story? Heck, I've been telling all my staff the past month! How many people will go out of their way to avoid that carrier, simply because a passenger was denied water?

"It amazes me how many companies watch the dimes instead of the dollars," he continued. "At Natural Foods, our most important policy is: Help people! Help your customers. Doesn't matter whether you make cars, or sell groceries, whether your customer is another business or the general consumer. You just don't lose a customer because you refused to do something they asked for, especially something simple and inexpensive like getting them a glass of water."

I thought back to my sales pitch to Mike of the previous week—and started to see why it had failed so badly. As

Mike had pointed out to me, I wasn't thinking about what Natural Foods needed. And I certainly wasn't thinking about what their customers needed. I was thinking about what we needed. Yes, I thought we had a competitive, good-quality product. But, as Mike made clear, quality is defined by the customer—in this case, by Natural Foods, or, more important, by the end users, the people who bought and ate our ice cream. And rarely had our company bothered to even ask them what they wanted. We didn't *listen*.

"You know," I said, "thinking about this, I can't help being embarrassed by how I originally approached you."

"Pete, you approached me the way 90 percent of the companies in every business approach me: as a salesperson. And I give you credit: You were more passionate than most. You clearly believe in your product, and your people, and that's a start. But you were focused entirely on *you*—why I should buy your ice cream—instead of asking me what I want, what I believe my customers want, and how you might help us provide it. It seems like a simple shift, but there's a big difference.

"You need to put aside your concerns for a moment about making your sales quota or increasing revenues, and think about taking care of the people who are your customers. Companies that do that will make more than enough money—and can feel good in the process."

But the smartest thing I did was to reach out to our employees and ask them to talk to their friends and neighbors and relatives, to find out what the people they came into contact with expected—and wanted. And one of the ideas—franchising high-end boutique ice cream stores of our own, à la Ben & Jerry's, to better brand our name and our ice cream among consumers—really excited me.

C H A P T E R   F O U R

We Don't Need Steve Jobs

When I popped in to see Mike one afternoon several weeks later, I told him of the progress we'd made in putting the first part of LEO into effect. Mike couldn't have been more pleased.

"Congratulations." Mike smiled. "Sounds like you're doing the right thing. I've found at Natural Foods that when we're listening to our customers as well as we should, they help guide us on how to meet their changing needs and desires. After all, no company can keep doing the same things for people that they did six years ago—or even six months ago!"

But there remained a sobering reality to my small celebration. The fact was, I was taking only the first steps of a long journey to quality at Dairy Cream, and I knew time was running out.

"So where do I go from here?" I asked, fearful of his answer.

Mike smiled again. "Ready for your next lesson?"

"You bet!"

"Okay. Well, the more specific we discover our customers' desires are, the more nuanced our solutions must be."

"I'm with you," I said.

"That brings us to the second part of LEO—*enrichment*. It's not enough to just listen to our customers. We must respond to them by enriching their experience and perception of our store, products, and services. And to do so, we need new ideas and innovators."

"How many innovators can a company afford?" I asked. "A Steve Jobs doesn't come cheap."

"I'm sure he doesn't. But we sell groceries," Mike said. "We don't need a Steve Jobs. We need clerks and stock boys and department heads with their eyes open and their brains working. And that's what the first step of enrichment is all about—realizing that enrichment involves *everyone*."

"Walk with me for a moment," he said, getting up.

We headed over to the information desk, where we found Jenny, the woman who had first helped me find Mike at my initial visit, chatting with a customer. When Jenny was free, Mike asked if we could talk with her. Jenny asked one of the checkout people to cover for her before joining us.

Thinking how odd it was to enlist the aid of a checkout person to help out at the information booth, I asked her, "Does this happen often?"

"Good question," Mike said. "Jenny?"

"Well, at one of our staff meetings some time ago," she explained, "we decided that everyone should learn a secondary job at the store, so we could more easily cover for each other for a few minutes, or even a day or two, if someone was unexpectedly out. That way, things still run smoothly, regardless of who's here. Also, you don't feel trapped doing the same job every day. And as a result, we've come to rely on each other a little bit more, which brings us closer together as a team."

"Great idea," I admitted.

"It was Jenny's, in fact," Mike said. "Natural Foods is built on a thousand great ideas. And I'm only good for a dozen or so, tops. As you've found out, if you want to get the best ideas, you've got to ask your people. They know more than anyone does about what they do every day."

"You know, Mike, let me switch with Margot," Jenny said. "She can tell you, Pete, about our checkout lines." A few moments later, Margot came over to talk with us.

"Through our weekly customer focus group at the store," Mike explained, "we discovered one of the most important things to our customers was convenience. It is as important to them as selection, service, and price, if not more so. So we decided to serve them better by cutting down their time in the checkout lines."

Great companies are built on a thousand great ideas. To get the best ideas, you've got to ask your employees.

"What a great idea," I said. "There's nothing I hate more than waiting in line."

"The idea was Margot's," he said, introducing her to me. "She saw the problem develop every day at her station."

At Mike's invitation, Margot explained how she had spearheaded their strategy to cut down on the cashier lines.

"Last year, I went out to Las Vegas for the first time," Margot said. "I had a great time, won a few dollars. But most important, I learned a lot about business. When you're in Vegas, you never, ever, have to wait for a slot machine or a blackjack table. They *always* have one open for you. If the crowd at a certain time requires ten tables, they always seem to have twelve dealers ready. So I asked one of the pit bosses about it. He said, 'Why should we make you wait to wager your money?" Made sense to me. You may love Vegas, or hate it, but you can't deny that they are the kings of customer service."

"Imagine what Vegas would be like if it was run by the Department of Motor Vehicles!" Mike said. "You'd never go back."

"Sad, but true," Margot said. "Anyway, at one of our meetings the week after I came back from Vegas, I thought, why should we make our customers *wait* to buy our products, to give us their money? Seems to me we should be *eager* to let them pay us, not make them wait. It's not only a source of irritation to them, it's just plain stupid for us. We work so hard to get them in the store and provide the things they want. Why should we undermine the process at the point of payoff?

"I realized that, like the casinos, we should *always* have extra cashiers ready. We should *never* make our customers wait to give us their money. Everyone on our team agreed. So we doubled the number of checkout lines to ten—then doubled it again to twenty! And someone suggested that we angle them to make them seem less obtrusive, and take up less space. And thanks to another suggestion by one of our teammates, we put the checkout lines at the far end of the front window, so people didn't see them when they came in. Instead, they walk into a dazzling array of our produce and products. On top of that, they now walk past more of our products to get to the checkout lines. The extra items they pick up en route have more than paid for the changes we made.

"And finally, we assigned one clerk to each of our twenty checkout lines in order to keep customers moving."

"But with your new system, don't you have a lot of clerks waiting around much of the time?" I asked.

"Take a look for yourself," she said, turning to the lines. "We have eight checkout clerks at their stations—it's two in the afternoon, not a particularly busy time for us—and six of the eight have customers. We decided to always have two more lanes open than we need—like the blackjack tables in Vegas."

"But you have twenty cashiers on duty? Where are the rest of them?"

Mike and Margot grinned. "Come with us," Margot said, leading me past the checkout lines. In the corresponding product aisles leading into each checkout lane, we saw a person in a dark green smock stocking goods, tidying up displays, talking with customers—but always keeping an eye on their aisle, and the green light above, which indicates when they are needed at their register.

"When one of your fellow checkout team members realizes they need another checkout line," Margot said, "they simply turn the green light on at your aisle. You look up, and you know you're back in the game. This keeps us flexible, it keeps our aisles looking first-rate, and it keeps our checkout process operating at top speed, zipping customers through as fast as possible."

"And it creates more of a sense of accountability among

each of our team members," Mike added. "Everyone is looking out for everyone else, as on any good team. While you're at the checkout counter, you need to keep your eye on the flow of customers, and open and close registers accordingly. And when you're not at the register, you contribute in other ways. If you're the guy who runs aisle twelve, the pasta aisle, you want to make sure it's looking good. You don't want your aisle to become sloppy on your watch.

"The bottom line," Mike concluded, "is that unlike most grocery stores, the customer experience here isn't one of waiting in line to check out—it's all about shopping. The less time you spend waiting to pay, the more time you'll have to shop for our products. And the faster you'll want to come back."

"Wow," I said. "No wonder my wife loves coming here, even during busy times."

"Well, I'm glad to hear that. That's our goal!" Mike said. "But Margot and her friends took it one step further. Someone on the cashier team came up with the idea of setting up our lines 'banking style,' with one line of customers feeding into whatever cashier lines were open, so you don't have to worry about picking the wrong line. It's more efficient, too, since every cashier usually has only one customer at a time."

"Clever," I said.

"Hey, the banks invented it, not us," Margot said. "We

were just smart enough to apply it to grocery stores. It's really helped us attract the after-work crowd, who are always in a rush to get home. It especially helps getting men through the doors."

"And what I love about it," Mike said, "is that we're borrowing the best ideas from lots of places. We're constantly looking for ways to improve what we do, to better serve our customers and make their experience a good one. We're constantly coming up with ways to do things faster, better, and more efficiently, and ultimately that leads to more customers, more satisfied customers, and greater profits."

CONTINUAL IMPROVEMENT

"Look," Mike continued, walking me back to the café, "innovative thinking helps us to do things better. Think of all the 'rules' that were broken by people who refused to believe 'that's the way things are,' so that we now take for granted gravity, democracy, flight, radio, and television."

"Space travel," I said, getting into the spirit.

"Exactly!" Mike said. "The list is long. But every one of the people who came up with those ideas was in a small minority. That's why we remember *their* names, and not the names of the thousands of people who said it couldn't be done simply because it had never been done before. The names of those people are lost to history, and maybe rightly so.

"If you want to stay ahead in your business, whatever business you're in, you need to keep reinventing the wheel. If you're in the car manufacturing business, you need to develop cars with better gas mileage, better safety features, more sophisticated navigational and entertainment systems, fold-down third-row seats, and more cup-holders. To keep ahead of the competition, you need to be thinking about how to improve your product and service every day.

You need to think about how to improve your product or service every day.

"The same thing is true here," Mike continued. "Who in his right mind would hire twenty clerks to work ten cash registers for eight customers checking out at two in the afternoon? Well, if you engineer it right, it works! And what does a clerk really cost us, if each one brings in even 1 percent more business? We weren't able to create all *this*," he said, sweeping his hand over the store again, "by making our customers wait ten to fifteen minutes to give us their money.

"Our success, at heart, comes down to three things:

"First, **a strong desire to change how we do things** whenever we see something we think we can do better;

"Second, **a willingness to think outside the box** to come up with the best possible solution;

"And third, **an urge to improve everything we do.** That means being attentive to every last detail."

"But how do you come up with all these ideas?"

"I'm not as smart as I look!" Mike cracked. "I ask the customers. I ask our employees, and *they* ask our customers, too! We have meetings, where we throw ideas around. That's the fun part. If you want to come up with creative concepts to please the customer, you have to think creatively, and work creatively. You have to borrow ideas shamelessly from other businesses and cultures. We simply get a few people sitting around a table, pick a concern, and generate as many ideas as possible for solving it. If you want to keep the ideas flowing, you can't criticize people for coming up with an idea that won't work."

"But what if they really *are* dumb ideas?" I asked.

"If you want their input, there *are* no dumb ideas!" Mike exclaimed. "Just let 'em fly. What you're looking for are the few ideas that stick. The key to finding them is to create the kind of environment that doesn't *penalize* creativity, but *rewards* it.

"Most of all, you need to think beyond the status quo," Mike went on. "Just because we've always done it one way, doesn't mean we have to keep on doing it that way. Decades ago, Robert F. Kennedy used to say that while many look at the way things are and say 'Why?' he looked at what *could* be and said, 'Why not?' That's the attitude I try to encourage. I want *all* of our employees to think that way."

Create an environment that *rewards* creativity.

PUTTING THE RUBBER TO THE ROAD

"But time is money, too," I said. "With all these meetings, isn't there a danger of becoming too pie-in-the-sky? Of losing focus?"

"There could be," Mike admitted, "if we weren't focused on coming up with specific, clear-cut projects that we know we can complete.

"We decide which ideas we want to pursue, reduce them to as few steps as possible, and then start 'nailing down' who's going to do what, and when. Without goals, or deadlines, or leadership, there's no focus, no urgency, no accountability. Whereas our way, things *happen*, trust me!"

"But you're a retailer, not a manufacturing company," I

responded. "Improving our manufacturing processes isn't that simple."

"Pete, the same principles apply. You know, we're a manufacturer, too. We bake our own baked goods, and cook most of our prepared foods right here. We don't just sell them. And if the quality of our breads and pastries isn't up to snuff, we hear about it. But we use the same principles—the desire to change, the willingness to think outside the box, the constant urge to improve in order to make the best, most nutritious, fresh, high-quality bread or baked goods possible. The team members who work in our bread factory have the authority to stop the production line at any time if they see something amiss or find that the dough lacks the proper texture or consistency. We're constantly looking for ways to improve the quality of our ingredients, the cleanliness of our operations, and the efficiency of how our dough is made and the bread is baked. We constantly check to make sure the temperatures of our ovens are accurate. If any part of the production line is out of alignment or in danger of breaking down, we fix it before a breakdown occurs. Everything about how we go about preparing the foods we make is focused on maintaining consistent high quality. Just as here at the store, we are constantly looking for new ideas to improve everything we do."

• • •

After leaving my meeting with Mike, I arrived at the Dairy Cream factory once again bursting with energy. Mike had ended our conversation with a few words I couldn't shake:

"Making quality part of everything you do doesn't just happen as a result of good intentions and a clever slogan. Quality isn't some vague value you achieve simply by cheering your workers on. You have to first ask them what's working and what isn't, which you're doing. And then you have to give them the kind of tools and incentives that allow them to achieve what works."

Seated in my office, I first called Malcolm Jones, our owner, to ask for the resources to follow up on some of our employees' ideas from the meeting the previous week. It was, of course, the last thing he wanted to hear. But I explained that I needed the money to try to do what he'd asked for—increase sales and profits.

"Delvecchio, you're making me mad. You think this is a joke? I expect to see results, and I mean fast, if you wanna keep your job."

Thinking of my kids, and our mortgage, my stomach did flip-flops. But I knew I was doing the right thing. I told him that all I wanted was a few bucks to buy paint, new light fixtures, some basic equipment, and some pizza for anyone willing to pitch in. Malcolm wasn't sold until I promised him that if he could give me what I needed, I could give him a couple dozen free man-hours of labor. He finally agreed to chip in a few thousand bucks—chump change for a business our size, but a near-record investment from a notoriously cheap owner.

"Now get me some results, or else!"

But when I hung up, I realized that this was only the first of two sales pitches I had to make. And the second was probably going to be much harder. Asking for some money to retool the factory was one thing; asking for a few hours of our workers' time was quite another.

I called two more back-to-back meetings with our shifts. Julie brought in the list of ideas they had come up with the previous week and read them off. After she finished, Kevin, the court jester, added a few more, like "Install company pool and spa" and "Build nine-hole golf course," which got a few laughs. It also underscored their skepticism that anything would come out of our meetings.

I launched right in. "This list of yours—repaint the factory; improve lighting along the line; add more safety equipment and a better mixer; redecorate the lunchroom—is a good one."

"But . . . ?" Kevin said, getting more chuckles from the crowd.

"But nothing. Let's do them. Mr. Jones just signed off on the improvements."

This got their attention.

"There is, however, a catch."

"It comes out of our paychecks?" Kevin said, generating more laughter.

"No," I assured them. "He's even willing to pay a little extra for premium paint and equipment. But he's not willing to pay for labor. So, if you're willing to come in this Saturday, from nine to three, to improve your workplace, we can do this. And Mr. Jones will throw in a tailgate lunch from Natural Foods."

I heard a few mumbled "Okays" while others just grumbled, until I cut through the din. "Folks, we spend eight hours a day here, minimum. And none of us likes the way this place looks from the outside, or feels on the inside. In exchange for a few hours, we can make the two thousand hours we spend here every year a whole lot safer, more efficient, and more pleasant."

There were some positive responses to that, but I needed everyone's support. "When was the last time Mr. Jones put any money into this place?" I asked. It was the kind of comment that could get me fired, but I was in danger of that already. "Well, he's given us the money we need to follow up on the suggestions you made. He's listening to you. And I'm listening to you. If we don't follow up, what does that say about us? That we're the ones who don't care. But if we come through, his attitude might change, right along with ours. We can't *afford* to pass this up.

"So," I said, looking out at them. "Who's with me?"

Half the hands went up immediately. The other half soon followed—even Kevin's. I smiled, relieved.

"All right," I said. "Let's break this down. Who wants to be on the paint crew?" We went over each project, assigning people to every task, from buying the light fixtures and equipment to prepping the places we were going to improve.

Near the end of our first half-hour meeting, I heard from a surprising source: Shy Sheila. "If we improve the place enough," she said, "we may even be able to invite consumers and schools in. Let them watch us make the ice cream, and taste it afterward."

"It's a smart way to promote the company and generate some community goodwill," Kevin admitted. Mike was right. Sometimes great ideas piggyback off of other ideas, large or small.

"Good!" I said. "This is a great first step. I want to reach out together with you and our customers to make our ice cream the best made, anywhere." I had already decided to create focus groups to determine exactly what it is that our store customers—and general consumers—like and don't like about our ice cream, and to find ways to make our product better. But I decided to hold that thought for later. For now, it was enough to get the internal customers on board.

We ended the meeting on a high note—one I didn't realize we had in our range.

CHAPTER FIVE

Striving for Perfection

I found myself driving to Natural Foods a couple weeks later without an appointment, confident that Mike would find time for me. I was bubbling over with the good news I had to share. I was still on fire from Saturday's big event, our employees' makeover of our work space—what Sheila called the "First Step." I had gotten T-shirts printed up for everyone with this phrase on the front, and passed them out first thing Saturday morning so we could work in them and look more like a team. People had boom boxes blaring, young kids were running around madly helping out, and a million volts of positive energy were being directed toward our work home—and each other.

One crew washed the outside of the building and painted it a shiny white. One of the more artistic of our employees painted a mural of a rainbow emerging from some puffy clouds to a big pot of ice cream. I was amazed at the hidden talents of our staff. Another crew scrubbed down the inside of the factory, painting it an attractive off-white, which brightened the interior lighting immediately. The effect was magnified tenfold when we installed brighter lights above every line.

We uncartoned some new safety equipment and replaced several older machines. But the pièce de résistance was the lunchroom. Just cleaning the dingy windows looking out on the parking lot made a huge difference. The lunchroom crew painted the walls an elegant beige, hung paintings and pictures of nature scenes, and recarpeted the fifteen-by-twenty room in an inviting yet durable brown. Kevin, the company cynic, had worked for a carpet installer in an earlier life and was happy to show off his skills. We had brought attractive, inexpensive chairs and tables from Ikea to complete the transformation.

With such a large turnout and with everyone working enthusiastically, we finished most of the tasks we had assigned by early afternoon and then sat down to a tailgate lunch, courtesy of Natural Foods, followed by Frisbee and touch football on the back lawn. I couldn't recall the last time I'd seen our employees enjoy themselves so fully. We really did seem like a team rather than company employees whose only common thread was the fact that we all worked at Dairy Cream.

For the first time in memory, I sensed that the men and women around me left the Dairy Cream factory at the end of the day almost reluctantly. And they came back again on Monday totally pumped. The energy level was so high that everyone seemed carried along by a wave of enthusiasm. Productivity, I noticed, was through the roof. But most of all, the attitudes and the atmosphere on the floor and in the back offices were more upbeat than I had ever seen. As two o'clock approached, I saw the second shift gathering in the new lunchroom, so I walked in and called an impromptu meeting on making still more improvements. This time I focused on production issues and the consistency of our products, the quality of the ingredients we purchased, and ways to improve the texture and taste of our ice creams. I planned to have a similar conversation with our marketing and packaging people. One of our longest-tenured employees, John C., suggested that we construct a new sign in front of the factory, proudly displaying our name—and our product—to the world. It seemed like a nice show of our newfound pride, and the perfect topping to a sundae of new initiatives. As we were getting up to leave, I told them I'd bring Mr. Jones down to show him what we'd done with his money—and work on him to get a little more.

SUBIR CHOWDHURY

"Have faith, folks," I said.

This time there were no guffaws.

THE AMERICAN DISEASE

When I arrived at Natural Foods, Mike could tell from the look on my face that things were improving at Dairy Cream. When I shared what we were up to, he smiled.

"Well done," he said. "Very well done." From him, those few words of praise meant a great deal to me. "You've learned a lot, and you've improved things almost immediately. It shows how committed you, and your employees at Dairy Cream, are to changing the way you do things. I think you're ready for the next step, the biggest step."

It was what I'd hoped to hear.

"Great," I said. "I know the L in LEO stands for Listen, both to our *internal* and *external* customers. And the E is for Enrich, up and down the organization. Can you explain what the 'O' means? I've forgotten the principle you said it stands for."

"Perhaps you can guess," Mike said. "If you *listen* to what your customers want, and you find innovative ways to *enrich* your business, what's next?"

I could have given the usual clichés—keep working hard, keep your eyes on the prize, and all that—but I suspected Mike had something more specific in mind. And I really didn't know what it was. I thought about the letter O, searching for a clue, but nothing came to mind. "Mike, you've got me," I said.

Mike said with a wry smile, "This last step might be the most important of all, and is probably the toughest."

I'd talked with Mike a good deal over the past months, but I had never heard him adopt such a serious tone. Whatever he was going to tell me next, I knew he believed it devoutly.

"The next step is to *optimize* what you're doing," he said. "Not just improve—*optimize*. How do you do that? By striving for perfection."

"Striving for perfection?"

"Yes. It's not enough to simply 'do your best.' At Natural Foods, perfection is a *real* and tangible goal, something we break down and try to achieve, piece by piece. To achieve perfection, you need to do several things:

"**First, you need to recognize the price of failure.** If you fail, your business, or division, may falter. This is not for the faint of heart.

"**Second, you need to do it right the first time.** That means *planning* for perfection from the very beginning, instead of looking for good enough and then fixing things after the fact. In other words, preventing fires, not fighting them.

"**Third, you need to get absolutely dogged on the details.**

"**Fourth, you need to develop a sense of what I think of as 'productive paranoia.'** I borrow it from a favorite phrase of legendary Intel chairman Andy Grove: 'Only the paranoid survive.' It means constantly worrying over what else you might do—about the competition, about opportunities you might be missing, about the next new thing. People, and companies, that get complacent ultimately fail.

"**And fifth, you need to instill in everyone on your team a passion for perfection, every minute of the day.** You need to transform it from a task into a mission, and you need to be very honest about how you are doing and about what you need to do to be the best."

"But how do I carry out these steps?"

It is not enough to simply "do your best." You must strive for perfection.

"If you're going to take the Optimize stage seriously, you need to see the situation for what it is. Pete, remember what I told you the first day you came in here? About how American business suffers from a national disease. We often *achieve* excellence, but we can't seem to *maintain* it!

"I think we've gotten better at listening to our customers, both internally and externally. But excellence in terms of constantly enriching and improving our products and service, and most of all, optimizing what we do, has never been a priority, much less a mission. As I've said before, America has *always* been great at innovation, from the cotton gin to the iPod. But we have a national blind spot that prevents us from seeing what it takes to keep the corporate machine humming at the highest levels, and from having the commitment to make that happen, every day."

"Isn't that human nature?" I offered. "I mean, it's always more exciting to attack the castle than maintain and defend it. It's more fun to get to the top than it is to work at the endless improvements and adjustments needed to stay there."

"Of course it is," Mike said. "But it's also human nature to want to sleep in, to talk whenever you feel like it, regardless of who's already speaking, and to become impatient waiting for a traffic light to turn green. But to create a successful society, we have to learn how to adapt human nature. The same is true of corporations. While it's exciting to *build* something new, we can't sustain excellence unless we find the energy and skills and motivation to maintain excellence—quality—in everything that we do."

"So how do I optimize what we do at Dairy Cream?"

"Again, the first step is to recognize the price of failure.

When you realize how painful and costly it is to fall short of perfection, the passion you need to prevent failure grows.

"Look at the *Challenger* space shuttle," he continued. "We devoted $2 billion and countless man-hours of our best and brightest people to make the shuttle. But we lost everything, including the lives of seven of our astronauts, because of a faulty O-ring that cost nine hundred dollars. When engineers cautioned about flaws in the shuttle, they were ignored, and their concerns were swept under the carpet because of cost concerns. Yet, the investigation into and cleanup of the *Challenger* tragedy cost us $500 million alone, enough to buy over half a million O-rings!

"People say, 'Don't sweat the small stuff.' That might be a good approach to downplaying the small irritations and stresses of life, but it's a horrible approach to running a business. When you're operating a space shuttle, the small stuff *is* the big stuff!

"The same principle applies to running a business. Taking care of the small stuff may not be life and death for us, but it can be, and often is, the difference between us selling our VCRs, and letting the Japanese do it for us."

Mike's point made sense. I remembered reading Rudy Giuliani's account of cracking down on crime in New York City in the early 1990s. He started by arresting the squeegee wipers—the guys who ran out to "clean" the windshields of cars stopped at traffic lights, in the expectation of a "tip." Giuliani and the New York commissioner of police felt that letting such brazen intimidation go sent a terrible message throughout the city. It suggested that the city would tolerate small crimes. But in the end it encouraged all crime to flourish. As the city, and the police, began to sweat the small stuff, the crackdown began to reduce crime across the board, from drug-dealing to homicide.

Then I recalled another example that was closer to home. "Remember when Coke spent millions on advertising to introduce its new bottled water, Dasani, to the European market? Its efforts collapsed when European scientists discovered that their bottled water had an easily detectable and removable impurity in it. Snazzy-looking label, though."

We both laughed. "Pete, you've hit the nail on the head. Great example. They got all the flashy stuff right. But they missed the whole point of their product: clean, healthy, *pure* water. That was the reason people were willing to pay a couple of euros for something they could get for free out of the tap. The price of failure, my friend, even a small, simple mistake, can be very costly indeed."

GET IT RIGHT THE FIRST TIME

"These ideas apply across the board," Mike continued. "A friend of mine, Larry, is a car dealer here in town, and he was telling me about all the fancy things they were doing to dazzle their customers—picking up their car, dropping them off, remodeling the waiting area—all of which, he said, were great improvements that increased business. But their service business tapered off after a few months. Larry couldn't figure out why. So he pulled together ten customers who had left the dealership to participate in a focus group. He asked them about their experience at their dealership, everything from the lighting to the atmosphere to the employees' uniforms and all the other things they'd been working so hard to improve. Everything Larry asked them about passed with flying colors. He was stumped. So finally he asked them, 'Well, what's the problem?'

"A middle-aged woman, who had been mild-mannered and polite throughout the interview, raises her hand and tells Larry, 'Mr. Brown, your dealership *is* very clean, and your people *are* very polite. And I love the fact that you pick me up, drop me off, and have donuts and coffee for us in the waiting room. But Mr. Brown, you need to fix my damn car! I've brought my car in three times trying to get the rattling sound in the engine fixed, and it's still rattling. All I've gotten is a $450 bill.'"

Mike and I cracked up. "We were howling over that one!"

"So what did Larry do?" I asked when I stopped laughing.

"He got his people to work harder at fixing the cars right the first time. More training, better systems, better hiring practices, and more accountability from his repair crew. Implementing rewards and penalties for their work. Larry soon discovered the main cause of the faulty work was the morning rush, when they had fifteen or twenty cars lined up, often without appointments, for service. They learned to spread their repairs out during the day, by taking appointments at every hour and driving their customers back to their homes or offices. It gave the service advisers the time they needed to ask better questions and work at a less rushed pace. And they learned to repeat back to the customer everything they said to make sure they didn't miss anything. They discovered that spending an extra five minutes at the desk with the customer saved them hours in redo work.

"The point is, the donuts were a plus. But they were no substitute for a car fixed properly the first time. Because that gets at the customers' most basic need, getting their car fixed."

"I see what you mean," I said. "The bells and whistles we come up with at Dairy Cream are important, but not at the expense of the quality of our ice cream, or service to our customers."

"Bingo!" Mike said. "The *only* solution to this is to make perfection a part of your company's mission. Spending money and time on recalls and refunds for defective ice cream or packaging is a losing effort. Your customers just won't stick around. If you spend more time and money at the outset to get your ice cream right, you'll save a ton of time, and profits, in the long run. Sometimes, real quality is invisible. If your products, and service, are flawless, people rarely talk about it. But the costs of poor quality are tangible, and their effect will cost you money, customers, and ultimately the success of your business."

"So how do I do that?"

> **The costs of poor quality are tangible; they will cost you customers and money, and ultimately affect the success of your business.**

"You can start by putting less emphasis on company firemen—the guys who are solving the problems or flare-ups that happen at every company every day—and more emphasis on fire marshals, the people who prevent them from ever occurring.

"At Natural Foods, a fire marshal is anyone who can detect a potential problem, and prevent it."

"In other words," I said, "*everyone*?"

"Exactly!" Mike said. "Of course everyone! Any building that waits for a real fireman to spot smoke and flames is a building that is about to burn down. Likewise with companies. When anyone, in any department, has an idea or sees something that can improve the way we do things, they are encouraged—required—to speak up. And they're *rewarded* for it rather than punished for it, whether the suggestion relates to their own department or team or not. If you want to create a business that is fireproof, you have to put aside issues of turf and territory.

"The fact is, if you want to get rid of the big problems, first get rid of the small problems."

"Huh?"

"When dealing with something as large as an organization, or a community, if you eliminate the small problems first, you don't give the big problems a chance to take root.

"Look around you," Mike said, pointing to the gleaming aisles of the Natural Foods store. "What do you see on our floors? Nothing, ever! Whenever something falls, we pick it up, or clean it. Floors that aren't spotless are the sign of a sloppy store. And that kind of sloppiness spreads quickly. Everyone's aprons are clean as well. We clean them after every shift and replace them whenever necessary. Everyone ties them in the back, at the waist. The tie strings never hang freely, or are loosely tied. Each team member's name tag goes on the upper right of the apron, so customers can read it when you shake their hands. These may seem like small things, but this kind of attention to detail adds up, whatever business you are in. It makes an impression. We believe it even affects the way our workers feel about themselves.

"I remember once reading about Vince Lombardi's Super Bowl champion Green Bay Packers," Mike continued. "They were always the best-dressed team in the league when they traveled. Suits and ties. Now, you can't claim that wearing a tie on a plane on Saturday will guarantee winning a football game on Sunday. But Lombardi was convinced that by dressing and behaving as the classiest team in the league, with the highest standards on and off the field, the attitude sunk in that they were different, that they were special. And they brought that attitude onto the field every Sunday."

I thought about the changes we had made at Dairy Cream, and how good they made everyone feel. Mike continued, "Bottom line: We now pay attention to the details, because our customers do. They notice if someone looks sloppy, if there is a busted bag of chips on the floor, if there's a light flickering overhead. All those things tell you we don't care. That no one's paying attention. And that creates a reaction, whether they can articulate it or not, with our customers.

"The opposite is also true," he added. "I'm sure you've seen dozens of workers tidying up this or fixing up that every time you've walked in. When our customers see our people cleaning things throughout the store, they're far less likely to add to our work by leaving things on the ground or not picking up after themselves. It's human nature: People want to keep well-maintained stores looking good.

Pay attention to the details—your customers do.

"Our prices are a little higher than most, but when you walk in, you know you've entered a different kind of store, a special place where quality, on every level, is the order of the day. I think our customers expect to pay a little extra.

"We have a Natural Foods way of doing everything, and the one common denominator is quality. Our customers recognize it; our workers take pride in it; and our competition envies it. Once you develop that kind of identity, by being dogged on the details, you work hard to keep it up."

PRODUCTIVE PARANOIA

"Can you explain what you mean by the next step, productive paranoia?"

"Well, we find it helps to be constantly looking over our

shoulders, being aware of what our competitors and other businesses are doing, and thinking about what else we can be doing for our customers. A bit of paranoia can be a tremendous motivator. The worst thing you can do is become complacent. Assume you're the best in your industry, and as a result you stop worrying about your competitors and start coasting when it comes to innovating and improving, and inevitably you get clobbered. You've got to be absolutely honest about how you're doing. It's easy to convince yourself you're doing well and block out the bad news or warning signs that would help your current cause when you start to lose your way. But fooling yourself about how you're doing is like sticking your head in the sand. It doesn't help solve problems. And it sure doesn't fool your competitors, or even more important, your customers.

"Pete, when you first came to see me, you were convinced you had a great product and were doing a great job. When I asked you how you stacked up against your competitors on a number of qualities, you didn't know. Rather than measuring how you were doing, you simply asserted it. You weren't being paranoid *enough* about how you were doing, and how your competitors were doing."

"Good point," I conceded. "And if we can't measure what we're doing, we can't improve it."

"Yup."

"That makes sense. Productive paranoia, huh? I guess we could use a little more of that."

A PASSION FOR PERFECTION

Mike smiled. "Need any help with a passion for perfection?" he asked. "As you've seen, it's what makes Natural Foods tick."

"I can see how powerful it is, by the way everyone in your store works to achieve it. It's a far cry from Dairy Cream at the moment. But I can see how vital it is. And I think I have some ideas on how to start making it part of our mission, too."

FACE THE NATION

By the time I returned to Dairy Cream, it was nearly time for the first of the focus meetings we had scheduled with groups of ordinary customers. The marketing group we had hired had arranged for us to meet with three focus groups spread out over several weeks.

Some of our employees felt that we weren't ready for such a step, because we'd only begun to implement changes to our manufacturing process.

"Maybe we are, and maybe we're not," I told them. "But

we can spend weeks, even months, trying to *guess* what our customers want from us. Why not bring them in now and find out what they think themselves? I thought back to something Mike had told me. **"Remember, quality is defined by the customer, not by us."**

I was originally tempted to invite only the department heads in to watch the focus group. But as Mike had pointed out, quality is for everyone. I figured that having our people hear the pros and cons of our products from the customers would be a lot more powerful than hearing it secondhand from me.

We had installed a camera and video monitor behind one-way glass in an adjacent storage room, where the workers waited nervously to hear customers evaluate our ice cream. Because we couldn't fit more than a couple of dozen people into the room, employees drew straws for the chance to watch, alongside our line managers and department heads. Employees from the later shift offered to fill in for the employees who were taken off the line. When I gave the focus group coordinator the signal, she brought fifteen preselected customers into our conference room. An array of ice cream cartons of a dozen of our flavors sat in the middle of the table. She invited them to try whatever they liked.

As they passed around the different cartons and began

eating, I heard several "hmm"s and "ahhh"s. Before long, they were ready to talk.

"Better than I remembered it," one woman who'd tried our ice cream before told the coordinator. It was a good sign, since we hadn't instituted many manufacturing reforms yet.

"I didn't realize Dairy Cream had so many flavors," another said. "I knew other companies made Strawberry Shortcake, but didn't know Dairy Cream made it, too." I cringed at this; it was a flavor we had invented.

"Anything else?" our focus group coordinator asked. "We'd love to know what you like, and what you don't." This seemed to be the opening several were looking for.

"Well," an older, portly man began, "I love your selection; you've got a lot of great flavors here. But I found one carton of Blueberry Cheesecake was filled with blueberries, while a second one I tried had almost none at all."

"Yeah," another said, "same with the Cookies-N-Cream—one carton's loaded with cookies, the other's all ice cream."

"The chocolate was silky smooth. But the vanilla," another complained, "had a rough texture to it."

"And what's with the packaging? This one has cream on half the *outside* of the lid!"

I glanced at our quality engineer, trying to conceal concern. But we both knew we had problems.

Several other complaints surfaced, as well as a lot of compliments. At least the news wasn't all bad. In fact, overall they liked our ice cream a lot.

"Okay," said the coordinator. "We appreciate your cooperation, and your candor. Is there anything else you want to add before we finish?"

"You've got some good stuff here. But it's not consistently good. If I buy the wrong carton, I'm going to be disappointed."

That one hurt, because it cut right to the quick.

"Thank you," the coordinator said. "That's just the kind of feedback we're looking for. We appreciate your time."

A DAIRY CREAM WAY OF DOING EVERYTHING

Several of us met with the outside marketing group we'd hired immediately afterward, amid the empty cartons in the middle of the table.

"Boy," said Bob, our quality engineer. "That was hard to listen to."

"Yes," I nodded. "But was any of it untrue? After all, they're our end users: They had no reason to lie."

"That's why it stung," he said.

I nodded. "Well," I said, "we heard what they had to say. What are we going to do about it?"

"We need to do a better job controlling the air content,"

one technician said. "If one batch is thick and the other is frothy, it's because of air bubbles getting into the mixing process."

"Okay, good," I said. "Let's find a way to measure the right thing, control and monitor that. We need to make it consistent."

"And the packaging problem has to be solved," one of our marketers said. "We know we've had quality issues, but we've never taken dramatic steps to do anything about it."

"Can you put a team together on that to fix it once and for all? If the outside of our carton is messy, customers will never pick it up in the first place."

One of our line workers then said something that stunned me: "The way we do it, the mix-ins just kind of tumble into the vat. There is no way to assure a consistent blend when we pour the ice cream into the tubs. That's why some cartons have a lot of mix-ins, and others little."

If we'd known that was a problem, we should have addressed it long ago. "Whenever *anyone* sees a problem, bring it to my attention or the attention of your immediate supervisor. We're all responsible for the quality of what we make. Sam, let's get a team on that immediately.

"The comments we're hearing, and the comments that we will hear in the weeks ahead, can be difficult to take. And I'm not going to kid you, it won't be easy to change. But now at least we're starting to find out what we have to do to compete. If we're going to get customers to buy our product instead of the competition's over the long haul, we need to do a better job all the way around."

Everyone is responsible for quality.

Everyone nodded vigorously. It was clear we were all on board.

CHAPTER SIX

Bringing It Home

Knowing what we had to do, and realizing we were desperate, over the next three months we addressed many of the problems that the focus groups, and our employees, had identified.

We replaced several key pieces of equipment, after sending out several of our engineers to study the manufacturing facilities and best practices of other companies. We asked our line workers for more feedback on ways to tweak production, and improve quality. We began to measure, and improve, every step of the production process, looking always to cut down on defects—or "variables" as the quality people call them—and raise the bar. We asked our engineers to come up with more robust cartons, without having to resort to costlier grades of cardboard. We took steps to ensure that no ice cream touched the package once the carton was sealed. We changed our mix-in procedure, installing sophisticated new equipment to precisely measure the mix-ins in each carton. And we started monitoring *everything*, from the percentage of air content in our ice cream to the temperature at which we stored the empty cartons.

We reduced the tolerance of variables on our mix-ins to 0.1 grams, and in the depth of each tub to two millimeters. Whenever we discovered a problem, from a broken package to colors that were less than true, we had a team diagnose and fix it.

The thing was, most of the improvements didn't cost a lot of money. The ones that had the biggest impact were achieved by our people looking at how we did things, and finding clever ways to improve them. The people power part of the equation was critical to improving our processes. We didn't have the resources to simply throw money at a problem. We used our heads instead of our wallets to make improvements.

At the end of this period of whirlwind activity, we found that we had a much-improved product. Next, we were anxious to get it in front of another focus group, to test it out with customers. Before the focus group meeting, however, I wanted to sit down again with Mike.

QUALITY IS CONSISTENCY

We met on a Monday, again at Natural Foods. Upon greeting each other, Mike asked, "How is your family?" So I told him. Despite the long hours I had worked to turn Dairy Cream around, things had never been better at home. I found that some of the same principles of quality made as much sense at home as they did at Dairy Cream. Listening to my wife and kids, working to improve our time together, paying attention to the little things, like what story they liked best or the name of their favorite stuffed animal, made as much of a difference as the more important things—that they did their homework, ate a good dinner. I think it showed that I care, in ways that went beyond words.

"I'm delighted to hear that," Mike said, smiling.

Then I told him about the dramatic developments at Dairy Cream over the past three months. Although I had filled him in on some of what we were doing early on, it had been a while, I realized, since we had talked.

"Pete," Mike said when I had finished, "I've talked to quite a few people over the years, but I've gotta say, no one has listened more closely, and followed through with as much determination and energy, as you and your team. I'm impressed."

"Thanks," I said gratefully, smiling. "It feels good to hear that. But we still have a long way to go. We haven't saved our jobs yet. One test coming up is a follow-up focus group to see what customers think of what we've been doing."

"When does it take place?"

"This Saturday," I said. "Our marketing group felt we could get a better cross-section of customers on the weekend—men, women, and kids."

"Good," Mike said. "Let me offer you a tip: Don't handpick the ice cream cartons for them. Let them choose randomly, and give them a large selection to choose from."

"Why's that?"

"I remember what my old hockey coach used to say to me," Mike said. "Don't judge a goalie on his best day, as almost anyone can get hot for a while; judge him on his worst. When he's not at his sharpest, will he lose you the game; or, can he still play well enough to keep you in it? I judge companies the same way: The real measure is not how they function at their best, on the basis of a single product or particularly good service one day, but how they do at their *worst*.

"Your goal is to instill the virtues of *sustained* excellence. Let me give you another example. A friend of mine, Donnie, is a golf pro. He's a scratch handicap, as good as they come, and he teaches duffers like me. He was telling me about the people he sees every week, guys who come to him and say, 'I'm a pretty good golfer, I'm just not *consistent*.' And Donnie tells them: 'Then you're not a pretty good golfer.' *Anyone* can hit a few good shots. The whole score 550 points with some good plays sandwiched between a bunch of mediocre ones. But to keep the opponent from scoring requires a successful defense from every player on the field, on every play of the game, every single game. Just one mistake from one player and the streak would have been broken. Michigan didn't set that record by having a loose approach to the game.

"Unfortunately, in our culture, the defenders are still unsung heroes. We like offense. We celebrate the home run hitters, not the fielders; the shooters, not the rebounders; and the quarterbacks, not the cornerbacks. But the best teams have great defenses: the Detroit Pistons; the Dallas Cowboys; and Pittsburgh's 'Steel Curtain.' Defense wins championships. And quality is the strongest defense there is in business."

PLAYING FOR KEEPS

The new focus group convened at 1 P.M. the following Saturday. The marketing group brought in fifteen people this time: five men, five women, and five kids. But before we began, a sixteenth "participant" slipped in: Mike McMaster himself, wearing a grin worthy of the Cheshire cat. I nonchalantly ushered him into the group, both excited about and worried over his reaction to what he was going to see and experience.

question, the *only* question, is: Can you keep it going for an entire round? And do it the next day? Everyone has ups and downs, even Tiger Woods. But the great ones' *worst* days are better than the average golfer's *best* day, and that's what makes them great. *That* is the kind of thinking I want to see every day on our floor at Natural Foods.

> **The real measure of performance is not how you do at your best, but how you do at your worst.**

"The people under you have put in a lot of time and made a significant personal investment to improve your factory. Do you think they'll work as hard to sustain it?"

I paused to think, and my answer surprised me. "Yeah. After all, they made the decisions, they did the work. Our improvements are the result of them. I think they'd hate to see things slide back to what they were."

"That's a huge step forward," Mike said. "When that's true, your people are no longer showing up just to receive a paycheck. They're part of a team, striving to achieve excellence. The next challenge is to instill in your people, and through your systems, the tools to sustain what you've done, and expand on it. And, as you've realized, the way to make sure that happens is to assign people to different tasks, establish deadlines, make those deadlines, and constantly work to raise the bar. At Natural Foods, our people are passionate about maintaining our store. After all, it's a store they helped create. In fact, we call it 'rebuilding' rather than 'maintaining,' because every day we have to fight the forces that would erode what we've done and return us to mediocrity. If you don't battle it and continue to build, entropy kicks in. So we battle it! But the real key isn't so much to fix things as it is to design them right in the first place so that problems don't occur.

"A lot of companies feel that quality costs money; that's one of the excuses they offer for not embracing quality in everything they do. But as we've both seen, the fact is, **quality is cheaper in the long run than 'good enough.'** The list of companies that go under every year because someone else does what they do, only better, is endless. And the reverse is just as true. Remember when the Koreans first introduced their cars to America in the late 1980s? The cars were a joke. People turned up their noses at them because of their poor quality and made fun of anyone who bought them. That was true for a decade. Then the Koreans became serious about quality and turned things around. If you're successful at Dairy Cream, I know you'll turn your company around as well. The fact is, when

you do things right the first time, you never have to twice. Your return on investment skyrockets.

Quality is cheaper in the long run than "good enough."

"The other thing about excellence that holds nies back, of course, is that making quality part mission is *hard work*. It doesn't have the sizzle o ment of launching a new product or service. It ta stant effort, and vigilance, from everyone, all t instead of the occasional splashy big play." A sp Mike told me the story of Fielding H. Yost, the coached the University of Michigan football te 1901 until 1927. "In his first year at Michigan, h press his team wouldn't lose a game. And they di ning the first Rose Bowl championship with an u record. Michigan scored 550 points that seasor age of 50 per game. But more impressively, Mich fense did not allow a single point in return!

"Tell the former coaches about the 1901 team's 550–0 point differential," Mike said, " be far more impressed by the zero than the 55

This time, we first gave the group a tour of our refurbished factory, showing off the new equipment. Afterward, we let them sift through the "final bins" to pick out whatever flavors they liked. Mike, I noticed, spent more time than most sorting through the cartons, no doubt trying to find the most poorly packaged carton he could. I was pleased that it took him so long to find one with a slight flaw: a small dent on the side of the lid. But it also showed me that we still had room for improvement.

I remembered Mike's recent maxim: You're only as good as your weakest sample. Because we weren't handpicking the cartons, we were at the mercy of their selection, and the quality of our product.

We escorted the group back into the conference room, offered scoops and bowls and spoons, and invited them to dig in while the cameras rolled behind the one-way glass.

I was undoubtedly reading too much into everyone's smallest reactions, as were my colleagues. But I was heartened by the conversations. They seemed to like what they were seeing and tasting. As they ate, they talked freely, offering lots of compliments.

"The Rocky Road is fabulous!"

"I love the Peanut Brittle."

Someone else yelled out, "Try this."

"How long has Dairy Cream been around?" a man asked. "I've never tried their ice cream before. I like it."

Although the praise continued to wash over us, to me each compliment only seemed like a criticism deferred. Did they *really* like it? After a dozen positive responses, I realized I would have to solicit negative views. "Anything you *didn't* like about the ice cream, or the selection, or the packaging?"

There was a surprising pause. Finally Mike spoke up.

"The carton of Double Chocolate Fudge has a dent on the side of the lid."

"I'm sorry," I said. "Please leave it there for us, and we'll figure out what the problem is to make sure it doesn't happen again." Our quality engineer came into the room to retrieve the lid.

"Anyone else?" I asked.

There was silence. And more silence. Then, one of the participants, a middle-aged woman, asked, "Can we purchase cartons to take home?" Another said, "I'd like some, too." One of the participants giggled, and several proceeded to clap. I felt my anxiety giving way to quiet jubilation.

"Thanks," I said, with more gratitude than they could know. "Thanks for coming down. Please help yourself to a few cartons of your favorite flavors on your way out."

As they filed out, every one of them picked up another carton or two for their families. Mike was the last to leave the conference room.

"So?" I asked him, my heart back in my throat.

"I'd like three cases," he said.

"Three cases?" I stammered. "Sure you can eat that much?"

"It's not for me. It's for Natural Foods. I want to try it out at our store."

I looked at Mike, then looked at my teammates, who were filing into the conference room.

"I never heard more welcome words," I told him gratefully. "We'll send several cases over. Our compliments."

I turned to the Dairy Cream team. "Everyone, I'd like you to meet Mike McMaster, the manager of Natural Foods." And at that moment, everyone realized what Mike's casual comment about taking several cases meant. It was as if we'd just heard that we'd passed the state bar exam. A giddy euphoria swept the room.

When Mike left the factory, the Dairy Cream workers gathered in the cafeteria, cheering, clapping, laughing, and hugging. There was still a lot of work to do; we were only at the beginning of our journey into the world of quality. But it was clear that we had turned a corner, and that by devoting ourselves to creating a culture of quality in everything we did, we had potentially saved our jobs, and our factory. And we did so not by cutting corners or rolling out razzle-dazzle marketing campaigns or laying off people, but by instilling a simple commitment to quality.

I called Jean at home to share the good news. When I told her about Mike's reaction and his decision to try out Dairy Cream's ice cream in Natural Foods, she exclaimed, "All right! Nice going, Pete. You did it! You've all worked so hard for this. I think this calls for a celebration! Let's go out for dinner tonight, the whole family."

Over the next few months, business was still touch and go. Malcolm had grumbled incessantly about the additional money he was putting out, although I think even he was grudgingly pleased by how much the factory had been transformed. And even he admitted how much better our ice cream tasted. But the real test was the perception of our customers. Gradually, our business picked up, and then more rapidly. Natural Foods not only sold out its initial orders of our ice cream, it increased the number of cartons it took each week fourfold over the next six months. Malcolm's grumbling and threats dwindled as our numbers went up.

And, in fact, Malcolm surprised me one morning by sweeping into my office unannounced and informing me that he was so impressed by the way I led our efforts to turn things around that he was making me company president. He would no longer take an active role in running the company, but would rely on my experience and leadership. It was an extraordinary turn of events. But, as Malcolm himself said, he never would have been able to transform the company in the same way, and my promotion was simply recognition of that.

But I knew, of course, that my efforts were only a small part of Dairy Cream's turnaround. The real work, and the majority of the ideas, came from our employees. And their efforts needed to be rewarded as well. So I immediately risked Malcolm's ire by deciding, as my first decision as president, to create an employee bonus system, based on performance, to reward the many people who had contributed to our success. Mike had said to me at one point that actions that are rewarded are the things that get done. And nothing, I knew, would motivate our employees more than a little extra money, and recognition for a job well done.

I began to notice more and more people not only buying our ice cream in the convenience stores and grocery chains, but talking about Dairy Cream to their friends and relatives as one of our region's undiscovered secrets. But it wasn't "undiscovered" for long. Several concessionaires at high school and college stadiums and arenas came to us, asking if they could carry our flavors. And the pièce de résistance was the opening of our first Dairy Cream franchised store, which was an immediate hit.

We still had a long way to go, but thanks to Mike, and all the hard work everyone at Dairy Cream put in, I felt we were on our way.

ACKNOWLEDGMENTS

For the development and production of this book I feel a deep sense of gratitude to:

- My Doubleday Random House editor, Roger Scholl, for his professional competence and project leadership—and for his continuous inspiration. Roger is the *best* editor I have ever worked with.

- Michael Palgon, the deputy publisher of Doubleday Broadway, who has been tremendously supportive of the book from our earliest discussions.

- My friend John Bacon for his enormous support and hard work from day one, for refining the manuscript with integrity and a sense of quality, and for his continuous help and belief in my work.

- Everyone at Random House for their dedication and hard work: David Drake, the director of publicity for Broadway and Currency; Meredith McGinnis, the associate marketing director who spearheaded Currency's marketing efforts; Janelle Moburg, vice president and sales liaison; Kim Cacho and her wonderful production staff: Luisa Francavilla; Michael Collica, who designed the book's interior; Jean Traina, who designed the cover for the book; Sheila Klee, the production editor; Rebecca Carter, Doubleday's foreign rights manager, and Louise Quayle, the domestic rights manager; Jean McCall, Amy Zenn, and Jessica Fink in special sales; and all the incredibly energetic and supportive people throughout the Random House sales organization.

- All of my dear friends and colleagues in the business, especially everyone at my firm, ASI Consulting Group, LLC (www.asiusa.com), for their continuous support.
- All of my customers, who have been enhancing my knowledge every single day since I started my professional career.
- All of my readers around the world, who have been the best supporters of my works.

I am very grateful to my parents, sisters, and in-laws for their constant demonstration of love and continuous support.

This book would never have become a reality without the support of my encouraging wife, Malini, and my daughter, Anandi.

SUBIR CHOWDHURY, a respected quality strategist, is chairman and CEO of ASI Consulting Group, LLC—the world leader on Six Sigma and Quality Leadership implementation, consulting, and training. His clients include global *Fortune* 100 companies as well as small organizations in both the public and private sectors. Hailed by the *New York Times* as a "leading quality expert," Chowdhury is the author of twelve books, including the international bestseller *The Power of Six Sigma*, which has been translated into more than twenty languages and has sold more than a million copies worldwide. Chowdhury's *Design for Six Sigma* (DFSS) is the *first* book on the topic and is credited with popularizing DFSS philosophy throughout the world. His *Management 21C* was selected as the Best Business Book of 1999 by Amazon.com in the

United Kingdom and was translated into more than ten languages.

Chowdhury has received numerous international awards for his leadership in quality management and his major contributions to various industries worldwide. In addition to being honored by the Automotive Hall of Fame, he received the most prestigious award of the Society of Automotive Engineers, the Henry Ford II Distinguished Award for Excellence in Automotive Engineering. He also received honorable recognition from the U.S. Congress, as well as the Society of Manufacturing Engineers' Gold Medal. The American Society for Quality honored him with the first Philip Crosby Medal for authoring the most influential business book on Six Sigma. He is also an honorary member of the World Innovation Foundation and the International Technology Institute (ITI). In 2004 Chowdhury was inducted into the Hall of Fame for Engineering, Science and Technology (World Level), and the ITI honored him with its prestigious Rockwell Medal for Excellence in Technology.

Chowdhury has an undergraduate degree in aerospace engineering from the Indian Institute of Technology (IIT), Kharagpur, India; a graduate degree in industrial management from Central Michigan University (CMU); and an honorary doctorate in engineering from the Michigan Technological University (MTU). In 2003, its golden an-